TREND
TRADING

Daryl Guppy

Wrightbooks

Daryl Guppy is also the author of:
Chart Trading*
Share Trading*
Trading Tactics*
Trading Asian Shares
Snapshot Trading*
36 Strategies of the Chinese*
and the Australian editor/contributor to:
The Day Trader's Advantage* by Howard Abell
Options—Trading Strategies that Work* by William F. Eng
*Available from John Wiley & Sons Australia, Ltd

First published 2004 by Wrightbooks,
an imprint of John Wiley & Sons Australia, Ltd
42 McDougall Street, Milton, Qld 4064

Office also in Melbourne

© Daryl Guppy 2004
Internet: <china@guppytraders.com>, <www.guppytraders.com>
The moral rights of the author have been asserted

Reprinted 2004, 2005, 2006, 2007 and 2009

National Library of Australia Cataloguing-in-Publication data:

Guppy, Daryl, 1954–.
Trend trading.
Includes index.
ISBN 0 7314 0085 2.
1. Stocks—Australia. 2. Investments—Australia. I. Title.
332.63220994

Cover design by Rob Cowpe

Acknowledgments: All charts created by Metastock© and Ezy Chart© using data supplied by Just Data and Online Trading Systems.

Disclaimer
The material in this publication is of the nature of general comment only, and does not represent professional advice. It is not intended to provide specific guidance for particular circumstances and it should not be relied on as the basis for any decision to take action or not take action on any matter which it covers. Readers should obtain professional advice where appropriate, before making any such decision. To the maximum extent permitted by law, the author and publisher disclaim all responsibility and liability to any person, arising directly or indirectly from any person taking or not taking action based upon the information in this publication.

CONTENTS

(Cont'd...)

Contents (cont'd)

PREFACE

A FLEA ON AN ELEPHANT

Trend trading is not about timing the market. It is about doing at least as well as the general market, and outperforming it. The task is not as difficult as the fund managers would have us believe. This book examines some of the tools investors and traders use to ride the rising ride, and lift above it. You have advantages as a small investor and we show you how to use them effectively.

Between March and September 2003 over 400 stocks listed on the Australian Stock Exchange increased in value by more than 30%, but only a few traders and investors were able to find and lock-in these trend-driven returns. Some caught a ride with a big opportunity, but lost it, turning a winning trade into a much smaller profit, or even in some cases into a loss. We examine some easy-to-apply trend trading methods to find these opportunities and to capture these types of profits. You can do this, and this book shows you how.

Many people invest in the market with the assistance of professional fund managers. You see the managers' advertisements in the newspapers proclaiming their expertise. They tell readers it is not possible to time the market. It is possible to participate in a rising trend. Ask a simple question of your fund manager or superannuation provider: did they match the broad market return in any year? Often the answer is a resounding and disappointing 'No'. Think for a moment about this answer. It means their team was unable to float with the rising tide, let alone add extra value through professional management.

I have given up trying to understand why people behave as they do in the market. Intelligent, sane, experienced, skilled people make serious errors. Losing money does not seem to be a deterrent and it does not modify their behaviour. Such reactions are beyond my understanding. I do not waste even my spare time in trying to understand *why* people do these things in the market.

I do, however, spend a lot of time trying to understand *how* people behave in the market. Shift to this focus and an entirely new range of relationships emerges. The study of the market becomes a study of human nature and crowd behaviour. The activity is tracked effectively in the patterns of buying and selling, in the structure of the price charts. They tell me little about the company, but speak volumes about the crowd of buyers and sellers. Tighten the focus a little more, and we discern a set of statistical or probability relationships.

Some are as simple as the propensity of a stock to continue rising after it has been mentioned in *Shares* magazine. We look at this in Chapter 2. Other relationships allow us to hitch a ride with a strong trend in the same way that a flea hitches a ride with an elephant. We do not create the trend, so we look for a crowd surging in the same direction we want to travel. They push a bow wave of profit ahead of them and we use their behaviour to successfully trade the market.

Working with the crowd, but not being part of the crowd, is a strange experience. There is a danger of being sucked into the whirlpool of emotion only to emerge, like so many others, financially poorer for the experience. Our skill and trading discipline protects us from disaster, and in this book we explore seven steps to build one particular approach to market success and survival. This is about trend trading. These are trades which may last weeks, or months, or years. The objective is to find a trend and hitch a ride for a defined period, for a defined return, or until we are aware the trend is no longer moving up.

We do not create the trend, and the level of our trade participation alone is not enough to maintain the trend. For trend continuation we must rely on the activity of many other traders and investors. Understanding what they are thinking and how they are behaving is the most significant aspect of successful trend trading. Understanding how we are going to manage the trade once we buy the stock underpins our trading profitability.

Mastering these aspects of trading is the focus of this book. Of the many different approaches, we have selected the approach we find most useful. Use this as a guide, but not as a universal solution. Understand how we bring together various indicators and analysis approaches to establish our trading solution. When it comes time to build or refine your own approach we hope these ideas will help you create a better solution for your own particular circumstances.

STOCK SELECTION SUCCESS

Good investors and traders know they cannot predict the market and they also know the outcome of any trade is not a 50/50 proposition. However they are a little more skilled at identifying the balance of probability. This is not guesswork. It makes the best possible use of technical and charting indicators to identify where the balance of probability lies. They recognise many of the popular indicators, and other indicators derived from them are very unreliable. Many of these indicators get it right 50% of the time and sometimes even less. People who use them must expect failure because the tools are flawed.

In addition to understanding the role probability plays in the market, successful traders and investors also match trade management with better money management created by good stop loss control. This turns a successful trade into a major contributor to portfolio returns. This ensures an unsuccessful trade has just a minor impact on portfolio returns.

Confused and common thinking is a major barrier to trading successes. Here is a list of inaccurate and confused assumptions:

☐ A trade can only move up or down, so the chance of a trade moving up is always 50%.

☐ Therefore it is very difficult to get the direction of a trade right more than 50% of the time.

☐ Consistent successful trade selection of better than 60% is suspicious because we know there is only a 50% probability of a stock moving upwards.

☐ Trading is really about prediction and we use charting and technical analysis to predict what will happen.

☐ All successful trades must be very large winners to overcome the 50/50 balance of winners and losers.

☐ Common indicators are reliable. They must be because they are so widely used and referred to.

☐ Common thinking leads to uncommon results.

These widely held ideas may help to explain why so many people fail in the market. They are not ideas we use and they do not underpin the way we approach the market.

Let's take the first cluster of misconceptions — a trade can only move up or down, so the chance of a trade moving up is always 50%.

The diagram in Figure 1 shows why this assumption is incorrect. It shows a stock that has been moving sideways for an extended period. The price action is confined to the thick box. Nothing has changed at the point shown by the end of the box. The stock price has three choices — not two. It may continue to move sideways, move up, or move down. Here we make an assumption drawn from Newtonian physics. Newton's law says the object — price — will continue to travel in the same direction until it meets an opposing force. Once it meets this force the direction of travel is deflected. In market terms this may be an important news event which has enough force to deflect or change the direction of the trend.

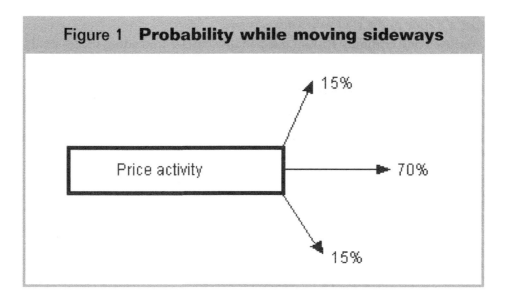

Figure 1 **Probability while moving sideways**

We cannot predict, estimate, know or guess at the news event from the information shown in this diagram. The event is unknowable so we must work with what we have, and it suggests a spread of the balance of probability as shown. There is an equal chance that prices will go up or down, but this balance is not 50% of all the available price options. Instead there is an overwhelming weighting towards a continuation of the existing price movement.

We show this continuation as a 70% probability. We are happy to admit this is informed guesswork based on our close observation of market activity.

The principle underlies the way we approach the market in our weekly *Tutorials in Applied Technical Analysis* newsletter, and this observation is verified by results from the ongoing, real-time monitoring of the notional case study portfolio. You might like to put this probability at 80% or even higher, but we suggest readings at this level do not leave enough room for the impact of significant events. A lower reading does not reflect the tendency of prices to continue to move as a continuation of their previous price direction.

If we have a 70% probability of the price continuing to move sideways then it leaves only 30% for alternative price moves up or down. Here we are happy to accept there is a 50% probability of an up or down movement. This means in terms of the total range of price movement we split the balance — 30% — evenly to suggest a 15% probability of rising prices and a 15% probability of falling prices.

Here is the most important point, usually missed by those who accept common understandings of the market, market behaviour, and the relationship the trader has with this and probability. There is a 70% probability of the current trend continuing. The diagram in Figure 1 shows this price activity as a sideways movement. This means it is *quite easy* to get the direction of a trade right more than 50% of the time. Just by trading in the direction of the sideways movement you have an 85% probability of prices continuing to move sideways or upwards (70% continuation + 15% up = 85%). This is an 85% probability of making a successful trade where price ends equal to or higher than your entry price.

TIPPING THE TREND OF PROBABILITY

When we tip the trend in one direction we get a very important change in the balance of probabilities. A sideways pattern is not dynamic. A sloping uptrend is very dynamic. This shows activity with a crowd of people very interested in buying the stock and this keeps pushing the price upwards.

Our interest is, as always, in the right-hand edge of this chart. The end of the price box shows us all the information we have. Newton's laws of physics still apply. Prices are most likely to continue in the same direction until they are met by an opposing or stronger force. This changes or deflects the direction of the previous price movement and changes the balance of probability.

A rising trend in prices is a measure of price acceleration and increases the probability of uptrend continuation. In Figure 2 we show an increase to 75%. In some cases, when combined with additional selection criteria like those discussed in the following chapters, this is increased to 80%. This plain, clear thinking stands diametrically opposed to mainstream and common thinking about market

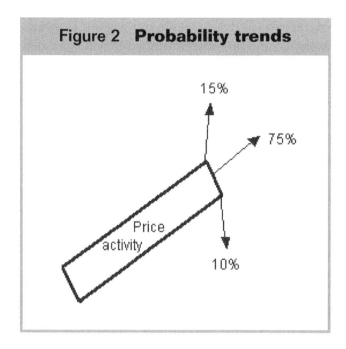

Figure 2 **Probability trends**

and price behaviour. In a trend there is not a 50/50 chance of price moving up or down. There is a 75% probability of the existing trend continuing. This trend acceleration also increases the probability of a price 'pop' or 'bubble' above the trend line. This is very important.

Unlike the sideways movement in Figure 1, the probability of an up or down move is not 50% of the balance or 15% each way. The probability of a higher price rise remains at 15% but the probability of a trend reversal — a drop in prices — is lowered to 10%. The overwhelming balance of probability is 90% in favour of the trend continuing, either at current levels or at slightly higher prices (75% continuation + 15% upwards = 90%). This is the raw power of trend trading. Pick a stock like this and the balance of probability is overwhelmingly on your side. Select a stock where the balance of probability is 90% weighted towards a continuation of the uptrend and it should come as no surprise that the overall trading success rate of stock selection in our newsletter case study portfolio is 73% or higher.

If trend continuation is this high then why doesn't the newsletter show a 90% success rate? The answer is simple. It is called human error, or more accurately, the tendency of traders to try to pick the bottom of downtrends by applying breakout trading techniques. These are exciting because they can lead to very large returns. They are also extremely high risk because we trade against the balance of probabilities. We use a range of specialist techniques and indicators to try to increase the probability of success, but we acknowledge this style of trading is inherently riskier than trend trading. The diagram in Figure 3 shows why.

With apologies again to Newton, we borrow his idea of gravity. Prices feel the impact of gravity, falling much faster than they rise. Compare any downtrend with an uptrend. The overwhelming majority of downtrends are much faster and swifter, and this changes the balance of probabilities.

A downtrend has an 80% probability of continuing and the dip probability remains around 15%. This is an acceleration of the existing trend, and our observations over many years of trading suggest the probability of these dips remains relatively constant. Combine these and you have a 95% probability of a downtrend continuation (80% continuation + 15% dip = 95%).

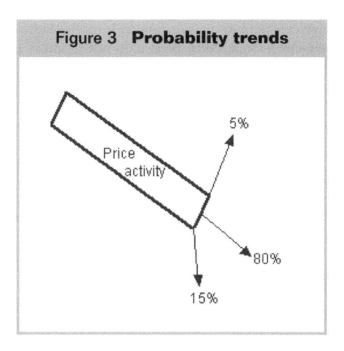

Figure 3 **Probability trends**

At any point in time in a downtrend there is only a 5% probability the trend will stop, reverse, and change into a new uptrend. We can work in that 5% probability area and increase our probability of success by applying a range of tools. However, on balance, we acknowledge the failure rate here is much higher than with other styles of trading. This failure rate is part of what drags our newsletter case study performance down to around 73% success. We also examine a range of other trading strategies in the newsletter and some are included in the case studies just to show how they do not work. The results are included in our portfolio tally and this further reduces the success rate.

A better understanding of the balance of probability in market behaviour makes it easy to understand why the two assumptions below are wrong:

1   Consistent successful trade selection of better than 60% is suspicious because we know there is only a 50% probability of a stock moving upwards.

This is wrong because the balance of uptrend continuation is much higher. When we trade with the strength of probability we achieve a higher success rate.

2   Trading is really about *prediction* and we use charting and technical analysis to *predict* what will happen.

Despite its frequent repetition by many investment writers, this remains inaccurate and untrue. It is common and uncritical thinking and it leads to mediocre performance or failure. It rarely leads to consistent success or market outperformance. Most people do not seriously examine the assumptions they bring to their understanding of the market. They dismiss the idea of prediction because it is fashionable — and then they spend hours looking for a system, a broker or an investment manager with a high success rate because they subconsciously believe this means they can predict the future.

Others are a little more advanced in their understating of probability. They believe there is a 50/50 chance of an up move or a down move so they are happy with a 55% success rate. Trapped by their own limited understanding, they cannot understand how it is possible to achieve consistent stock selection with success rates of 70% or better and so miss the real opportunity to build trading success.

RISK DOES NOT EQUAL REWARD

These crippling misunderstandings do not stop with the concept of probability and trend behaviour. A common belief implies all successful trades must be very large winners to overcome the 50/50 balance of winners and losers. This brings together several assumptions, shown in Figure 4.

High reward means high risk, or so we are told, and like children warned of the dangers of playing with fire, we accept the warning without question. High reward does equal high risk, but only if we choose to sit back passively and do nothing to manage risk. Investment and trade management is about the management of risk.

The idea that once a trade is selected the reward in the trade is about the same as the risk in the trade is shown in the first part of Figure 4. It comes from the assumption that the probability of rising prices is the same as the probability of falling prices. It further assumes the range of this rise or fall is evenly balanced. We could spend a lot of time showing why this is not correct, but we do not need to.

The error in thinking is resolved by understanding the role of a stop loss and the relationship it has with money management. No matter what the range of the downside risk, shown at the right of Figure 4, the stop loss effectively caps the risk at 2% of total trading capital. Our own action in the market using stop loss orders limits the risk by capping the level of loss.

The stop loss limits our risk and allows the rewards to run. We have simplified this diagram to show how even moderate returns are successful in counterbalancing the very small losses in unsuccessful trades. Successful trades do not need to be large winners to grow portfolio returns. The key to success is the way losses are kept small. Those who fail to understand this also often have a lot of difficulty with the concept that a 60% loss in an individual trade is acceptable if the dollar value of the loss is less than 2% of total portfolio capital. A more detailed discussion of the implementation of these concepts is included in Part VI.

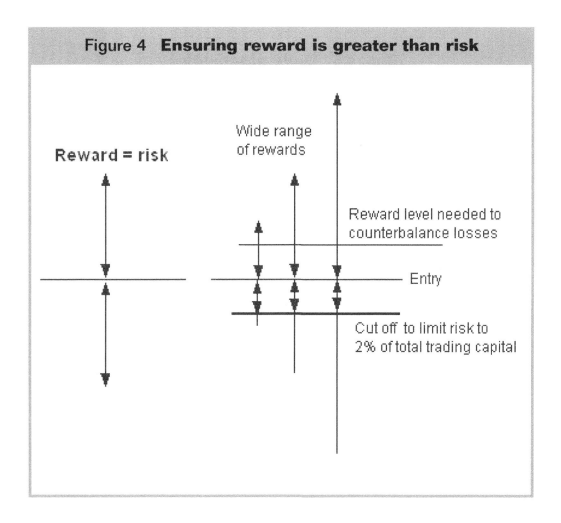

Figure 4 **Ensuring reward is greater than risk**

Reward = risk

Wide range of rewards

Reward level needed to counterbalance losses

Entry

Cut off to limit risk to 2% of total trading capital

The strongly trending chart in Figure 5 shows the final common assumption blocking market success. Many assume common indicators are reliable because they are so widely used and referred to. Others develop more indicators derived from these common indicators, tweaking them with proprietary and secret modifications. The truth is very few popular indicators are consistently reliable and many give no better than a 50/50 chance. Use them, or indicators derived from them, and it is no wonder trading selection success is around 45% to 55%. Some of these indicators are less reliable than a coin toss, but because they are mentioned in most trading books and endorsed by high-profile writers, we assume they must work.

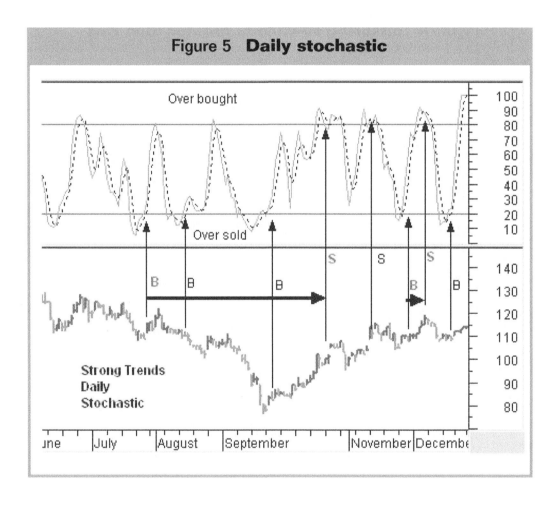

Figure 5 **Daily stochastic**

Consider the bar chart with the stochastic display. Of a total of eight trading signals, there are only two completed trades, shown by the thick black arrows. This is the first buy followed by the first sell. With eight signals we could reasonably expect to see four complete trades defined by an entry and exit signal.

10

Here we see two, giving a reliability rating for this indicator of 50%. The real problem is deciding which of the buy signals is a valid buy signal, and then deciding which of the sell signals is a valid sell signal. Easy to do retrospectively on the chart but devilishly difficult to do in real time.

It gets worse. Of the two trades identified, only one is successful and it is a small winner. The other is a large loser. This is despite the major trend change on the price chart with returns of over 30%.

Common thinking leads to common results. Uncritical thinking leads to poor performance. Thinking it is impossible for anyone to do better than yourself limits your ability to improve your trading. In this book we aim to show readers how a better understanding of the role of probability in the market results in a higher success rate in selecting and managing trend trades. It can be achieved consistently, and with better money management techniques, this is turned into better portfolio returns.

Seven success steps

Most of the material covered in the book is new, including the work on Darvas, the use of trend lines, the structure of selection processes and tests and the extended applications of the Guppy Multiple Moving Average. Inevitably there is some repeated material and concepts but I trust it is presented in a new way that adds to your understanding. Each part examines the tests required to identify, select and manage a trade.

Where do we start and what do we need? The first part, 'Gone fishing', provides a starting point. Common solutions rarely lead to uncommon profits so we spend a little bit of time examining some common ideas to see if they are really useful. This includes several simple methods of finding suitable trading opportunities. The market is complex, but solutions for breaking into it need not be. Simple tools give us access to good profits in the market.

The final chapter in the first part introduces the first of eight ongoing tests for readers. One of the most pernicious and incorrect of common misconceptions about market success suggests we need exclusive information or systems or techniques for success. This series of tests at the end of each part provides all readers with exactly the same information, yet every reader makes a different decision and ends up with a different profit result. The tests are based on similar work we did with newsletter readers so you can compare your results and reactions to theirs.

Sift through any collection of stock charts and some immediately stand out as clear and obvious trading opportunities. We show how this visual test is applied in the second part, 'Hey good looking'. This is not a complicated task and perhaps this is why so many new investors ignore it. Their preference seems to lie with what can only be described as ugly charts when prices fall dramatically from the top left of the chart to the bottom right. These are investment bargains and they come with an invitation to financial disaster. We discuss ways to avoid these attempts to separate you from your investment capital.

The third part, 'Line of lode', introduces a different approach to the application and use of trend lines. These are probability tools directly related to the management of the trade. Many traders use trend lines to define price action, often with a sneaking suspicion that they might be able to predict the future. This part considers these classic applications and then moves beyond them to examine the relationship between the trend line and better trade management. This turns the trend line into a powerful management tool.

Not all trends are created equal and Part IV, 'Testing character', includes an updated and complete discussion of the way the Guppy Multiple Moving Average (GMMA) indicator is used to assess a trend. The GMMA was introduced in *Trading Tactics* in 1997. Since then the indicator has evolved into more advanced and sophisticated applications. For many traders it has become the core way of understanding trend behaviour and indicating the type of trading opportunity. This part provides a detailed discussion of the trading and investment applications of the GMMA.

Before a stock is added to our portfolio we need a price check to more precisely define the trend and our entry point, and to commence the calculations necessary to manage risk. This is examined in Part V. Our preferred tool is the count back line. This was introduced in *Share Trading* in 1996 and this technique has also evolved with more sophisticated applications. It is used as a stop loss to protect trading capital when a trade is first opened. We show how this is applied to mid-trend entries. We also show how the count back line is combined with the GMMA as a protect profit tool as the trend develops. This is a powerful trend trading combination.

'Calculating size', Part VI, covers the key processes in nailing down risk. Risk is the cornerstone of the market, and yet so many people accept the assertion that high reward equals high risk. They believe they are powerless when confronted with the force of the market. This is simply not true and we examine some of the methods designed to effectively manage risk while leaving reward uncapped. The necessary figures are easy to produce, but implementing an effective stop loss or protect profit strategy is much more difficult. Our reaction to risk changes with experience, and unless we recognise these changes we may stumble on the path to success.

'Modern Darvas', Part VII, is an important detour. The approach developed by Nicholas Darvas represents an entirely different way of understanding trend behaviour. Originally developed and successfully applied to markets in the mid-1960s this approach was overwhelmed by the appeal of complex computer-driven analysis of the market and by increasing market volatility. We examine the classic Darvas application. We retain the logic of his understanding of trend behaviour and update the technique for application in modern, volatile markets.

We use six tests to select the best trend trading candidate, and no test is complete without a test result. In 'Performance plus' we discuss some of the ways our performance is diminished. We start a trade with the best of intentions, and then turn it into a trading wreck. This is Jekyll and Hyde trading where our best laid plans and intentions are thrown overboard when it comes time to act. There are no easy solutions to resolve this behaviour, but our discussion is designed to help you recognise the problem. We also examine a technique to separate luck from skill when assessing your trading results.

This part also concludes the 'No secrets' trading tests. Readers who resisted the temptation to flip forward to find the test answers can enjoy the opportunity to measure their performance and reactions against those who took the original test in real time. These test results confirm trading success rests on what you do with information which is also freely available to all your competitors. Success may appear difficult or impossible when everybody knows exactly the same information, but this is just a mirage. Profits come from the way we use information and we can all be successful. This is the true secret of performance plus in trend trading.

Word trends

Just like prices in the market, words are not random. They string together, first in notes, then in articles and chapters, and finally in parts to form a book. Before the words come ideas formed from trading experience, tweaked and stimulated by questions from people who attend our trading workshops, by questions from newsletter readers and others who have read my books. The ideas are challenged and forged in the heat of the market. They withstand scrutiny from industry professionals in Australia, Asia and the United States as the ideas are presented in professional development workshops.

The subject trend in this book gained impetus from the questions posed by Chen Jing, who wanted to know if the strategies could be applied to her home markets of Shanghai and Shenzhen. Like many new traders she felt success depended on using information not held by others and the 'No Secrets' chapters are designed to answer this concern. Additional specialised material was drawn from articles published in our weekly newsletter, *Tutorials in Applied Technical Analysis*, by Adam Cox, Leon Wilson and Matthew Ford. All have contributed to the ideas included in this book and I thank them for their assistance.

Leehoon Chong gave her time again to rigorously hunt down poor expression and the numerous spelling and typographical errors in the early drafts. My mother Patricia added her unique editing skills, proving old teachers of English never willingly surrender their red marking pens. Neither writing nor trading are possible without the support of my wife and son, who have long resigned themselves to the side effects of extended periods of intense concentration while the first draft is created and subsequent drafts rewritten. The time to write this book, free from the everyday demands of running Guppytraders.com, is made possible by the office work managed by Kathryn Flynn.

The end-of-day charts in this book are created by the Guppy Traders Essentials charting package, or MetaStock. A few charts are created by Ezy Charts. End-of-day data comes from JustData and is downloaded with their Bodhi Freeway service.

Common thinking does not lead to uncommon results in the market. Many market myths, or commonly accepted practices, often stand between us and market success. We look at some of these from new perspectives to show how you can find an edge that delivers better market returns. Your skill makes the difference between successful and unsuccessful trading, but we must remember that, like a flea on an elephant, we are just along for the ride.

Daryl Guppy
Darwin
February 2004

PART I

GONE FISHING

CHAPTER 1

HOW DO I START MAKING MONEY?

There are over 1,500 stocks listed on the Australian Stock Exchange, and with diligent research, you might get to really know perhaps 10 of them, or even 30. This ignores the other 1,470 stocks, many of which offer excellent trading opportunities. You need a short-cut that allows you to use your knowledge, and the actions of others, to guide you to better opportunities. We put together several short-cuts and a combination of solutions in this book.

Many people use trading as a part-time occupation to deliver a full-time income and this is a useful approach. The shift from earning money to making money earn money for you is important. Unless you accept that the objective is to make your money work for you, your approach to the market is most likely to be a gambler's approach, looking for quick money. A successful trader develops a different view of the world of money, and the relationship between capital and income.

A typical example of these different views is between those who want to immediately develop a replacement income for their wages, and those who want to use trading to supplement their income. The latter group focus on the most effective use of capital. They are not after a big hit — the gambler's approach. They look for the best return on their capital rather than focus on the size of the dollar return.

Protecting your capital, growing your capital and finding the best return are the core tasks for the trader and investor. Where and how to start are common questions. Some people examine their current job with its heavy time demands and decide the life of a share trader sounds easy in comparison. The common questions about becoming a full-time share trader include:

1   Do I need to become a full-time share trader to benefit from the market?

2   What is the difference between traders and investors?

3   How should I prioritise my learning curve?

4   What seminars, books and resources should I invest in?

5   Where do I get independent analysis?

6   What should I read?

7   Do I need exclusive, and often expensive, information?

8   Where do I start?

In this chapter we examine the first six questions. The last two questions call for dedicated chapters. This is our starting point for the market. Unless we believe it is possible to learn how to succeed in the market we cannot take the first step. Look ahead for a moment. After we embark on this journey we soon face a daunting obstacle — how to find suitable trading or investment opportunities. This is easier than it first appears. The more difficult task is reducing this list from 10 or 15 to just a single stock. Finding the best candidates means we subject each stock to a further six tests. Each part in this book is built around one of these tests, except the detour in Part VII, in which we look at Darvas-style trading. They are combined in the final performance test. The tests are:

☐   A selection test — covered in this part.

☐   A visual test.

☐   A trend line test.

☐   A character test using a Guppy Multiple Moving Average.

☐   An entry test using a count back line.

☐   A position size test.

☐   A performance test.

FULL-TIME OR PART-TIME?

Do I need to become a full-time share trader to benefit from the market? The short answer is 'No'. Full-time share traders are relatively rare and they tend to work for institutions. Full-time private traders are rarer. It is a skilled profession but unlike many professions, it also offers a part-time component. Trading skills are applied to a single trade, or to multiple trades.

When I first started, trading provided a very useful supplement to my wages income. Bank interest on my meagre savings was very high and delivered an extra $1,000 a year. Active management of market investments delivered $10,000 or more a year. Trading was clearly the best use I could make of my savings capital.

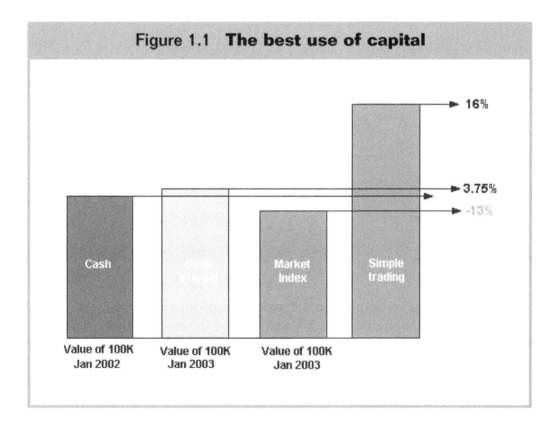

Figure 1.1 **The best use of capital**

The chart in Figure 1.1 shows some sample returns made from part-time trading achieved by a group of my students in Darwin who attended an eight-week course. They made their selections in lesson 1 at a time when they knew

19

little about trading the financial markets. We applied a simple trend trading strategy discussed in the next chapter. Their weekly management of the trades delivered a 16% return on capital over eight weeks.

TRADER OR INVESTOR?

What is the difference between traders and investors? This is a popular question that is often answered incorrectly. The correct division is shown on the left in Figure 1.2.

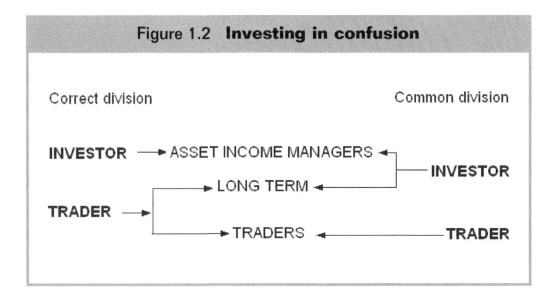

Figure 1.2 **Investing in confusion**

The investor is an asset income manager. He buys an asset such as a house, a government or corporate bond or a share because the asset delivers an income stream. He is particularly concerned about his return on capital as defined by the interest paid, the coupon rate or the dividend rate. When he makes these calculations he starts from the price he paid for the asset and looks at the income generated based on the original price.

If the current price of the asset falls, but the income generated remains much the same, he sees no cause to sell. If the price of the asset rises dramatically he may be tempted to sell to collect a capital gain. This extra capital is then employed to buy another asset such as a rental property, more bonds or other dividend-paying shares available for a low cost.

When the investor makes a decision about how well, or poorly, his asset is performing he measures the rate of income against his original cost — not the current market price of the asset.

The trader has a different objective. He wants to buy a product from a supplier at one price and sell the product to the consumer at another price. His income comes from the difference between the two prices — the price he paid, and the price he receives. Trading is the activity which drives business. It does not matter if you are selling tinned food, televisions, computers, office furniture or shares. The underlying principle is unchanged. We buy an item for one price and intend to sell it to a customer at a higher price.

The successful businessman trader buys items he knows other people want. He buys items in demand because he can resell those items at a higher price. If golf is the current fad there is not much appeal in filling the store with tennis racquets. He buys golf clubs at wholesale and sells them at retail plus 10% wherever possible. We buy shares in a rising trend because we can resell them at a higher price in a few days or weeks or months. Every now and then we get an unexpected bonus on the sale. Others call it a dividend.

Here is where common usage conflicts with the correct understanding of these activities and it is shown on the right hand side of Figure 1.2. When we commonly talk about investing we include both asset income management and trading activities. We bundle the two together and this makes it very easy to fool ourselves when things go wrong.

It works like this:

☐ The 'investor' buys a dividend-paying stock at a good price and holds it for the 'long term'. He is an asset income manager.

☐ The 'investor' buys a stock in a strong industry sector with a bright future. He pays a high price for it because he intends to sell it at some time in the future to collect the capital gain. He thinks he is investing, but in fact he is trading. He buys an item — the share — because he believes others will want to buy it from him at a later date, perhaps in the 'long term', for a higher price.

☐ The 'investor' buys a once-strong stock which has been in a slump for several years. He buys it because he believes the downtrend is about to end as demand for the company's products improves, or management gets better, or for any one of a hundred reasons. He buys this bargain because he believes others will want to buy it off him at a later date, perhaps in the 'long term' for a higher price, so he is prepared to wait. He has no income from the asset while he waits. His profit depends entirely on capital gain. He is trading, not investing.

☐ The 'investor' buys a strongly performing stock that does not pay a dividend. It continues to rise in price for a few months, and then it rolls over into a downtrend. The downtrend continues for several years and the 'investor' still holds onto the stock. In fact, he might even buy some more because it is now cheaper than when he first bought it. His intention is to sell the stock at some time in the future for a higher price than he paid for it. His profit depends on the difference between his buy price and his sell price. He might believe he is an 'investor' because he is dealing with a well-known, high-profile, well-respected listed company, but his purpose is not different from the 'investor' who buys a small bio-tech company hoping to sell it for a higher price at some time in the future. Both are trading, not investing, because their reward comes from capital gain.

The activities of an asset income manager are very different from those of an 'investor'. However, common usage of the term 'investor' combines and confuses asset income management with the business of buying and selling a product — listed market equities or shares. When we talk of investors in this book we are *not* referring to asset income managers. We are talking about 'investors' who aim to make a capital gain from their activity and who believe the 'long term' will assist them.

Take the time to re-examine your own 'investments'. If you purchased them with the intention of selling them at a higher price in the future then this book is for you.

TRADING TIME AND RISK

Popular opinion suggests the difference between trading and investing is also related to the time taken in each trade. Traders are short term, holding a stock for days or weeks. Investors are long term, holding a stock for months or years. Like many commonly accepted ideas in the market, these definitions are quite wrong and misleading. The difference between traders and investors is about their understanding of risk — not time. A trader may ride an uptrend for many months, but this does not make him an investor.

The real difference between traders and investors is in the way they approach the risk of market exposure, and is summarised in Figure 1.3. Investors usually believe the risk is mainly found prior to buying the stock. Their focus is on analysis and stock selection risk. Investors often spend a lot of time selecting the best stock. They favour fundamental research methods, looking at market share, company activities, management quality and financial reports. This research is important.

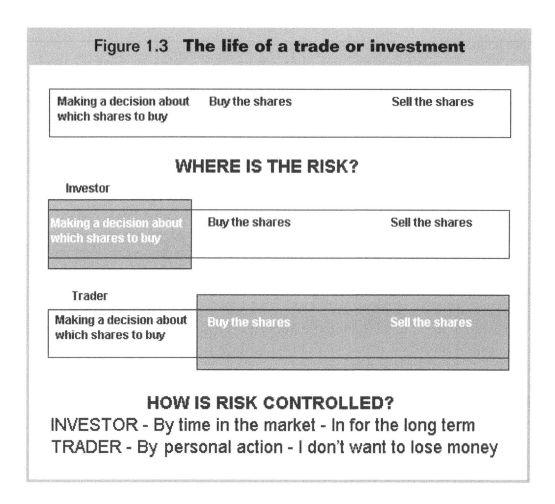

After an exhaustive analysis process the investors buy their selected stock and then largely forget about it because they believe the most difficult part of investing is in finding the right stock. The investors usually believe they have made the right choice. They are prepared to ride out any ups and downs because they believe these are minor fluctuations in the price. When the uptrend turns into a very clear downtrend they stay with the stock because they believe their analysis is sound. Larry Williams, a US trader and author, suggests investors are the biggest gamblers in the market because they make a bet and stay with it.

The trader takes a different approach. He does not abandon analysis of the stock and the company. He takes the time to research the trading opportunity. He may use the same analysis methods as the investor, or he may look for different types of analysis conclusions. The difference is not in how he selects stocks, but how he manages them once purchased.

The trader recognises the time of maximum risk is when he buys the stock. He knows the market has the power to destroy his profits, or his investment capital. He accepts this market test and he accepts the answer provided by the market. If the market does not agree with his analysis, then prices will fall.

Unfortunately if you go to some markets you might be robbed by a pickpocket. You protect yourself against robbery by being vigilant, perhaps by keeping your hand on your wallet or purse all the time. But it does not matter how well you prepare, you know there is a chance you might be robbed so you take extra care. The financial market is a dangerous place because it can snatch your hard-earned money away very rapidly. We must be prepared to act to protect our capital, and our profits. The trader understands this. He knows the real risk in the market comes after he buys a stock so he is ready to take his money and run away at the first sign of trouble.

This is the essential difference between traders and so-called investors. It is not how long they intend to hold the stock. It is how they react when a price fall starts eating into their profit or destroying their capital. The trader takes his profit, or a small loss, and leaves.

The smart investor does the same. This does not always call for a quick decision. Major trends usually decline slowly so the investor has many days or even weeks to sell. By February 2002 it was clear the S&P/ASX 200 uptrend had ended. The index moved broadly sideways for eight weeks before the new downtrend started. This did not call for a quick exit, but those who delayed lost most of their profits by March 2003.

The investor believes his stock selection is correct and he hopes the market is wrong, so he holds on. By the time it is very clear the uptrend has finished the investor is too frightened to sell because he has lost so much of his profit, or his capital. He cannot afford the loss so he keeps the stock and hopes one day it will make money.

The investor does better in the market if he learns how the trader treats market risk when a trade or investment is open. They both have the same objective — to make money from rising prices. The trader achieves this by actively managing his trade. The investor achieves this by actively managing his investment in the face of market price moves. How long they intend to be in the market has nothing to do with making money from rising prices.

The students in Darwin applied a discretionary trading approach which is as relevant to investors as it is to traders. This trading style puts the trader or investor in the driving seat. The trader assembles a collection of his preferred indicators, assigns a level of importance to each, and then makes a decision based on his understanding of the indicator readings and trading signals. This inevitably involves some subjective judgment, and this opens the door for error. The trade is managed in the same way, and this requires a high level of confidence.

Mechanical trading seeks to remove human intervention — and hence subjective behaviour — as much as possible from the trading equation. Typically such systems rely purely on mathematical relationships. However in establishing any system there is subjective human input to determine the most desirable outcomes. Trade management requires discipline and a great deal of faith in the system as traders are tempted to second-guess the trading signals.

Intuitive trading develops from experience, and should not be confused with the gut feelings used by novice traders. Experienced traders are subconsciously aware of certain patterns and market set-ups. When they see them they act intuitively, drawing on many years of trading experience. This requires a high level of confidence and skill, and trades are managed with certainty. These trading processes are difficult to explain. In this book our emphasis is on developing discretionary trading approaches.

Pursuing a part-time occupation is not the same as turning it into a full-time occupation. An extra $10,000 a year is a welcome bonus, coming from just a few hours a week, squeezed in between other job commitments. If you do not get around to opening a new trade it does not have a significant impact on your standard of living. If a trade takes longer to develop than you expect then the lack of cashflow does not disrupt your weekly grocery shopping. As a part-time trader, you do not have to rely on the income generated from trading.

Full-time trading is an entirely different beast. There is no regular income from wages. The pressure suddenly increases because many people feel the need to see a regular weekly income from their activity. They do not like dipping into their savings to meet the weekly food bills. They believe they have to make a certain amount each week to at least match their old wage income. The tendency to gamble becomes much stronger and some trades are closed early simply to generate cashflow to meet weekly living expenses. This pressure is even greater if they do not already have a substantial level of savings to draw on for living expenses when necessary.

In my case, when my three-year work contract finished I was making enough from part-time trading to not have to worry about looking for traditional full-time work. I took on full-time trading only after I was already making a living from it.

You become a full-time trader by graduating from a part-time trader and when your trading income is greater than your current wage income. In this situation you have already accumulated sufficient savings to make full-time trading, with its irregular income flow, a real possibility of success.

But you do not need to become a full-time trader to enjoy the benefits available from trading the market. Most people are able to successfully use part-time trading to provide an excellent supplement to their existing income. This may reduce the pressure to take on overtime, and make longer, unpaid holidays a realistic option, or even hasten the drift towards part-time work. These possibilities are all achievable when wage income is supplemented by part-time trading income.

This approach is the most appropriate for most people, and it is also a vital first step for those who aspire to full-time trading. Trading success is possible, but it is not for everyone. Treat it as a serious part-time occupation first, and then make the transition based on success.

Our objective in this book is to examine trend trading techniques using a group of our preferred indicators. This is not difficult, or time consuming. The approaches and tools are applied successfully to both investing and trading strategies. At heart we want to know how to find big fish, how to catch them, and how to land them successfully so we can generate a steady income from the market. This could be a weekend hobby, a nightly obsession, or a full-time occupation. The choice is yours, and the trend trading techniques we discuss will assist you on the path to success.

LEARNING STEPS

How should I prioritise my learning curve? Traders tend to follow the same type of learning curve, and although there is no short-cut, there are ways of recognising where you are on the curve and avoiding some of the mistakes made by others. Everyone's journey is the same, but different in detail.

Most of us assume there is a direct relationship between our knowledge of trading and charting tools and our trading success. This belief is based on our success in other activities where we generally experience a direct relationship between knowledge, skill and success.

This is a straight line relationship, shown in Figure 1.4 as a thick black line sloping up from poor knowledge and poor ability to expert knowledge and wizard performance. We accept not all of us will become wizards, but we expect our native ability to improve with more knowledge and understanding.

Learning about trading does not work in this way. When we start trading we believe our lack of analysis skills stands between us and success. To some extent, this is true. There are advantages in learning how to use the tools of charting and technical analysis correctly. Many of our early trading mistakes come from simply not understanding how to apply a stochastic, or failure to understand the entry and exit signals. We improve our chances of success in the market with basic education, and for a while there is a steep and successful learning curve.

The learning curve of the typical trader is shown by the curving lines in the bottom section of Figure 1.4. The first curve moves quickly upwards. The more we know about the tools of analysis, the better our trading becomes. We generally move quickly from poor, or uninformed, ability to average. Then something strange happens. Our trading performance plateaus. Trades that worked in the past stop working. The number, and perhaps size, of our losses grows. This is where many traders are washed out of the market because the number and size of their wins is not large enough to overcome their losses. We want to get off this poor performance plateau and we believe the easiest way is to learn more about the market and technical indicators.

This is often when the trader decides to purchase an expensive tool box charting program to access more indicators. Some people consider specialist programs that give them the ability to extensively construct and test trading systems and indicators. A significant group goes hunting for short-cuts and they are fodder for the tip sheet newsletters. Another group believe success comes from a black box system advertised in a glossy brochure. This looks like a short-cut but more than a few are mugged along the way.

The thirst for knowledge is driven by the belief that the more we know about the subject, the better our performance will be. We are still stuck with this vision of a straight line relationship between knowledge and skill.

For many people the quest for additional knowledge results in confusion. Market clarity is replaced with many competing approaches and subtle distinctions. The difference between indicators like Williams %R and a rate of change calculation is only a matter of degree. Depending on your trading style, it may or may not give you a significant edge. We all feel a compulsion to explore the 200 indicators in the MetaStock charting package to see if there is one combination that will improve our trading results.

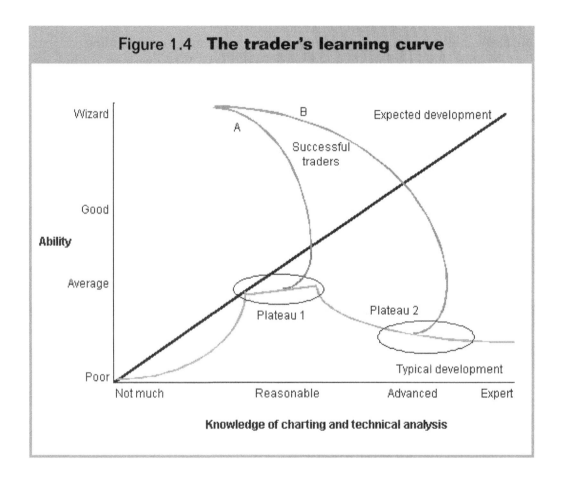

Figure 1.4 **The trader's learning curve**

This confusion is compounded by muddled attempts to apply a range of systems. This week we are fascinated by the Relative Strength Indicator and we take several trades based on this idea. Next month we believe the ADX indicator is more important, based on a magazine article. We try a few trades based on these ideas. The result is our trade planning disappears under the assault of so many choices.

Unless we are careful our trading performance declines to a new lower plateau. We are still performing better than the beginner, but our performance is now less than average. This is analysis confusion, and it may take many months, or years, to work our way out of this. The way out of the labyrinth still rests with education but the shift is from the mastery of the theoretical subject matter to the practical implementation of trading. Owning an expensive tool set and knowing the correct names of each chrome-plated spanner, screwdriver and set of pliers does not make you a motor mechanic. This book is designed to help you take the next step.

Sadly the typical trader is eliminated either on the first plateau or on the second. There are also a few spectacular falls from other points on the curve. Traders fall off the plateau because they simply run out of money or stop making money, and that dampens their enthusiasm.

The difference between average traders and successful or wizard traders is shown by lines A and B, and our objective is to show you how to change your learning curve to match these. No matter which plateau you start from, the outcome is the same. It marks an important shift in attitude and understanding.

While our trading is on the plateau we develop a belief that because the market is a complex system the best way to understand it is by using complex indicators. The first step on the new learning curve is taken when we discard this notion. The Darwin students' trading results at the start of this chapter are evidence that simplicity works.

We have shown the successful trader's learning curve as arching back towards a reasonable level of knowledge. This is a little misleading. In reality the curve shows the way we select a 'reasonable' amount from our total trading knowledge and apply it to the market and our trading approaches. This selection is always a move away from complexity and towards simplicity. Although we know a great deal about systems, indicators, trading methods and money management we make a conscious decision to apply just a handful of this knowledge to our trading. We need the additional knowledge before we can make the decision to exclude some of it. We cannot trade successfully from a position of ignorance, but like an artist, the best pictures are built from what we choose to leave out.

Successful traders know a lot about the market but they approach it using simple techniques. Books like Schwager's *Market Wizards* series, Toghraie's *Real People: Real Traders* and Nick Radge's *Every-Day Traders* all underline this observation. Each plateau provides us with a constellation of choices. Our choices expand as our knowledge grows, and the second plateau provides more choices than the first. A few typical traders take the short-cut to trading success from the first plateau. Most traders slip slowly into the second plateau in a process which is measured in years rather than months. By making a conscious selection of just a few proven or preferred methods we improve our trading success quite substantially. This is the real secret of success for market wizards.

We emulate this by understanding the process. Rather than being just part of the general confusion and following the typical learning curve, we can recognise what is happening, take steps to avoid the obvious pitfalls and accelerate our take-up of the upper learning curves. If we know our position on the curve, we can prioritise the resources and tools we need for each stage.

The diagram shows the curve in relation to knowledge of charting and technical analysis. It does not show an axis related to money management. If we could do this, we would show these upper learning curves also curving away from each plateau to show an increase in knowledge about money management techniques. More knowledge continuously improves trading performance. It is the hidden partner in trading success.

RANKING RESOURCES

What resources, books, software, seminars or learning tools should I invest in? The difference between coaching and tipping is important. The beginner knows he does not know much, so it is tempting to buy a weekly publication that purports to provide a list of stocks to buy. Some may be published by obscure groups or organisations, while others are published by well-known identities. In all cases, the tip sheet provides buying, and occasionally selling, advice. Generally the reasons for buying are rarely explained. Subscribers are asked to accept the buy recommendation based on the experience and reputation of the tip sheet publisher. Alternatively they are encouraged to accept that buy recommendations are the result of some specialist technical technique. Parts of the technique may be revealed, but readers are never entirely certain how the final buy recommendation is made. Any technically based search is likely to turn up 10 to 20 potential trading candidates, so unless we know why one candidate was selected in preference to the others we can never learn how to emulate these decisions.

Tip sheets do not teach. Traders learn nothing useful from them. In many cases, all they learn is bad habits, particularly when it comes to handling the inevitable trading errors. Tip sheets are in the business of publishing and marketing. The financial market is their chosen field, but it could just as easily be horse racing, property development or Tupperware. These are harsh comments, but an extended and serious examination of tip sheets provides the evidence.

From a coaching perspective, understanding how to handle trading errors is vital for survival. From a marketing perspective, errors in stock selections are a negative. Readers want successful tips, which is why they buy the newsletter. Advertising highlights how many tips the newsletter got right, and shows dramatic returns on a few selected trades. It makes for good advertising and increases circulation. Unfortunately it bears little relation to the real world of trading.

Tip mistakes — stocks that go down instead of up — are quietly ignored and very rarely discussed in detail again in the tip sheet. Publishers are able to do this because the churn rate of subscribers is high, and the attention span of readers is short. Readers want the next hot tip and are not interested in the losers. After 12 months many subscribers have stopped reading the tip sheet because trade losses have robbed them of trading capital. It is easy to hide the losers behind the hype of a few winners.

Ignoring losers mirrors the way many new traders approach their own portfolio performance. They ignore Telstra trading at $5.00 — which they purchased at $8.00 — and focus on other stocks that have gained 15% over recent weeks.

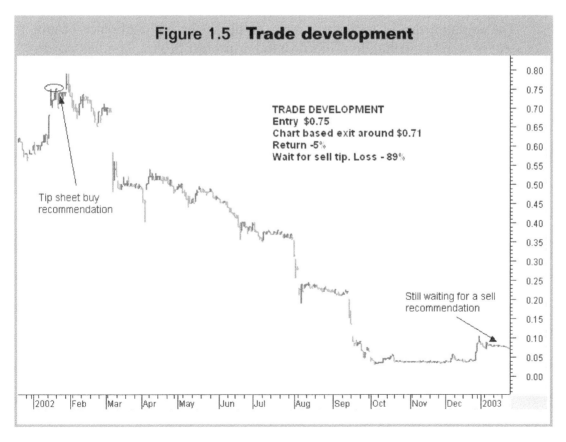

Figure 1.5 Trade development

TRADE DEVELOPMENT
Entry $0.75
Chart based exit around $0.71
Return -5%
Wait for sell tip. Loss - 89%

Tip sheet buy recommendation

Still waiting for a sell recommendation

Here is a performance reality check with examples culled from several tipping services. We start with Figure 1.5 and simply note the absence of any sell advice as the stock lost over 90% of its value. Take the time to do the same by listing the buy recommendations from a tip service and then matching them with sell tips for the same stocks. The results are enough to frighten any serious investor or trader.

One market report recommended the purchase of a mining stock. No sell advice was issued — not even when it was clear the stock was going to be delisted! This 100% loss was not included in portfolio accounting. Another market report recommended a media share at $0.75. Two weeks later the trend collapsed. A year later the stock was trading at $0.10. No sell advice was issued to subscribers.

Another market report recommended a stock to readers at $0.85 and suggested readers hold onto the stock when the trend collapsed to $0.64 after a clear trend peak at $1.00. Readers were encouraged to hold onto the stock throughout the downtrend because they were told it was going to climb back even higher than $1.00. It took another 16 months to reach $1.01.

The common thread with these types of tip sheets is the absence of any concept of stop loss selling to protect capital or protect profits. In other words, there is *no risk control* because the success of the tip sheet rests on its ability to get the tips right. They are not interested in teaching their readership how to trade, perhaps because much of their income comes from magazine and newsletter sales.

Tips are for waiters. Tip sheets are not for traders, although later we show how they are used in a trading strategy.

A good coach or coaching newsletter should spend as much time analysing their losers as they do their winners. A coach explains how he reached his conclusions. He demonstrates how decisions were made. He examines ways the decision could be improved. The coach concentrates on risk control — on what to do when things go wrong. He recognises failure is part of the game. Failed trades are recognised and accurately accounted for in any portfolio report. The coach demonstrates in advance how he intends to manage the trade, how his stop loss is structured and why he has chosen one particular method rather than another.

The coach analyses every trade for ways to make it better. He develops a clear trading plan setting the conditions for selection, entry and exit. The final aspect of the plan is how much return the trade could make.

To stay at the top of his game, champion golfer Tiger Woods employs several coaches. He has a coach for his golf swing. He has a putting coach. He does not have a tip sheet.

How do you get a coach? There are three ways:

1   Hire a personal trading coach and be prepared to pay for his time and expertise. It has taken the trainer many years to learn this skill so it is not available for a pittance. Coaches include Nick Radge at Reef Capital, www.reefcap.com, Robert Deel at www.tradingschool.com and Oliver Velez at www.pristine.com. They all work with a small number of selected students.

2   Attend workshops. These may be general trading workshops, or workshops on specific techniques. They are not free or under $100. Seminars at these price levels are a marketing hook to attract customers who are potential clients for very expensive trading programs, systems or products. If you want genuine coaching in a real workshop environment where you are expected to learn how to trade by yourself then expect to pay between $200 and $2,000. The presenter's trading experience did not come for free, and he does not give it away for free.

3   Subscribe to a teaching or coaching newsletter or magazine. In terms of magazines, *Active Trader*, *Technical Analysis of Stocks and Commodities*, *Chartpoint* and *Your Trading Edge* offer teaching resources. They do not discuss current individual buy and sell opportunities. Their focus is on exploring techniques and tools. *Shares* magazine leans more towards stock selection advice than education.

Our weekly newsletter, *Tutorials in Applied Technical Analysis*, is one of the very few coaching newsletters available worldwide. It provides an opportunity to look over my shoulder, and the shoulders of other traders, as we find, assess, select and manage different types of trading opportunities in current market environments. We know many people do not have the time or discipline to explore and apply different trading techniques so the newsletter provides a way to properly explore these ideas with disciplined application. The newsletter is an ongoing smorgasbord of techniques and opportunities. We use notional case study trades, managed and monitored in real time with weekly reporting, to demonstrate and evaluate a variety of trading techniques.

This is not individual coaching, but the insights into the reality of trading are as close to coaching as possible in a newsletter format. Most of our income is derived from trading the market — not from newsletters.

ANALYSIS INDEPENDENCE

Where do I get independent analysis? Trading and investment analysis should be objective. One of the strengths of charting and technical analysis is its use of objective figures — price activity — which are readily available to anyone interested in the market. How individual traders choose to apply and interpret those analysis techniques is a matter of subjectivity.

The fundamental analyst relies on figures created by the company in annual reports and press releases. He works with figures generated by outsiders, such as auditors and accountants. He also works with figures produced by others for particular purposes. The application of fundamental analysis is a subjective process from the very start because very few of the figures used are independently verifiable. Even the balance sheet is a carefully massaged document.

A significant problem for traders and investors who rely on the research and analysis of others is the objectivity of the research and recommendations. When a research company is being paid by a company to do the work then it is not uncommon for the report to put the best possible gloss on the situation. When a brokerage is preparing a report on a company, and it is also handling trading work for the same company, then the same constraints apply. The result is few sell recommendations are produced by the analysis industry. This applied even in 2000 after the tech market crashed.

READING IS CHEAP

What should I read? New traders starting out on the path to part-time or full-time trading should read, read, and read. This is the cheapest part of any market education. Follow up areas of interest with specific reading, then explore the ideas with paper trading to see how they work, and if they work for you. The market has many opportunities. Some are more complex than others. We do not have to follow every opportunity. However, it is useful to know what is available before we make a decision about what suits us.

There are many excellent books available, and we mention many of them throughout this book. In no particular order we suggest any books written by

Alan Hull, John Murphy, Martin Pring, Robert Deel, Jack Schwager, Louise Bedford, Chris Tate, Tony Oz, Thom Dorsey or Alexander Elder are worth buying.

Under the Traders Reading button link on www.guppytraders.com we have posted reviews of several hundred trading books. Many trading books are expensive, and there is nothing more annoying than spending $80 to $120 on a trading book only to find it is not particularly useful. The objective in these book reviews is to give you some idea of the content and usefulness of new trading books as they are released. If we review a book, it means we have read it. The reviews are written from the perspective of a trader. Books are ranked from 'must have' books for serious traders to 'bedside reading' for those who have a consuming interest in all things related to the market. Use the rankings and the reviews as a guide to books you have heard about, or areas of interest you wish to pursue in more detail.

In terms of my own books, this summary guide may be useful.

SUBJECT	BOOK	MARKET EXPERIENCE
Want to know more about trading?	*Share Trading*	Beginner to experienced
Want to know more about charts?	*Chart Trading*	Beginner to experienced
Want to know more about tactics?	*Trading Tactics*	Beginner to experienced
Want to improve your trading results?	*Better Trading*	Experienced to professional
Want to understand short-term trading?	*Snapshot Trading*	Experienced to professional
Want to survive difficult markets?	*Bear Trading*	Beginner to experienced
Want to understand low-risk trading?	*Trend Trading*	Beginner to experienced

New traders start small and part-time. Apply just one technique on paper. When it works successfully several times think about taking a single trade using the technique. Build on successes, and make sure the inevitable failures do only limited damage.

You did not get to your current career position in a single bound. Nor will you get to be a full-time trader in a single bound. Every success, no matter how small, is important. Concentrate on the return on capital and real money will follow. Long-term, part-time trading to supplement your income offers a good compromise solution. We do not dismiss it out of hand. Let's go fishing for market opportunity.

CHAPTER 2

FISH FINDING

Finding market opportunity is not very different from a weekend fishing trip. Both present a wide variety of possible locations. Finding where the fish are clustered, and then hooking onto the best of them presents familiar problems and solutions. The fisherman may choose to talk with others, gathering hot tips about the best fishing spots. In market terms, this is the same as following hot tips generated by experts, newsletter writers or your next door neighbour who works for a particularly interesting company.

Other fishermen know the general area they want to fish so they head out quickly from the boat ramp, before turning to their fish finder to help them locate where the fish have gathered. This is a little like the technical analyst who trawls through his database looking for stocks which meet particular conditions.

Smart fishermen are more cunning. They let nature do the work for them. First they anchor near some snags, or a rocky bar. Then they cut up some old bait, or burley, and throw it over the side. This burley in the water attracts small fish. Their feeding attracts other fish, and before long the real predators arrive. Having lured the fish to him, the fisherman casts into the middle of the feeding frenzy and gets a nice hook up. It might not be the biggest fish, but he can confidently cast in the same area many times and catch fish.

We use the same techniques in the market. For burley, we use specialist newsletter publications or magazines like *Shares*. Their research brings bigger fish, and as we show later in this chapter, we fish with a high probability of success.

Any edge we gain from a new trading method is very short-lived. Information spreads quickly, and extensively. If we use a secret technique then we only have a temporary edge. It is unlikely we are smart enough to stumble across a new indicator or trading approach or a brand new trading method. It is more likely any method we use is soon 'discovered' by many other traders who are working at a solution to the same problem and who are much smarter than we are. Despite the widespread use of standard indicators, many people use them to trade the market effectively. Many successful traders use quite simple methods, including the same trend lines and moving averages as you do. They trade the same markets, base their decisions on the same end-of-day data, and use the same charting packages as the trader working from home. Yet some traders are very successful, while others struggle to return a profit.

It is not the information you have that is important. It is what you do with the information that counts. We all start with the same information — the same chart and the same entry point — but the final trading results are quite different. The main reason for the difference lies with our individual response to fear and greed. Each of us has different exit points based on how much cash we worry about losing, or the amount we think we deserve from the trade.

Hot tips

I am often asked to give hot tips, and I am often given hot tips. Whether we give them or accept them, our reaction to tips tells us something about our chance of long-term survival. I do not give tips and I do not accept tips because they are inconsistent with my approach to trading the market.

We all know of somebody who has made a small fortune from a hot tip. They are not shy about telling us. We do not get to hear about those who have lost money following hot tips, although there are many more losers than winners. They are simply too embarrassed to tell other people about their experience. Everybody gets bad tips, while good tips go to only a few. There is always the feeling brokers and dealers get information first and they benefit from it. This is true, but in an increasingly transparent market, this information edge is getting smaller. These professionals still make money from this edge because they have the knowledge and skill to analyse this information quickly. Their trading edge comes not from the information, but their quick understanding of what to do with it.

Stand on the floor of the futures exchange and watch the floor traders' reactions to the news tickers. They know what to do instantly while you and I are still struggling to work out the significance of apparently minor news events. The difference is analysis skill and this is the real trading advantage.

Forget for the moment the unethical and illegal relationship between insider trading and hot tips, and consider how these short-cuts prevent the development of trading skills. The real appeal of a hot tip is the possibility of making money without working. The tip entices us with the suggestion that fundamental and technical market analysis is not required for success. Tips attack the discipline required to develop and apply consistent analytical skills to the important problems of investing and trading. Undermine this discipline and it is more difficult to apply discipline when it comes to managing the trade.

The hot tip delivers a conclusion without supporting evidence. Trading becomes an act of faith and it implies absolute trust in the person who gave the tip because we are unlikely to find additional information, or unearth confirming data. We surrender responsibility for success or failure to somebody else. We rely on another tip to tell us when to get out, or when to salvage a losing trade because we were not able to apply a consistent analysis to the entry. After all, it was a tip.

I am a private trader and so I accept full responsibility for my trading results. I do not wish to work for somebody else. If I accept hot tips I am really working for somebody else because I have turned my back on my own analysis skills in favour of a quick fix with no plan. There are people who will take the responsibility for managing your trading portfolio. They charge a fee for their professionalism, for their consistent analytical approach and for their planned approach to investing your capital. These tips come with a guarantee of professionalism.

Serious traders are interested in making money from the market as a result of correct analysis. Some rely heavily on fundamental information, while others use charting and technical analysis tools. No matter which approach or combination they choose, each trading or investment decision is based on sound analysis. The market is analysed in a disciplined and consistent way. Trading improves because the trader is able to identify repeated errors arising from his consistent approach to market analysis. He knows where he went wrong, and why, and this improves his systematic approach.

His analysis uses continuous and credible independently verified data. The market applies a process of natural selection because the data is available to anyone and everyone. Only the best trading methods and the most reliable data sources survive. Unsuccessful trading methods are abandoned or modified using other reliable data available. Our skill in understanding the market develops steadily, and with it, our confidence. Traders do not always get it right, but when they are wrong they know why. Because they understand what they are doing and why, they are more inclined to develop good risk control strategies based on money management. Analysis requires discipline and discipline also helps when it comes to trade management. We ignore hot tips unless they are confirmed by our independent analysis.

THE EDGE OF ARROGANCE

Your market survival depends on finding a trading edge — a technique or approach to put you ahead of the competition. This makes intuitive sense, and often the first intuitive reaction is to find information before anybody else knows about it. At worst, this is insider trading based on information coming from company sources or closed boardroom meetings. At best, the information comes from superior analysis of known facts.

There is an unacknowledged arrogance in this approach. At heart it suggests Mr Smith, or Sondberg, or Cheung, none of whom have accounting qualifications, can burrow through company reports and find a conclusion the most skilled analysts or company directors have somehow missed. It is unreasonable to expect a person whose largest life-time investment is his house or apartment to have the slightest chance of out-guessing or out-managing skilled entrepreneurs like Kerry Packer or Hong Kong magnate Li Ka-shing.

This arrogance is only one step removed from the belief that a brokerage analyst, who may be slightly better qualified, is able to pick apart company reports and evaluate company performance and direction much more effectively than the company Board. And to top off this arrogance, we expect the brokerage analyst to be an expert in not one company, but a dozen or more.

A small understanding of these factors is better than no understanding at all, but it is foolish to suggest this information somehow gives us an investment or trading edge over our competitors. In all likelihood they have the same information we do, and may even have received it earlier than we did. It is only when we put this so-called information edge into perspective that we can concentrate on developing a realistic trading edge.

Those traders who prefer the objective analysis of price activity — the technical analysts and the chartists — are not immune from this same type of arrogance. Their search for the definitive edge takes a different form and it is usually a variation of a search for a perfect indicator to forecast the market turning points. The novice technical analyst often believes he can discover a new relationship, or a new twist to an established indicator. He believes such an indicator gives him an edge in the same way other traders believe early access to company news gives them an edge.

Operating in parallel to the financial analysis industry is the trading system industry. For a few thousand dollars, and a chance to buy one of the last remaining licences, you can use software for just a few minutes a day to automatically generate remarkably accurate buy and sell signals. Both these industries sell a product to people who believe the key to market success lies in knowing something before others do so they can predict the future. Persistent failure simply confirms you have chosen the wrong analysts or system. It is difficult to shake these ideas, and perhaps it partly explains the widespread failure rate amongst market participants.

CASTING BURLEY

At Guppytraders.com we have several research departments employing around thirty staff in total. Every day they search the market for opportunity. The annual costs for our research departments range from a $77 subscription to *Shares* magazine to up to $700 for other similar services. A single successful trade covers these combined costs. You have access to exactly the same research, and in these chapters we demonstrate how to use the material generated by our common research departments.

We believe market success comes from what you do with the information also available to everybody else. We assume we do not get access to early information, outstanding analysis or the early warning technical indicator tool. We accept we are probably the last in the information chain but this does not hinder trading success.

Our trading philosophy rests on five foundation beliefs:

1 Everybody has the same information that we do, or more.

2 Price behaviour reflects crowd emotion.

3 Today's price is a continuation of yesterday's crowd emotion.

4 Future price behaviour is best analysed in terms of a probability matrix.

5 Risk is directly related to price and is manageable.

These beliefs underpin our broad trading strategy and specific market trading tactics. Our trading edge comes from what we do with information. It does not come from early access to information. Trading results depend on skill and risk management and these in turn depend upon a variety of behavioural characteristics we developed long before we started thinking about trading the market.

In a series of workshops over several years, we demonstrated the practical application of these beliefs. We call it a *Shares* strategy because it is based around information published in *Shares* magazine. The same approach is applied in the same way to information from a variety of specialist financial publications. The key requirement is the readership must primarily purchase the publication for its information on shares and trading. These publications usually also provide some form of hot tip service.

The *Shares* strategy is a robust trading approach based on using the observed statistical relationships to set up a probability matrix as shown in Figure 2.1. The strategy is disarmingly simple: buy stocks which are mentioned in *Shares* magazine and which are also in an established uptrend on the chart because they have an 80% probability of remaining in an uptrend for eight weeks.

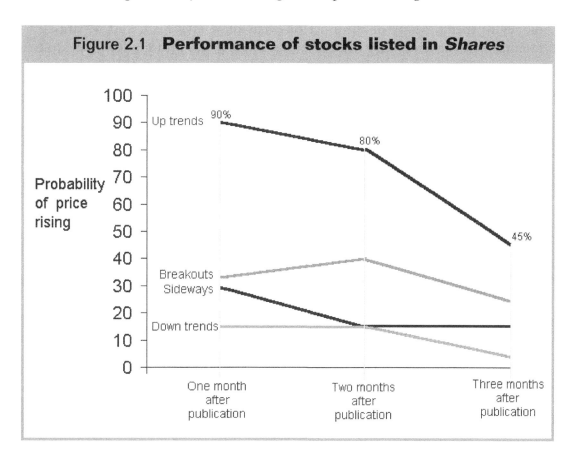

Figure 2.1 **Performance of stocks listed in *Shares***

The strategy is robust and returns a profit most of the time. The level of profit varies, but it is a profitable trading strategy. The strategy is time-based, lasting for a maximum of eight weeks unless an earlier stop loss exit is triggered. The exit is managed carefully in week eight to lock-in the best exit price.

The strategy is not based in trying to analyse what the writers and analysts in *Shares* magazine think about each company. They have done the research and we do not want to duplicate this. We are not interested in the accuracy of their research or analysis but we are interested in the observed statistical impact on stocks which are mentioned in the magazine. Some workshop participants found this an uncomfortable idea. They felt more comfortable with an information edge — find the best write ups — rather than with a statistical probability edge.

In market terms, *Shares* magazine and other specialist newsletters are like burley thrown into the water. These publications attract people who are interested in the market. People buy these publications for one purpose only — to learn how to make money with the shares mentioned each week or month.

These are specialist publications and they attract specialist crowds who have money to spend. Many of them act on what they have read, and we are all familiar with the temporary readers' bump where prices lift for a few days after a favourable news report. If we look at the broader picture a different set of relationships emerges. Get your company mentioned in *Shares*, and there is a good chance a small crowd gathers around your stock. When crowds gather they get emotional. When they get emotional they provide traders with opportunities.

What happens to a stock mentioned in *Shares* magazine? With *Shares* magazine the statistical relationship favours a continuation of existing uptrends. One month after publication, 90% of stocks that were in an uptrend remain in an uptrend. Two months after publication, 80% of uptrending stocks are still trending up. Three months after publication only 45% of uptrending stocks remain in an uptrend. The rest have either declined or started to move in a sideways pattern.

This is the core of the strategy. If we select a stock mentioned in *Shares* magazine which is in an uptrend then there is around an 80% probability it will continue to trend upwards for around eight weeks. This is a high-probability strategy.

Stocks in a downtrend have around a 15% chance of turning into a new uptrend by the end of the first and second month after publication. Three months later, less than 5% of downtrending stocks are still in an uptrend. Stocks moving sideways have a 29% chance of moving up at the end of the first month. However this is a minor blip, and the probability of a continued uptrend drops to 15% over months two and three.

Stocks that have started to move in a breakout from a downtrend fare slightly better in the first month with a 33% probability of rising. The second month lifts this to 40% and reflects the rally and retreat behaviour of breakouts. During the first month some stocks rally, and then retreat below the original breakout level. By the end of the second month a new rally has carried prices higher but less than 25% of breakout stocks continue with this rally into the third month after publication.

There are always a few stocks with readers' bumps. These stocks move up sharply in the first month of publication, and then by the end of the second month the pre-existing trend prevails every time. If it was a downtrend, then the stock moves back into a downtrend after the readers' bump. If it was in an uptrend, the readers' bump bubble collapses back to the original uptrend.

A word of caution. These are broad statistical relationships. Some months do better, or worse, than these general relationships. However we have found these broad relationships are accurate and provide a good basis for a trading strategy.

PERFORMANCE BIAS

We workshopped this strategy with nine large groups spread throughout Australia. We gave each group exactly the same information, and applied exactly the same trading strategy. Despite this, there was a substantial variation in the results. This is perhaps the most important observation of all because it can be directly transferred to our own trading. Results did *not* depend on information — it was the same in all workshops. Results did *not* depend on the trading system or technique — it was also the same.

Results depended on the way our personal — or collective — bias influenced our stock selection. Some groups made 'better' selections than others. Results were directly correlated to the way the trades were managed. Holding onto losers in some cases destroyed *all* open profits from other, successful trades.

Let's put this another way. You can destroy any excellent trading system in two ways. First by your stock selection. Most trading systems offer several choices at the end of each scan. Most analysts offer a choice of several stock selections. As you do not have the money to trade all selections, you must make a choice about which selection gets your cash.

The second path to destruction is your trading discipline, or lack of it, which undermines a successful trading approach. This is not just developing the discipline to sell when stop loss points are hit. It is also the discipline to sell to lock-in profits rather than trying to second-guess the system and hold on for just a little bit of extra profit.

Each workshop started with a list of all the stocks reviewed in the same single old issue of *Shares*. We do not look at what the journalists have written about these stocks because we are not trying to guess which is the best analysis. The list is a starting point, and the first step is to divide the list into four groups:

1   Stocks in an established uptrend — 80% probability of continuing up for the next eight weeks.

2   Stocks in a downtrend.

3   Stocks just starting to break upwards from a downtrend.

4   Stocks moving sideways.

The workshop objective was to trade four stocks with a nominal $40,000, so the first action list had to be reduced using several selection tests until just four candidates remained. The remainder of this book examines these selection tests in detail, so we just provide an outline here. The selection starts with a visual, or eyeball, scan of each chart. Stocks in an uptrend are noted and moved into the next action list. All others are dropped from consideration.

The second selection filter uses the Guppy Multiple Moving Average (GMMA) to understand the nature of the trend. Those stocks not matching the criteria are eliminated.

The third filter step is based on the ease of trade management. Stocks for which the trend is easily defined using a straight edge trend line are easier to manage than stocks where there are multiple similar trend line choices. With a single definitive trend line there is less room for argument and quibbling when the exit signal comes. This makes it easier to apply trading discipline.

The fourth test looks at ways to match price and risk with a verifiable trade management technique. The fifth test makes selections based on trading size, price and risk factors.

In some groups the final selection came down to an emotional decision. With perhaps five stocks standing after applying the selection tests the group had to make an intuitive decision on which stock to drop so they could end up with the four required. On a personal level this reflects the difficulty of any trading decision. Every selection process starts with many candidates and the list must be narrowed down, usually to just a single trade opportunity. Often the final decision between a handful of candidates is based on emotion. Our personal bias has a full opportunity to come out and play.

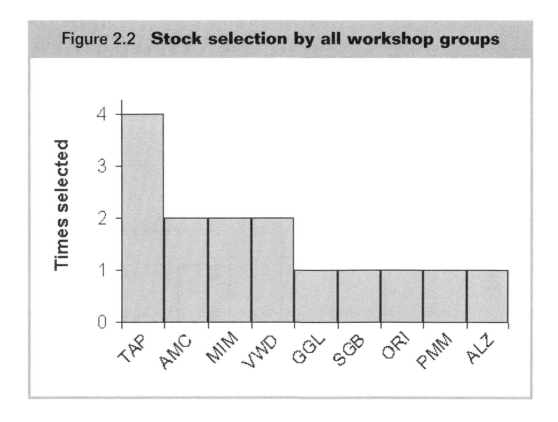

Figure 2.2 **Stock selection by all workshop groups**

With access to exactly the same information and using exactly the same trading system, the workshop groups could only agree on a single stock as shown in Figure 2.2. TAP was selected by every group. AMC, MIM and VWD were the next most selected stocks. Of the remainder, each was selected by only one group.

What accounts for the difference? It is not the information or the strategy because these were the same in all cases. The difference comes from the collective bias of the group. It is difficult to generalise, but Brisbane workshop participants were more optimistic. They had the highest number of stocks remaining after the first eyeball scan. With their bullish view they seemed to believe any chart showing sign of an uptrend — no matter how steep or how undeveloped — was likely to keep on climbing. By the end of the selection process they had to eliminate three stocks based on emotion.

In contrast, Sydney participants were more conservative. They dropped fast-moving stocks in the first eyeball scan. Their choices tended to favour slower moving trends and blue chip stocks. Many of these were subsequently dropped after GMMA analysis, but the conservative bias remained.

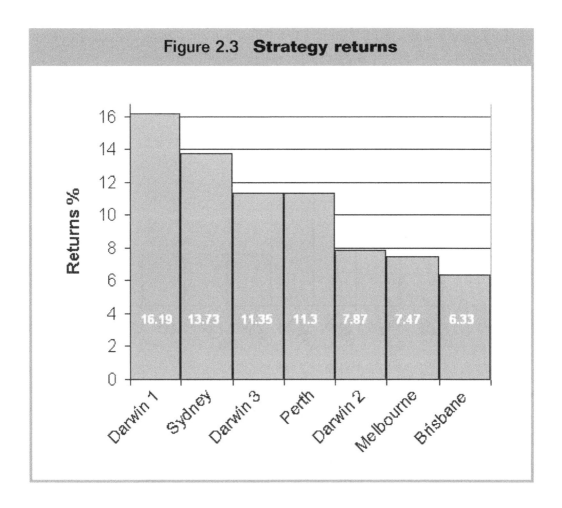

Figure 2.3 **Strategy returns**

In stark contrast to all was the first group of Darwin students. Many of them were beginners and this gave them a decided advantage. They had few preconceptions about charts, indicators and trends because for many of them the eight-week course was their first sustained contact with chart analysis. At the end of the first lesson, they looked at the same charts as the other workshop groups. Unencumbered by charting theory the Darwin students simply concentrated on the eyeball selection of stocks moving upwards. There was no time to apply the GMMA or the trade management analysis. Relying just on eyeball selection, they narrowed the choice down to four. They did exceptionally well with a 16.19% return over eight weeks.

Across all groups, using exactly the same list of stocks, returns ranged from a low of 6.33% to a high of 16.19%. The variation comes from the inevitable role our bias plays in the selection process. Had we asked participants to read the articles in *Shares* magazine and use these as a filter to select four stocks, there would be an even greater variation in results because we are so susceptible to emotional analysis that uses terms like 'good', 'excellent', 'high potential', 'hot stock' and 'set to soar'. This emotional information influences the way we interpret the price action on a chart.

Even without this emotive guidance we still bring emotions to bear on our eyeball analysis of charts. We had over 100 people at any one time all looking at the same charts and trying to answer the same question. Getting agreement on anything other than the most basic analysis question — 'Up?' or 'Down?' — was difficult.

The statistical probabilities in this strategy suggested an 80% success rate so we expect around 20% of the stocks selected would fail to perform, and this was confirmed in practice. The profitable returns shown above depended upon traders selling the losing trades as soon as the stop loss point was hit. Holding onto the losing position severely reduced profits, and in some cases turned an overall profit into a loss.

The workshops had many objectives. One of them was to demonstrate how trading success does not depend upon having exclusive information. The other was to show how trading success depends on how you use the same information that everybody else has. Success depends on skill, and skills can be learned.

This particular strategy is time-based. Like a weekend fishing trip, we pack up after a set period, irrespective of how the fish are biting. At the end of eight weeks, these trades are closed. A similar strategy is built around following the uptrend until it finally ends. This may be weeks, months, or even sometimes years in the future. We use different methods to locate these opportunities and they are examined in the next chapter.

Chapter 3

A HITCHHIKER'S GUIDE TO THE SHAREMARKET

Not everyone is comfortable hitching a ride with the market unless they know the driver personally. The prospect of hitching a ride for eight weeks based on a statistical probability without researching the company does not appeal to everyone, because we like to think we have a closer relationship with the company and the stock we purchased. However, when we ride a trend we are essentially hitchhiking and we go along for the ride. It may be more comforting to convince ourselves that if we have researched the company we somehow know the driver and this makes the ride safer. In this chapter we want to take the next step, and recognise it is the character of the ride that counts. This is not a giant leap and many investors and traders have already moved down this path when they use charting and technical analysis tools to identify a strong upward trend.

In *Share Trading* I wrote about 'Walking a mile with the crowd' by taking a bite out of an existing trend. The strategy discussed in this chapter illustrates another way to achieve this objective. In the market I do not mind hitching a ride with strangers because I understand I am *not* a partner in the business.

The capital-raising exercise by insurance company AMP in 2003 is a good example of the way shareholders are not partners. The way the announcement was made, and the arrangements for new capital raising, confirmed that groups other than the large institutions are essentially ignored when larger companies make decisions. Smaller shareholders were not told of these decisions until after the event, and they were not invited to participate on the same terms as the institutions.

Some financial journalists asked tough questions about the relationship between the Australian Stock Exchange's continuous disclosure rules and the AMP announcement. When did AMP change its view that the December 2002 results were good and conclude in early 2003 business was so bad that there was no alternative but to raise more capital? When did AMP start discussions about capital raising with its advisers and initiate discussions on the book build? The journalists also asked why AMP decided the market price would not be materially affected by this announcement.

These observations are more than just a repeat of the gripes felt by many small shareholders. These observations, and AMP's actions, challenge the core of our understanding about the market, and the way we approach the market.

PARTNERS?

The shareholder often believes he is a partner in the business. This partnership agreement comes from the earliest days of dangerous voyages to the Spice Islands and British India. These voyages were initially funded by a small group of businessmen — partners. Later the group expanded and became joint stock companies. The idea was for shareholders to share the risks and the rewards. This is the classic, and outdated, understanding of the relationship between shareholders and the company.

It is a powerful idea and its ghost may be heard in the wails of shareholders when companies announce unexpected results or reward poorly performing executives with obscenely large pay rises. Shareholders believe they have been misled because they believe they are partners — and partners are entitled to be informed.

This classic idea is perpetuated by investors like Warren Buffett. Driven by envy, small want-to-be investment kings fail to see the important difference between Warren Buffett and themselves. His success takes several important steps beyond those available to the small investor. When Buffett invests in a company he often either takes a seat on the Board or has a powerful influence on the behaviour of the Board. He is a true partner in the business in a way we can never be, even with our 100 shares. Many shareholders want to rub shoulders with kings, with the titans of industry. An ordinary share, purchased on the open market, gives the impression they are a significant part of something larger. This is a dangerous illusion.

If you are *really* a partner in a business then you may:

☐ Participate in management decisions.

☐ Help with hiring and firing of key personnel to ensure the business is developing successfully.

☐ Set the strategic direction and help formulate responses to emerging competitive challenges.

☐ Accept extended periods of low returns because you have the ability to influence the type of management decisions taken.

☐ Put in more capital to assist business growth.

Even a silent partner has a role to play in managing the company, although they may choose not to be active for extended periods. A shareholder is not a partner. Of the tasks listed above, shareholder participation is usually limited to putting in more capital to assist business growth by way of capital raisings or reconstructions.

If a shareholder attempts to behave as a partner he is limited to writing letters to the Board, or asking questions at the Annual General Meeting. If he is prepared to run the risk of being labelled a shareholder activist, he may attempt to get a seat on the Board, or perhaps agitate for an extraordinary general meeting. In most cases this shareholder is vigorously opposed by those with whom he believes he has a 'partnership' arrangement by virtue of his share ownership. The festering performance at NRMA Insurance over management direction highlighted the difficulties when shareholders believe they are partners with a right to be involved in management decisions. Despite all the evidence to the contrary, many shareholders who call themselves investors believe they are partners in the company and entitled to a level of management respect. This is one of the most fatal beliefs in the market.

FLEAS ON AN ELEPHANT

The alternative is to realistically accept who we are in the market and the role we play. If we discard the deceptive idea that we are a partner and accept the notion that we are merely a traveller — a flea on an elephant — then we immediately open up a different range of opportunities. We are simply along for the ride, and like a hitchhiker on the side of the road we flag down a vehicle going in our direction. We do not know the vehicle's ultimate destination, but we know if it is travelling in the same direction we want to go. Later the vehicle might take a side road, travelling in a different direction. If it does, then we get off, stand on the side of the road again, and catch a ride with another vehicle moving in our direction.

If we are lucky, we hitch a ride on a truck going straight to our destination. This is a one-way ticket to profitable returns. However, most times we find our journey is made up of a collection of shorter trips. We still get from point A to point B, but we achieve this by a series of rides. When the vehicle — the stock — takes a sharp turn, we simply get off and wait for the next ride going in our direction.

Please note this hitchhiking approach says nothing about the length of each ride. This is not a time-based strategy where we hitch a ride for eight weeks. This strategy hitches a ride for as long as the trend continues to move upwards. This is not investor versus trader, short-term versus long-term. Such dichotomies are not useful in understanding the essential nature of market success.

Better selection methods help us to identify market vehicles that allow us to hitch a ride for extended periods while travelling in our preferred direction. Hitching a ride with Woolworths between 1999 and 2002 or Toll Holdings between 1998 and 2002 carried shareholders on a long, uninterrupted ride in the right direction.

Compare this smooth uninterrupted ride with the progress of the second journey in Figure 3.1. Getting from A to B is more difficult and requires four separate rides. The ride with the first stock ends with a trend collapse and the trader jumps off when the trend direction changes. The ride with the second stock ends with a sideways consolidation. Prices simply stop rising and drift sideways: time to find another stock to hitch a ride with. The third stock sputters in a sharp but brief rally and is abandoned quickly. The trader rejoins a trend with the final stock selection. Both diagrams show traders hitching a ride from point A to point B. Neither attempts to predict or control what happens. Each concentrates on how he will react to any change in price direction.

This simple concept is astoundingly difficult for many market participants to accept because they do not want to surrender control. They are loath to admit they do not have an ability to influence the driver — the company management. They believe they are partners, and will not accept that they are just hitchhikers along for the ride.

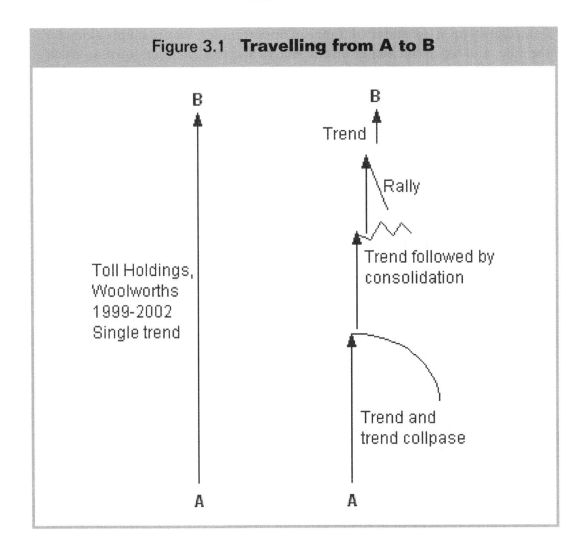

Figure 3.1 Travelling from A to B

B

Trend

Rally

Trend followed by
consolidation

Toll Holdings,
Woolworths
1999-2002
Single trend

Trend and
trend collpase

A   A

HITCHHIKING

If they accept they are hitchhikers they are able to make better use of the two decisions they can control: the time of their entry and the time of their exit. Entry is based on selecting a vehicle going in the direction you want to go. The exit means jumping off when the vehicle changes direction. If you stand on the side of the road at Wangaratta, hitching a ride to Sydney, then you select vehicles travelling north. Even a lost tourist with a bad sense of direction is unlikely to hitch a ride with a vehicle travelling south, yet investors frequently try this approach. This hitchhiker's strategy is called buying blue chip bargains.

If the vehicle stops going north, and turns east or west, or does a U-turn and starts travelling south, the hitchhiker knows it is time to get out and wait for another vehicle travelling north. The hitchhiker has the freedom and the ability to exercise this choice. He knows he is at the mercy of the driver. He accepts he is a traveller, not a partner.

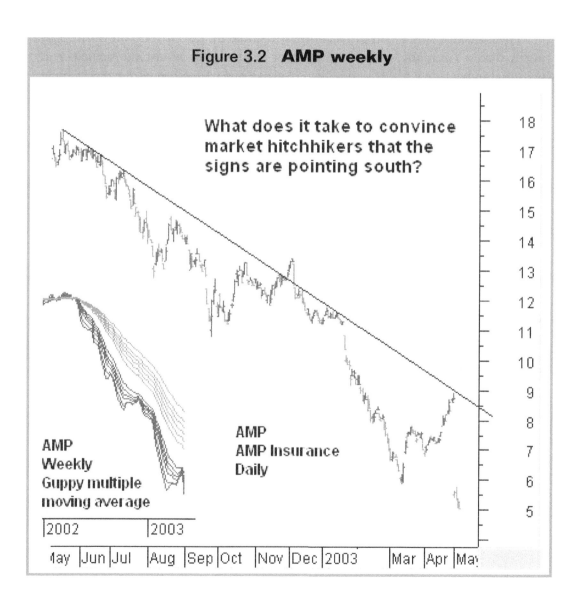

Figure 3.2 **AMP weekly**

Consider the weekly AMP bar chart with a Guppy Multiple Moving Average indicator[1] in Figure 3.2. Think of this indicator as a sign on the side of the road. You want to go north and this sign is pointing south. The sign does not tell you about the road conditions ahead, but it tells you the direction of the traffic. The sign does not warn you of a precipice ahead or a major pothole. The chart indicator does not warn you of an unexpected bad earnings report, a company collapse or any of the details driving the share price south.

The indicator simply says this company is travelling south. If you want to go north then a company with this indicator relationship is not the vehicle you want to hitch a ride with. If you believe you are in partnership with every vehicle you flag down then the direction you end up travelling may come as a very nasty surprise. The market is intolerant of those who deceive themselves and it destroys outmoded ideas very quickly, and perhaps this is why so few are able to do well.

There are two major ways to identify stocks we want to hitch a ride with. The first uses the research of others to identify where a crowd might gather. This includes an independent analysis of the stocks mentioned in *Shares* magazine, in tip sheets and other widely circulated trading advice newsletters.

Those who want a more technical approach often use a variation of a moving average crossover search. A casual glance through the charts shows a number of uptrends which are relatively well-established. There is nothing particularly unusual or remarkable about these trends and a substantial number are easily defined using a 10-day and 30-day exponential moving average combination. Many people look for the point of crossover when using two moving averages. This is not useful if we want to catch a stock moving north because the crossover point does not identify a high probability point.

Go back for a moment to the hitchhiker. He knows he has a better chance of getting from Melbourne to Sydney if he hitches a ride with a TNT Express truck than if he flags down an ordinary family car. Using a moving average crossover point is like selecting any TNT truck as it pulls out of the TNT depot. It is the right truck, or conditions, but there is still a low probability it is going to take you in the direction you want. The further you are along the road to Sydney, the higher the probability the TNT truck you select is travelling all the way to Sydney. Catching a trend shortly after it has proven it is sustainable and travelling upwards increases the probability of success.

---

1 This indicator is discussed in more detail in Part IV.

STRESS TESTING

Trend trading is not breakout trading. Our objective is to take a bite out of an established trend by hitching a ride with the price action. The choice of potential rides is enormous so we subject each candidate to several stress tests. Failure on one test is enough to drop the stock from consideration.

The tests are:

- ☐ A visual test.

- ☐ A trend line test.

- ☐ A character test using a Guppy Multiple Moving Average.

- ☐ An entry test using a count back line.

- ☐ A position size test.

- ☐ A performance test.

We examine each of these tests in detail in the next six parts. They are combined in the final performance test. This is really a personal test the market makes you take. Once the stock is purchased it is up to you to decide how effectively you apply your trading plan. We have a known stop loss price. Will you act on it if it is hit? You get to manipulate the performance test results by deciding when you will make an exit to cut a loss or protect a profit. Your action decides success or failure. This individual action was the most significant factor in the variation of results in the *Shares* strategy discussed in the previous chapter.

Your decisions and your trading discipline decide if your selected trade passes the performance test. Most times, the problem is not with our selection of stocks. It is with our inability to act on our carefully prepared trading plan. This is a problem of trading psychology and we look at some aspects of this in Part VIII.

It costs money to take this test in the market so we have developed a much cheaper eight-part performance test to help you gauge your strengths and weaknesses. The test unfolds in the last chapter of each part of the book. The test objective is to help you understand how your reactions impact on your trading success. We have considered some useful methods of finding trading candidates but not all candidates are equally attractive, so the next part applies a visual test to find those which are good looking.

CHAPTER 4

NO SECRETS

Our trading edge does not come from access to restricted or specialised information. It comes from our trading skill, which is developed through education and experience. The results are determined by our reactions to greed and fear. This is a big claim, and in the series of 'No secrets' chapters we put this claim to the test, with your participation.

Given exactly the same information as our competitors we make quite different decisions because each of us has a different personality. When deciding to buy or sell, we include a veritable container-load of extraneous baggage. Even if we apply a mechanical trading system, such as those black boxes advertised in glossy hard-sell brochures, we are no better off because ultimately we send the buy or sell order.

This is a difficult idea for many would-be traders and investors to accept. We want to believe specialist knowledge and inside information gives us an edge. We are wary of simplicity because the market appears so complex. We are reluctant to accept easy-to-understand approaches because we have been led to believe the market is best left to skilled professionals. When markets get tough, the professional fund managers protect their position with an ingenious argument: things are so difficult, they claim, that even professionals are having a bad time. How can you, an ordinary person, expect to do better? Their unsurprising conclusion is that we should give them our money to manage.

As you read more of this book we show you how simple steps are used to identify steady trading and investment opportunities. Between March and August 2003, over 400 stocks added more than 30% to their price, and over 100 added more than 100% in the same period. Many of these opportunities were found using the simple methods discussed in the remainder of this book. More were found using methods discussed in *Snapshot Trading*.

EVERYBODY WINS

Difficult as it is to accept, we can use commonly available market information and still trade successfully. Even more difficult to accept is that we can use exactly the same trading tools and approaches as many others, and still make a profit. We love the idea of exclusivity. Package a set of common indicators, put it in a shrink-wrapped box and sell it for $100 and many people ignore it. If it is so common, and so cheap, it must not be any good. Take the same product, but lift the price to $9,000, and many people flock to your door. At this price it is not only good, it is also exclusive, so we must have an edge because others do not know the techniques.

During trading workshops I am often asked if I feel the effectiveness of the trading methods I am teaching will be diminished as more people understand and use them. The reasoning behind the question is outdated. The person relying on this outdated reasoning assumes the only way to beat the market or to establish a trading edge is to know something others do not, or to use a little-known technique. This reasoning is false because information spreads more quickly and extensively than in the past, so any edge we gain by these methods is very short-lived. If I use a secret technique then I only have a temporary edge. There are thousands of traders all working with the same or similar software, searching the same markets, so the odds of my developing an original idea are very low. The idea may be new to me, but it is rarely new to the market. Any method I use is soon 'discovered' by many other traders who are working on the same problem and who are much smarter than I am.

The widespread use of standard indicators enables many people to effectively trade the market. Many successful traders use the same trend lines and moving averages that you do, yet some traders are very successful, while others struggle to return a profit. We explore some of the reasons for these differences in the trading example spread over the next eight sections of the book.

Some readers ask, 'If everybody uses technical analysis won't it destroy any technical advantage?' A moment's thought soon shows how false the argument in this question is. Most people use fundamental analysis to make their trading decisions, yet this does not lead to any standardised trading or investing approach and there is still a very wide range of investment outcomes. We want to encourage you to put these misconceptions aside.

GREED

The 'No secrets' chapters at the end of each part are designed to illustrate the single most important factor in your trading success — you and your relationship with greed.

Greed keeps the trader in deteriorating trades: he hopes prices will climb back to old levels so he can exit, or he hopes prices will climb back to break-even after his stop loss has been passed. Often the only opportunity we have to understand if we have greed under control is in a real trade and it is a very expensive learning process. We give you the opportunity to apply a performance test without the expense, and to test your performance and judgement against the results achieved by others who have taken the same test. We intend to achieve this using this test for readers:

☐ This book has eight parts. At the end of each part is a 'No secrets' performance test. Every reader has the same information, the same stock and the same group of indicators. You must answer the same question: 'Is it time to take an exit?'

☐ In the 'No secrets' chapter at the end of the following part we show our analysis of the previous charts and our exit decision so you can compare your reasoning and decisions with ours. This is useful, but we want to take this test a step further.

☐ This test was originally run in real time with readers of our weekly newsletter, *Tutorials in Applied Technical Analysis*. Each week we asked readers to email us if they believed we should exit the trade. We compiled their results and their reasons for getting out of the trade at any point. Their comments and analysis are included in these notes and make an interesting comparison point for your own analysis.

☐ At the end of this exercise with our newsletter readers we compiled a table showing the number of people making an exit decision at each point.

The differences are very revealing and we discuss them at the end of Chapter 39. This means you can compare your action with the decisions made by this wider group. What percentage of other readers agreed with you, and did their reasons match yours? Are you duplicating the mistakes made by many others, or are you able to develop a trading edge based on skilled trading?

The answers to these questions help you improve your trading skills, so when you take the real performance test you have a better understanding of the factors contributing to success. This test may change your opinion about the importance of early information.

Start your test

In the first three chapters we provided some evidence that it is not the information you have that is important. What is more important is what you do with the information. In this test series we all start with the same information — the same chart and the same entry point — but the final trading results may be quite different. In the real world, some differences are the result of the trading tools we each apply and some are due to our trading methods. We remove these differences in the test below by limiting the information to a single stock and a defined set of indicators. The 'No secrets' notes and test are designed to show how greed and fear provide different exit points based on the same objective data.

We start this test with an unnamed stock and an entry at $0.32. It is a breakout entry, and, as the chart shows, the entry is managed by a variety of techniques. An entry at $0.32 is consistent with the count back line technique, the Guppy Multiple Moving Average (GMMA), and a moving average crossover. These indicators are discussed in more detail in coming chapters. We have also included a Relative Strength Indicator (RSI) and MACD_Histogram display. We have selected the entry point and the same group of indicators so all readers start the test from the same point with exactly the same information.

In the original test we printed a new chart every week showing eight important decision points. The trade covered 18 weeks, but we concentrated just on the major decision points, and in the eight 'No secrets' chapters we give you the same information we provided our newsletter readers on a weekly basis. We ask you to examine the charts, and note down your answer to this question: 'Stay in the trade or take an exit?' Be warned, somewhere in this trade period, or eight-chapter exercise, is an exit point, and a point which shows the consequences of not acting on the exit.

In the 'No secrets' chapter at the end of the next part we discuss how we, and other readers, applied the indicator analysis. Then we show how the trade developed in the following period and ask you again to make an exit decision based on the most recent chart. You have an important advantage in this exercise because you can exit at the best point prior to the most recent day on the chart and back as far as the previous chart. You could of course flip forward to the next section and see how the chart developed before making a decision but this is cheating and will not help you understand the role your personality plays in your trading success.

On the other hand, it may be more revealing than expected! The desire to cheat, to get an unfair advantage, a desire to know the future, or know something before others, makes a perfect candidate for black box trading systems and unnecessarily complex analysis approaches, based on obtuse trading methods.

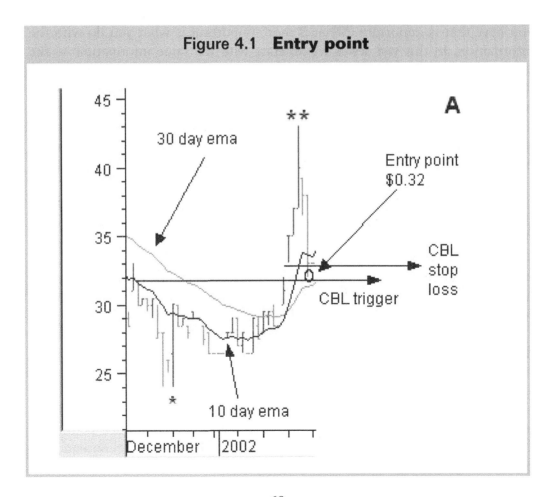

Figure 4.1 **Entry point**

We start the analysis with the chart A in Figure 4.1 on the day of the entry decision. We use two moving averages, a 10-day and a 30-day exponential moving average. The crossover of these two averages occurred six days prior to the last chart point shown. Prices moved up very quickly, so as a trader we waited for the pullback and the opportunity to buy on anticipation of a rebound. It is a classic breakout trading strategy.

The count back line (CBL) used as an entry tool is calculated from the pivot point low shown with the * below the price bar in December. The use of this indicator is discussed more fully in Part V. Clearly there was a close above the CBL line at $0.32. Once this happens we shift the count back line calculation into a stop loss mode. This is calculated from the most recent high, marked with the ** above the price bar in January. We have plotted this CBL stop loss line a little below the value at $0.33 so it is easier to see the relevant price action. Every reader gets to buy at $0.32 as prices hit an intra-day low below this stop loss line. It is brilliant trading, but it's not enough to give us a long-term edge.

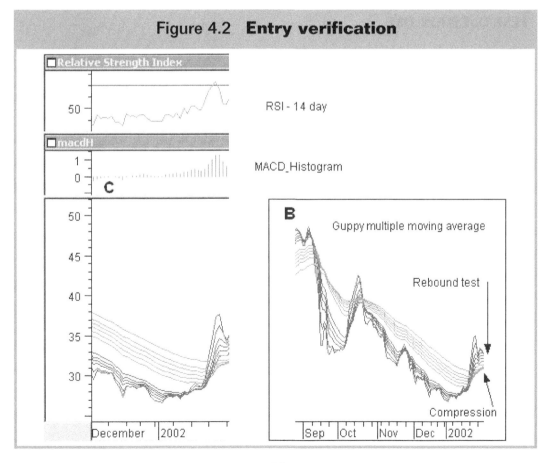

Figure 4.2 **Entry verification**

We think this trade entry is safe, and we use an extract in Figure 4.2 from the 12-month Guppy Multiple Moving Average display, shown in chart B, to verify this. The GMMA is discussed more fully in Part IV. The short-term group of averages has been successful in breaking above the long-term group. The long-term group — the investors — has compressed and begins to turn up. We expect the short-term group to pull back towards the long-term group, find buying support from the long-term group, and then rebound. We want to join in the rebound. It is a relatively aggressive entry into a new breakout trend.

Chart C shows the same time extract as chart A. It includes an expanded view of the GMMA and the status of the RSI and MACD_Histogram plots. These are the five basic indicators traders apply to the management of this trade. Later, if the rebound is confirmed, we may add a straight edge trend line as an additional management tool. With each new 'No secrets' chapter we show the updated decision point display for each indicator.

TEST QUESTION ONE

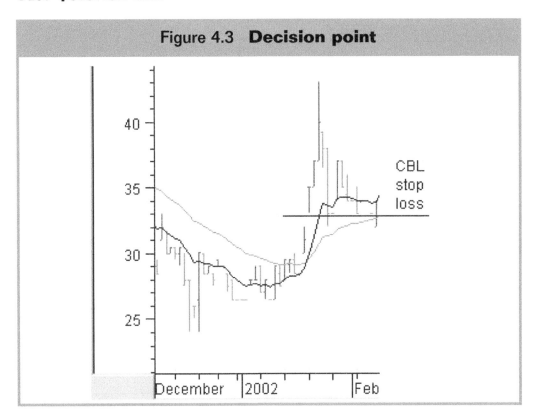

Figure 4.3 **Decision point**

The first decision point comes six days later. The first chart extract in Figure 4.3 shows the count back line calculations when used as a trailing stop loss. The indicator group shown in Figure 4.4 provides some conflicting signals. Some readers take this as evidence the initial trend is weakening, with reduced probability of the trend continuing upwards. Other traders rank the indicators, paying more attention to some than to others. The choice is yours. We offer no guidance.

If you believe there is a suitable time in the period between the charts in Figure 4.1 and 4.2 at the start of this chapter and updated charts in Figure 4.3 and 4.4 to exit the trade, then add a handwritten note to the end of this chapter. Explain why you feel the indicator conditions are strong enough or the trend is weak enough to take a precautionary exit on this trade. Or simply write 'No exit required', followed by an explanation and analysis of each indicator.

We discuss the analysis of these chart and indicator relationships in the next 'No secrets' chapter. Then we show how the trade developed to the next decision point, and ask you to make another decision.

This is a learning exercise. Our interest, and yours, is in the way different traders reach different decisions based on exactly the same data. Be warned: this trade may end at any time. It would be unwise to assume we have selected a long and easy trade in this example. Cheat in this test if you wish by flipping forward to the final assessment, but remember you cannot cheat in the market.

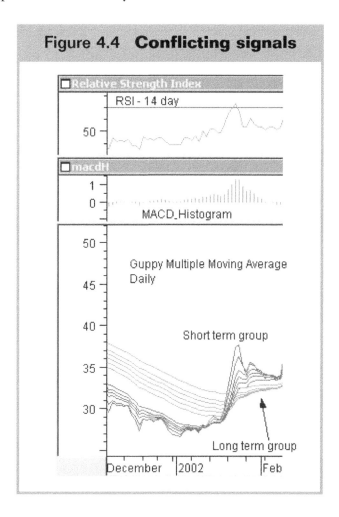

Figure 4.4 **Conflicting signals**

Notes:

_____

_____

_____

_____

_____

_____

_____

_____

Part II

HEY GOOD LOOKING

Chapter 5

HEADS UP

The fisherman reaches his favourite fishing spot using his preferred method. It might be based on a tip from a fishing mate or it may involve clambering along the edge of a mangrove creek to find a rock bar where the barramundi lurk. Perhaps it is a precise site located using the latest GPS technology or he may use burley to attract small fish and then bigger fish. No matter how he selected his spot, once he starts fishing he must select the best tackle. Will he fish the bottom with a running hook and sinker, or slap the water with a lure to entice the barramundi to strike? He tests various methods and combinations until he gets a strike. Experienced fishermen have a test routine, starting with the selection of hook size. A bigger hook filters out the small bait fish, but is stout enough to catch the larger target fish.

Traders approach the market in the same way, and the structure of this book is based on the seven tests we apply for selecting the best trading opportunities. Our intention is to catch a good trade. Sometimes we hook onto a much larger trade which provides a good talking point with a 60% or more return. Most times we simply catch enough trades to keep food on the table. The trader locks onto many trades delivering 10% to 40% returns. He throws back the smaller trades, those offering less than 10%. Every now and then he loses a trade just as a fisherman loses a fish. When the fishing gets nasty, the fisherman aims to lose just a hook or sinker, not the entire fishing rod. Traders aim to lose just a small amount of capital when trading turns rough.

The seven tests we use in trade selection are:

1 A test to find an appropriate stock to trade. We use the research created by others and followed by the crowd, or technical scans of the market to join an emerging or established trend. We covered some of these processes in Part I.

2 A visual assessment test of the candidates, by eyeballing a chart. This is the focus of Part II.

3 A trend line test, to confirm the trend and to determine ease of trade management.

4 A character test, to determine the nature of the trend using the Guppy Multiple Moving Average (GMMA).

5 A price test, to set stop loss and protect profit conditions using the count back line (CBL)

6 A size test. This sets the exact parameters for the trade, including risk management.

7 A performance test. This is the simplest test of all. Either the trade makes money and we pass the test, or it loses money and we fail the test. The 'No secrets' chapters at the end of each section are an ongoing performance test.

Every day there are hundreds of trading opportunities in the market and they come in all shapes and sizes. This is a beauty contest and beauty is in the eye of the beholder. A trade that appeals to me might not appeal to you. As private traders we have the luxury of selecting the type of trade we think is most attractive. It is a personal choice matching our preferences, inclinations, aptitudes and skills. We have already seen this personal bias in action in the introductory chapters on the *Shares* strategy. Different workshop groups using exactly the same list selected quite different stocks.

Come to the market and there are many head-turning trading opportunities. It takes discipline to focus on just a single type of trading opportunity. It is a discipline worth cultivating because distractions in this business can be very expensive. Even with this focus, the range of choices usually exceeds the amount of capital we have. The first and cruellest market law states a 10% loss cannot be made up by a 10% gain, and we look at this in more detail in Chapter 27. The second of these cruel market laws tells us we never have enough money to trade all the opportunities we find.

The seven tests we apply are used to select the most attractive trend trading candidates from any group of stocks. In the process we ignore some outstanding returns found in different types of trades. We may also miss some excellent returns from trend trades that have failed one of our tests. No technique is perfect. We settle for a robust technique that puts some successful trades on the table every time we go fishing in the market.

We apply a simple eyeball test of the stocks on the list of potential candidates and we want to make an intuitive judgement about the trend of each candidate. There are four primary trend combinations. The trend may be going up, down or sideways, or it may just be too complicated to be able to tell. We want just one of these possibilities: the trend moving upwards. This type of price action has a higher probability of continuing in the same direction for the coming days, weeks, months, or sometimes years.

CHILD'S PLAY CHARTING

Locating charts with this characteristic is so simple that a child can do it. As experienced traders, we make this task more difficult because we bring so many other decision-maiming factors to the table. The more experience we have, the more difficult it is to look at a chart of price action simply and understand the clear messages contained within it. Instead we are distracted by the fundamental knowledge we have collected about the company. Our analysis is skewed by recent news events and the way we think they might impact on the stock. Experienced technical analysts find it difficult not to imagine what the stochastic or Relative Strength Indicator display might look like.

All of these preconceptions obscure the plain and simple message available from a chart of price action. The price is either going up, or it is not. If it is not, or if there is some doubt about the uptrend, then we drop the chart from our list of potential candidates. We invariably miss some candidates which look miserable now, but which turn out to be very good or even star performers in the future, and this is perfectly acceptable. I do not normally indulge in guessing games when money is at stake. I never play guessing games in the market where substantial capital is at risk. This is not a lottery. This is a calm assessment of the balance of probabilities, and the clear direction of the trend is an excellent starting point.

Better still, this screening requires tools no more complicated than an eyeball. We simply look at the chart on the screen. Alternatively, print it off and hang it on the wall, or move back from the computer screen. Does it still look like it is going up? If the answer is still yes, then we add the stock to the list of candidates ready for the next trend line test.

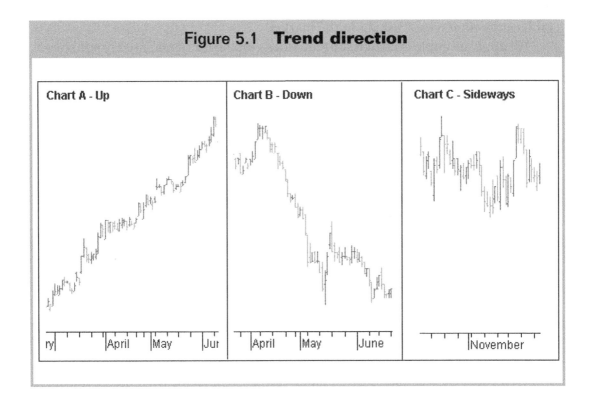

Figure 5.1 **Trend direction**

This is really simple, as shown in Figure 5.1. There is no question chart A is in an uptrend while chart B is in a downtrend and chart C is moving sideways. We use the rest of this chapter to examine the detail involved in making this choice, but we could also stop right here. This chart display does not just summarise what we do in this second step in the seven-step selection test — it is the entire test. It is so simple that many people instinctively move on, looking for greater complexity, more detail and more complications. They are all unnecessary, and one of the most significant steps in trading success is to recognise that simply trading with a well-defined trend is a tremendously powerful strategy.

Louise Bedford, author of *The Secret of Candlestick Charting*, refers to this eyeball test as the Tim Tam test. She suggests you borrow the young child from next door and ask her to look at the charts with you. She will have no preconceptions, no emotional attachment to particular stocks and little pecuniary interest in the outcome of her choice — just the reward of a Tim Tam chocolate-covered biscuit. The child's task is to simply respond with 'Up', 'Down' or 'Dunno' when shown each chart. The consultation fee is a packet of Tim Tams and has the potential to save you thousands of dollars.

The key to success in this selection test is the ability to temporarily suspend your preconceptions and emotional reactions to the company under consideration. Your original test list may have been selected on the basis of PE ratios, or culled from Martin Roth's *Top Stocks* series which applies excellent fundamental analysis, or perhaps the list is based on favourable newspaper coverage. For the moment you have just one task — forget all of this work and concentrate only on what the price action is showing.

When this eyeball selection test is finished you might like to re-assess the candidates against your other yardsticks. You may find confirmation of the choices made based on the trend of price activity. On other measures the stocks may be attractive, but if the chart shows a sustained downtrend in prices it is flashing a serious warning signal. Trade this stock and it may kill your capital.

TREND BEAUTY

Uptrends are one of four primary combinations of market activity and they are further subdivided into three combinations, as shown in Figure 5.2 as thicker lines. These divisions reflect the development, growth, and eventual end of an uptrend. The first component appears just after a downtrend has turned to an uptrend, shown by the thick line in area B. This is where the new trend is at its weakest. Like a child learning to walk, there are many false starts before he strides confidently into the future. Trading in these areas calls for breakout trading skills, a high level of stop loss discipline, and the ability to accept many false starts. Joining the trend in area B calls for experience and skill, although typically it is new traders who are attracted to this price action.

The second area is the strong, well-developed trend, shown by the very thick line. This is the most stable section of the trend. We discuss tools for recognising these trend situations in coming chapters. An entry in area C is perhaps the best entry point. It carries a lower risk of trend failure and the trade is easy to manage because trend volatility has declined. There is less chance a sudden price move will trigger stop loss conditions or destroy trading capital and profit.

The third area of the trend includes the period where the uptrend eventually declines and collapses. Usually there are a variety of warning signals alerting us to this weakness. The signals should be heeded because trend collapses may fall very quickly, consuming a considerable amount of profit if we delay the exit. Joining a trend late in its development, in area D, is the least preferred entry option.

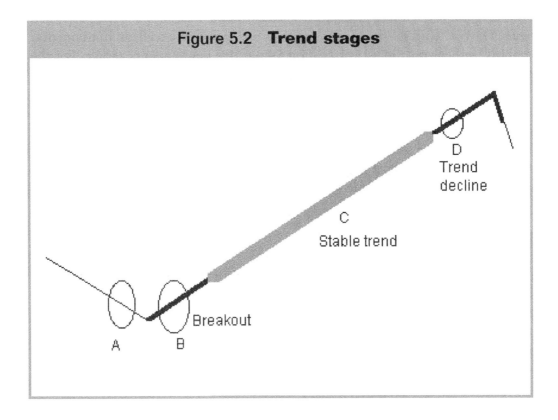

Figure 5.2 **Trend stages**

The most dangerous area for a trade entry is in area A. The trader is betting against the prevailing trend by moving in anticipation of a trend change. Disaster is often just around the corner as the downtrend regains momentum and the stock continues to move downwards. Unfortunately this area attracts the new investor who believes his fundamental analysis is capable of identifying good companies unfairly hammered by the market. Backed with this profound belief in his analysis or the ability of his broker or tip sheet mentor, he buys the stock and grimly holds onto it through adversity. While everybody else is grabbing a life jacket, these fellows have chained themselves to the company safe bolted to the floor of a sinking ship. We should leave them to their fate, and vow not to join them.

When we first glance at a bar chart we look for evidence a trend has started, or that it is well established. We use a consistent timeframe for analysis. My preference is to display 260 trading days, or one year of data, in each screen. Keeping the time displayed the same for each new chart standardises the comparison of trend slope and behaviour. In this test selection process we do not analyse each stock in depth. It is enough to simply conclude price is going up, and the stock requires no other feature to be added to our short-list. At this second stage in the selection process we are not particularly concerned with the steepness or slope of the trend, but in test three we use this to trim the list further.

BAR CHART BEAUTIES

We want to build a list of robust opportunities so we start with the bar chart. We can tell a lot about a stock by just looking at the bar chart. Please examine the seven stocks in the following pages, identified only by a letter. You have a simple question to answer based on the trend you observe. Buy it or not? Your decision is based on the last day's trading shown on these daily charts. You are thinking of buying the stock tomorrow. We give you our brief analysis and selections at the end of this chapter. We have zoomed in on the relevant price details so not every chart shows a year of price action. However, we have been careful to ensure this close-up does not distort the price and trend activity.

None of the charts includes volume. At this stage of the selection process, volume is an unimportant factor. Stocks with low volume or erratic trading activity are weeded out in later tests. Our primary interest is in the direction of price and trend because this is the very foundation of success.

Figure 5.3 Chart A

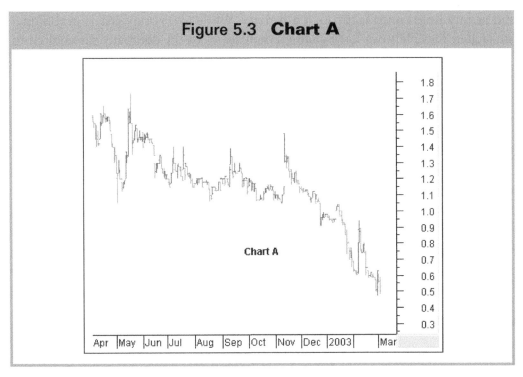

Chart A

Figure 5.4 Chart B

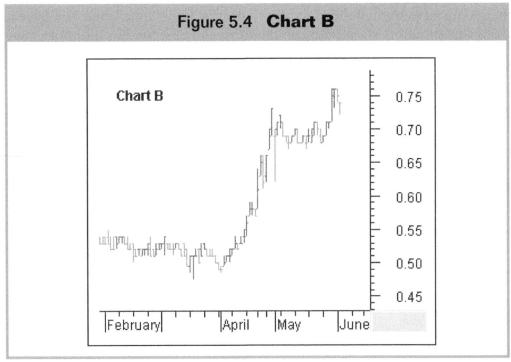

Chart B

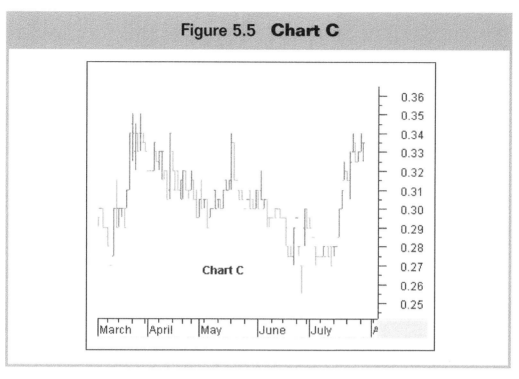

Figure 5.5   Chart C

Chart C

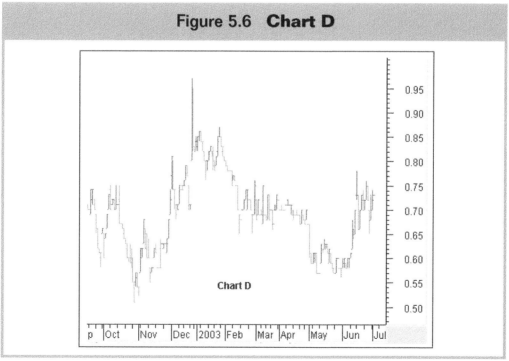

Figure 5.6   Chart D

Chart D

Figure 5.7 Chart E

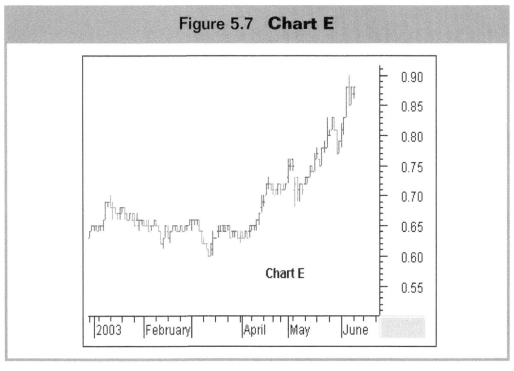

Chart E

Figure 5.8 Chart F

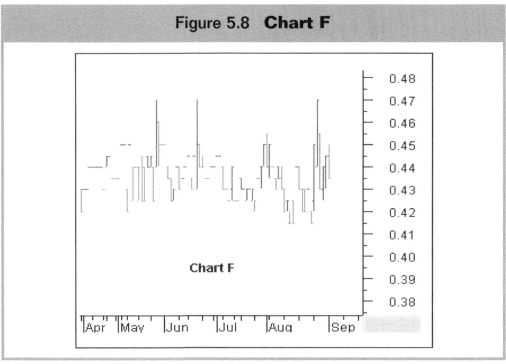

Chart F

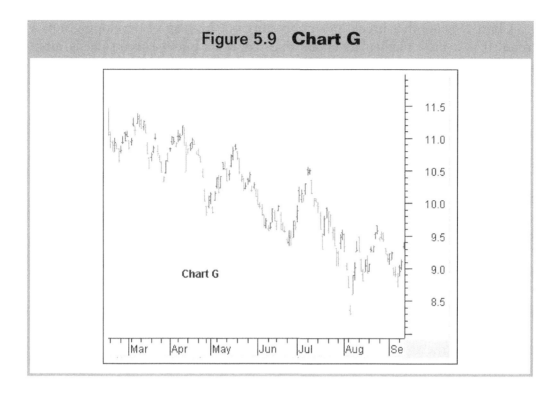

Figure 5.9 **Chart G**

BEAUTIFUL ANALYSIS

Chart A is a simple reject. There is no evidence of an uptrend. Buy this at $0.57 and you sit on a 63% trade loss a few months later.

Chart B offers a clearer entry into an established trend which started eight weeks earlier so it has had time to prove its strength. Buy at $0.74 and a few months later you take a 154% profit from the trade. This goes on our list.

Chart C is a breakout opportunity. The downtrend prevailing for several months has been broken. The new trend is only just established and is still in the initial rally breakout stage. We do not add this to our list of candidates although it suits those traders who wish to trade breakout events. They stand to make 42% from this trade over the next few weeks. We miss this opportunity, although we might decide to add this stock in a week or so if the trend is able to confirm its continued strength.

Chart D is another breakout opportunity on the cusp of developing into a trend. It is a little further advanced than chart C, but the trend needs more confirmation. If prices can push up around $0.77 then we have some confidence the new trend is in place. Buy at $0.77 and traders collect a 30% return over the next few months.

Chart E is an excellent established trend trade. The trend has been in place for around eight weeks and is well established. This is a smooth rise with steady price movements. This trend does not have a lot of volatility, or large ranging days. The difference between the high and low for each day remains relatively constant. This is steady trend accumulation and this characteristic makes the stock a prime candidate for future analysis. Add this at $0.87 and traders take home an 87% profit over the next few months.

Chart F is a disaster. There is no clear trend so it is dropped immediately from the list of potential candidates.

Chart G is in a downtrend so there is no reason why it should remain on our list of candidates for the next test.

Do you agree with these choices? Would it make a difference if we told you that amongst the stocks we dropped was blue chip BHP Billiton, chart G. We also dropped more commonly known stocks Ambri, chart A, Sally Malay Mining, chart C, and Magna Pacific, chart F.

Those we selected were speculative no-name Adecel, chart D, and lesser known stocks Timbercorp, chart B, and Great Southern Plantations, chart E. This knowledge may make you feel uncomfortable about the choices. External knowledge distorts our selection process because we try to match what we know about a stock with the price activity. We like the stock, and we think it is going to go up, so we look for evidence on the chart to support this preconception. We examine some more of these obstacles to objectivity in the next chapter.

We applied tests three through six to those stocks that survived test two. At the end, only Timbercorp remained. Did we select a real bar chart beauty? You be the judge based on the performance test. The Timbercorp trade returned 154%.

We increase our chances of success if we ensure our initial selection process concentrates on what the market is telling us rather than what we want to tell the market. Who cares if we think a stock is good? What counts is what the market thinks and this is revealed through the price activity recorded on a bar chart. Beauty is in the eye of the beholder and this beauty is a bankable commodity.

CHAPTER 6

OVERCOMING BIAS

*H*ere is a simple question: why would you hold onto this stock in Figure 6.1 if you purchased it in area A? You would not hold onto it, you reply. Sorry, but the evidence shows that thousands of traders did, and not just with this particular stock, but with many others with similar chart patterns. Not only did they hold onto it, but when they were asked for more money they cheerfully paid up. The name of the chart is not important although many readers ruefully recognise it as Telstra.

The reason why sensible, rational, educated, intelligent people do this is one of the major conundrums of the market. We have no solutions to resolve this riddle, but in this chapter we explore some approaches that may help you recognise and avoid this situation.

In the previous chapter we examined the application of a simple test. Yet we look at this sample chart of Telstra, and as shareholders, we convince ourselves it is about to go up. Objectively the chart message is clear and using the processes in the previous chapter, we have no hesitation in dropping it from any search list. Filled with good intentions we start our own search and analysis — and select a stock like Telstra as an investment opportunity.

This chart clearly records the destruction of your capital had you purchased it in area A and held onto it. Every time you looked at the chart you would have found reasons for not selling.

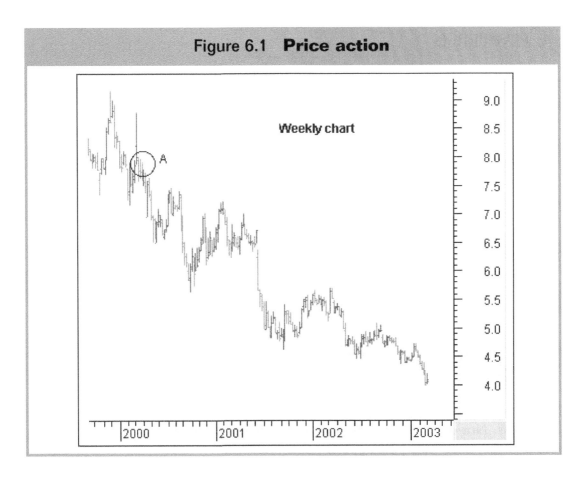

Figure 6.1 **Price action**

These excuses are amongst the most creative on earth. They have to be because if they were weak we would accept the price pattern evidence and sell the stock before it reached the very bottom of the chart. Excuses for taking no action might include:

☐ It is a quality stock.

☐ It is an industry leader.

☐ It is oversold.

☐ It is so low it must rebound soon.

☐ I cannot afford to take the loss.

☐ I like the company story.

☐ I am in for the long-term investment.

☐ It pays good dividends.

☐ You cannot time the market.

I am sure you could add a dozen more from your own personal collection of excuses. Categorising excuses does not help resolve the problem but it is interesting to note the same excuses are routinely applied to blue chip stocks, mid-cap stocks, speculative stocks, IPO startups, fly-by-night bio-techs and dodgy mining exploration minnows. This is what they mean by 'falling in love' with a stock. Give the ugliest stock some of your money and suddenly you are attached for life! This is destructive behaviour. Successful traders do not indulge in this. Developing solutions to minimise the impact of this behaviour is a very important step towards market success. So how do we achieve this?

CONFRONTING GUILT

First we need to get some issues, and some guilt, out in the open. There is not a single trader or investor who has not had one, or more, of these loser stocks in their portfolio at one time or another. Experience is no protection against this type of disaster. It happens to all of us so you are not alone in this experience, but just because it happens to everybody, it does not mean we talk about it. This is one of the secrets kept in the closet which is unfortunate because if we refuse to acknowledge the problem, it becomes very difficult to resolve.

Just because everybody holds some of their losers, it does not mean it is the right thing to do. Holding onto losing stocks is a bad habit, and it blocks the road to success. Although it is very easy to say we should have dropped this stock somewhere, anywhere, before it reached the very bottom right-hand corner of the chart, it is much more difficult to put this thought into action. This confirms trading and investing is as much an emotional decision as a rational one. In turn, this suggests we may have more success if we tackle the problem from a behavioural perspective.

When we explore this behaviour we must constantly remind ourselves we are not idiots. We may do some very foolish things, but we are not stupid. The solution to change is not found in attacking our self-esteem. Formal research suggests investors are smart, intelligent, successful, educated and business-oriented people. Our informal research, conducted by talking to colleagues, to thousands of other investors and to fellow traders in conferences across the world confirms these conclusions. In life we generally know what we are doing, what we want, and how to get it — except when we start to work in the financial markets.

The survey results in *Wealth of Experience* by Bowerman and Duffield support this conclusion.

The market rewards many of those behavioural characteristics that lead to failure in other business. The market's ego is larger than ours and every day it sets out to prove this — it wants to show us who's boss. Most times it succeeds. Over the long term it succeeds admirably and diminishes the ego and confidence of individual traders, investors, fund managers, analysts and superannuation funds. It does, however, reward those who have the humility to accept that the market rules, and trade on its terms.

It has taken me a lifetime to develop my personal behavioural habits. Like most people, I am comfortable with these habits and it is very difficult to change them. This is not just a trite observation. It underpins some significantly large industries which rely on our inability to change. The diet industry is a familiar example. Few people are able to change their eating behaviours for long enough to consistently achieve the desired outcome. Trading is a much more serious affair. Success or failure in a diet is an unimportant lifestyle issue for most.

Let's up the ante. Doctors and surgeons are frequently frustrated by patients on the road to recovery after a life-threatening heart attack. Often survival requires the patient to make significant lifestyle changes to exercise routines, eating habits, work practices and personal behaviours. After a few months recidivist rates start to climb. Despite a close brush with death, many people find it very difficult to make and sustain these changes.

Trading and investing fall somewhere between these extremes. It is much more serious than a diet, and not quite as serious as a heart attack. This experience could cost you $5,000 to $50,000 or more every time you repeat it. This happens to people who track down the last cent in transaction costs to achieve a reconciled cheque book balance every month and yet pay scant attention to a declining investment value measured in thousands of dollars.

It gets worse. Sharp business acumen is blunted when trading the market, so eventually they are forced to take a loss of perhaps $10,000 or $30,000. This is not pocket money. For most people it hurts so we expect to learn very quickly from this experience. Instead we plough back into the market using exactly the same methods, approaches and decision-making tools that delivered the original loss.

The truth is we cannot easily understand why this behaviour takes place. We do have some ideas, and although we think they are interesting, we also think it is more important to recognise these behaviours in ourselves so we can take action, not to change them, but to minimise the harm they do.

Harm minimisation

I suspect I am a chocoholic. I have never met a chocolate I did not like and a box of chocolates in the house is an open invitation to consume them. I know resistance is useless and I know it is very difficult to change my behaviour. I have been through the inconvenience of the last minute rush to replace the box which was designed as tonight's birthday gift and which had been accidentally consumed by late afternoon. The guilt and the cost of replacing expensive chocolates are still not enough to change my behaviour for more than a very short time.

My addiction is not so strong that I go out of my way to find chocolate in the supermarket, or make a special trip to the corner store, although I admit Easter is tough. I cannot change my behaviour, but I can minimise the harm my behaviour causes. It is simply a matter of not allowing chocolate into the house or office. Chocolate is the problem. Without chocolate in the house, there is no problem so my behaviour does not become a problem. My behaviour has not changed, but the trigger which initiates the behaviour has been removed.

The easiest way to avoid the problems in the financial market is simply not to be involved. For some people this may be the only option but for those reading this book it is not a solution. We want to enjoy the benefits of market participation while avoiding the associated personal disasters.

Harm minimisation depends on two factors:

1   Recognising the destructive behaviour. Large losses are a strong hint there is a problem.

2   Sidetracking the behaviour by removing the trigger. This may mean changing the way you see the market.

We start with the core of the problem — ourselves.

Business inhibitors

Trading the market is a business, but it is not like any other business you may have been involved with. The character and attributes rewarded in a normal business environment frequently remain unrewarded in the business of trading the market. Some of the attributes become a major disadvantage in terms of success.

Writing in *The A to Z of Healthy Small Business*, Amer Qureshi suggests 14 critical factors for business success. This representative list provides a useful reference point for understanding the differences between business success and market success.

☐ *A strategy.*

This underpins every approach to business.

☐ *A good product or service.*

Trading is an unusual business. We are a consumer, not a producer. We buy and sell a product — shares — which are offered in a marketplace. We do not create or manufacture the shares or the companies. Our objective is to buy a good product that is easy to sell at some time in the future. We have no control over the quality of the product once we have purchased it. It may get better or worse quite independently of any action we take. This overthrows the traditional business ideas relating to product and service quality. This financial market business rewards us for what we do with the product, not for how we select it.

☐ *Motivation — a passion for what you are doing.*

This underpins every approach to business.

☐ *An ethic of hard work.*

The underpinning of every successful business. We work harder at our own businesses than we would work for a boss in a similar situation. Reward and success and effort are directly linked. These links are the first ones broken in the financial markets and this is the most difficult difference to accept. This is a business where rewards really do go to those who work smarter rather than harder. Success may come from as little as a few part-time hours a week because it depends on just two actions — when we buy and when we sell.

This break in the link between hard work and success is hard to accept. This link is a persuasive idea, and some unscrupulous operators take it a step further. They prey on our belief that something more expensive must be more worthwhile than something less expensive. Follow this belief and the sellers of expensive trading systems capture another victim. Trading successes can be astoundingly simple and call for just a few hours work a week.

☐ *Determination and attitude.*

Let us take a closer look at this factor in the classic business sense. This often means staving off defeat when the odds appear to be against you. Tenacity is rewarded, and the business magazines are full of stories of entrepreneurs who believe in themselves and their product. They overcame shortage of capital, buyers who did not believe in the product, and a market reluctant to accept their service. This heroic struggle for acceptance in the consumer market is portrayed as an admirable trait.

This type of determination is very appropriate if you have some control over the quality and development of the product, idea or service the business is producing. Unfortunately, the product your market business sells — a share in a company — is not something you have any control over.

Tenacity and determination to hold onto a falling share is not very often rewarded in the financial market. The determination is directed in the wrong place. It does not matter how long you hold onto a share because this does not improve your chances of affecting the company which issued the share. Determination to succeed in your business of trading is important. Determination to hold onto a particular share despite adversity is not a step towards success.

☐ *Luck — lots of it.*

Much of conventional business success rests on being in the right place at the right time. It may be as simple as striking up a conversation with the passenger beside you on a long flight. This is less likely to be a factor in financial market success where this type of luck takes the form of a hot tip. The market leaves little room for luck, and offers scant rewards for it. Long-term success depends on skill consistently developed and applied. When luck plays a role, it is more likely to be incremental, allowing you to sell a stock at the exact all-time high for an uptrend.

The conversation with your fellow flyer leads to contacts or ideas. You have control over the implementation of the ideas and the development of the relationship. In the financial market this control is not possible. You are an observer of events and your only choice is in deciding when to take action in response to price action driven by forces outside your control. I welcome the lucky windfall, but I never plan for it.

☐ *A good bank manager.*

I have a simple trading rule — I do not borrow money to trade. My bank manager has no role to play in my trading business. If you trade on the margin then your bank manager has a very limited role to play. Margin calls are automatic and leave no room to manoeuvre. Our bargaining skill, rhetoric and ability to write a fancy business plan have no role to play when the margin call arrives. We simply either come up with more cash to cover the call or sell stock to meet it.

☐ *A great accountant.*

In classic business the accountant is a partner assisting with day-to-day decision-making, asset allocation and taxation advice. In our financial trading business he is used after the event to manage taxation considerations. He is not involved in making the buy or sell decision, or in deciding what shares should be added. The timing of these decisions is dictated by market activity.

☐ *Some start-up capital.*

This underpins every approach to business, but with one important difference. In financial market trading the start-up capital can be as low as a few thousand dollars. This makes market trading attractive to many part-time players. Once the first purchase is made there are no ongoing costs. There is no lease to pay, no wages to settle, no maintenance or repairs required and no theft to guard against. A business is undercapitalised when it must borrow against future income to meet ongoing costs. Our financial market business need never be in this situation.

☐ *Single-mindedness.*

This is great for business and fatal in financial markets. It is too often confused with bloody-mindedness where a single-minded determination to succeed overcomes all obstacles through sheer tenacity. These are admirable qualities unsuited to market trading.

We are not trading a company, we are trading the price action of the company. This is the relevant measure of our success or failure in the investment. We pursue business objectives with single-mindedness because we are able to influence or determine the outcomes through our own action. Not so with the market. Our share is buffeted by storms created by thousands of factors beyond our control, and at times, beyond our knowledge. The skill we need is to be able to distinguish between when it is time to hold on tight and time to let go.

☐ *An understanding partner and family.*

This underpins every approach to business.

☐ *Foresight.*

Take this to mean the ability to anticipate problems and develop plans to overcome them and this factor is vital in classic and financial market success. Understand this to mean the ability to foresee the future and we open the way to disaster in financial markets.

There are tremendous rewards for those who anticipate a future demand and fill it with a timely well-priced product. This is the driving force of business innovation in developed and developing economies. It provides the engine that powers the market. It does not help us a great deal in a financial market business because we are not venture capitalists. We are not making a significant contribution to the capital of the company. We own a handful of shares, and as discussed in earlier chapters, we are just along for the ride. Unless we know the business intimately — as intimately as its directors, accountants and divisional managers — we can only hazard a guess at the future and the company's ability to handle it successfully. There is no denying sometimes the guess is right, but the field of guesswork is littered with failures as industries squabble over standards and fight for market share. Cool logic — and a touch of emotional attachment — still says the Macintosh operating system is superior to Windows, but Windows dominates the computer desktop.

Successful trading limits the role foresight has to play. In its place we try to identify the balance of probabilities, and locate stocks where this balance favours a continuation of an existing trend. This approach underpins the processes covered in this book. Select a successful trade and it may look like foresight. However this confuses a rational assessment of the probability of specific price action with the ability to foresee the future.

❑ *Management ability.*

In a very significant sense this is unimportant in financial trading. We do not manage others. We do not have to manage inventory, worry about stock ordering, cashflow, salaries and the myriad other factors that fill the manager's time. Typically we must seek only to manage ourselves because we make the critical buy and sell decisions. We do not need to manage staff, product processes or quality supervision.

We need to set-up trade management processes which are part of a trading plan. However, these are not the same as the management skills in running a business. Ultimately success in market trading comes down to our ability to manage ourselves rather than managing others. It is not a widespread skill.

❑ *Calmness under pressure.*

Pressure comes from competing demands on time coming from multiple sources. Remaining calm while those around you drift into hysterics is a recipe for business success and an almost totally irrelevant skill in your personal financial market business.

There is just one relationship you must handle. It is the relationship between the current price of your shares and what you are going to do. You can buy more, sell, or do nothing. These are not competing demands on your time. It is a simple decision. It may well be an emotional decision and it is certainly better if taken calmly and rationally. However, it is not quite the same as balancing the demands from advertising, marketing, product development and distribution, all of whom want a decision by 3 pm today.

You may have cause to regret not taking a decision in your financial market business, but any pressure is self-imposed. You do not have to make a decision, so it becomes much easier to put off a decision, as shown by the chart at the beginning of this chapter. It is easier to distort this decision and we look at some of these processes below.

There are significant differences between the attributes required for business success and success in the financial markets. If we bring our business attitudes to the problem of trading the markets we soon find we are ill-equipped. The financial market is not an extension of our business career. It is an entirely new field of endeavour with a different set of rules rewarding humility and those who move beyond common perceptions. We must understand success in this business rests entirely with ourselves. There is no evading this responsibility and it is surprising how difficult this is to accept.

This personal responsibility starts with our assessment of a chart of price action, which is also sometimes our first step on the road to failure.

O<small>BJECTIVE ANALYSIS</small>

It is difficult to look at anything objectively. Even Federal Treasurers have been moved to describe a set of numbers as 'beautiful'. When we look at numbers displayed as a chart, it is very difficult to view the chart dispassionately. We bring our own preconceptions and biases to our view of the chart. Two people looking at the same chart may reach quite different conclusions. This is quite acceptable as each develops a different trading plan. Each plan could be successful, but only if discipline is applied to manage risk correctly if the trade fails to develop as anticipated by the analysis. Each believes his interpretation is supported by the chart activity. They subconsciously select tools to confirm what they already believe they know.

We should accept that for all intents and purposes we are not going to be able to rid ourselves of this bias. It is with us for life. In many cases this bias is unimportant so whether a glass is half full or half empty is not usually a life-threatening decision. Deciding if a stock is moving out of a downtrend and into an uptrend certainly has a significant impact on our money.

As soon as you start your analysis you bring certain assumptions to bear. Consider chart A and chart B where we want to determine the potential for the uptrend to continue. We use a simple straight edge trend line to visualise the trend balance. Our focus is diverted to looking for evidence to support this, particularly if we had already purchased the stock in area A in Figure 6.2. We have lost some profits by not selling at the very top of the trend, so we like to find reasons to support a continuation of the trend.

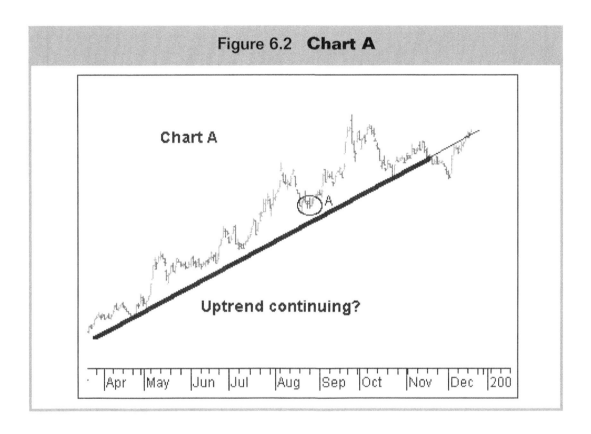

The thick section of the trend line on chart A defines the uptrend and the way the line has acted as a support area. Prices moved down to the line and they rebounded away from it. The most recent break below the trend line is a sign of potential trend weakness. However prices have rallied upwards and used the trend line as a resistance point. Importantly, in the last days shown on the chart extract, prices have started to move above the old trend line. This suggests that the new price activity could be part of a trend continuation. A bullish interpretation of this chart supports a resumption of the uptrend. Join this now, and we expect to participate in steadily rising prices.

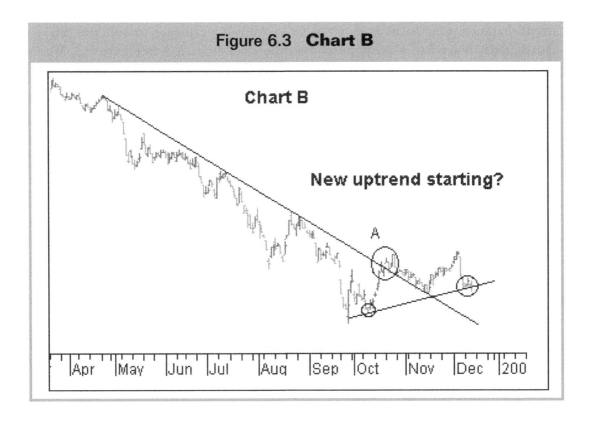

Figure 6.3 Chart B

It comes as no surprise to many readers that chart A and chart B are exactly the same. One has been inverted or turned upside down. Some charting packages

Generally traders tend to be bullish. We prefer buying lower and selling higher and in this sense we are optimistic. This bias accompanies us when we turn to chart B in Figure 6.3. Is this breakout likely to continue as a new uptrend? The breakout is clear and those who acted on this signal early may have purchased stock in area A. This decision also affects the way we subsequently analyse the chart.

It takes a lot to stop a downtrend. It is not unusual after the initial breakout for prices to fall back, perhaps using the old downtrend line as a new support area. What is important is the way price rebounds from this. The new uptrend line captures the significant rally and retreat behaviour. The two significant rebound points are circled. How realistic is our bullish enthusiasm? How much does it distort our analysis, and is there a way to reduce or offset this?

No SURPRISE

It comes as no surprise to many readers that chart A and chart B are exactly the same. One has been inverted or turned upside down. Some charting packages like Guppy Traders Essentials include an easy-to-use invert chart icon button. Others like MetaStock use a more complex process to achieve the same result. Some charting packages do not have this facility. Inverting the chart is an essential way of revealing bias, and offsetting the impact it has on your trading decisions.

As soon as we open the chart we are preconditioned to a particular style of analysis. Chart A is about uptrends. Chart B is about downtrends. We tend to be bullish, so in chart A we tend to lower the trend line and use just the points in May and October to set the line. This gives the trend more room to move and stops us having to make a decision that might cut into existing profits. The price action at the end of the chart now has a real possibility of being part of a trend continuation. It is comforting to have our preconceptions confirmed so we do not rigorously examine our analysis.

Open chart B and we look for a trend breakout. We want to buy low and sell high and the breakout opportunity is the prime example of this type of trade. We hunt for an opportunity to make money so we tend to be more discriminating about defining the trend. The world of profit is still ahead of us and we would like to get as much as possible by executing an early entry into the new trend. We take more risks with profits we might make than we do with profits we already have.

We know both these charts are of the same stock, but we have reached opposite conclusions. We say chart A is a trend continuation and chart B is a trend change. The contradiction comes from the way we apply our bullish bias to each chart.

The contradiction cannot be resolved until we know which chart is inverted. In this example it is chart A. Using the inverted chart rule matrix in Figure 6.4 we select the analysis conclusion we applied to the normal chart B, and match it with the conclusion we applied to the inverted chart A. This is shown with the * and the trading action simply states our bullish bias is too strong. These rules assume we plan to enter into a long-side trade, buying lower and selling higher. Success relies on a continuation of the trend, either established or the new trend.

We cannot have it both ways, even though our bullish bias would like to do this. If the trend is going to *change* in chart B then it cannot simultaneously be going to *continue* as an entirely different trend in chart A. Step back to reality, and to the chart that is displayed the correct way up. It is only our bias that makes us think this breakout has a chance of survival. The chart shows AMP Insurance, and this bias encouraged traders to buy AMP on this false breakout at $12.00. In the coming year it was to sink as low as $4.30 in a continued downtrend before any hope of a genuine trend change emerged.

Figure 6.4 Rules for using inverted charts to defeat bias

Normal chart	Analysis	Inverted chart	Analysis	Conclusion and action
Up trend	Continues	Down trend	Continue	Balanced view - enter
	Continues		Weak	Bullish bias too strong - exit
	Weak		Weak	Balanced view - exit
	Weak		Continue	Trend defeats bullish bias - exit
Down trend	Continues	Up trend	Continue	Balanced view - avoid
	Continues		Breakout	Bullish bias too strong - exit
	Breakout		Breakout	Balanced view - enter
	Breakout*		Continue*	Bullish bias too strong - avoid

Be aware of your bias. Use it to help your decisions rather than letting it hinder them. It could be a beautiful chart but it is even better if it is a genuinely beautiful trading opportunity. Use your natural bias to help confirm the difference.

CHAPTER 7

NO SECRETS

At the end of the last part we set both the entry conditions for this ongoing performance test trade and the first set of potential exit conditions. We asked you to write a trading note if you believed the charts showing the decision point justified an early exit from this trade. The purpose of this trading exercise is to explore the way traders make different decisions based on exactly the same data. Although there is a most profitable outcome for this trade this does not necessarily make it the only solution. Every trader has a different capacity for fear and greed. This means traders look at the same information and make different decisions. Some exit too early, some exit near the top, and others exit too late, giving up some of the profit from the trade.

The objective of this trade exercise is to use the trading example to track your responses to selected decision points. The test results, shown in Figure 7.1, from our original wider survey amongst our newsletter readers provides comparison of your reactions and your analysis with theirs. The first chart shows the percentage of readers who took an exit. The second chart shows the return generated by this exit. Were you part of the 1% of readers who opted for an exit based on the previous chart decision point?

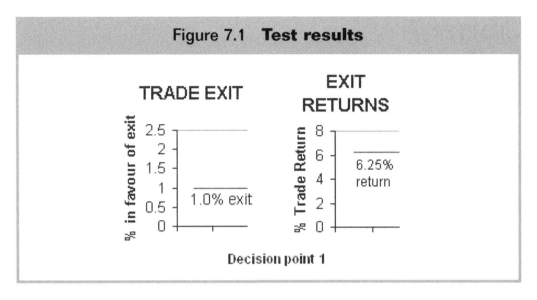

Figure 7.1 **Test results**

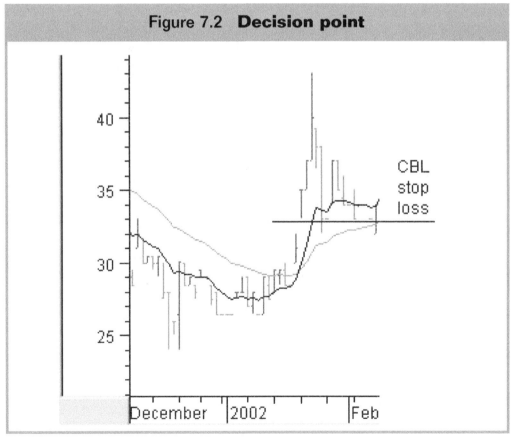

Figure 7.2 **Decision point**

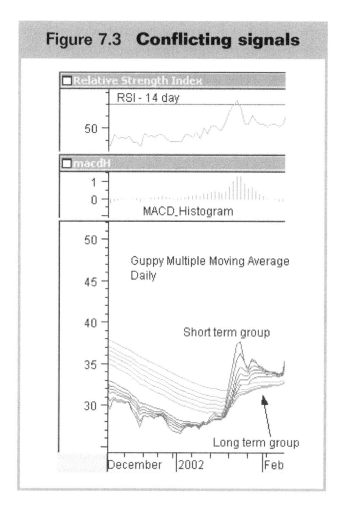

Figure 7.3 **Conflicting signals**

Relative Strength Index

RSI - 14 day

50

macdH

1
0

MACD_Histogram

50

Guppy Multiple Moving Average
Daily

45

40

Short term group

35

30

Long term group

December | 2002 | Feb

Based on the charts in Figures 7.2 and 7.3 — reproduced from the previous part — a few readers decided it was a good time to exit. We give them a good exit at $0.34 which returns 6.25% on the trade. Few trading decisions are clear-cut. Prices may close below our stop loss level, but this does not mean we act on the signal immediately. Traders may use the same indicator combination but interpret them in different ways. They may act in advance of the indicator signal, taking a defensive or fearful exit. Others wait until the exit signal is generated, and then delay action until prices fall further. They hold on because they hope prices will tick back up and reward them for their patience.

OUR ANALYSIS

The table in Figure 7.4 summarises our analysis of the charts and indicator signal decision point given to readers at the end of Part I and shown here as Figures 7.2 and 7.3. It also includes a summary of the exit analysis reasons given by readers who took the original tests and who sent exit emails at this decision point. Most cited the MACD_Histogram crossover as the reason for the exit.

The table includes our reasons for staying in the trade. These outweigh any exit signals so the trade remains open. None of these reasons for abandoning or staying with the trade are absolutely correct. There is no right answer, and this is one of the characteristics that makes trading so difficult to master. As this trade develops over each new part, readers will develop a better idea of how other traders make their exit decisions. Use this information to improve your own trading.

	Figure 7.4 **Analysis summary**	
INDICATORS	**STAY IN TRADE**	**EXIT TRADE**
Count back line	No close below the CBL line.	Open below CBL line could be a sign of weakness.
Guppy Multiple Moving Average	The short-term group has rebounded from the long-term group. Separation between two groups prior to rebound is good. Long-term group continuing to move up.	Both groups of averages have narrowed, showing trend weakness.
Moving average crossover	No moving average crossover.	No signal.
RSI	No action. Wait for next RSI peak to plot potential divergences.	No signal.
MACD_H	None applicable.	MACD_H has crossed below zero reference line generating a sell signal during the last week.
Trend line	Too early to place trend line.	Too early to place trend line.

TEST QUESTION

The charts in Figures 7.5 and 7.6 show how the trade developed over the following days to the next decision point. There is now sufficient action to allow traders to plot a straight edge trend line. The rally started, then retraced, and then rebounded. This retracement and rebound provides the second plot point for a straight edge trend line, defining the potential trend. On this chart extract the trend line also provides a potential exit signal. Should you act on it? The choice is yours. We offer no guidance.

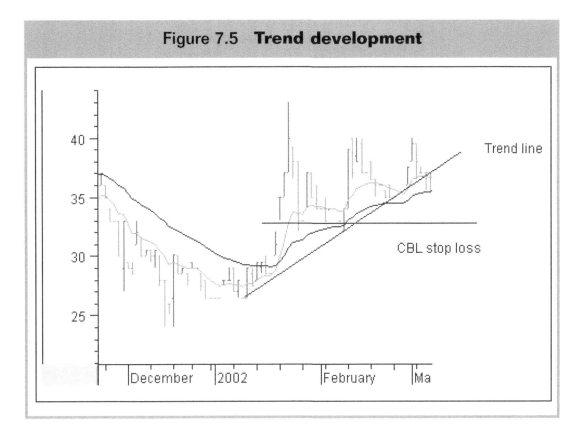

Figure 7.5 **Trend development**

The other indicator groups provide some conflicting signals. Some traders take this as evidence the initial trend is weakening, and decide there is a reduced probability of the trend continuing upwards. Other traders rank the indicators, paying more attention to some than to others.

If you believe there is any suitable day in the 18-day period between this decision point and the previous chart to close the trade, then please note the reasons for your decision at the bottom of the following page. It is your decision and you have the same information as every other reader. The result depends on skill and trading discipline — or your ability to resist the temptation to cheat by turning to the end of Part VIII. If you have already voted for an exit after the previous notes, then please respect your decision. In this exercise, just as in real trading, once you sell the stock you miss the opportunity to take part in any subsequent highs.

In 'No secrets' Chapter 20 we show how the trade developed from this point. We discuss the analysis we applied to each indicator as shown in Figures 7.5 and 7.6.

97

Figure 7.6 **Trend development**

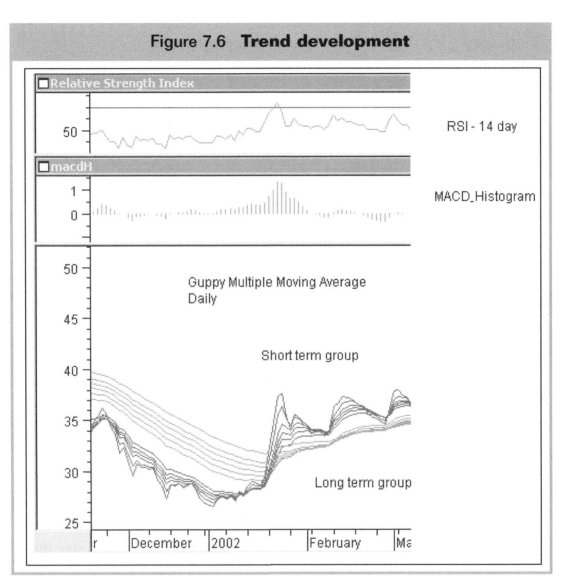

Notes:

_____

_____

_____

_____

PART III

LINE OF LODE

CHAPTER 8

CLASSIC TREND LINES

Greedy fishermen in quiet Southern Australian waters often throw two lines overboard. This is not good practice in the Northern Territory because the target fish are more aggressive. When a barramundi 'whoomps' down his meal the sound echoes around the lagoon. Others come quickly to feed at the same table. Imagine your dilemma if you get a simultaneous hookup on both lines. The first is on the landward side of the boat, and the barramundi is powering towards the shelter of the tangled mangrove roots. The second is on the river side and the fish is heading for deeper open water. Which line do you cut, and which do you grab? Personally I go for simplicity and play the fish heading for deeper, unobstructed water. It is the same approach I use with trade selection. The classic trend line is used to select the most easily managed trades and this boosts our chances of landing a successful trade.

The first trend trading test gathered a selection of candidates. The second visual test discarded those not moving upwards. This part deals with the third test and uses straight edge trend lines as a selection tool to find the better candidates from the smaller list of survivor stocks from test two.

Plotting and using straight edge trend lines causes more confusion and more questions than almost any other single aspect of charting. Much of this confusion comes from the way we understand the role of the trend line in charting analysis. Some traders feel the trend line is a predictive tool, and this leads to considerable frustration. Others treat the trend line as a planning tool with a loose link to probability. The consequences of each of these beliefs are quite significant because they reflect an important division in the way we understand market behaviour.

101

We start with a discussion of the way trend lines are understood in classic charting analysis. In the next chapter we examine an alternative way to apply trend lines to develop better trade management solutions.

A straight edge trend line is simply a straight line drawn with a ruler or plotted in charting software with a mouse cursor. Other trend line varieties include a curving parabolic trend line or a wriggling volatility-related plot, such as a moving average or Average True Range calculation. In this chapter we are interested only in straight edge trend lines.

An uptrend is confirmed when each new high is higher than the previous high. The trend line is drawn touching the *lows* of these bars. A close below the lows indicates the bears have beaten the bulls and signals a trend change. A downtrend exists when each new low is lower than the previous low. The trend line is drawn touching the *highs* of these bars. A close above the highs indicates the bulls have beaten the bears and signals a trend change. The more times the trend line is touched but not broken by price movements, the more significant, or accurate, the line is. Trend lines may be: short term — a few days; medium term — a few weeks or months; or long term — a few months, or even years.

TRENDS ARE NOT RANDOM

There is a difference between the trend and the trend line. The trend is the general direction of price movement and is a result of market behaviour. We look at yesterday's prices and make a decision about what action we would take if prices move to different levels today. A higher high may encourage us to sell to lock-in a profit. A lower low might trigger a stop loss exit. These rising prices are not random. What happened yesterday is a result of analysis in action. People look at the stock in many different ways and analyse it using many different methods. Some people make a decision to buy or to sell based on this analysis. For many people this decision involves a range of emotions and this emotional quotient is included in the price traded during the day.

What we do today depends on analysis and emotional reactions. Prices in the market are not random events, nor are they independent events like a series of coin tosses. Today's price is linked to yesterday's price by an analytical and emotional thread. This is an important observation because it confirms that trends in prices are not a matter of random behaviour. Price trends rest on analysis and emotion which are not always mixed in equal proportions. Prices trend because investors have memories, so a trend is created by regular and sometimes repeated patterns of investor behaviour.

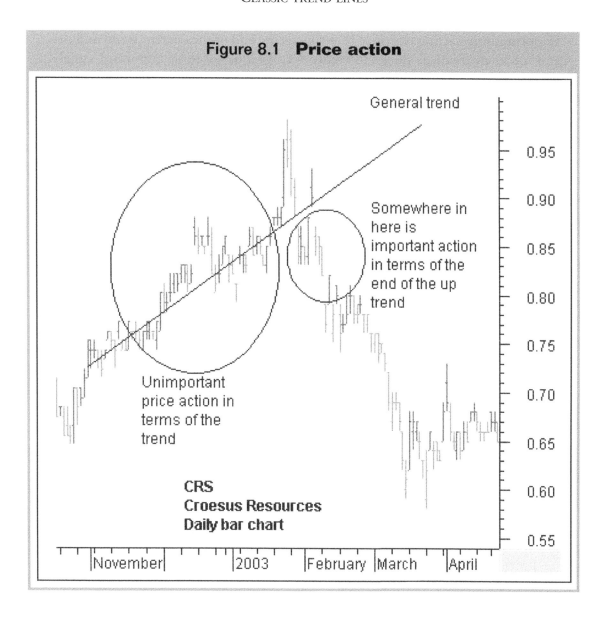

Figure 8.1   **Price action**

The general trend of a price movement carries prices upwards or downwards. Buy and hold AMP Insurance and the general trend has been downwards. Buy and hold National Australia Bank and the recent general trend has been upwards. The general trend does not help us distinguish between important and unimportant price action.

Unimportant price action is part of the normal price movement in a trend. Prices may move up and down, but they do not signal a change in the trend.

Important price action is a price that signals the end of the current trend and the start of a new trend, as shown in Figure 8.1. We look for these important signals at the end of a downtrend so we can buy into a new uptrend. We also want to see the signals at the end of an uptrend so we can sell before a new downtrend starts.

A single line through the middle of a price trend tells us which direction the trend is moving. An eyeball analysis of the chart does the same and this low-tech method works very effectively as part of the second trading test discussed in the last part. These approaches are a starting point but they do not help us to distinguish between important and unimportant price action.

The classic trend line plot has a single construction rule:

☐ The straight edge trend line is plotted beneath a rising trend. The objective is to define the lower limits of the existing trend using the information available at the time.

We use the line to define the limits of price action. Typically we use a close below this line as a signal the trend is failing and it is time to take an exit. When we first plot a trend line this potential exit signal is clear.

We define the uptrend on the bar chart using a best fit straight edge trend line. The objective in deciding where to plot the line is to capture the majority of the low points in the existing trend. Which existing trend we are defining depends on our intended trade. The chart in Figure 8.2 shows four trend lines, all plotted using the information available on the last day shown on the chart and projected into the future:

☐ Trend line 1 defines the general direction of the trend. It does not help us distinguish between important and unimportant price moves in terms of signalling an end to the uptrend.

☐ Trend line 2 is accurately placed. It does not start at the very low of the previous downtrend. It starts several days later, but connects all the significant low points up to the time we see on the chart. If prices fall back towards the value of the trend line we expect them to bounce away and continue moving in an uptrend.

☐ Trend line 3 is guesswork. It connects just two low points. There is very little evidence these two points are significant in terms of the trend. They may be in the future, but when they are compared with the many other confirmed points used to plot trend line 2 it suggests trend line 3 is less likely to be valid.

☐ Trend line 4 picks up three points in a steep short-term trend. This line is suitable for a trader with a short-term perspective.

Figure 8.2 **Trend lines**

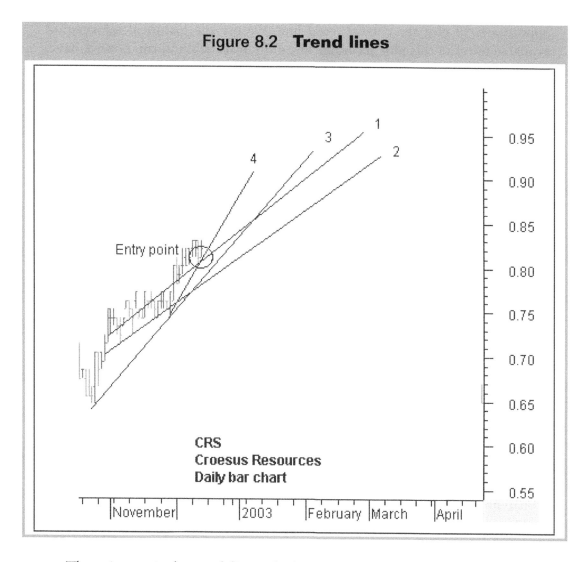

There is no single trend line solution encompassing all timeframes. Each timeframe has its own valid trend line solution. The danger comes when we start a short-term trade using trend line 4 and then change the trade into a longer term trend trade using trend line 3 when prices close below trend line 4. This is bad trading because we ignore our original trading plan.

BACK TO THE FUTURE

The objective of the trend line at this stage is to ensure the current uptrend activity is properly captured. The current activity on the chart gives us the opportunity to plot the correct trend line. We use the historical information available to make this plot accurate. The more historical information we have, the more accurate the current trend line plot and projection. If we are attempting to plot a new uptrend with just a few days or weeks of activity, it is a little more difficult to plot the trend line because we do not have enough information. Using existing information we plot a line that most-effectively captures and defines the price action in the past — trend line 2.

Once the retrospective plot is completed we project the trend line into the future. The classic objective is to use the trend line projection to define the future trend and to help decide which price action is significant or insignificant in terms of a trend change. This step causes most confusion and it highlights the differences in the way we use a trend line.

If we believe the line has a predictive role then we are frequently frustrated as future price action invalidates our trend line plot. Prices close below the trend line, we take an exit, then prices recover and the trend continues upwards. We are faked out by a false dip below the trend line so we believe we have incorrectly plotted the trend line.

An extension of this approach is the preoccupation with deciding how to set the correct plot for the trend line using as little information as possible. There is a tendency to believe there is a single correct trend line solution and if this is found early enough, it is possible to plot an accurate predicative trend line. This belief sends traders on a fruitless search for an algorithm or set of precise rules to plot the definitive trend line. The search is unsuccessful because it is based on an incorrect understanding of the role of the trend line in trade management.

The trend line does not predict the future. The trend line we plot defines the probability of a particular set of price relationships continuing. In simple terms, the more often a trend line is hit and the more often prices bounce away from the trend line, the more valid the trend line plot. And more importantly, the more significant any close below the trend line.

The chart in Figure 8.3 shows how price action developed after our initial trend line plot:

☐ Trend line 1 remains a general guide to the trend and is not useful for trading. For clarity, we have removed it from this chart display.

☐ Trend line 2 is confirmed by future price action. It remains valid. There are two low points below this line, but price rebounds quickly the next day. This is a judgment call, verified with Guppy Multiple Moving Average indicator analysis techniques discussed in the next part.

The decision is also confirmed by the way prices open higher and move higher on the following day, and this would have been clear in the order lines as trading opened.

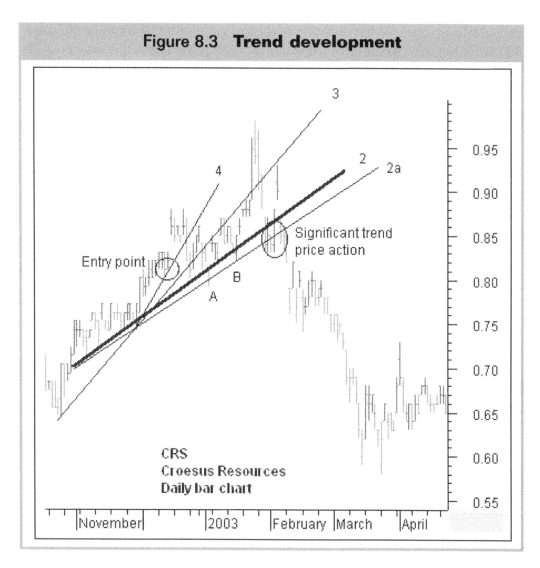

Figure 8.3 **Trend development**

The break below trend line 2 is signalled by seven days of clear closes below the value of the line. Looking at the historical chart the trend break is very obvious, but this does not mean it is rapid. Once the first trend break signal is delivered, we look for confirmation of the signal. This is either a lower opening the next day or a series of days where prices are unable to close above the trend line. In this example there is a seven-day period where the trend break is clearly signalled and an exit is possible at reasonable prices before the new downtrend kicks in as prices accelerate downwards.

Why not shift trend line 2 downwards to the position shown by trend line 2a? The problem is that only one of the lows at point A or B can be included. No matter how you fiddle with the starting point or the slope, it is only possible to get the line to touch one of these lows. Trend line 2, however, touches many lows and this makes it more valid.

☐ Trend line 3 is obviously incorrect, and this is quickly proven. Initially based on two points, there is no third low to confirm the placement of the line. Prices move back towards the line, then close below it on a consistent basis.

Traders who used trend line 3 plotted it incorrectly because it was based on too little information. However, if traders had used this trend line an exit was signalled and confirmed by the multiple closes below the line. An exit taken here would have been false, but still a profitable trade based on the common entry point shown on the chart.

☐ Trend line 4 is an accurately plotted trend line. This short-term trade ends with a dramatic drop below the trend line and is confirmed the next day. Short-term trades require closer management because these short-term trends may collapse very rapidly. Trend line 4 was valid for the style of trade used.

TREND PROBABILITIES

Newtonian physics suggests objects continue to move in a single direction until they meet a stronger force. Behavioural analysis suggests people continue to do the same thing until they meet a stronger force that prevents them from continuing. The market combines these two observations. Prices continue to rise until there is an event strong enough to cause people who own stock to change their mind about owning the stock.

This is a platitude, but a useful one. We know things are continuing as they have been because prices stay above the sloping trend line or, more accurately, the balance of probabilities favours a continuation of the trend. A close below the trend line signals a shift in this balance of probabilities. We know there is an increased probability of change when prices close or move below the trend line.

This means multiple trend line plots in different timeframes co-exist on any single chart and every trend line plot is tentative. As more price information becomes available, we may adjust the trend line to take this into account.

This adjustment brings its own set of dangers and temptations. Faced with a close below the trend line we need to resist the temptation to lower the trend line to avoid taking a loss or collecting a reduced profit. The trend line is used to define the current intended trade. It should not be adjusted significantly while the trade is open. Once the trade is closed we may adjust the trend line plot in the light of subsequent price activity that shows the trend is continuing.

Those who like to use trend lines as a tool for prediction argue some trend line plots have a higher probability of success than others. They tend to believe there must be a single plot that increases the probability to a very high level — almost to the level of predictability. This approach means they are uncomfortable with the fluid nature of trend line plots and tentative trend line plots.

The core area of dissatisfaction with trend lines comes from the difficulty in plotting an accurate trend line for future market behaviour, based either on prediction or probability. This is reflected in the questions I often get when showing trend lines on charts: 'Why did you place the trend line there?', I am asked. 'Six weeks ago you may have placed the trend line somewhere else, and you would not know the price break below the trend line was false. Acting on that exit signal would have taken you out of a winning trend where the trend really just kept on going up after a minor pullback.' Sometimes the questioner concludes we somehow cheat when we plot the line.

This conclusion is wrong because we use what we know at the time the trade is opened to plot the best trend line. This plot may ignore previous trend line plots because in the light of the information displayed on the chart we now know they were invalid, or useful only for shorter term trends. It is silly to deny the use of all the information we currently have. We adjust the plot of the trend line in the light of past price information available to us on the chart display on the day we make the trade entry decision.

In this sense the trend line plot is always tentative. It relies on new price information to prove or disprove it is correctly plotted. This is the most important area in discussing trend lines. The classic focus tends to be on the best plot of the trend line so we can use it with confidence to predict or establish the probability of price action in the future. The success or failure of this probability prediction is used as a measure of the success or failure of the way we have plotted the trend line.

Although it is a common question, it is also a distracting and wrong question because it does not help us improve our trading. Trend lines are used more effectively when they deliver trade planning and management solutions. We examine these alternative applications in the next chapter.

CHAPTER 9

LINE MANAGERS

Trend lines are most useful when they provide trade management solutions. For many years I accepted the classic interpretation of trend lines and spent a lot of time refining rules for plotting them. This included some work to create an automatic trend line tool for charting software. Over the course of many trades I began to observe the lack of relationship between trend line placement and successful trades. The classic understanding and application of trend lines is a distraction because the tendency is to focus on a single solution to correct trend line placement. This approach separates indicator construction from the purpose of using indicators. Our purpose is to successfully trade the market, and the trend line is a planning and management tool, not a solution. We examine the significant difference in these approaches below.

We plot a trend line to understand how the trend is developing so we can decide when to buy the stock and later sell it as the uptrend changes to a downtrend. Plotting a trend line is not an academic exercise. It is part of a trading plan. There are three aspects of this relationship. They are:

1   The market.

2   The trend line.

3   Our trading plan, which includes the management of the developing trade.

Many traders concentrate on the first two aspects of the relationship and assume the third will follow. Classic approaches focus on the relationship between the market and the trend line, so we still like to believe the line somehow defines the market as shown in Figure 9.1. This is why we are so concerned with the accurate placement of the line.

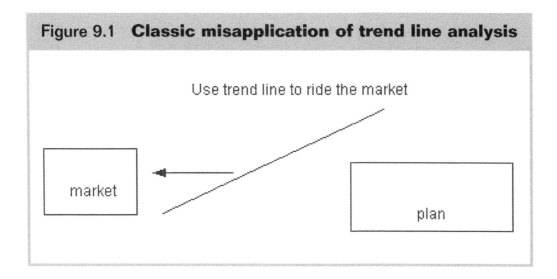

Figure 9.1 Classic misapplication of trend line analysis

Use trend line to ride the market

market

plan

We know the market is not aware of any trend line we plot on a chart but this does not stop us from acting as if there is a relationship. Our assumptions grow easily so our plan is to use the trend line to define the trend and so ride the market. The key relationship in this thinking is between the trend line and the market. This is why the placement of the trend line is so important. If it is wrong, then we miss out on riding the market trend.

The discussion in the previous chapter concentrated on better placement which was defined by the ability of the line to define or capture future price action. The misuse of a trend line as a tool for prediction provides an easy target for the detractors of charting and technical analysis — and rightly so.

The relationship between the trend line and the market shown in Figure 9.1 has become the core assumption of classic trend line analysis. The assumption is wrong because the trend line plot is entirely for our own use and signals our analysis of the market or stock. We understand the correct relationship more clearly if we re-state the purpose of the trend line.

☐ The purpose of the trend line is to define our analysis of the stock, based on the probability of the trend continuing, so we can develop a trade management plan.

The purpose of the trend line is *not* to define the way the market will behave. The trend line plot defines our *intended trading plan*. The more effectively the trend line is plotted, using the rules discussed in the previous chapter, the better we are at defining the balance of probability and identifying any changes. However, the success of our trade does not depend on how well we plot the trend line. The success of our trade depends on how well we react to price moves below the trend line.

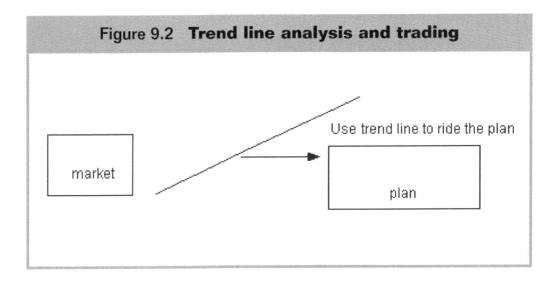

Figure 9.2 **Trend line analysis and trading**

The correct relationship between the three aspects — market, trend line and trading plan — is illustrated in Figure 9.2. Our trading action is linked directly to the values of the trend line. We use the trend line to ride the plan. We do not use the trend line to ride the market, somehow dragging the plan behind it. The difference between the two trend line concepts is very important as they reflect different approaches to the market.

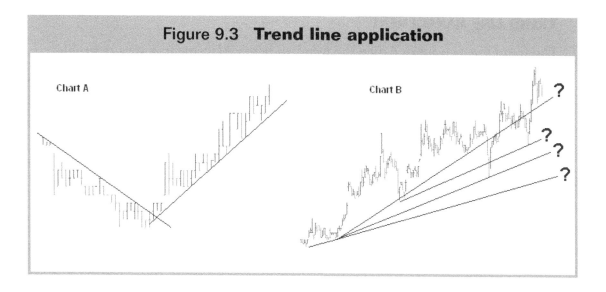

Figure 9.3 **Trend line application**

The chart extracts in Figure 9.3 summarise the most important application of the trend line for trade management and selection. The tool tells us what we should do sometime in the future. It is not a tool that tells the market what it is going to do, or a tool to predict how the market might behave. A close below the trend line tells me to close the trade because, in terms of my analysis, the trend is no longer reliable. Later we might argue about the accuracy of our trend line placement, but we should never doubt the importance of acting on the exit signal generated by our placement of the trend line.

Compare the stocks shown in chart A and B from a trade management perspective and note your answers to these questions.

☐ Which stock provides an easier trade to manage?

☐ Which stock gives the clearest and most reliable exit signals?

☐ Which chart removes the temptation to haggle by selecting a lower trend line?

☐ Which chart display eats away at our resolution and trading discipline?

Chart A provides a clear and simple management solution and for this reason it is preferred to chart B. Remember, in this stock selection process we usually have to reduce the opportunity to just a single trade. We look for reasons to drop a trade from the list because our practical objective is to reduce a list of 20 or 30 attractive trades to just one that offers the highest level of trading success, and this ultimately depends on our ability to manage the trade.

TREND LINE MANAGEMENT

The trend line is used to define the trend so better placement is very desirable, but more importantly, the trend line is used to define how we are going to manage our trade. The only features we control in a trade are our entry and exit decisions. Our analysis of the market or a stock ties the entry and exit to a specific set of conditions. These may be a close above the count back line, the crossover of two moving averages or the close on the value of a trend line.

We cannot be certain any of these indicators or trigger conditions are correct but we are interested in a higher level of probability rather than certainty. In selecting an indicator to use as an entry or exit trigger we try to match the indicator with the character of the stock or trading opportunity to ensure the balance of probability is tilted in our favour. The remaining balance — the chance things go wrong — is an important consideration in our trading plan. We apply a strict and disciplined range of calculations to set stop loss conditions, activated if our entry decision turns out to be incorrect. These are discussed in Chapter 26. This stop loss exit decision to protect capital is not related to our understanding of the individual stock, our belief in its future, the strength of our analysis or any other specific stock-related information. The stop loss exit decision is related to a loss of trading capital caused by an adverse price movement.

Obviously we aim to select the best combination of indicators to reduce the occasions where we are shaken out of a trade incorrectly. We aim to ensure the exit signal means the trend really has come to an end. However, the long-term accuracy of the selected method is not as important as the discipline of consistently acting whenever the signal is generated. We cannot afford to develop a trading plan and then ignore it once we buy the stock. We track a case study notional trading portfolio in our weekly newsletter, *Tutorials in Applied Technical Analysis*. The results from the past eight years are ongoing evidence of the importance of strict stop loss and the contribution it makes to successful trading.

TREND LINE TRIGGERS

If we accept the trend line plot is important because it forms the basis of entry and exit action in our trading plan, does this mean we plot a trend line anywhere on a chart? The trend line stands between us and market activity. When we build a trading plan we use price points to make our entry and exit decisions. These price points are triggers for action. The trend line remains a means of defining which price values are significant and which are unimportant. The nature of the trend we are trading — daily, short-term, long-term — determines which price values are significant for our intended trade.

The trend line is an aid to defining the value of those price points in a trend. The trend line should define as accurately as possible the trend we are trading to provide exact price triggers for action. However, the success of the trade depends on how we react when those price triggers are tripped. Based on our analysis, we believe a close below the trend line is a signal the trend has weakened, or has ended. We act on this price trigger because it is consistent with our analysis and not necessarily because it accurately defines developing market behaviour. The price action in Figure 9.4 shows how trend line analysis is combined with trade management.

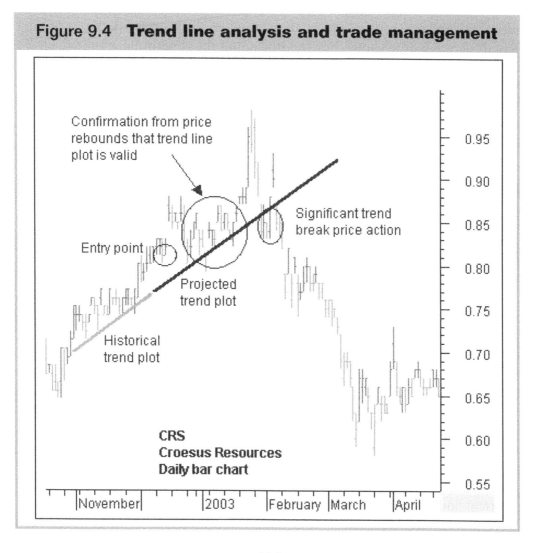

Figure 9.4 Trend line analysis and trade management

The exit does not have to be consistent with what actually happens with the trend in the following days or weeks. At the time our trend line analysis triggers an exit we cannot know if our trend line plot is accurate or inaccurate. Only future events tell us. If the line is proven accurate because a new downtrend emerges after the trigger signal then we use exactly the same methods to plot the next trend line.

If the trend line plot is shown to be inaccurate, and the trigger signal turns out to be false because prices rebound and continue upwards, then we may reconsider the methods we use to plot the trend line. Or we may decide this incident is isolated and continue to use our methods of trend line plotting.

We must trust our analysis. If we do not, then our trading becomes pure guesswork and gut instinct. The analysis provides the framework of our trading plan. It determines when we buy the stock, and the conditions under which we sell it. As soon as we buy stock, the success of the trade is dependent upon when we take an exit. For this decision we rely on our analysis which is summarised by a trend line projected into the future. We only know if this trend line is right or wrong retrospectively, but when we exit we know immediately if our trade has been profitable or unprofitable.

TREND LINE TRADING PLANS

This line of argument is counter to the classic understanding of the relationship between trend line plots and market activity. I found a trend line more useful as a trade management tool after I had a number of trades where the trend line was accurately placed but the trade was a failure because I did not follow my trading plan. I came to understand the success of the trade was not related to the trend line, it was related to the plan based on the trend line.

More importantly, I observed when I place a trend line incorrectly — subsequent price action proving the retreat was temporary and not a trend change — but acted strictly in accordance with my plan, that the trades were successful and made a profit. The success of the trade rested upon my reactions when trading plan triggers were activated based on the trend line plot. The accuracy of the trend line had little impact on the success of the trade. Having a totally accurate trend line did not make a successful trade if I did not follow the plan. Having an inaccurate trend line did not preclude a successful trade if I followed the trading plan. Once I understood the correct relationship between the market, the trend line and the plan, I stopped sweating over the exact retrospective and future placement of the line.

A better trend line more effectively captures current and future price action and signals the genuine end of a trend. A more successful trader acts on the entry and exit signals consistent with the analysis underpinning his trading plan. The trend line has no influence on the market, but it has a significant influence on your trading plan. This relationship is the key to using trend lines successfully in trading.

The trend line defines the trend but, more importantly, it defines our trading plan. The relationship is between the trend line and our plan, not between the trend line and the market. When we get a close below our trend line the logic of our plan tells us the balance of probabilities has shifted so we get out. This discipline plays an important role in the success of our trading — learn to act on plan signals.

We can always rejoin the trend if the break may be false or a new parallel trend line develops at slightly lower levels. There is an additional transaction cost but treat it as an insurance premium. The trend line break could have signalled a total collapse and ignoring the signal could have cost thousands of dollars. We do not know at the time what will happen, but according to our plan we know an exit signal has been delivered. We act on the one thing we control — our entry and exit decision, which is based on trend line analysis.

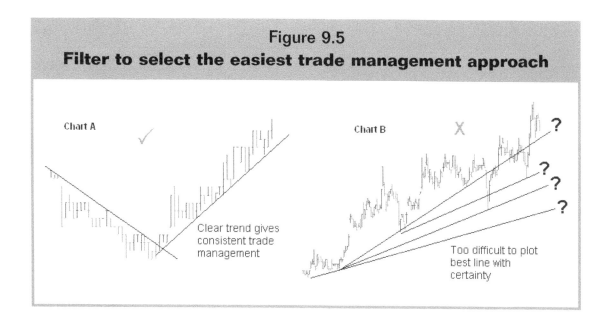

Figure 9.5
Filter to select the easiest trade management approach

Chart A

Clear trend gives consistent trade management

Chart B

Too difficult to plot best line with certainty

The trend line is the third selection test. The first test found a selection of candidates and the second visual test dropped those stocks not moving upwards. We apply the trend line as a filter test and look for trade opportunities which are most easily managed using this tool. Stocks compatible with easy trend line placement like chart A in Figure 9.5 survive this selection test because their ease of trade management increases the probability we will make clear exit decisions when the time comes.

Trades offering multiple choices of equally valid trend line plots are much more difficult to manage because it is easy to find excuses for not acting on the first exit signal. When we have trouble clearly defining the trend we can expect indecision when it comes time to exit the trade. Equipped with skill and experience, traders can effectively manage these more difficult exits but we do not need to accept this additional challenge when clear, simple, easy-to-manage trades are available. Stocks with multiple management choices are dropped in favour of those offering a clear solution.

Although our focus in this book is on longer term trend trades, it is also useful to understand the application of a slightly different trend line created by a parabolic curve. In the next chapter we detour to examine the opportunities offered by this type of fast-moving trend which may last for weeks, or more than a month.

CHAPTER 10

CURVE BALLS

arabolic trends, or curving trend lines, are a distraction from longer term trend trading but they offer a specific set of trading strategies which deliver very useful returns. It is very difficult to identify these trends early in their development and in most cases the trend is half way through its lifespan before we recognise it. They provide specific parabolic trend trading opportunities. They also deliver a fright to traders who purchased stock earlier on the basis of a quite different trend behaviour. This is why it is useful to recognise this change in the character of the trend, and to develop appropriate trading strategies.

In a parabolic trend the dominant characteristic is the way the trend starts slowly, and then speeds up. We select a parabolic curve to define the trend because the trend cannot be adequately defined by a single straight edge trend line. The developing trend could be defined by a number of short-term straight edge trend lines, as shown in Figure 10.1. Each of these lines is validly placed, but they are only an accurate definition of the trend for increasingly shorter periods. The parabolic nature of the trend is formed by looking at the inside of the curve created by these multiple short-term trend lines.

The trend line construction requirements remain the same as the classic construction techniques discussed in Chapter 8. A straight edge trend line just touches as many significant lows, or clusters of lows, as possible. The parabolic trend line must do the same. The parabolic trend is an exponentially calculated curve and it captures the acceleration in price activity. The curve starts as a near horizontal line, and the slope of the curve increases as price action moves higher. The parabolic curve eventually develops to a point where the last points on the curve create a vertical line. The curve is then completed, and so is the trend it defines.

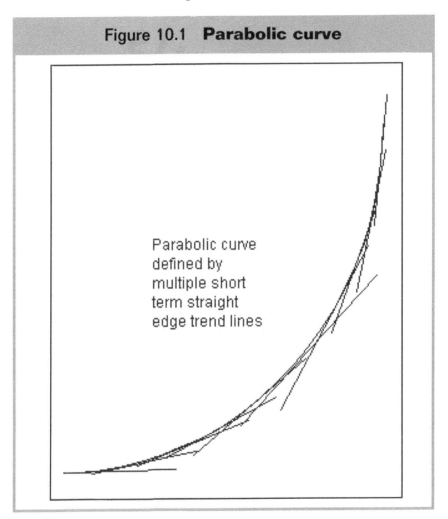

Figure 10.1 Parabolic curve

Parabolic curve defined by multiple short term straight edge trend lines

We use the parabolic trend line tool in the Guppy Traders Essentials charting package, or toolbox, to plot these trends. The curve is not constructed like an ellipse so this common charting software drawing tool does not provide a substitute for a parabolic trend line plot.

In an ordinary uptrend, we use a straight edge trend line to define the trend. The trend is defined by the ability of prices to stay *above* the trend line. It has no pre-determined end or time limit. The parabolic trend line is defined by the ability of prices to stay to the *left* of the parabolic curve. This is easily achieved while the slope of the parabolic curve is gentle, but once the end of the curve becomes vertical then the curve can no longer move forward in time. The end of the curve has a fixed date, say 29 April. Price activity is not fixed, so on 30 April the stock will trade and no matter what price is achieved, the bar for the day will fall to the *right* of the parabolic trend line.

This gives two specific characteristics to parabolic trends:

1   Parabolic trends often collapse very rapidly, often with prices gapping downwards.

2   Parabolic trends have precisely defined time limits.

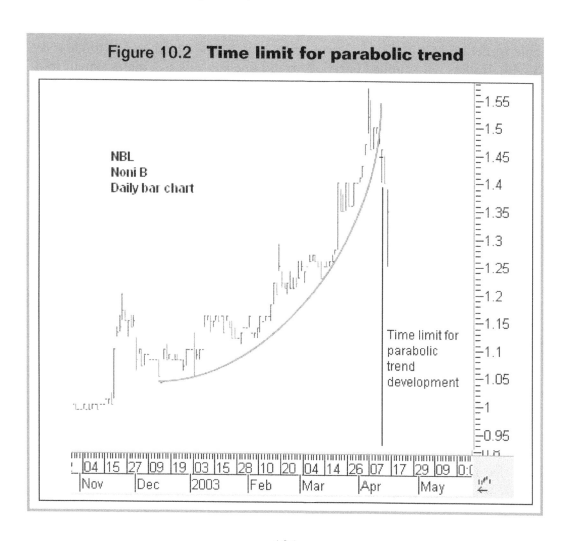

Figure 10.2   **Time limit for parabolic trend**

The chart of Noni-B (NBL) in Figure 10.2 illustrates a parabolic trend line and shows two exit points. The first is a close below the parabolic trend line. The second is the day on which the parabolic trend goes vertical. This is a time-based exit, irrespective of the prevailing price.

We know trading is not about prediction. It is about identifying the balance of probability. Some trades have a very high probability of developing in a consistent way, and the parabolic trend is one of them. This probability is so high that at times it resembles prediction.

On the day the projected parabolic trend line went vertical, NBL prices gapped down, opening at $1.45, dropping to $1.40 and then climbing back to close at $1.46. Good traders take an exit at $1.45 because this is the day the parabolic trend approached vertical and they expect a price drop. Traders who waited for end-of-day confirmation and who took action on the next trading day were also able to get an exit at $1.45. Prices opened at $1.45 and then fell to close at $1.40. Traders who applied parabolic trend line analysis as a management tool were able to achieve an exit at $1.45. At worst, the exit would have been at $1.40 on either of these days.

Traders who did not apply parabolic trend line analysis and management faced a substantial reduction in their open profits by the close of trading a few days later, with prices dropping as low as $1.25. Getting a reasonable exit became difficult.

Although traders are reasonably confident about the way the parabolic trend comes to an end, it is more difficult to decide what happens after the parabolic trend ends. There are significant dangers for those who attempt to ride out the collapse of a parabolic trend.

STRAIGHT UP OR PARABOLIC?

A parabolic trend is a momentum-driven trade and it is easy to confuse with a trend moving sharply upwards. Recognising the difference is important because the parabolic trend calls for a different type of management. The Australian Foundation (AFI) chart in Figure 10.3 highlights the recognition difficulties. We consider entering this trade on the day after the last bar shown on the chart so we need to know which type of trend line is most appropriate. The solution comes from the basic construction rules for each type of trend line.

The rules for a straight edge trend line are:

☐ Price action is easily defined with a single straight edge line.

☐ A straight edge trend line touches as many significant lows, or clusters of lows, as possible.

- The trend is defined with a single straight edge trend line.
- The straight edge trend line does not set a time for the end of the trend.

  The rules for a parabolic trend are:

- Price action is best defined using a series of very short straight edge trend lines, or a curve.
- The parabolic trend is best defined with a curved line.
- A parabolic trend line touches as many significant lows, or clusters of lows, as possible.
- As the curved parabolic trend line approaches the vertical, it sets a time for the end of the trend.

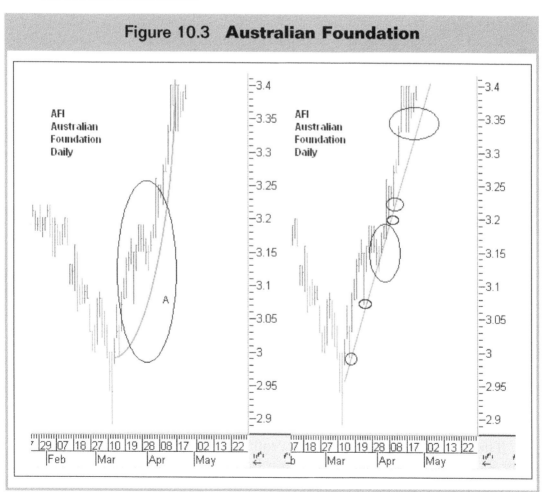

Figure 10.3 **Australian Foundation**

Using these construction definitions we see the parabolic trend line is not appropriate for AFI. Area A shows the relationship between price action and the plotted parabolic trend line. We look in vain for a cluster of lows, or even a single low point, to define the trend in this period. We expect to see several lows touching this trend line and prices rebounding. This does not happen, and this makes the use of the parabolic trend line invalid for the analysis or management of this type of trade.

In contrast, the straight edge trend line is plotted along multiple clusters of low points, shown in the circled areas. Move the line to the left, and too many significant lows are excluded. Move it to the right, and too few significant lows are included. The plot captures the bulk of the significant lows. This is the most accurate, and the most appropriate, style of trend line plot, and confirms this is a momentum trade best managed with a straight edge trend line.

EX-DIVIDEND TREND OFFSETS

When a stock goes ex-dividend there is a fundamental change to the known value of the stock. This change has nothing to do with company performance, with perceived value, nor with estimates of future performance. The stock is now worth less than it was yesterday because new shareholders are no longer entitled to a defined dividend payment. This usually results in a drop in the share price by at least the value of the dividend, and sometimes more. To avoid being shaken out of a trend trade by this adjustment we adjust the placement of our trend line. This applies to straight edge trend lines but not to parabolic trends. We stay with the earlier NBL example and look at the impact of a $0.04 dividend on trading activity.

When NBL opened ex-dividend, prices dropped from the previous close at $1.50 to $1.45. If we had been using a straight edge trend line as a stop loss point then the solution to the ex-dividend day is straightforward and shown in Figure 10.4. The value of the dividend is projected down from the low of the day prior to the ex-dividend day. On the chart extract this is shown as a thick vertical line. The straight edge trend line shown is not plotted accurately, but we use it because we want to keep the charts comparable and demonstrate the principle. The straight edge trend line is then moved downwards by the amount of the dividend and plotted as a new, parallel, offset trend line.

If the trend line is used as a protect profit stop loss point, then this is the only time a stop loss point is moved downwards. Using an offset straight edge trend line when a stock goes ex-dividend is a sensible solution to the price change that occurs when the value of the stock changes as a result of an independent action. The impact of the dividend is removed from the trend line plot and trade management.

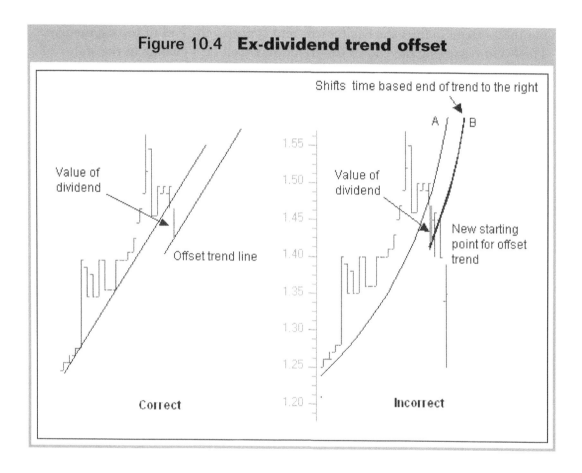

Figure 10.4 **Ex-dividend trend offset**

This offset principle, shown on the right-hand chart in Figure 10.4, does not apply with a parabolic trend. Again, please note the parabolic trend line is not plotted accurately. We use it only to show the principle. In this example the original parabolic trend line A is offset by the value of the dividend and plotted as parabolic trend line B. This is invalid, and the essential difference between the two trend line construction principles explains why.

A straight edge trend line has no time-based end. As long as prices remain above the line, the trend is intact. The parabolic trend line has a time-based component. Prices must remain to the left of the trend line. When the line moves to vertical, just the passage of time will inevitably move prices to the right of the line and signal an end to the trend.

This time-based component is an immutable part of this parabolic trend definition because it captures the way crowd excitement is accelerating. The parabolic trend defines the excitement and captures the end of the excitement. The event triggering the end of the trend may well be a change in the status of the stock — it goes ex-dividend — but the parabolic trend is a function of time and slope. The crowd has already taken dividends into account. If it remains excited, then prices will not adjust by the dividend value and the nature of the trend will continue to conform with the parabolic trend line parameters.

Parabolic trends represent a detour in our analysis, but if we do not recognise them, they have the ability to hijack our trading plan. The parabolic trend spans trend line analysis, trade management and the character test we want to apply in the next section. The parabolic trend has a specific character which is traded in a particular fashion. When these trends develop as part of a longer term trend they provide the opportunity to take unexpectedly high profits. It is not an opportunity to miss.

CHAPTER 11

NO SECRETS

At the end of the last part we examined a new set of potential exit conditions and asked you to use them to decide if you should exit the trade. The purpose of this ongoing trading exercise is to explore how traders make different decisions based on exactly the same data. Although there is a most profitable outcome for this developing trade, that does not necessarily make it the best or only solution. Every trader is unique, so each person looks at the same information and makes different decisions. Some exit too early, others exit near the top, and others wait too long, giving up some of the profit from the trade.

When we asked the same exit question of readers of our weekly *Tutorials in Applied Technical Analysis*, in the original trading test only 6% took an exit as shown in Figure 11.1. We give them an exit at $0.37 for a quick 15.63% return.

Few trading decisions are clear-cut. Prices may close below our stop loss level, but this does not mean we act on the signal immediately. Traders may use the same indicator combination but interpret signals in different ways. They may act in advance of the indicator signal, taking a defensive or fearful exit. Others wait until the exit signal is generated and then delay action until prices fall further. They hold on because they hope prices will tick up again and reward them for their patience. As profits grow it is tempting to look for reasons to collect them.

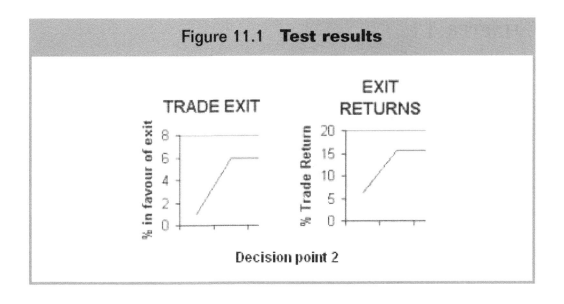

Figure 11.1 **Test results**

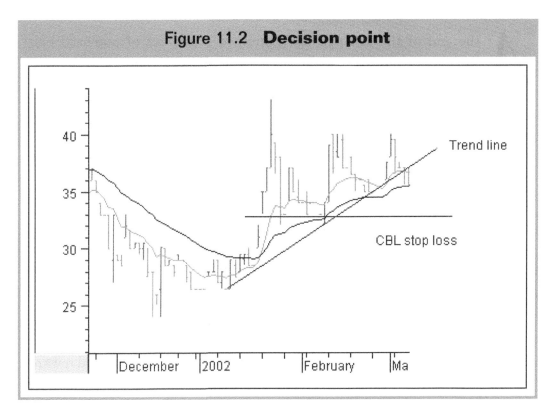

Figure 11.2 **Decision point**

The charts in Figures 11.2 and 11.3 are repeated from Chapter 7 and most people who exited at this decision point cited the closes below the trend line as the main reason. Some felt this trend line signal was supported by the MACD_Histogram. They seemed to ignore the consistent sell signals generated by the MACD_Histogram at the previous chart extract. A few traders applied a trend line to the Relative Strength Indicator (RSI) peaks and used this to confirm their exit decision, but unfortunately RSI trend lines are one of the least effective applications of the RSI to stock trading.

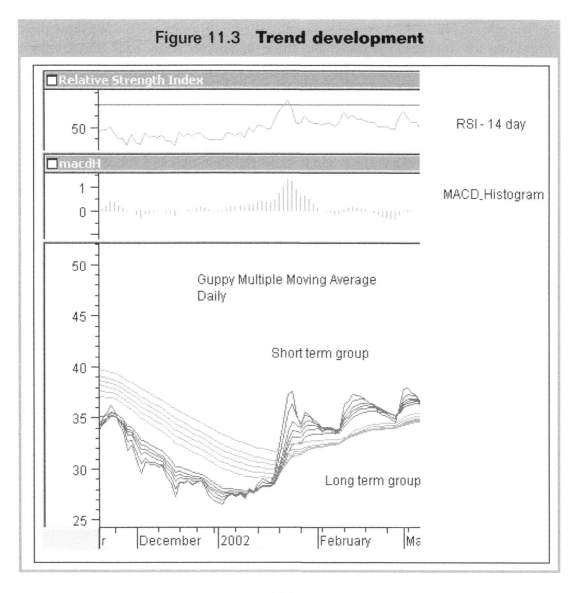

Figure 11.3 **Trend development**

This shows an interesting characteristic amongst traders. Once we get one exit signal — the close below the trend line — we tend to look at other indicators with a bearish view. Instead of looking at them objectively, we go hunting for reasons to confirm the decision we have already made. Looking for confirmation is different to looking for verification. We must try to assess each indicator signal on its merits, and not in a bullish or bearish light.

OUR ANALYSIS

The table in Figure 11.4 provides a summary of indicator analysis. We show the reasons for staying in the trade, and these include the count back line, Guppy Multiple Moving Averages and moving average signals which do not flash an exit. The reasons for exiting the trade are compiled from reader feedback in the original test.

What was your decision at the end of the previous section? Our conclusion is the trade remains open. None of these reasons for the exit or for staying with the trade is absolutely correct. There is no right answer, and this is one of the features that makes trading so difficult to master. As this trade evolves over the next few sections of the book, readers will develop a better idea of how other traders make their exit decisions. Use this information to improve your own trading.

Figure 11.4 **Analysis summary**

INDICATORS	STAY IN TRADE	EXIT TRADE
Count back line	No close below the CBL line when used as a trailing stop loss.	No signal.
Guppy Multiple Moving Average	Long-term group is moving upwards and still showing signs of increasing separation. Short-term group is compressed and ready for rebound.	Short-term moving group moved to the top of the long-term group on the last retracement. This next retracement could break the weak long-term group which is not widely spread. Defensive exit.
Moving average crossover	No moving average crossover.	Short-term average is turning down. This confirms the weakness seen in other indicators.
RSI	No action. Wait for next RSI peak to plot potential divergences.	RSI peaks are trending lower as shown by trend line which indicates trend weakness.
MACD_H	None applicable.	MACD_H unable to stay above the zero reference line.
Trend line, support and resistance	Retracements seem to have found temporary support at $0.35.	Closes below the straight edge trend line signal an exit. Potential resistance at $0.40 confirms exit decision.

TEST QUESTION

The next significant trading decision is several weeks away, towards the end of March on the chart time scale. The charts in Figures 11.5 and 11.6 show how the trade developed in the following weeks and end at the next decision point. Now traders start to worry about momentum-driven trades and the way profits rapidly disappear when a stock retraces or collapses. The indicator groups provide some conflicting signals. Some traders see this as evidence the initial trend is weakening, and conclude there is reduced probability of the trend continuing upwards. Other traders pay more attention to some indicators than to others. The choice is yours. We offer no guidance.

Get out or stay? It is a simple question for you to answer in a short note written at the bottom of the page. At the end of the next part we show how the trade developed from this point and discuss the analysis we applied to each indicator as shown on the charts.

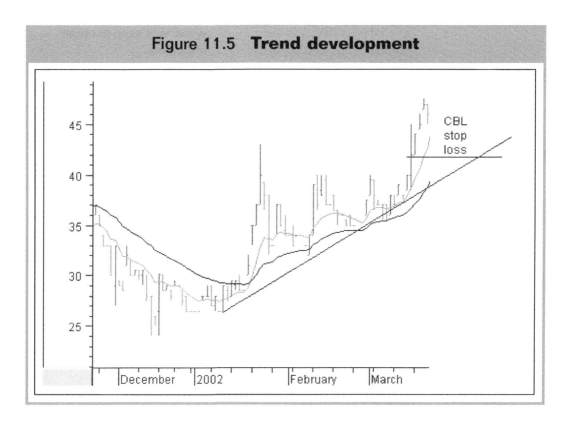

Figure 11.5 **Trend development**

Figure 11.6 **Trend development**

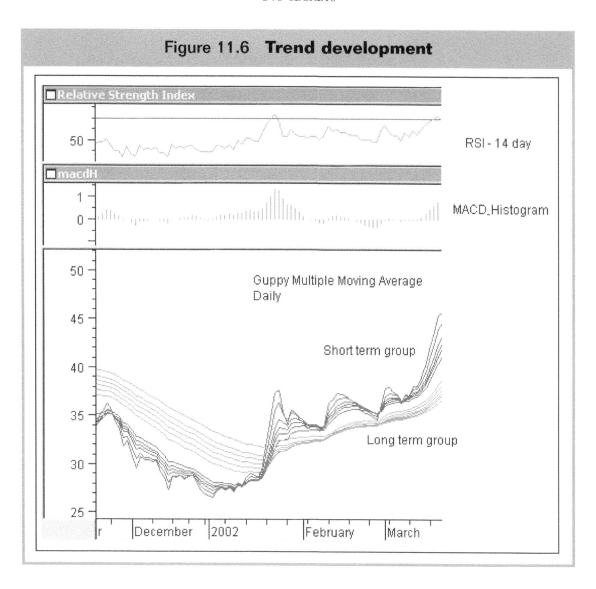

Notes:

PART IV

TESTING CHARACTER

CHAPTER 12

BUILDING CHARACTER

Some trends turn out to be nasty characters with concealed weaknesses leading to sudden trend collapses. Others just plod along slowly, adding to your profits day after day. They do not attract our attention as much as those stocks which shoot up rapidly in a sustainable short-term trend lasting weeks, or in an accelerating parabolic trend that brings disaster when it reaches its use-by date.

Identifying the difference in the nature of the trend — fast, slow or parabolic — and the character of the trend — well supported and dependable, bedevilled by trading activity, dominated by a trading bubble — provides us with a significant trading edge. It allows us to select the most appropriate trading strategy and the best trading tools for managing the selected trade. It is foolish to treat a rally in a prolonged downtrend as the beginning of a new uptrend. When the rally collapses there is a tendency to hold onto the stock if our analysis supports a continuation of the uptrend. We convince ourselves the rally retreat is temporary and the uptrend will resume. Such hopes pave the way to financial disaster. Understanding the nature and character of the trend is the purpose of the stock selection test four. The test prevents us from taking this particular path to financial perdition.

We started this trade identification and selection process with a market fishing trip, following the burley trail created by others, or slipping off to our favourite fishing hole located using a scan of our stock database. This is stock selection

137

test one. Within a short time we are surrounded by a host of opportunities so we must decide which to throw back and which to keep. Our task as traders is to keep only the best so we use a series of six further tests to identify the best from the opportunities available.

We want to walk with the crowd as it propels prices steadily higher in an easily defined trend. We use the eyeball search as the second test to catch those stocks already moving in uptrends. We want to shift the balance of probability more in our favour so we look for stocks that have proven they can move upwards. Many initial candidates fail the eyeball test.

In the previous section we showed how trend lines are applied and used as test three to select easily managed trades. This reduces our original list of potential trades but there are usually still too many to trade with our available capital. We reduce this list further by applying stock selection test four. All the survivors from the first three tests show an uptrend, but the character of the uptrends is different.

The stocks in Figure 12.1 are clear examples of different types of trends. Not every chart you look at has this clarity. We use the Guppy Multiple Moving Average (GMMA) to define the character of the trend. This is much more useful than using just two moving averages because the GMMA captures the character of the trend and the relationship between two dominant forces in the market — the traders and the investors. The GMMA was introduced in *Trading Tactics*. Since then the indicator has remained the same, but the range and sophistication of its application to a variety of trading situations, markets and financial instruments have increased substantially. Over the next few chapters we look in detail at these developments and their application to a variety of trading situations.

Remember, in this test we look for a steady trend with a high probability of continuing. The first three chapters in this part are particularly relevant to this process. The remaining GMMA chapters are also important from a trade management perspective. These applications of the GMMA help us make a better exit decision by determining when the trend is really coming to an end so we avoid making an incorrect exit based on a price collapse that later turns into a rebound continuation of the trend.

We apply the GMMA to each candidate on our selection list. Those without good trend character and a suitable nature for our purposes are dropped from our final list. The GMMA is a standard tool in Guppy Traders Essentials, MetaStock, OmniTrader, Ezy Charts and other end-of-day charting programs. It is included in Marketcast, MetaStock Professional and NextVIEW intra-day charting packages. The GMMA is included as a systems selection test and exploration option in OmniTrader, giving users advanced and sophisticated screening and filtering capabilities. The indicator is constructed by combining the groups of moving averages as discussed below.

Figure 12.1 Different types of trends

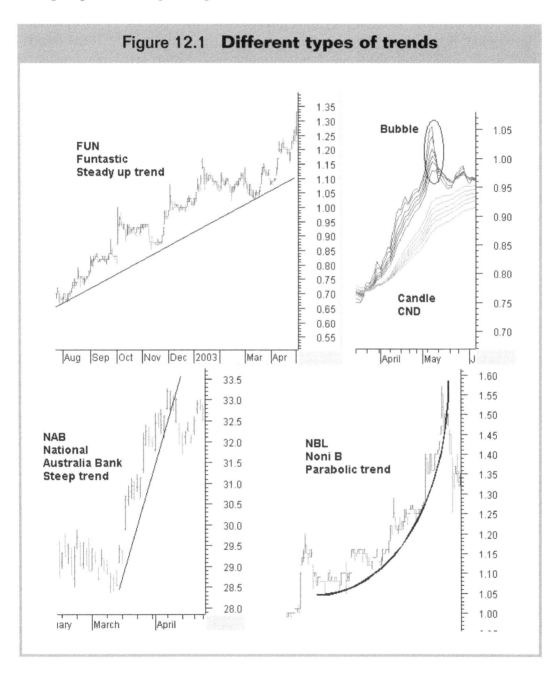

TRACKING INFERRED ACTIVITY

The GMMA indicator tracks the inferred activity of the two major groups in the market. These are investors and traders. Traders are always probing for a change in the trend. In a downtrend they take a trade in anticipation of a new uptrend developing. If it does not develop they get out of the trade quickly. If the trend changes they stay with the trade, but continue to use a short-term management approach. No matter how long the uptrend remains in place, the trader is always alert for a potential trend change. Often traders use a volatility-based indicator, like the count back line or a short-term 10-day moving average, to help identify the exit conditions. The trader's focus is on not losing money. This means he avoids losing trading capital when the trade first starts, and later he avoids losing too much of open profits as the trade moves into success.

We track the traders' inferred activity by using a group of short-term moving averages. These are 3-, 5-, 8-, 10-, 12- and 15-day exponentially calculated moving averages. We select this combination because three days is about half a trading week. Five days is one trading week. Eight days is about a week and a half.

The traders always lead the change in trend. Their buying pushes up prices in anticipation of a trend change. The trend survives only if other buyers also come into the market. Strong trends are supported by long-term investors. These are the true gamblers in the market because they tend to have a great deal of faith in their analysis. They believe they are right, and it takes a lot to convince them otherwise. When they buy a stock they invest money, their emotions, their reputation and their ego. They simply do not like to admit to a mistake. This may sound overstated, but think for a moment about your investment in AMP Insurance or Telstra. If purchased several years ago these are both losing investments yet they remain in many portfolios, and perhaps in yours as well.

The investor takes more time to recognise the change in a trend but he always follows the lead set by traders. We track the investors' inferred activity by using 30-, 35-, 40-, 45-, 50- and 60-day exponentially calculated moving averages. Each average is increased by one trading week. We jump two weeks from 50 to 60 days in the final series because we originally used the 60-day average as a check point benchmark for the long-term trend.

These moving average combinations reflect the original development of the GMMA where our focus was on the way a moving average crossover delivered information about agreement on value and price over multiple timeframes. Over the years we moved beyond this interpretation and application of the indicator, and we discuss these developments in the following chapters. The GMMA grew from two observations about moving averages. First is the lack of clues about future behaviour and second is the lag in the moving average crossover signal.

The classic uptrend signal is generated when the short-term moving average crosses above the long-term moving average. The perfect examples shown in trading books are just too perfect when they show a moving average crossover followed by a new uptrend. Real trading is often much messier and the chart extracts in Figure 12.2 highlight the problem. When a moving average combination converges almost to the point of a crossover it provides no useful information about the probability of future behaviour.

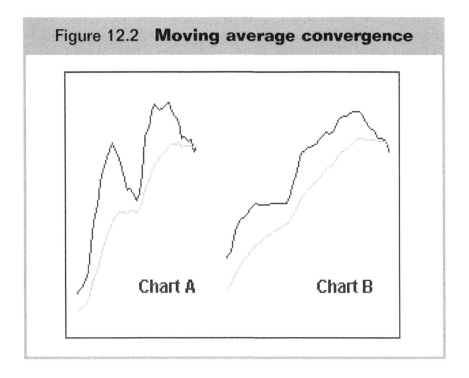

Figure 12.2 **Moving average convergence**

Chart A   Chart B

We cannot tell which of these convergences is most likely to lead to a collapse of the trend, or a continuation of the trend. Make the correct choice and we get to stay in a trade where the trend continues steadily upwards. Select the wrong chart, and the trend collapses very rapidly. These two charts show a decision point based on a 10- and 30-day moving average crossover. They both look exactly the same. Had we purchased stock previously, then this signal would have us reaching for our sell orders. Unfortunately one of these stocks goes on to add 63% in the following months. The other loses 17%. Can you select the winning stock based on the moving average display? It is a matter of luck, not judgement.

Despite the so-called power and reliability of a moving average crossover, at significant turning points we cannot usefully choose between chart A and chart B because we cannot understand the trend using this indicator combination.[1]

Although pairing moving averages is a useful trading tool, it is not very helpful in understanding the nature of the trend. It simply does not give the trader enough information to decide where the balance of probabilities lies.

The GMMA provides a clear view and understanding and this is the information we use when applying it to the exit question posed above. The eventual developments for charts A and B are revealed in the footnote below.[2]

The second starting point for the development of the GMMA was the lag between the time of a genuine trend break and the time a moving average crossover entry signal was generated. Our focus was on the change from a downtrend to an uptrend. Our preferred early warning tool was the straight edge trend line, which is accurate and simple to use. However, some breakouts were false and the straight edge trend line provided no way to separate the false from the genuine.

On the other hand, the moving average crossover based on a 10- and 30-day calculation provided a higher level of certainty that the trend break was genuine. However the crossover signal might come many days after the initial trend break signal. This time lag was further extended because the signal was based on end-of-day prices. We see the exact crossover today, and if we were courageous, we could enter tomorrow. Generally traders waited for another day to verify the crossover had actually taken place, which delayed the entry until two days after the actual crossover. This time lag often meant price had moved up considerably by the time the trade was opened.

---

1 We explore the reliability implications of these crossovers in Chapter 17. For the moment we just note this lack of reliability was a starting point that helped initiate a search for a solution which provided better understanding of the nature and character of the trend.

2 Chart A in Figure 12.2 shows Chiquita Brands. This stock moved upwards over the next six months, adding 63% to the price at the point of this crossover. Chart B shows Capral Aluminum, which lost 17% in the six months following this crossover signal. If we focus just on moving average crossovers we lose all the additional information a moving average tells us about the way the market values the stock and supports the existing trend.

The standard solution calls for a shorter term moving average, which moves the crossover point further back in time so it was closer to the breakout signalled by a close above the straight edge trend line. Some combinations are shown in Figure 12.3. The drawback is that the shorter the moving average, the less reliable it becomes.

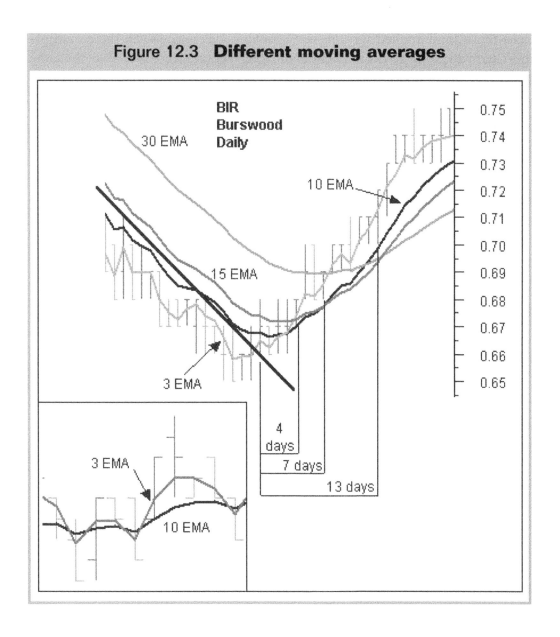

Figure 12.3 **Different moving averages**

FINDING THE GMMA

Serendipity and luck had a role to play in the development of the GMMA. In exploring these combinations I initially worked with a single test stock. The charting program I had at the time limited the number of simultaneous moving average plots on the screen. For convenience I used the maximum number of six short-term averages. Later I cleared the screen display, leaving the original bar chart intact, and applied six long-term moving averages. When these multiple short-term and long-term exponential moving averages were placed on the same underlying bar chart five significant features emerged. They were:

1   A repeated pattern of compression and expansion in a group of six short-term averages.

2   A repeated pattern of compression and expansion in a group of six long-term averages.

3   The pattern of behaviour was fractally repeated across different timeframes. These short- and long-term groups were useful in understanding the inferred behaviour of traders and investors.

4   The degree of separation within groups and between groups provides a method of understanding the nature of the trend and trend change.

5   The synchronicity was independent of the length of the individual moving averages. At major trend turning points compression occurred across both long- and short-term groups and this provided early validation of signals generated by the straight edge trend line.

This conclusion emerges from these features and it underpins the GMMA:

☐   The relationship between moving averages and price is better understood as a relationship between value and price. The crossover of two moving averages represented an agreement on value over two different timeframes. In a continuous open auction, which is the mechanism of the market, agreement on price and value was transient and temporary. Such agreement often preceded substantial changes in the direction of the trend. The GMMA became a tool for identifying the probability of trend development.

These broad relationships and the more advanced relationships used with the GMMA are summarised in Figure 12.4. We examine the identification and application of each of these relationships in the remaining chapters of this part.

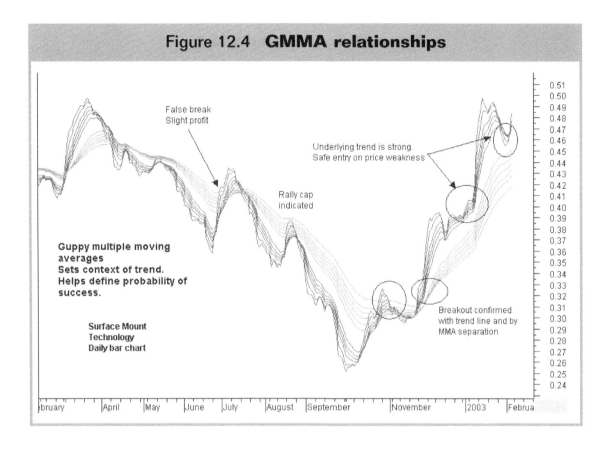

Figure 12.4 GMMA relationships

False break
Slight profit

Underlying trend is strong.
Safe entry on price weakness

Rally cap
indicated

**Guppy multiple moving
averages
Sets context of trend.
Helps define probability of
success.**

**Surface Mount
Technology
Daily bar chart**

Breakout confirmed
with trend line and by
MMA separation

The chart illustrates the most straightforward application of the GMMA and it worked well with 'V'-shaped trend changes. It is not about taking the lag out of the moving average calculation. The GMMA is used to validate a prior trend break signal by examining the relationship between price and value. Once the initial trend break signal is validated by the GMMA the trader is able to enter a breakout trade with a higher level of confidence.

The Commonwealth Bank (CBA) chart in Figure 12.5 shows the classic application of the GMMA. We start with the breakout above the straight edge trend line. The vertical line shows the decision point on the day of the breakout. We need to be sure this breakout is for real and likely to continue upwards. After several months in a downtrend the initial breakout sometimes fails and develops as shown by the thick black line. This signals a change in the nature of the trend line from a resistance function prior to the breakout to a support function after the breakout.

145

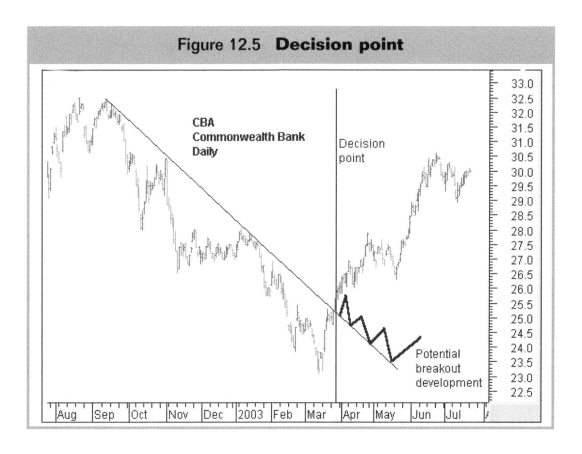

Figure 12.5 **Decision point**

FINDING CHARACTER

The GMMA is used to assess the probability that the trend break shown by the straight edge trend line is genuine. We start by observing the activity of the short-term group. This tells us what traders are thinking. In area A in Figure 12.6 we see a compression of the averages. This suggests traders have reached an agreement on price and value. The price of CBA has been driven so low that many traders believe it is worth more than the current traded price. The only way to take advantage of this 'cheap' price is to buy stock. Unfortunately many other short-term traders have reached the same conclusion. They also want to buy at this price. A bidding war erupts. Traders who believe they are missing out on the opportunity outbid their competitors to ensure they get a position in the stock at favourable prices.

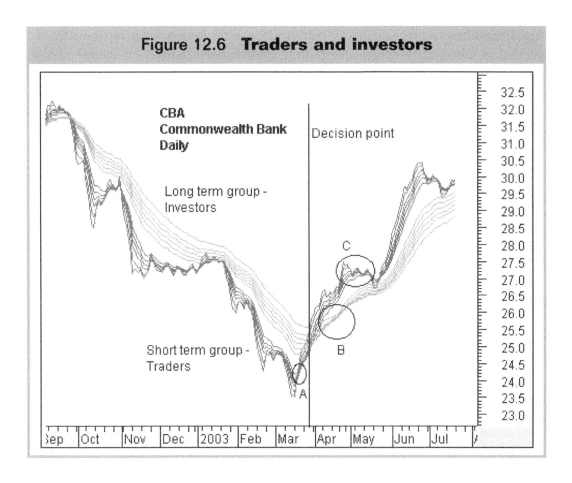

Figure 12.6 **Traders and investors**

The compression of these averages shows agreement about price and value. The expansion of the group shows traders are excited about future prospects of increased value even though prices are still rising. These traders buy in anticipation of a trend change. They are probing for a trend change.

We use the straight edge trend line to signal an increased probability of a trend change. When this signal is generated we observe this change in direction and separation in the short-term group of averages. We know traders believe this stock has a future. We want confirmation the long-term investors are also buying this confidence.

The long-term group of averages at the decision point shows signs of compression and the beginning of a change in direction. Notice how quickly the compression starts and how this signals the decisive change in direction. This is despite the longest average of 60 days which we would normally expect to lag

147

well behind any trend change. This compression in the long-term group is evidence of the synchronicity relationship that makes the GMMA so useful. This compression and change in direction tells us there is an increased probability the change in trend direction is for real and sustainable. This encourages us to buy the stock soon after the decision point shown.

The GMMA picks up a seismic shift in the market's sentiment as it happens even though we are using a 60-day moving average. Later we look at how this indicator is used to develop reliable advance signals of this change. This compression and eventual crossover within the long-term group takes place in area B. The trend change is confirmed. The agreement amongst investors about price and value cannot last because where there is agreement some people see opportunity. Many investors missed out on joining the trend change prior to area B, and now that the change is confirmed they want to get part of the action. Generally investors move larger funds than traders so their activity in the market has a larger impact.

The latecomers can only buy stock if they outbid their competitors. The stronger the initial trend, the more pressure to get an early position. This increased bidding supports the trend and is shown by the way the long-term group continues to move up, and by the way the long-term group of averages separates. The wider the spread the more powerful the underlying trend.

Even traders retain faith in this trend change. The sell-off in area C is not very strong. The group of short-term averages dips towards the long-term group and then bounces away quickly. The long-term group of averages shows investors take this opportunity to buy stock at temporarily weakened prices. Although the long-term group falters at this point, the degree of separation remains relatively constant, confirming the strength of the emerging trend.

The temporary collapse of the short-term group comes after a 12% appreciation in price. Short-term traders exit taking short-term profits, and this is reflected by the compression and collapse of the short-term group of averages. As long-term investors step into the market and buy CBA at these weakened prices, traders sense the trend is well supported. Their activity takes off, and the short-term group of averages rebounds, separates, and then runs parallel to the long-term group as the trend continues.

The GMMA identifies a significant change in the market's opinion about CBA. The compression of the short-term and long-term groups validates the trend break signal generated by a close above the straight edge trend line. Using this basic application of the GMMA, the trader has the confidence necessary to buy CBA at or just after the decision points shown on the chart extract.

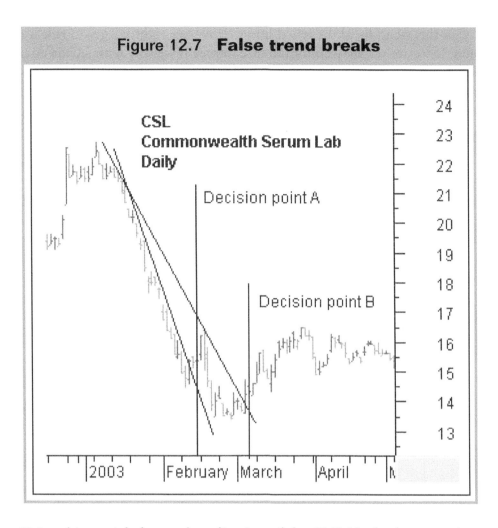

Figure 12.7 **False trend breaks**

Using this straightforward application of the GMMA also keeps traders out of false breakouts. The straight edge trend line in Figure 12.7 provides the first indication the downtrend may be turning to an uptrend. The Commonwealth Serum Laboratories (CSL) chart shows two examples of a false break from a straight edge trend line. We start with decision point A. The steep downtrend is clearly broken by a close above the lower trend line. If this is a genuine trend break then we have the opportunity to get in early well before any moving average crossover signal.

This trend break collapses quickly. If we had first observed this chart near decision point B then we may have chosen to plot the second trend line as shown. This plot takes advantage of the information on the chart so we know the first break was false, and by taking this into account we set the second trend line plot. Can this trend break be relied upon? If we are right we get to ride a new uptrend. If we are wrong we stand to lose money if we stay with a continuation of the downtrend. The straight edge trend line by itself does not provide enough information to make a good decision.

PROBABILITY AND GMMA

When we apply the GMMA in Figure 12.8 we gain a better idea of the probability of the trend line break actually being the start of a new uptrend. The key relationship is the level of separation in the long-term group of averages and the trend direction they are travelling. At both decision point A and decision point B, the long-term group is well separated. Investors do not like this stock so every time there is a rise in prices they take advantage of this to sell. Their selling overwhelms the market and drives prices down so the downtrend continues.

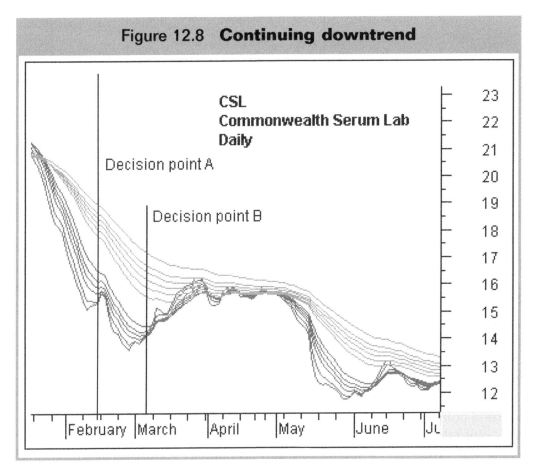

Figure 12.8 **Continuing downtrend**

The degree of separation between the two groups of moving averages also makes it more difficult for either of the rallies to successfully change the direction of the trend. The most likely outcome is a weak rally followed by a collapse and continuation of the downtrend. This observation keeps the trader and investor out of CSL.

Looking forward we do see a convergence between the short-term group of averages and the long-term group of averages. Additionally the long-term group begins to narrow down, suggesting a developing level of agreement about price and value amongst investors in April and May. In late March the 10-day moving average closes above the 30-day moving average, generating a classic moving average buy signal.

Using the GMMA we ignore this signal and the other GMMA convergence relationships. This decision is based on a more advanced understanding of the relationships revealed by the GMMA, and we examine these strategies in the next chapter.

ANNEX TO CHAPTER 12

VOLATILITY CLUSTER BEHAVIOUR

Analysis by Adam Cox originally published in
Tutorials in Applied Technical Analysis.

Some technical indicators seem to be more robust than others. Some seem to work fine only to fall apart at the most inopportune time. But why? Is there a specific reason? Is the answer simply to use more indicators? Like most traders I have asked these same questions over the years. To satisfactorily answer these questions, however, I had to start off at what I call step number one — develop a 'market philosophy'. In other words, start the trading equation from the bottom up to understand the share price time series. Although share price time series may be classed as having a type of random walk, they have a rich texture. We start with a brief look at one of the elements that gives 'body' to some of this texture.

'Heteroskedasticity' describes a fairly simple concept and in essence means variance or volatility changes over time. I am using the term volatility loosely here in lieu of variance or standard deviation. The Greek word 'Hetero' means to be different, whilst 'skedasticity' simply means variance.

This phenomenon may be called 'volatility clustering'. Share price time series have a rich texture. To examine volatility clustering we may take the difference of each price as illustrated in Figure 12A.1. This technique is used a lot by econometrics to create what is known as time series 'stationarity'. This stationarity simply allows the time series' mean and standard deviation to be measured. Westpac's return series displays a familiar bell-shaped distribution curve, shown in Figure 12A.2.

Figure 12A.1 Return transformation illustrated

Time	Price	Return	
1	10		
2	10.20	(10.20-10.00)/10	= 2%
3	10.50	(10.50-10.20)/10.20	= 3%
4	10.35	(10.35-10.50)/10.50	= -1.4%

ASYMMETRIC VOLATILITY

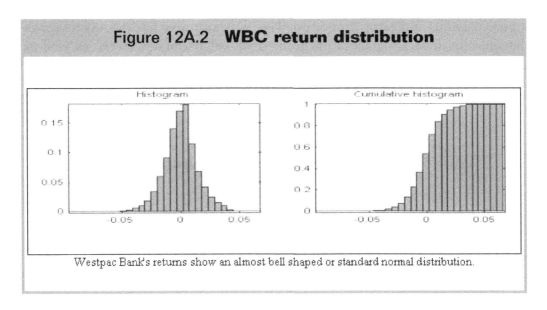

Figure 12A.2 **WBC return distribution**

Westpac Bank's returns show an almost bell shaped or standard normal distribution.

Share price time series also display another phenomenon: asymmetric volatility, related to heteroskedasticity. Shares tend to display more volatility on the downside than the upside. This phenomenon may be explained by the leverage effect. Volatility appears to be higher on the downside because margin loans are called-in when the share price falls. Margin loan–based selling drives price lower and with more momentum than upside price raises. This phenomenon cannot be attributed to short selling alone. An investor with a current long position may exit that position at-market, whereas the short seller may not make a new low by his selling.

The GMMA captures the behaviour of heteroskedacticity and auto-regressive processes at 'levels' rather than being an oscillator. The GMMA describes this phenomenon in an effective and deliberate manner shown in Figure 12A.3. Daryl Guppy writes in *Trading Tactics* '…the signal we read is not price, but behaviour'. This indicator has the advantage of showing these phenomena or behaviours at levels, as well as displaying long and short directional characteristics; something a pure volatility indicator does not indicate. Many oscillator-based techniques, including the stochastic oscillator, are simply averaging processes, and cannot reconcile the effects of volatility clustering.

The GMMA describes heteroskedasticity and serial auto-correlation in a simple and robust manner, whilst retaining price direction qualities, something a pure volatility indicator cannot do. This indicator also has the advantage of dynamically illustrating these phenomena or behaviours at levels, as well as displaying long and short directional characteristics; something a pure volatility indicator cannot do.

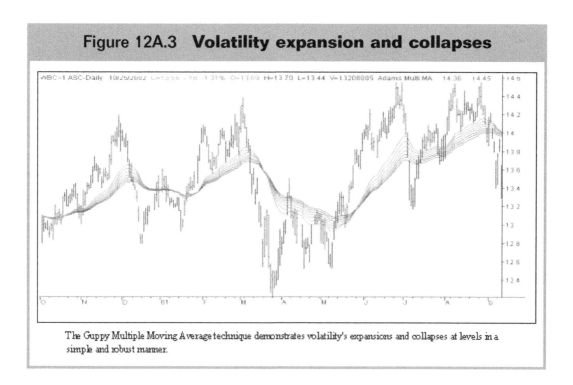

Figure 12A.3 Volatility expansion and collapses

The Guppy Multiple Moving Average technique demonstrates volatility's expansions and collapses at levels in a simple and robust manner.

CHAPTER 13

TRACKING TRADERS AND INVESTORS

The financial market is dominated by traders and investors, not by bulls and bears. Terms describing the attitude of the market do not describe the operation of the market. A trader may be bullish or bearish. This changes, but the traders' fundamental approach to market activity — a shorter term view and aggressive risk management — does not change. The market is not a single unified body where everybody thinks the same way. At heart it is a mechanism for resolving strongly held and contradictory views often backed by substantial sums of money. For every buyer who believes a stock is about to go up there is a seller who believes the stock is about to go down. The market trading mechanism allows these contradictions to be resolved. The seller gets his money and the buyer gets his opportunity.

This broad market mechanism is inhabited by two groups — traders and investors. Their activity defines the nature and character of every trend. Understand how they are behaving and we have a powerful tool to analyse the trend and select the best trading tactics.

The Guppy Multiple Moving Average (GMMA) provides a guide to the inferred activity of each of these groups. Our individual behaviour is not remarkably different from others in the market. How we think and react is magnified many times by other market participants. By understanding more clearly how and why we react to a given situation we make better judgments about how others may react.

Experienced traders understand that psychology has a vital part to play in trading success. Our first understanding of this impact is when we confront fear and greed in an unrestrained fashion. Making more money than we ever dreamed possible for what looks like little work is a heady experience. It has many interesting and unexpected consequences on our behaviour. Some of them are not very pretty to observe.

Fear becomes an intimate companion when our hard-earned cash is gobbled up in a falling market. This is no thrill ride with a guaranteed safe ending like a theme park rollercoaster. We react in quite unexpected ways and they are not always pleasant. Greed and fear are the base emotions triggering psychological reactions. When we move beyond these raw emotions we find many other factors come into play.

Experienced traders find success rests as much upon understanding more about themselves and their motivation as it does on understanding the market. Everybody has different psychological reactions in detail, but it is useful to examine the broad psychological factors inhibiting or enhancing trading success. These are ultimately reflected in GMMA relationships.

INVESTOR BEHAVIOUR

We start with investor behaviour, and in particular, the specific problems faced by fund managers. These include the need to shift large sums of money in the market, the regulatory environment, and the unusually high level of herd instinct prevailing in this industry as they consistently compare ratings, portfolio holdings and performance amongst their peers.

Institutional funds operate on the basis of portfolio weightings. At the top level these weightings determine how much they hold in cash, bonds, Australian shares or international shares. On a more specific level these weightings are applied to each sector. A fund allocates a set proportion of their holdings to each of the major sectors, such as retailing, mining, transport and utilities. At a tactical level, this asset allocation policy also applies to stocks within the sector. The weighting formula helps decide just what proportion, or weighting, in the portfolio should be allocated to the retailer Woolworths rather than Coles Myer. In some cases, there are prudential requirements which specify the focus of the fund and limit their exposure, or weighting, in particular sectors or markets. The weighting of stocks in the fund portfolio is under constant review and is adjusted regularly.

Many funds were underweight when gold started to rise in price in early 2003. As gold rose it became more important for funds to include more gold stocks in their portfolio. The market weighting allocated to the gold sector had changed and this provides a useful way to understand how the GMMA reflects investor behaviour.

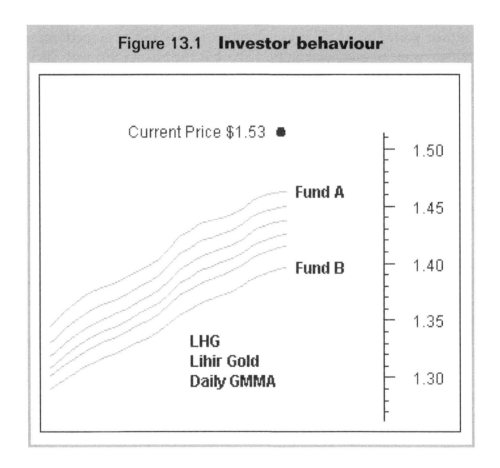

Figure 13.1 shows an extract from the long-term group of averages in the GMMA display for gold producer Lihir Gold (LHG). Imagine each moving average line represents the buying activity and intentions of a single fund manager. The upper average represents the buying activity of a single fund A and the

longest, and lowest, average shows the buying activity of fund B. Although each fund wants to add LHG to their portfolio they have different levels of need and urgency. Fund A has been caught flatfooted by the rise in gold. They are 'underweight' and need to urgently add a gold miner like LHG to their portfolio so they can participate in the better performance in this sector, but also to ensure the asset allocation between sectors accurately reflects the underlying sectors driving the market.

Fund B has been much smarter. They have about the correct weighting for gold in their portfolio. As the price continues to rise and to outperform other sectors they want to add some more LHG but there is no urgency. They can afford to wait for prices to dip quite substantially before taking any action.

The wide spread in the GMMA group shows how this thinking is reflected in market activity. While LHG trades at $1.53 the investors are not really interested in competing with the traders who are pushing prices higher. Fund A buys stock once prices drop to $1.47 as they cannot afford to wait until prices drop any further. Given their need to add gold stock, and their assessment of value, they become buyers at $1.47.

Fund B, which already has most of the stock they need, do not become buyers until prices drop to $1.40. At this lower level LHG is enticing enough to turn fund B into an active buyer. The degree of separation in the long-term group reflects the different levels of urgency behind investor behaviour. Those who believe they are missing out on a great opportunity are prepared to pay more than those who already have plenty of stock and who will only buy at bargain prices.

The width of separation confirms the strength of the trend. As traders offer stock at lower prices, from $1.47 to $1.45, and perhaps at $1.40, there are many funds who buy at these price levels. The selling pressure is absorbed by the investors across a $0.07 price range. If the long-term group of averages was compressed, then selling pressure would be absorbed across, perhaps, a $0.02 range, which makes it easier for selling to overwhelm the number of available buyers. The result is a weaker trend and a higher potential for trend collapse.

Private investors are not driven by exactly the same requirements as fund managers, but the same influences are present. If you held LHG from an earlier investment purchase then your behaviour as prices rise is similar to fund B. If you did not hold LHG during the rise in gold prices your reactions as an investor closely resemble those of fund A. These common and basic behaviours help create the GMMA displays which allow us to draw inferences about investor behaviour when assessing the strength and character of the trend.

TRADER BEHAVIOUR

Market activity is based on the difference between price and value. What we do on a personal level is repeated by many others and the action is highlighted by trader-style activity. When we buy a stock we prefer to pay a lower price than what we believe the stock is worth now. We look for a bargain, joining the bid, rather than meeting the ask. If we believe the real value of Telstra (TLS) is $6.71 and it is currently trading at $6.00 then we buy TLS at $6.00. It does not matter how we decided the real value of TLS is $6.71. We might use fundamental analysis, rely on a brokerage report, back our own judgement, or use a variety of charting and technical analysis techniques. We could even compare the current price of TLS with a 30-day moving average where the value is $6.71. What is important is how we act on this information. If we reach this conclusion by ourselves and if nobody else reaches the same conclusion, then it is very easy to buy TLS at $6.00. We do not have to beat anyone to this price because no-one else is aware of this critical difference between the current price and future value.

Of course this happy situation does not prevail in real markets. Once TLS hits $6.00 there are many people — hundreds, if not thousands — who are all aware of the same price and value relationship. Not all act on this understanding. Some may not have the money available. Others may want to wait until prices fall even lower, perhaps to $5.90, before they decide to buy. However, we know quite a few people believe TLS is a good buying opportunity at $6.00 when we see their orders in the order line.

We turn on the market depth screen shown as a table in Figure 13.2, eager to buy TLS at $6.00. Unfortunately there are already nine other orders in front of us. Here is the core problem for us as individuals, and it underpins the volatility, and limits of volatility, in the market. It is no surprise there are nine other people who want to buy TLS at $6.00 because they have all read the same analysis and used the same tools as us. We all believe the agreed real value of TLS is $6.71. This is not surprising as we all followed the same map, and ended up at the same place — but we have a problem. There are only 1,000 shares available at $6.01 but ten buyers are prepared to pay only $6.00 and they want a total of 20,000 shares.

The table shows a simplified order structure, and to make the example easier to follow, we are going to freeze the sell order line. The table shows ten traders who have all reached the same analytical conclusion. They put this analysis into action by placing a buy order in the market. The only way they can execute this analysis is by outbidding their competitors. This is an emotional experience. The closer price creeps to the agreed real value — $6.71 — the more desperate the traders become because they worry they might miss out on buying the stock.

Figure 13.2 Matching price and value

	Buy order line		Sell order line		
Trader A	$ 6.00	2000	1000	$ 6.01	
	$ 6.00	2000	1000	$ 6.11	
Trader B	$ 6.00	2000	1000	$ 6.21	
	$ 6.00	2000	1000	$ 6.31	
	$ 6.00	2000	1000	$ 6.41	
	$ 6.00	2000	1000	$ 6.51	
	$ 6.00	2000	1000	$ 6.61	
	$ 6.00	2000	**1000**	**$ 6.71**	Agreed value
Trader C	$ 6.00	2000	1000	$ 6.81	
Our initial order	**$ 6.00**	**2000**	1000	$ 6.91	
	$ 5.90	2000	1000	$ 7.01	

How long is the difference between price and value likely to last? The answer determines how we approach this buying opportunity. We want to buy 2,000 shares. If we believe the difference is likely to last for a while then we join the end of the order line, as shown in the diagram. If we believe the difference is unlikely to last then the only way to get this quantity is by bidding up to $6.11, beating our competitors.

We decide that the only way to get our shares is by bidding up to $6.11. What happens next depends on many factors. The difference between price — $6.11 — and our projected value — $6.71 — is still quite large. Trader B — who holds the third order in the queue — is worried this sudden jump to $6.11 might mean he misses out on getting into TLS at a favourable price, so he decides to lift his buying order. He wants 2,000 shares so he is forced to buy 1,000 at

$6.21 and another 1,000 at $6.31. Even at these higher prices, the price is still below the estimated $6.71 value for TLS. Trader B has purchased stock on the right side of the price and value relationship.

Trader A — who was at the top of the order line at the start of this exercise — now looks like missing out completely. Depending on his confidence in his analysis and his emotion, he may decide to chase price. After all he thinks TLS is good value at $6.71, and the price rise to $6.31 is evidence others believe TLS is worth more than $6.00. Driven partly by analysis and partly by emotion, he lifts his bid, paying $6.41 and $6.51 to buy a total of 2,000 shares.

Trader C — who has developed a nasty habit of getting the analysis correct but missing out on the trade because he is too timid to chase prices — decides to bite the bullet. He fills his order for 2,000 shares with purchases at $6.61 and $6.71.

CYCLES OF VOLATILITY

This is a compressed and simplified example, but what happens next is important because it completes the cycle of volatility. When price and value merge, volatility falters. We use our own sample trade to illustrate the relationship. We thought TLS was undervalued at $6.00. We paid an average of $6.06 to buy TLS, which was cheap compared with our estimated real value for TLS of $6.71. Now that the price of TLS is equal to the estimated value of TLS there is little reason to remain in the trade. Unless we can reasonably establish TLS is worth more than $6.71 there is no point in holding onto the stock. If it is worth more than $6.71 we hold the stock until price reaches the new level of value.

On this analysis, when price is equal to value, we sell TLS and take home our profit. In this example we sell 1,000 at $6.71 and 1,000 at $6.61 because we do not believe TLS will trade at over $6.71 as this is the real 'value' of the stock.

Our selling may trigger a cascade effect amongst other traders. Remember, traders are interested in controlling risk in two ways; first by protecting capital and second by protecting open profits. The price decline eats into trader A's open profit. He too has seen prices rise to the estimated real value of TLS and now he worries the price decline is the start of a downtrend. It is not the profit he hoped for, so he sells his shares to protect what little profit remains. To simplify and highlight the relationships for this example we assume selling 2,000 shares drops the price down by two order lines, in this case to $6.41.

Traders want to protect capital and trader C is now sitting on a loss. He sells his 2,000, driving prices down again by two notches to $6.21. This in turn triggers another wave of selling. This action is recorded on the daily chart and we see trading open at $6.01, rise to $6.71 and then fall back to $6.01. Magnify the timeframe from a single day to ten days, or twenty days, and we magnify the volatility. Our estimates of value may change, and the relationship between price and value changes, but our reactions to these changes remain constant.

The reactions of individuals are duplicated many times in the broader market. The processes we apply on an individual level are replicated by many other people in similar ways and at much the same time. We are unknowingly part of a group, united by our common analysis and our common approach to risk management. We are traders who have defined objectives in the market and closely defined methods of active risk management. Our activity creates volatility because our trading objective is to more closely match price and value. When price and value are separated it is our buying and selling activity that brings the two together.

Our behaviour is not remarkably different from others in the market. How we think and react is magnified by other market participants and is reflected in the behaviour of the short-term and long-term groups of averages. The GMMA captures these inferred relationships, and in the next chapter we show how to use this information to join an established trend with greater confidence.

CHAPTER 14

TREND TRAVELLERS

The Guppy Multiple Moving Average (GMMA) is so vital to the application of the fourth stock selection test based on understanding the trend character that it was necessary to take a detour in the last chapter to explore the construction philosophy. Armed with this understanding traders confidently assess the nature and strength of the trend.

There are three basic types of ongoing trend behaviour and we consider an example of each in this chapter. They are:

1 Fast moving steep trend.

2 Longer term steady trend with limited trading activity.

3 Long-term trend with consistent trading activity.

These types of trend opportunities pass our eyeball test two and trend line test three. How we decide to trade these trends and select the entry tactic depends upon our understanding of the relationship between traders — the short-term group of averages — and investors — represented by the long-term group of averages. This analysis test further identifies better trading opportunities and reduces the list of potential candidates. We focus on the activity of the traders because the trends are underpinned by committed long-term investors. Although not risk free, these opportunities offer low-risk access to rising markets and the ability to manage the trade with less intensity. A quick glance at the chart every few days is all the management supervision required.

These trend trading opportunities use the clearest of the GMMA relationships. We are not concerned with how the trend change was initiated. We are not called to make a judgment about the degree of compression at the point where the old trend changes to a new uptrend, nor is timing a vital issue. In the classic trend change situation discussed in Chapter 12 there are considerable advantages for those who recognise the trend change early. When we join an established trend the timing is less important because the rising trend is likely to continue for many days or weeks.

Our interest is in the nature and character of the established trend. We look for low-risk, high-probability trend trades. Our intention is to either take a bite from the trend or to get out of the trend *after* it has started to deliver trend weakness or end-of-trend signals. Both strategies are more difficult to execute than they appear. Logically, it makes sense to get out while the going is good — take a bite from the trend or get out as soon as possible after the trend has turned because we know we cannot reliably identify the very top of any trend move. In practice greed gets in the way. We want to take a very large bite from the trend, or we hang on after the trend has turned waiting for the opportunity to exit at a higher price. The GMMA helps our analysis of the trend, but trading discipline turns this analysis into trading success. For comparison we also examine the effectiveness of a standard two moving average combination indicator.

FAST MOVING STEEP TREND

We do not have to be amongst the first to see an opportunity to be able to benefit from it. Often we see trends that developed over several weeks and we have just one question: is it safe to join the trend? This becomes more relevant when the trend breakout from the consolidation area has been very steep as shown with David Jones (DJS) in Figure 14.1. Using the information available on the bar chart extract we need to decide the best trading tactics.

Using just the bar chart we are likely to avoid entering the trade. The trend run up has been steep and substantial. This has the characteristics of a momentum-driven trade, and these have a nasty habit of collapsing very quickly. The pause and decline in prices might be the beginning of a trend collapse. On the other hand, this temporary lull may be the beginning of a trend continuation. To make a better decision we need to understand the character of the trend.

Often traders rely just on two moving averages. The 10-day exponential moving average is shown as the thick black line. It is well above the 30-day moving average. The current price action is above the 10-day moving average but this just confirms this is a strong, fast-moving trend. It gives us no additional information about the probability of the trend continuing. Once we move beyond a simple crossover analysis, the information provided by two moving averages is limited.

The information we extract from the GMMA display in Figure 14.2 is much more detailed and useful for making a decision about joining this trend. The vertical line shows the decision point on the previous bar chart extract. The first feature we note is that the activity of the GMMA in area A is not relevant to our analysis of the stock at the

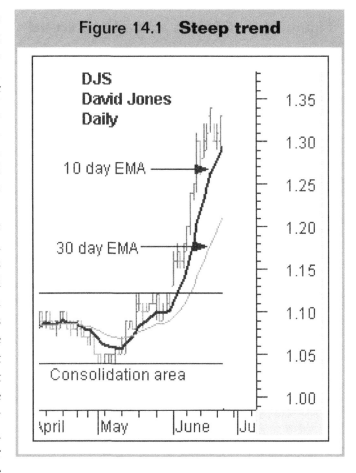

Figure 14.1 Steep trend

decision point line. It would have been difficult to accurately use the GMMA to identify the breakout from the consolidation area. This does not devalue the GMMA's usefulness in making an assessment about the nature of the trend once it has developed.

We first want to know how the long-term investors are thinking. This is an optimistic crowd. Once the uptrend has started the long-term group of averages quickly separated into a broad band. The wider the band, the more stable the trend and the more strongly it is supported. Although the slope of the trend is steep, the long-term group suggests there is a scramble amongst investors to buy this stock. The development behaviour of the long-term group duplicates the way the short-term group has spread out.

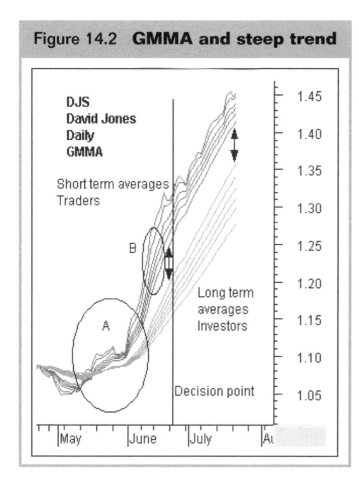

Figure 14.2 **GMMA and steep trend**

DJS
David Jones
Daily
GMMA

Short term averages
Traders

B

A

Long term
averages
Investors

Decision point

The behaviour of traders also provides important information about the stability of the trend. If the trend break is dominated by speculative trading then we expect to see considerable expansion and compression activity in the short-term group of averages as traders sell and collect quick profits. There is a small example of this in area A but this is the only instance of this activity.

The short-term group of averages quickly separated and remained separated by around the same amount. By the time they reach area B the averages are moving broadly parallel to each other. The expansion has stopped, and there is little evidence of compression which characterises trading activity. This trend is well-supported by investors, and by traders who may have entered with a short-term timeframe but who are now inclined to hold onto the stock while the trend continues.

Finally, the degree of separation between the averages, shown by the double-headed arrow, has stabilised. The two groups of averages are maintaining the same degree of separation and moving parallel to each other. Looking forward, the second double-headed arrow shows how the degree of separation remained constant as the trend continued.

Although this is a steep trend driven by momentum the GMMA analysis shows it is a low-risk trend trade at the decision point. This type of pattern passes our stock selection test four.

In summary the GMMA provides this identification information for a mid-trend entry:

☐ Short-term group is well separated and moved into a parallel pattern.

☐ Very little compression and expansion activity in the short-term group means less speculative trading.

☐ Long-term group separated quickly and develops a steady parallel relationship. Group is widely separated.

☐ Distance between groups of averages has started to stabilise, confirming trend continuity.

LONGER TERM STEADY TREND WITH LIMITED TRADING ACTIVITY

Trend stability depends on two factors. The first is the level of support offered by long-term investors. This is shown by the degree of slope and the degree of separation in the longer term group of averages. The second is the level of speculative trading activity. This is shown by the frequency of compression and expansion behaviour, and the degree of rally and retreat shown in the short-term group of averages. The DJS example showed long-term investor support and a low level of speculative trading activity. Using these key analysis features we more easily analyse the type of trading opportunity in Boral (BLD) displayed in Figure 14.3.

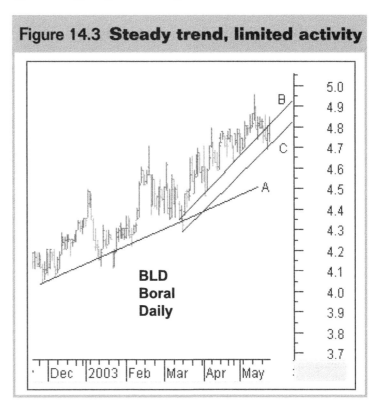

Figure 14.3 **Steady trend, limited activity**

BLD
Boral
Daily

We start, as all traders should, with the bar chart. It is confusing. The trend has clearly accelerated away from the longer term trend line A. The acceleration was defined using trend line B, but current price action suggests the trend is in trouble. We have the option of plotting new trend line C which offers the opportunity to join this general uptrend at a point where prices have temporarily fallen. One of the problems is that prices could still fall all the way back to the projected trend shown by line A.

Superficially it appears BLD is offering an opportunity to enter an established uptrend. The bar chart does not give us enough information to make a confident decision. In contrast the GMMA indicator provides a lot more information about the character of the trend and the most appropriate trading tactics.

We start the analysis by examining the activity of the long-term investors in Figure 14.4. The vertical line shows the decision point on the previous bar chart. The long-term group of averages is well-separated and moving in a broadly parallel pattern. There is no expansion in the averages. This has already taken place so now there is just steady buying when prices weaken. This strong parallel pattern with good separation indicates investors are still prepared to accumulate stock.

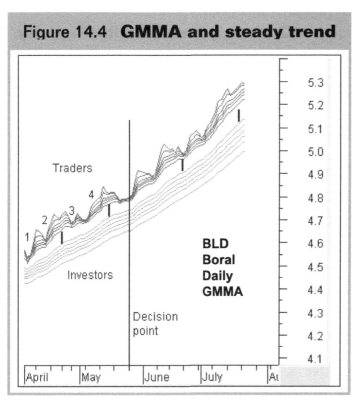

Figure 14.4 **GMMA and steady trend**

The degree of slope is not as steep as the DJS example. This steady upwards climb is steeper than trend line A, but not as steep as trend lines B or C on the bar chart. We do not define the steepness of the trend in absolute terms by assigning a value to the degree of slope. It is clear the trend in BLD is less steep than DJS. This gentler slope is a characteristic of long-term enduring trends well supported by long-term investors. This strong underlying trend has a low probability of a sudden collapse. Our primary focus in this chapter is on entry analysis for joining a trend. When this type of trend ends it is most likely to involve a slow rollover, giving investors ample opportunity to make a dignified exit.

The second feature of interest is trading activity which is revealed by the level of compression and expansion in the short-term group of averages. There are four complete examples of compression and expansion on the chart prior to the vertical decision point line. This is gentle trading activity. There is no fast and dramatic run up in prices followed by an equally dramatic collapse. Instead we see a steady, slow, almost cyclical expansion and contraction like waves constantly lapping at the coastline during a rising tide. The limited nature of this trading activity confirms there are no wild swings in volatility in this trend. There is no excitement, but there is a steady, rising trend.

The final feature we assess is the degree and nature of the separation between the two groups of averages. The thick vertical lines are all the same length. Prior to the decision point, the degree of separation remains approximately the same. The short-term group and the long-term group are moving parallel to each other. There is a greater level of trading activity, but it is not strong enough to pose a serious threat to the integrity of the trend. When prices pull back, investors step in. When traders sell there is barely a falter in the uptrend. Looking forward on the chart we see the degree of separation remains relatively constant over the coming months.

These GMMA relationships show BLD is an excellent stock for position traders and investors who want to join a well-established, stable trend. Both benefit from regular opportunities to buy the stock as prices make a temporary retreat within the context of the trend. These retreats may trigger an exit signal based on a straight edge trend line analysis, but they are unlikely to pose a serious threat to the continuation of the underlying trend. GMMA analysis confirms a low-risk trend trade at the decision point and stocks with these GMMA relationships pass the fourth stock selection test. In summary the GMMA provides the following identification information for a mid-trend entry:

☐ Long-term group is well separated in a parallel pattern. Investor support is strong and steady.

☐ The compression and expansion activity in the short-term group occurs over a small range suggesting low volatility and limited trading activity.

☐ Traders are not probing for a change in the trend as dips do not carry the short-term group down to the long-term group of averages.

☐ Distance between groups of averages is constant. A parallel separation confirms trend stability.

LONG-TERM TREND WITH CONSISTENT TRADING ACTIVITY

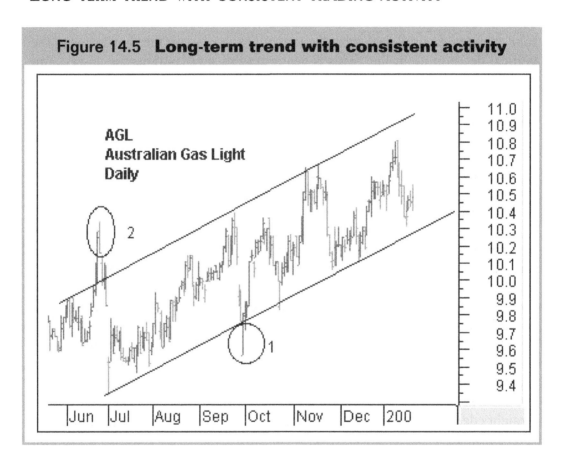

Figure 14.5 **Long-term trend with consistent activity**

AGL
Australian Gas Light
Daily

The first glance at the Australian Gas Light (AGL) price action in Figure 14.5 shows this is a more volatile trend. The pattern of rally and retreat is pronounced. These trends carry prices significantly higher with dramatic retreats which can overshoot, as shown in area 1. This is a dangerous and uncomfortable trend, even though in the long term it offers significant returns. It is dangerous because of the degree of volatility within the trend. Traders are constantly driving prices down and on one of these occasions this will signal the end of the trend. The difficulty is in deciding which dip is a buying opportunity and which signals the trend has ended.

It is difficult to plot a straight edge trend line. The lower plot line shown is not perfect, but it captures the majority of the major dips. A parallel trend line does a good job of defining the upper limits of a broad trend channel. Even this suffers from overshoot, as shown in area 2.

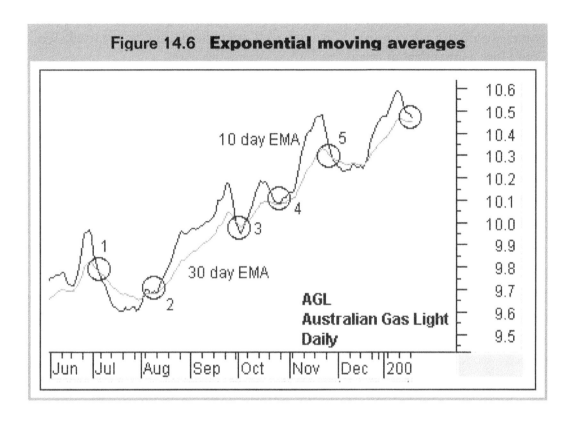

Figure 14.6 Exponential moving averages

Our key question in applying test four is to decide if it is a good idea to buy into this trend on the basis of the price weakness shown at the end of the bar chart display. We suggest the GMMA provides a more comprehensive answer, and an analysis of a chart using just two moving averages shows why. The second AGL chart in Figure 14.6 shows a 10-day and 30-day exponential moving average. You could shorten or lengthen the time periods, but the same problems remain. We have no way of telling if the current retreat in prices is temporary, as it has been in areas 2 through 5, or if it is part of a larger trend dip as in area 1. The most we infer from these relationships is that this combination of moving averages delivers many false signals.

The classic solution to the problem of false signals is to lengthen the 30-day average to perhaps a 40-day average so the false signals are eliminated on the historical chart. This is a type of curve fitting, when the indicator is adjusted to meet the specific character of a single stock. We need an indicator combination that works well with a wide variety of stocks. Even if we did lengthen the 30-day moving average we expose ourselves to another problem. When the trend collapse comes we do not get confirmation until well after the decline has started. We could lose a great deal of profit.

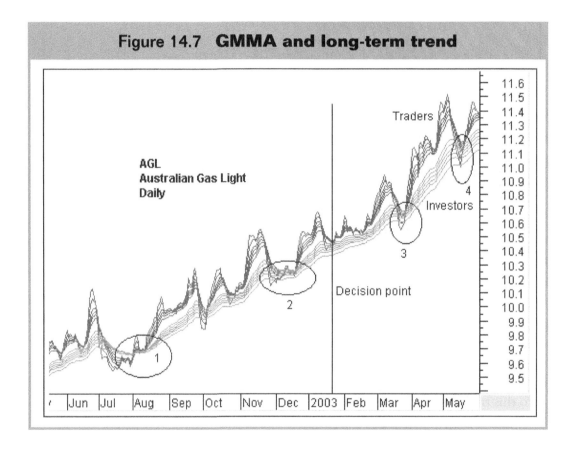

Figure 14.7 **GMMA and long-term trend**

The GMMA indicator provides us with a greater depth of information. The vertical line in Figure 14.7 shows the decision point from the bar chart. We examine three features:

1 The degree of separation and compression in the long-term group of averages.

172

2   The degree of separation and compression in the short-term group.

3   The degree of separation between the groups.

We start with investors. This is a nervous trend. The separation of the long-term group of averages is relatively narrow. After the resumption of the trend in area 1 the stock has not enjoyed dedicated and committed investor support. The long-term averages have not separated strongly as with BLD or DJS. This narrowness makes this trend more vulnerable to attack and decline.

When prices are driven down we see nervous investors taking the opportunity to sell rather than buy. This is shown by the way the long-term averages compress and this comes from selling activity as investors off-load stock to lock-in a better match between price and value. If investors believed lower prices represented good value they would actively bid against other investors to accumulate stock, maintaining the degree of separation seen in previous examples.

There is regular compression and expansion activity so traders are active in this stock. Traders push prices up, take short-term profits, and then watch how the market behaves as prices are driven down. This frequent rally and retreat activity suggests traders believe the trend is not well-established. They are worried about the trend collapsing which is why they take the short-term profits. The collapse of prices probes the strength of the trend.

Each pullback weakens the trend. In area 2 it causes a compression of the long-term group. The traders' rebound is slow to develop. In area 3 the short-term group dips below the long-term group before rebounding. This happens again in area 4 and each larger and stronger dip confirms a slowing of the trend and increases the probability of trend collapse. In June the trend reverses, dropping from a high of $11.50 to below $10.60.

The third GMMA relationship of interest is the degree of separation between the two groups of moving averages. On this chart there is no pattern of consistent separation and this confirms the relatively unstable trend. This information allows us to make a better decision. For traders the GMMA confirms there are short-term trading opportunities. They are traded in their own right, and without the secure protection of a sound underlying trend. These trades call for speed, caution and discipline.

For investors the GMMA suggests joining this trend for an extended period carries a much higher risk than either DJS or BLD. The more often a trend is probed for weakness by falling prices, the greater the potential for a trend collapse. This trend has the potential to collapse quickly so this stock fails the stock selection test.

In summary the GMMA provides the following identification information for a mid-trend entry:

☐ Long-term group is narrow suggesting a relatively weak trend. It may continue for many weeks but it is vulnerable.

☐ Trading activity is high and there is a high level of volatility.

☐ Traders are probing for a change in the trend. These dips cause compression in the long-term group and dip below the long-term group.

☐ The volatility of the level of separation between the two groups of averages confirms the underlying instability of this trend.

The GMMA provides the trader with a greater level of information about the nature, character and stability of the trend than information obtainable from other analysis methods. This information allows the trader or investor to develop a more appropriate strategy. In a sound, well-established trend, less management supervision is required and the entry price is not as critical to the success of the trade. In an unstable trend subject to high trading activity the entry price is important and these conditions call for more frequent management, making them less suited for longer term investing.

The AGL chart introduces the prospect of trend entry based on price weakness. Even though we may accept that joining a strong trend is a successful trading strategy, we always look for an edge. We think we do better if we join the trend when prices drop temporarily. It is a classic strategy, but the danger is that when prices drop they may signal the start of a new downtrend. In the next chapter we consider how the GMMA helps us distinguish between temporary price weakness and a trend collapse.

CHAPTER 15

USING PRICE WEAKNESS

T he ultimate challenge for any trend trading indicator is to distinguish between temporary price weakness and trend weakness. Get it right and the trader joins a strong trend at a better than expected price and this increases profits. This is a key method traders and investors use to join a trend which has been established for weeks, or months. You do not have to join a trend near its very beginning to make money. Steady, consistent, unexciting but impressively large profits are accumulated by joining a trend after it has broken the previous downtrend and set a new direction.

Get this distinction wrong and the bargain entry helps you pay top price as the trend suddenly plummets. It is not so much a heart-in-the-mouth feeling as a cash-in-someone-else's-pocket nightmare. Avoiding this mistake is vital to investment success. The Guppy Multiple Moving Average (GMMA) indicator is used to understand price pullback behaviour within the context of an established uptrend. This is part of the character assessment which forms the fourth stock selection test. Stocks passing this test are retained, while those failing are dropped from our list of trend trading opportunities. We use the GMMA because it is a more effective indication of the nature and character of the trend. The conclusions we draw from the GMMA cannot be drawn from a two or even a three moving average combination. The key relationship is the way traders and investors are behaving.

We look at three situations in this chapter. They are:

1   Timing entry into relatively minor pullbacks in strong momentum trends.

2   Rebound entries after a significant collapse in prices.

3   Safe trend entries when other tools have signalled a false trend collapse. This also touches on the way the GMMA is used to more effectively manage exits and to avoid exits on false trend breaks.

MINOR PULLBACKS IN STRONG MOMENTUM TRENDS

We all know the feeling when during a search of the market we stumble across a stock like Timbercorp (TIM). It has established a good, fast uptrend, moved sideways, and then continued the uptrend. For whatever reason, we missed the early part of this trend development. We want to join this trend as prices drop back towards the straight edge trend line. We have three questions to answer:

1   Is the underlying trend strong?

2   Is this price collapse temporary, or the start of a new downtrend?

3   How can I enter at the lowest possible price just prior to a rebound?

The bar chart in Figure 15.1 does not provide useful answers to these questions. Although we have a major recovery point on which we plot the uptrend with some confidence this is countered by the tentative

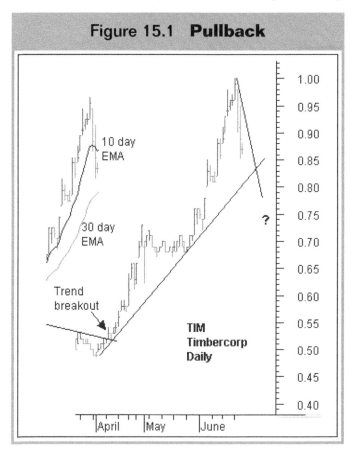

Figure 15.1   Pullback

plot of a downtrend line. The move from $0.70 to $1.00 has been very fast and often this type of momentum collapses very rapidly. If this trend rebounds we could collect a substantial return. On the other hand, if we enter near current prices they could also continue to fall very rapidly.

Turning to a 10-day and 30-day moving average display does not provide any useful additional information. A classical application of these tools suggests any trade should remain in place as there has been no moving average crossover, but if the trend collapses quickly the moving average crossover signal sacrifices a lot of open profits. For traders looking to join the trend, the moving averages do not help answer the three questions above.

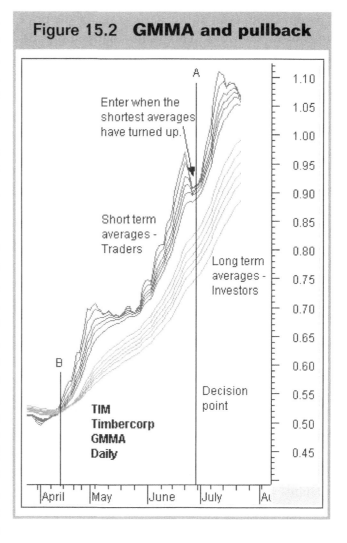

Figure 15.2 **GMMA and pullback**

The GMMA display in Figure 15.2 provides the trader with more information. The decision point is shown by the vertical line A. The key to any trading decision is the strength of the underlying trend. The long-term group of averages is well separated, moving upwards, and moving in a broadly parallel fashion. This has all the characteristics of a strong trend. This conclusion helps to answer the second question.

The price retreat is unlikely to be the start of a new downtrend. The tentative downtrend line on the bar chart can be removed. If this price fall was a serious threat to the trend we would see the long-term averages beginning to compress.

The direction, even at this early stage of the price drop, would start to level off and move sideways. This is not happening and supports our conclusion the underlying long-term trend is sound.

Ideally we would like to enter at the lowest price of the temporary collapse. Sometimes we get lucky. Close observation of the behaviour of the shortest of the short-term averages helps to make a more consistent decision about early rebound entries. We know the underlying trend is strong, so we concentrate on the behaviour of the 3-, 5- and 8-day averages in this grouping. Once they all begin to reverse we buy at the best possible price in anticipation of the rebound continuing. Even if we miss this point by several days, our understanding of the nature and character of the trend gives us the confidence to pay slightly higher prices to join.

The answers to the last two questions also highlight the synchronicity of the GMMA. This new trend began with a breakout from the downtrend in April. The point of the breakout was identified by the straight edge trend line and a crossover of the 10- and 30-day moving average. The vertical line B on the GMMA chart shows this breakout point.

Remember the construction of the GMMA. The shortest average is 3 days and the longest is 60 days. Using this as a moving average crossover combination is almost inconceivable because the signal would lag behind price action by many days. However when these averages are combined in a GMMA we see an unexpected synchronicity. We understand the behaviour and intentions of traders and investors immediately and are able to take appropriate action.

This same synchronicity applies with the temporary TIM price pullback. The rebound of the shortest moving averages confirms the price collapse has reached its limits and the upward trend is ready to resume. A stock with this relationship passes the GMMA character test and remains on our stock selection list.

REBOUND ENTRIES AFTER A SIGNIFICANT COLLAPSE IN PRICES

The hunt for trading opportunity is not always as clear cut as TIM. The Campbell Brothers (CPB) chart shown in Figure 15.3 beckons with possibility, but it repels with many negatives. This looks like a trading opportunity with a high level of risk, but also a high level of reward. Fast breakouts have powerful retreats which are often followed by a powerful new uptrend. Trading at around $4.70, CPB does not offer any price leverage advantage, but the price action is similar to many lower priced speculative stocks. Many traders ignore this type of stock and move onto those with clearer opportunities. Using a GMMA we have the tools to make a more valid assessment of the opportunity, and locate a better time for entry.

We start with the negative features clearly displayed on the bar chart. The first is the pattern of a fast rise, followed by a sideways drift and weak rebound which has culminated in the current sell off. Although it is difficult to plot a straight edge downtrend line, the price action in recent weeks has a definite downward bias to it.

The second dominant feature is the double top at $5.00. This is not a true double top, which by definition forms at the top of an uptrend. This is an intermediate double top which occurs within

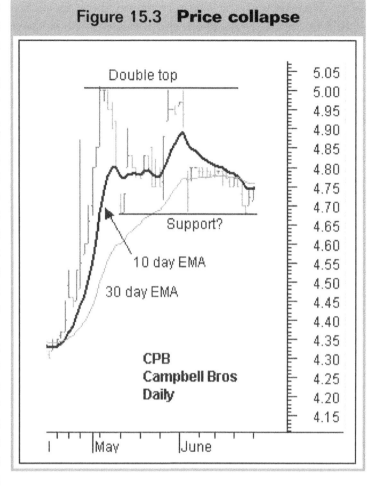

Figure 15.3 **Price collapse**

the context of a developing trend. It is not a strong reversal pattern, but it is a bearish development. Traders who purchase this stock watch carefully as prices again approach $5.00 looking for potential strong resistance.

The final bearish signal is the way the 10-day moving average has crossed below the 30-day moving average. This is a classic trend reversal signal, but it is not always reliable.

On the bullish side of the equation, the weak support level offers a little hope price may rebound and the trend continue. We are interested in this type of opportunity because of the rebound possibility. They can be very strong and when they follow the initial breakout, this rebound can be the start of a prolonged, powerful trend. We could wait for more trend confirmation, but in this case we want to use the GMMA to give us an analysis advantage.

We start with the long-term trend at the decision point defined by the vertical line in Figure 15.4. The trend momentum has slowed and this is readily clear from the bar chart. The GMMA shows the long-term group has not narrowed. Instead the averages are moving sideways in a parallel pattern with a minimal amount of compression. If investors had panicked we would see a rapid compression in the long-term group of averages as they scrambled to get out. Without the compression we are confident the trend is supported and this increases the probability of a price rebound.

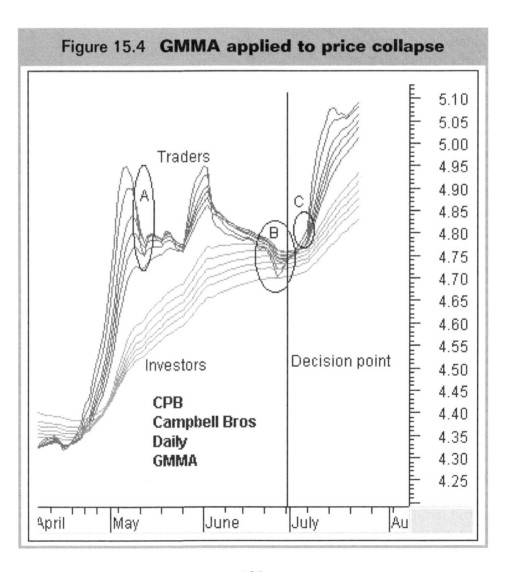

Figure 15.4 **GMMA applied to price collapse**

The sell-off in area A was due to traders taking short-term profits. Those who missed the original breakout were buyers and prices moved back to the $5.00 level. The failure to break above this level — and thereby establishing a double top pattern — quickly drove price down. Traders watched the pattern develop and sold out quickly in anticipation of a trend decline.

The key feature of interest is shown in area B where the short-term group of averages has penetrated the long-term group and then turned up. This rebound activity suggests the trend has been supported and has a high probability of continuing. Aggressive traders use this rebound and early compression in the short-term group of averages as an entry point. More conservative traders may wait three or four days until area C where the compression of short-term averages is complete. A stock with these GMMA relationships could pass our fourth test. It is not as appealing as the strong trend shown in the previous chart, but it still reveals an opportunity to join an established trend at a moment of price weakness.

Compression tells us there is an agreement of price and value across multiple timeframes. As traders attempt to take advantage of this agreement, they must outbid their competitors and we see an expansion of the moving averages. Despite the 60-day moving average used in the long-term group calculation, this group quickly resumes its upwards march in area C. Both the degree of separation and the parallel characteristic in this long-term group are quickly restored as the trend continues upwards. For traders who are comfortable with this type of opportunity, the GMMA provides a better way of understanding the potential development of price action.

SAFE TREND ENTRIES

The final example of price weakness in strong trends uses Harvey Norman (HVN) in Figure 15.5 to illustrate the way the GMMA verifies an exit signal generated by other methods. Our decision point is shown by the vertical line. For traders and investors who already hold HVN this approach allows them to decide if they should hold or sell the stock. For those thinking of buying HVN on a moment of temporary price weakness, the GMMA helps define the trend more effectively and to put the initial trend break signal into a broader context. Using the same analysis the existing HVN investors may use the pullback to add to their existing position. In Chapter 18 we look in detail at the way the GMMA is used to manage exits.

The price drop is a clear break of the uptrend which had prevailed for three months. The uptrend was an important reversal in the downtrend which started in January 2003 and persisted until this breakout in April 2003. This uptrend had also risen above the longer downtrend in HVN which had been in place since January 2002. How we handle this break below the straight edge trend line is important, particularly if the break is false.

The GMMA helps us to make a better decision and we start with the long-term group of averages to understand how investors are thinking. The price dip does not put a dent in the direction or spread of the long-term group of moving averages. This is a strong, well-supported underlying trend where investors are involved in steady buying at moments of price weakness.

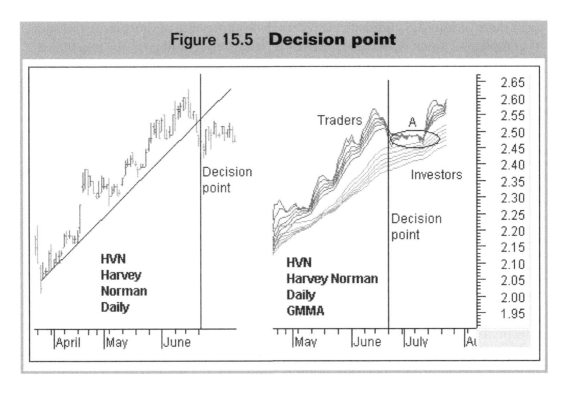

Figure 15.5 Decision point

As shown in area A, both traders and investors have ample evidence the underlying trend remains intact despite the trend break signal delivered by the straight edge trend line analysis. This allows traders to take new positions, and existing shareholders to add to existing positions. The GMMA allows us to verify the signals generated by other indicators and to identify trading opportunities which are overlooked by others. This significant trading edge comes from a better understanding of the trend and the context of short-term trader-driven price action.

We use the GMMA as a tool to understand the character and nature of the trend in this fourth selection test. We keep stocks with strong, established trends and drop those where the GMMA reveals trend weakness. This reduces the list of potential trading candidates, and they are subjected to a fifth selection test based on price relationships.

This application is an important strand in using the GMMA but the indicator is also used in make better trading decisions in a variety of breakout, rally and trend exit situations. The next three chapters take a detour and examine these in detail. They are not directly related to the style of trend trading forming the core discussion in this book. Readers who are more interested in these trend trading strategies may wish to move directly to the 'No secrets' chapter at the end of this section. Those who are interested in the way the GMMA is used to help manage trend trade exits should also read Chapter 18.

CHAPTER 16

RALLY BREAKS

Understanding the nature and character of the trend is one of the most important pieces of information available to the trader. Aggressive traders look for early signals of a trend breakout because an early entry provides the key to substantial profits as the trend develops in future weeks and months. Understanding the difference between a rally and a trend change allows the trader to establish a better trading plan and to apply the most appropriate trading tool. This is particularly important in the context of a prevailing downtrend because it prevents us from mistaking a rally for a true breakout.

Bargain hunting, or bottom fishing, usually attracts disparaging comments from experienced traders and professional fund managers. They suggest it is impossible to do this consistently and successfully. Investment advisers often point to their own poor performance in this area as evidence, arguing if they cannot get it right, then the average mum and dad investor cannot succeed either. There is a certain hypocrisy in these statements as the investment industry spends a lot of time, money and effort in trying to find bargains and the bottom of downtrends. In the world of fundamental analysis it is called value investing and is often summarised as buying good companies at cheap prices before the rest of the market recognises the true bargain.

It is more useful if we acknowledge we all like to bargain hunt. Heavyweight stocks at low prices are tempting, just like any stock sold down from previous highs. We all like a bargain, and in the financial market, this means hunting in high-risk areas. Most of us cannot resist this temptation, so it pays to learn how to hunt more effectively and with a higher level of safety. This comes from a better understanding of the nature of the opportunity.

The key principle in bargain hunting is the attempt to buy the stock as close as possible to the end of a downtrend, and just before it starts in a new uptrend. This calls not just for good timing, but also excellent recognition skills. A breakout — a trend change — looks deceptively like a short-lived rally. For the first days, or even weeks, the two may be virtually indistinguishable. Good rewards go with picking a breakout, but there are substantial penalties for trading a false breakout, or treating a rally as a breakout. To illustrate the difference, and the way the Guppy Multiple Moving Average (GMMA) is used to separate the two events, we start with the classic analysis of the BRL Hardy (BRL) bar chart in Figure 16.1.

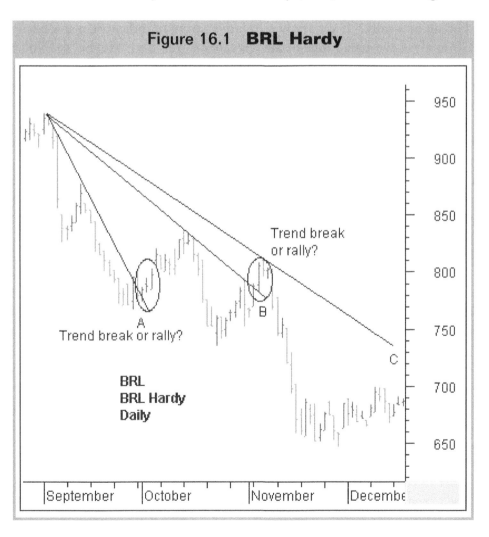

Figure 16.1 **BRL Hardy**

First we need the context of the chart. BRL enjoyed a sustained, steady uptrend from 1998 to March 2002, lifting from around $4.50 to $11.50. This is a steady success story. In March 2002 the uptrend was broken by a series of price retreats. The new downtrend had carried price to a low of $7.70 at the time shown in the circled area A. For months financial commentators suggested BRL had been unfairly treated by the market. This steady stream of commentary, coupled with the nature of the company and the degree of price collapse, has all the ingredients necessary for a bargain hunt.

Using the information available at the time in September, we plot the first of the straight edge trend lines. The price activity in area A moves above the trend line and suggests a trend break. The straight edge trend line is a powerful tool for identifying trend breaks. There is one question we ask at this point: 'Is this a trend break or a rally?' If we apply a Relative Strength Indicator, a stochastic or MACD analysis we get a range of answers, from 'Yes' and 'Maybe' to 'No'. It is difficult to make a rational decision about this breakout. We all hope it is the beginning of a new uptrend because this would deliver exceptional profits. Sometimes this hope is powerful enough to encourage us to hold onto the stock as prices retreat, and then rebound as shown in area B.

If we chose to ignore the possible trend break in area A, we are soon faced with the same problem again in area B. The new trend lines take into account what we now know happened to the September rally in area A. If we came to this chart in early November we use the September high as a new point to plot trend line B. It is easy to convince ourselves these two trend lines are part of a fan pattern, which often precedes a major breakout.

Buy this second potential breakout, and it does not take long to realise it is also false. By mid-November this rally has collapsed. Looking at the chart in December we use the November peak as the second point in a downtrend plot. Using a variety of indicators to understand what is happening at point A and point B still gives us a variety of answers and no real assistance in deciding if this is a genuine trend break, or just a rally.

The GMMA helps develop a better understanding of the nature of the opportunity. We use it here to show how the trader avoids trading because he knows there is a high probability the trend break signal is false. This is also useful for traders who are shorting the stock. Recognising a short-lived rally means they hold the short position with confidence and are not shaken out by a false move. More aggressive traders may use this analysis to trade the breakout as a short-lived rally. They have the advantage of early recognition which means they are prepared for a price collapse and react accordingly.

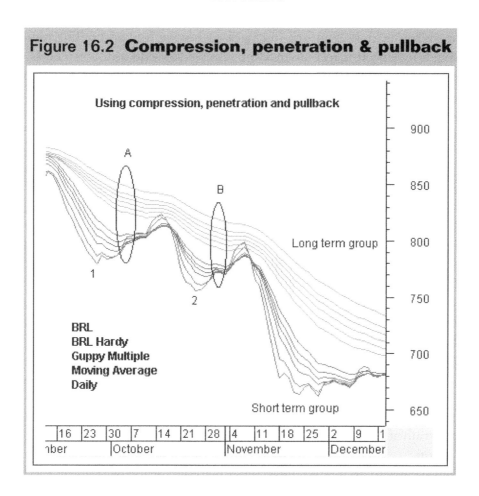

Figure 16.2 **Compression, penetration & pullback**

The GMMA display in Figure 16.2 shows the same points identified on the bar chart display. We are interested in three relationships.

1 *Compression*. The level and degree of compression in the long-term group.

2 *Penetration*. The ability of the short-term group to penetrate into the long-term group.

3 *Pullback*. The extent of the retreat by the short-term group.

We start with a simple observation. The longer term group is above the short-term group. We prefer to display the long-term group in red because it reminds me this is the dangerous part of the trend. If we are fighting the long-term trend, then we need to take extra precautions. When the long-term group is above the short-term group we recognise the need to dampen our enthusiasm and hope when trading from the long side — buying low and selling high. It is surprising how easy it is to convince ourselves a stock in a downtrend is really about to start a new uptrend. This hopeful understanding is a fatal way to start a new trade.

With this background, the first feature we assess is the compression in the long-term group because the investors have the power to cap a rally, or to lend a helping hand to a breakout. Traders lead the market, but investors are the driving force. The wider the separation in the long-term group, the greater the strength of the prevailing trend.

At both area A and B, the long-term group is well separated at the time of the initial trend break signal. Subsequently there is a very small degree of compression which tells us investors see this price rise as an opportunity to get out at slightly better prices than anticipated. When prices lift, the investors are selling. If they were buying, the long-term group would start to compress.

The observation of this relationship alone convinces traders these potential trend breaks are likely to be a capped rally, as the short-term group of averages moved towards the bottom of the long-term group. Immediately we have an advantage because we know this is most unlikely to be a trend break. If we buy the stock we do not delude ourselves it is about to turn around and climb back to $9.50 or higher. There is not much money to be made between $7.70 and $8.10 and it is a desperate market when a 5% return starts to look attractive. This small rally may offer a better derivative trading opportunity using a warrant or an option.

When we get to area B we have the advantage of knowing how the initial rally developed and we assess the degree of penetration. Think of the short-term group as an axe chopping away at the trend. This is a thick, well-developed trend, as shown by the degree of compression in the long-term group, so it needs a very powerful axe to chop through this thick timber. The first blow of the axe is unlikely to penetrate substantially. Put enough blows in the same area, and the trend will weaken.

With BRL the first rally barely penetrates the long-term group before investor selling drives prices down again. There is a low probability the second rally will penetrate much further because the long-term group remains well separated. The second rally does slightly better, but it too is quickly driven downwards. Additionally, the second rally is unable to move as high as the first. It is weaker not just in height, but in strength.

These conclusions are based on observation. We do not need to get out a measuring tape. The short-term average in the first rally moves just above the lowest red line in the long-term group. In the second rally, the short-term group moves above the second lowest red line in the long-term group. We do not find it particularly useful to classify the penetration characteristic in this way. We find the visual relationship easier to apply.

The final factor in GMMA analysis is the extent of the pullback after the rally is defeated. If we had any doubts about the strength and invulnerability of this downtrend, then the lower pullback in area B confirms it. When the first rally is defeated, traders lose hope. In their scramble to get out from under this falling trend, they take panic exits, driving the short-term group even lower than its previous lows. This type of pullback confirms the strength of the downtrend, and the low probability of an upturn in prices leading to a change in the trend.

Flip back to the original bar chart in Figure 16.1 for a moment. Our challenge was to decide the nature of the price break identified by the close above the straight edge trend line. At both area A and B it was possible to convince ourselves a trend break was developing. Many investors thought this way but the GMMA clearly indicated the breakout was most likely to be a short-lived rally and the indicator sets the cap conditions. This is a useful trading edge.

CHANGING NATURE

The key advantage of the GMMA is that it helps the trader understand the changing nature of the trend in a way a standard moving average analysis is unable to achieve. If we can distinguish a true developing trend break from a short-lived rally we have a tremendous advantage over our competitors. Bargains do exist in the market, and the GMMA validates the opportunity. Our preference is to use the GMMA in conjunction with straight edge trend line analysis. Aggressive traders use the GMMA to enter in anticipation of a trend change, truly catching the bargain basement prices.

The bar chart display of Iluka Resources (ILU) in Figure 16.3 sets out the main decision points. The break above the straight edge trend line is shown by the vertical line on both this and the GMMA chart. This is a relatively slow trend change and is more characteristic of market behaviour than a rapid 'V-shaped' rebound. Price moves above the trend line, and then moves sideways with a slight upwards bias for the next few weeks. There is plenty of time to make a decision here before prices move to new $4.40 highs in a strong uptrend. From March through May traders reasonably ask: 'Is this a new trend break?' If the answer is 'Yes' then they concentrate on getting the best possible entry price around $3.80, buying these lows with confidence. If the answer is uncertain, they may be forced to join the trend at around $4.30 as the trend break is dramatically confirmed a few days later. The best analysis puts money in our pockets.

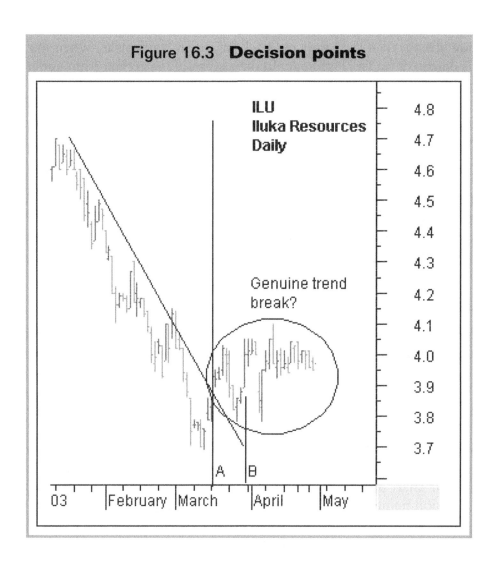

Figure 16.3 Decision points

We start with compression analysis at the point of the breakout, shown by the vertical line A in Figure 16.4. The long-term group is well-separated, suggesting any price rise is likely to be capped. This calls for caution. Although we now know this trend line break was accurate we could not make this decision with confidence at the time. Entering ILU at point A was a gamble and our objective is to avoid gambles in favour of taking trades with a high probability of success. We are interested in this stock as a potential breakout opportunity so it stays on our watch list for another week or so because we want to observe the behaviour of the rally, and the way it retreats. Line B points towards a shift in the balance of probabilities. The long-term group has begun to compress in reaction to the rally behaviour of the short-term group. The thick line shows the degree of separation at line A. Compression tells us investors are buying and expansion tells us they are selling. At line B the long-term group has compressed, revealing investors are beginning to compete with traders to buy ILU as price rises. This compression moves ILU further up the watch list.

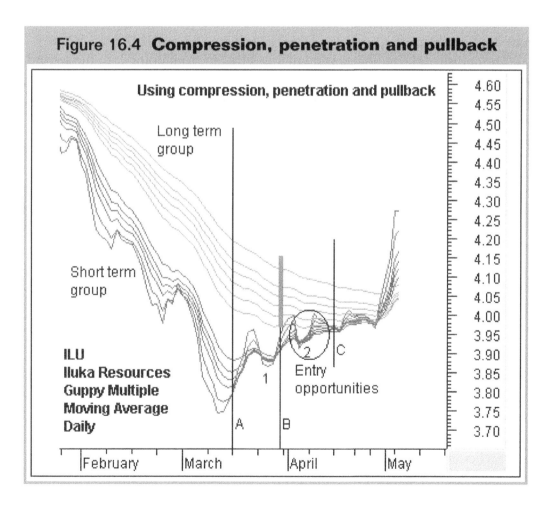

Figure 16.4 Compression, penetration and pullback

A few days later, the rally is capped, and prices decline. We compare the level of penetration in two ways. We first note the second rally succeeded in penetrating the long-term group of moving averages. The first rally did not achieve this. Second, we note the roof of the second rally is higher than the first. The peaks in the short-term group of averages are rising, suggesting increasing strength. At the peak of the second rally the long-term group of averages is compressed quite noticeably. Investors are now buyers, starting to compete amongst themselves to get hold of stock. This is a bullish signal.

Confirmation comes with pullback analysis. First the pullback in area 1 is lower than the pullback in area 2. Traders are not prepared to let price fall as far as it did previously. In March many thought $3.85 was a good entry point but by early April many traders think $3.92 is a good entry point. We know this because the traders come into the market at this level, buying stock and preventing it from falling any further. Investors who are interested in selling stock do not have to drop their offer price any lower as traders will buy ILU at $3.92.

The nature of the pullback at point 1 is different from point 2. In the second pullback and rebound, the compression area of agreement develops rapidly and quickly moves up as the short-term group of averages separate. This is active trading and this sequence of higher rallies and lower pullbacks in the short-term group of averages sets the conditions for an early entry into a high probability trend break.

We have used ILU as an example because it shows an extended period where trend break GMMA relationships are observed almost in slow motion. From April through May the long-term group compresses. The short-term group continues with higher penetrations of the long-term group with each new rally. The subsequent pullbacks show smaller retreats. The trader and the investor have a clear analysis path confirming this is a new trend break and not just a short-lived rally. We reach these conclusions before a 10- and 30-day moving average crossover takes place at the point shown by line C. This weak crossover signal is followed by a heart-stopping convergence of these two averages a few days later. In contrast the GMMA analysis provides clear evidence of the nature and strength of the developing trend change and gives the trader confidence to buy ILU at $3.80 as prices dip back in early April.

This GMMA trend analysis is used to recognise a rally in a downtrend as with BRL, and distinguish this from a rally that is part of a developing uptrend as with ILU. This early recognition provides us with a trading edge because we make a better decision about how to trade the developing price action. We know what to expect, and we plan accordingly. The analysis applied to ILU is for aggressive traders hunting bargain breakout opportunities. Although many traders are attracted to this, not all trade them successfully, or are comfortable with the risk involved.

Excellent trading opportunities exist once the breakout has been confirmed. It is useful to understand the nature of the trend change by retrospectively applying GMMA analysis to understand the compression, penetration and pullback relationships. The GMMA is applied in real time to assess the best entry opportunities after the breakout is confirmed. In the next chapter we show how GMMA analysis provides a better solution for trading genuine breakouts. This is not relevant to trend trading, but it is an important part of the broader application of the GMMA as a trading tool.

CHAPTER 17

BREAKOUT TRADING

Aggressive traders attempt to identify a change in the downtrend — an uptrend breakout — as soon as it happens, or even before. This aggressive trading carries a higher level of failure because unless the trader has excellent trading discipline, there is the danger of holding onto a stock as it continues to go down in the hope it will eventually rebound.

A more common, and in some ways safer, approach is to trade the trend breakout in the days or weeks after it has happened. This reduces profits when compared with an earlier entry, but this reduction is counter-balanced by the increased probability of a sustainable new trend. Few traders are content with joining these trends at any price. Most try to get the best entry possible, based on a pullback in price. If we understand the nature of the trend and the breakout using the techniques discussed in the previous chapter then we take advantage of these points of price weakness confident in our analysis of the developing trend.

Our objective is to identify established trends, but we recognise greed has an important role to play. Despite steady trading success, there is always the temptation to move the entry to a point a little earlier in the trend because we stand to make bigger profits. The shift from trend trader to breakout trader is subtle, but like the slow change from black to grey and then to white, there comes a time when we are clearly in one situation and not the other. Woe betide our wallet if we fail to recognise the change. We use the Guppy Multiple Moving

Average (GMMA) to separate breakout trading activity from trend trading approaches which aim to join a strong developing trend.

The GMMA is applied in real time to assess the best entry opportunities after the breakout is confirmed. It gives us an answer to the question: 'Is this price collapse part of a general new trend collapse, or an entry opportunity?' This is a significant question because young trends are weak so there is a higher probability of trend collapse.

A breakout takes place when price moves away from its existing pattern. This includes the change from a downtrend to an uptrend, or from an uptrend to a downtrend. It also includes a price move above a well-established support or resistance level. A breakout price activity is different from the general pattern of price activity existing during previous days or weeks. Breakout trading carries high risk because there is no guarantee the breakout will persist. Many breakouts are false, so traders look for other indicators to confirm the breakout is for real. Real breakouts are very profitable. Conservative traders look for breakouts, but then look for confirmation the trend has changed.

Breakouts come in two important formats. The most common is the 'V-shaped' breakout where a clear downtrend develops into a clear uptrend. This is clear retrospectively, although at the time the process can be frightening and many traders delay the entry because they worry about a trend collapse. Less common is a breakout from a trading range, or a prolonged sideways movement. This is an important characteristic of bear market recoveries and it presented a common pattern in the first months of 2003. It also applied to stocks that have been locked in a downtrend for extended periods. These rarely bounce in a 'V' recovery. Instead they drift sideways for months, but when they eventually break out they can deliver very attractive profits. We start with this pattern.

BREAKING WITH THE BULLS

In assessing the GMMA relationships in breakout trades we consider four relationships. The first two apply to the longer term group of averages, and the second group to the short-term group of averages. We look for:

- ☐ *Compression*. Early in the breakout the long-term group compresses as investors reach agreement on the value of the stock.

- ☐ *Direction*. Compression indicates agreement. The direction of the compression provides clues to the future development of the trend. We look for compression and upwards bias.

195

- ❑ *Collapse.* It takes a lot of effort to break out of a downtrend. These rallies are short lived, and we expect them to collapse. The nature of the collapse in the short-term group provides clues to the strength of trader activity.

- ❑ *Rapid bounce.* A fast bounce and recovery in the short-term group confirms increased trading activity and this forces interested investors to bid higher to get stock.

The Eagers (APE) bar chart in Figure 17.1 highlights some of the problems traders face in many breakout trades. The first is when we miss the initial breakout so by the time it shows up on a once-a-week search of the database, the initial opportunity has passed. We leave it on our watch list to see how it behaves when prices collapse after the initial rally. At the decision point shown we need to decide on the probability of a bounce occurring. Get this correct and we trade from around $5.40 to $6.10 or even higher if a full trend develops.

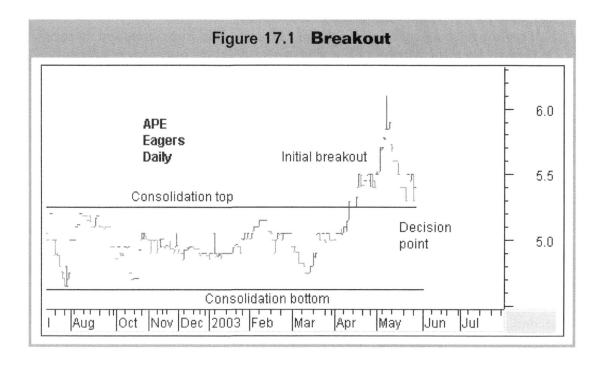

Figure 17.1 **Breakout**

The GMMA indicator helps us make a better decision at the decision point shown by the vertical line in Figure 17.2. We start with the analysis of the long-term group. No trend survives without buying support from long-term investors. We may intend to take a trading approach to this opportunity, but unless investors are there to lend a helping hand, we do not get the opportunity to join a prolonged trend.

Compression is an easy question to answer. Already the long-term group is well separated. It shows no sign of compression in response to the drop in prices seen on the bar chart and shown here by the collapse of the short-term group of averages.

The direction of the long-term group is still upwards, even though the speed of the rise has slowed slightly. The compression and direction suggest this trend has strength so we trade with increased confidence and take advantage of this temporary low in prices.

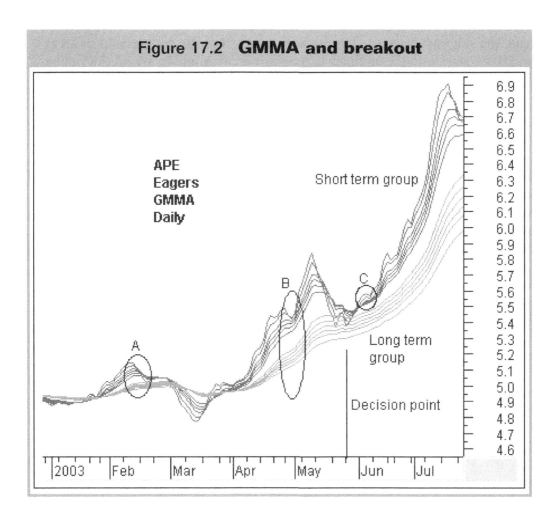

Figure 17.2 **GMMA and breakout**

This analysis is confirmed when we turn our attention to the short-term group. Trader activity always leads investor activity as traders probe for weakness in downtrends, and test the strength of uptrends. We see an orderly collapse in prices. Traders are not panic-stricken and it does not take long before new traders come into the market and start buying. They see the fall in prices as an opportunity rather than an alert signal to abandon a weak trend. The period of compression and agreement is short, and the expansion starts quickly.

If we choose to wait a few days, the rapid compression preceding a rapid bounce is revealed. At this decision point many traders buy APE in anticipation of this type of rebound because the first three factors — compression, direction and collapse — are consistent with a breakout developing into a longer term trend.

This conclusion begs the question of how we decide this is a real breakout from the sideways pattern. The answer comes from the comparison of areas A and B. We start with the pullback in the short-term group. In area A this pullback never develops into a rebound. In area B, the degree of pullback is smaller, and the pullback quickly develops into a rebound that carries the short-term group to new highs. This is further confirmed by the long-term group. In area A this group does not get a chance to separate so they do not expand. At the time of the pullback in the short-term group, the long-term group is just a thick line. Compare this with the pullback relationship in area B. The long-term group is well-separated and clearly moving upwards. This analysis confirms that the breakout spike to $6.10 has a higher probability of becoming part of a broad uptrend development rather than just a temporary rally or spike.

TRADING WITH A 'V'

It is easier to apply GMMA analysis to the classic 'V-shaped' trend breakout where a downtrend quickly develops into a new uptrend, as shown in Figure 17.3 of Macquarie Airports (MAP). The danger in these young trends is the breakout may turn out to be just a short-lived rally. Our fears are confirmed when the breakout falters and prices dip back from the initial highs. 'Is this a buy point, or an exit signal?' In a classic, text-book example of the 'V-shaped' trend reversal this question does not arise. Price clearly changes direction, and does not look back. In this situation there is no point in waiting for a price pullback, or a rally collapse, so it is important to recognise these breakout characteristics early. We reach some initial conclusions at the decision point shown. Wait a week or so, and the conclusions are clearly confirmed.

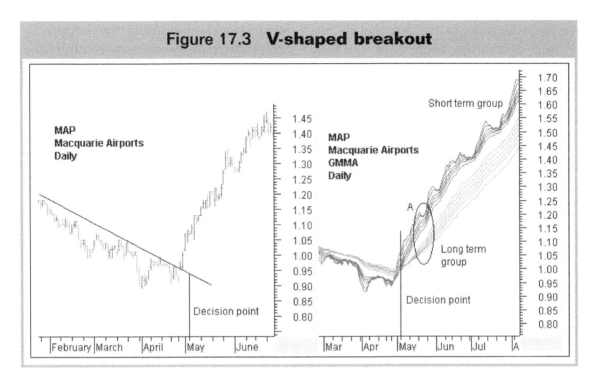

Figure 17.3 **V-shaped breakout**

The key is the behaviour of the long-term group. The averages have gone from separated and down to compressed and up. The direction of the long-term group has changed rapidly. Remember the longest average in this group is a 60-day calculation, yet by the time of the decision point, all the long-term averages have turned up. This is an early confirmation of the trend break and of the strength of the trend. This type of information is not available from any other indicator, and certainly not from just two moving averages using a crossover signal.

The long-term group has also compressed and this tells us the investors are in agreement about the value of the stock. They are not waiting for a pullback before taking action. They are worried they will miss out, so they aggressively outbid each other to establish a position.

Traders see this and choose not to sell. Look at the character of the short-term group of averages. They compress a few days before the decision point line, and then move upwards and spread out quickly. There is a lot of steady buying activity here. Compare this relationship with area C GMMA display in Figure 17.2. We are being aggressive at this decision point, but the nature of this expansion suggests strong trader and investor support. When traders come to sell, there are other traders who are prepared to buy at these prices. They are not waiting for a price pullback to get an entry. As a result there is no compression in the short-term group and they quickly move into a parallel relationship. The circled area A is further confirmation of this. See this pattern and you know you have no choice but to take the current price if you want to join this robust trend.

RALLY AND RETREAT

Most times a trend breakout follows a series of attempted breakouts — the rally and retreat behaviour discussed in the previous chapter. When the breakout develops we see a pattern of rallies, retreats and rebounds. The Freedom Group (FFL) chart in Figure 17.4 illustrates how these occur and shows how we apply GMMA analysis to make a better judgment about the advisability of an entry at decision point 1 and 2. Although we are cautious in applying the GMMA as a means of anticipating a trend break, the FFL display shows how this is achieved.

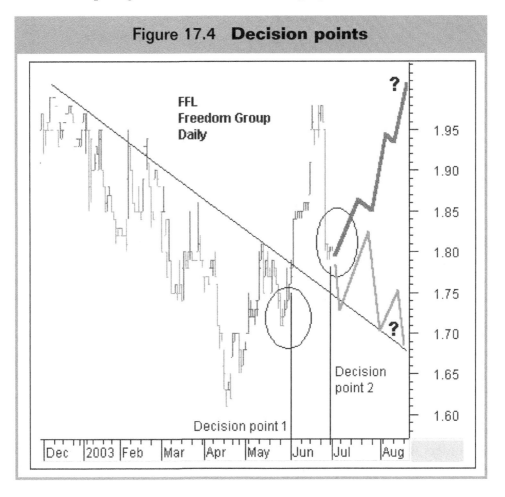

Figure 17.4   **Decision points**

The bar chart shows a downtrend defined by the straight edge trend line. Prices have consistently moved up to the line, and then dropped down. This pattern of rise and retreat has defined the downtrend so there is no obvious reason why we would be interested in decision point 1. There has been no break above the trend line. Decision point 2 which follows the collapse of the initial breakout rally is the more traditional application of the GMMA to breakout trading. Our concern is if we buy in this area prices may drop to the trend line, rebound, then retreat to the trend line again as shown by the lower thick line. We use the GMMA to decide whether this is a likely outcome, or if prices are likely to rebound in a new uptrend as shown by the upper thick line.

The GMMA provides answers to both decision points. The key analysis favouring an entry at decision point 1 starts with the long-term group of averages in Figure 17.5. Traders need investors, so we need to understand investor behaviour and start with the compression and directional behaviour shown in the area circled. The long-term group is beginning to compress as some investors are beginning to think FFL has a brighter future. Compression tells us investors are not taking advantage of temporarily higher prices to sell. It tells us they are beginning to buy as prices rise. Some of them begin to worry they might miss out on an opportunity.

Investor action is most likely driven by fundamental analysis. We do not need to read their analysis to know it is bullish because the direction of the compression is upwards. This is a bullish signal in a downtrend from the most conservative market participants.

Shift our attention to the trader activity, and rally collapse and rebound behaviour attracts our interest. This is not a sharp rally. The collapse does not resemble that shown in area A. This is a slower decline. Traders are not in a rush to take profits. The short-term group slips below the long-term group, and then rebounds as shown by the rapid compression. There is a lot of excitement here as traders jostle each other to buy stock. They believe FFL is going to lift and the investors also believe this. The long-term group continues to compress and the direction is up, even after the minor stumble in late May. This is a very bullish environment. Aggressive traders have no hesitation in buying at decision point 1 because of the developing investor activity. Traders lead the way, but we only follow when investors are showing increased willingness to become buyers. This GMMA analysis signal leads the price break above the trend line by several days.

The FFL bar chart presents a different set of problems at decision point 2. We have the opportunity to join a developing trend at a point of price weakness but we have to know this is not a point of trend weakness. The important relationship is shown by the long-term group. The group is not compressed. The wide spread developed at the top of this initial rise is largely maintained as the long-term group begins to turn down slightly. This degree of spread is also maintained as we move beyond decision point 2.

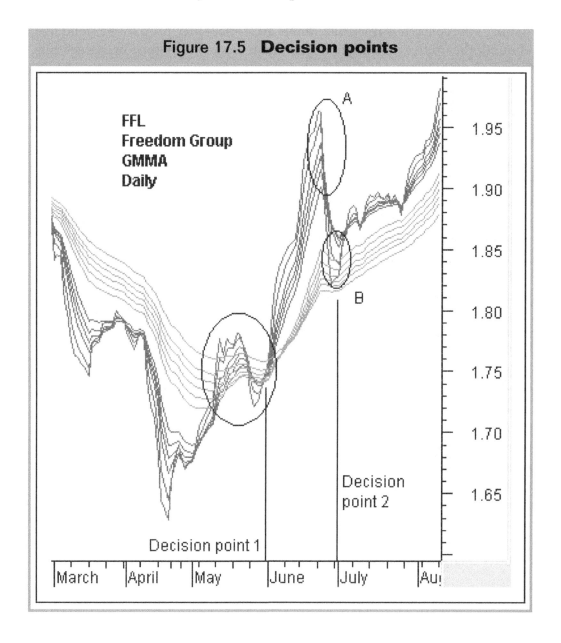

Figure 17.5 **Decision points**

EXPANSION AND COMPRESSION

The underlying feature of the GMMA is the compression and expansion relationship. Compression shows agreement while expansion shows disagreement. If the long-term group turns down and begins to compress we infer investors are selling. When the long-term group slows, moves sideways, or takes a slight dip and remains well-separated we infer investors are still buying stock. They are not fools. They will not pay more than necessary, so as prices dip, driven by trader selling, the investors do not have to pay as much to buy. In unison, they lower their bid prices and we see a dip in the long-term group but the averages remain parallel with each other.

The direction of the long-term group is not down. This is certainly a pause, and a broad move sideways, but it is not a reversal. We are confident this trend is intact, and strong.

Knowing the ground is firm underfoot, we turn to understanding how traders are reacting. The price collapse is sudden but so is the rebound. There is a significant gap between the 3- and 5-day averages and the rest of the averages in the short-term average group. Short-term traders have sold down the stock aggressively, but those with a slightly longer timeframe are not so eager to sell. The most aggressive sellers dip into the long-term group of averages, but the least aggressive see the price dip as a buying opportunity. The rebound starts quickly as the shorter averages turn up in a scramble to buy back into the stock.

A successful breakout quickly drags the long-term investors with it. This group separates rapidly and does not react significantly to the inevitable breakout rally collapse. This relationship confirms decision point 2 is a safe entry point and there is a strong probability this new uptrend will continue.

Investor activity helps us as traders to better understand the nature of the breakout opportunity and to assess the probability of a young trend continuing. Typically traders spend a lot of time on an entry decision and less time on the exit. The GMMA is a useful exit tool because it helps us understand the nature of the developing trend failure so we select the most appropriate exit indicators and apply them at the most appropriate time. In the next chapter we show how it gives us an answer to the question: 'Is this price collapse part of a general new trend collapse, or an entry opportunity?'

CHAPTER 18

BETTER EXITS

Joining a trend is only part of a trading solution. The real difficulty comes in the final performance test, and the result we get depends on how well we manage the exit. We use the Guppy Multiple Moving Average (GMMA) to assist with better exits so this chapter is an early instalment in the discussion of the final performance test. Good traders understand trading is about identifying the balance of probabilities because the odds are always stacked against us.

The probability of an event occurring is the ratio of favourable outcomes to the total number of possible combinations. The odds of an event happening is the ratio of favourable outcomes to unfavourable outcomes. In the market these differences have important impacts. The total number of possible favourable outcomes in a trade is finite. You make a profit, break even, or lose money. The total number of possible outcomes — not combinations — is three. There is only one favourable outcome so the odds are against you in every trade. The ratio of favourable outcomes is always 1:2.

We offset the odds in trading by identifying the balance of probabilities — the total number of price combinations. We have suggested the balance is most easily seen visually using a straight edge trend line and a GMMA. A stock trending upwards for six weeks has a high probability of continuing to trend upwards tomorrow. The range of price combinations is skewed in an upwards direction. A stock trending upwards for three days has a lower probability of trend continuation.

The price of a stock today is not independent of yesterday's stock price. This is why coin toss analogies and random walk theory are so irrelevant to the market. Prices are not independent events. When you buy a stock your decision is influenced by the price it traded at yesterday. The event — you buying a stock — is not independent of the previous event — someone else bought or sold the stock.

Successful trading recognises the odds are stacked against us, so traders look for tools to identify situations where the balance of probability is tipped in their favour. When a trade is implemented, traders are alert for changes in the balance of probability because they know the odds are still stacked against them.

We buy stock for a single reason — we expect it to go up and make us money. We sell stock for many different reasons. Where possible we try to lock-in the maximum profit possible from the trade. This does not mean getting out at the very top of the trend or not long after the trend has turned down. As part of a good exit solution, we also want to avoid getting out of a trade on false trend breaks. This happens when prices dip, and then recover and continue the trend.

No single exit indicator or group of indicators is going to provide the best solution to these wide variety of exit demands. The GMMA is useful in deciding when a trend is weakening, and this allows us to apply the most effective protect profit tool given our trading objective. In a fast-moving bubble trade, the collapse of the bubble is managed using a volatility-based stop loss such as 2×Average True Range or the count back line. In a slower moving trend trade we may decide to apply the count back line after the initial trend weakness signal is delivered by the GMMA.

There are four exit conditions where the GMMA is useful. They are:

1   The failure to bounce and recover which indicates trend weakness.

2   Multiple declining bounces. The steady slow collapse of the trend.

3   A bubble trade exit.

4   The sharp drop through the long-term group of averages. This is a clear trend change signal.

Each of these exit conditions is managed using a specific selection of tools. The GMMA tells us which tools are most appropriate. The GMMA is designed to help the trader understand the nature and character of the trend. It is not used as a stand-alone entry or exit tool. The key relationship is set by the traders. Trading activity leads the market and investors follow. We have an advantage if we move with the traders.

BOUNCE FAILURE

Most times we start with a bar chart display before applying a GMMA. We have not included a bar chart with these examples because we want to concentrate exclusively on the GMMA relationships. We examine two relationships when applying the GMMA to exit analysis. The first is the relationship in the long-term group of averages. The second is the character of any bounce in the short-term group of averages after a price drop. A trend continuation depends on continued trading activity so when prices drop we want to see new traders taking advantage of these lower prices. Their trading shows they are confident about the future. If this group does not bounce, then the key leaders in the trend have failed and complete trend failure becomes a higher probability.

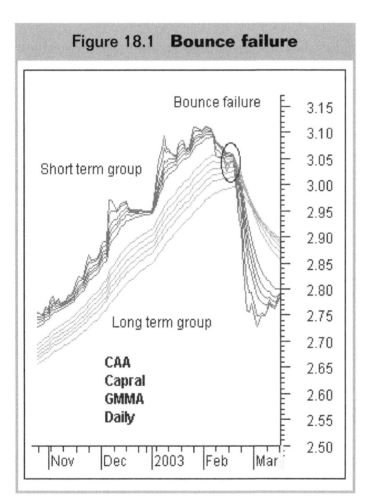

Figure 18.1 **Bounce failure**

The Capral Aluminum (CAA) chart in Figure 18.1 shows a wide spread in the group of long-term averages. Investors are comfortable with this stock. Traders are not panic-stricken, but they have sold the stock down steadily over previous weeks. Once their selling drifts into the long-term group of averages we look for a rebound as new traders come in. They have to outbid investors who are holding stock, or adding to their positions. New traders do not arrive so the rebound fails to develop, leading to a sharp compression and fall in the short-term averages. This is the exit signal, even though the long-term group of averages is showing few signs of compression. When traders jump ship there is a strong probability the trend is faltering or about to end.

This pattern says nothing about the speed of the collapse. With CAA the collapse gains momentum very quickly. The GMMA relationship tells us these lows are not temporary dips. They are initially created by traders desperate to get out, and are very quickly followed by investors who are trying to lock-in profits. We do not wait for the GMMA crossover. We use the information about the changing nature of the trend to take an early exit.

MULTIPLE DECLINING BOUNCES

Many trends roll over slowly, making it easy to convince ourselves the trend is pausing rather than changing. These slow collapses give us plenty of time to fine-tune an exit, but only if we recognise the beginning of a trend change. Recognition starts with the way the long-term averages move sideways and begin to converge. Eventually they begin to turn down with a slow and graceful swan dive.

The key relationship signalling a trend change is the behaviour of traders. Each new bounce away from the long-term group is weaker. When prices move up, traders who have not sold their previous positions swamp the market with sell orders so any rally is very short-lived. Desperate to get out, traders keep offering stock at lower prices as the rally retreats. As a result the short-term group of averages dips even further into the long-term group. The next rebound is weaker, and the retreat more severe.

The Gympie Gold (GYM) chart in Figure 18.2 tracks this behaviour over several months. The retreat and penetration in area 3 is much greater than in area 1. It is the reluctance of the long-term group to act as buyers that suggests a weakening of the trend. In a strong trend, the ability of the short-term group to threaten the trend is countered as aggressive investors buy the stock as price falls. Deeper penetration by the short-term group shows investors are losing interest. The final rebound in area 4 is a complete failure. However by this stage the trader should be well-prepared for a potential trend change and be ready to act quickly to lock-in profits.

When increasing penetration is combined with compression in the longer group of averages the warning of a trend change is loud and clear. This compression shows agreement on value. Investors also believe the stock is fully

207

valued so when prices dip investors are no longer buyers. When prices lift the investors join traders as sellers which results in compression in the long-term group.

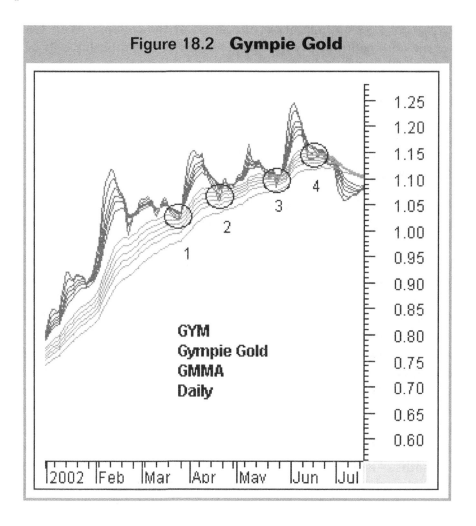

Figure 18.2 **Gympie Gold**

GYM
Gympie Gold
GMMA
Daily

The GYM chart shows this relationship developing over three months. A similar relationship — deeper penetrations and compression in the long-term group — can develop over a few weeks and appear much closer to the eventual end of the trend. These repeated deeper blows are early indications of trend weakness. Traders use this early warning to tighten protect-profit conditions in an attempt to get out as close to the top of the final rebound rally as possible.

The GMMA relationship means they are alert for other confirming indications of trend change or weakness.

At best, this GMMA combination is evidence of a weakening of trend momentum. At worst, it precedes a significant trend change. Traders tend to get out of this stock and move into more attractive trading opportunities. Investors may decide to take a defensive exit, and buy into the stock again only when there is evidence an uptrend has resumed. There is no need for speed here. This trend change may take weeks to fully develop, but do not use this extra time for indecision. The height of the rally rebound is less important in this analysis.

BUBBLE EXITS

We examine bubble-style trading in more detail in the next chapter. Bubble exits are not entirely unexpected. Traders looking for fast-moving stocks are always trading bubbles of price enthusiasm. Investors and traders who selected a stock in a steady trend may unexpectedly find themselves trapped in a bubble trade. This gives them a choice. They can apply bubble exit strategies to capture unexpected profits, and then buy back the stock as the bubble collapses and rebounds from the long-term group. In this case they apply a volatility-based stop loss condition. Other investors may decide to ignore the bubble, confident prices will remain in a long-term trend and continue to rise. The danger in this approach is when the trend bubble collapse is fast and severe, destroying the existing uptrend.

The key feature of a bubble is the way the short-term moving averages move well above the long-term group with a wide degree of separation. This fast move may invalidate the appropriateness of the protect-profit indicators used in the early part of the trend trade. We cover identification and management issues for bubble trading in the next chapter.

SHARP DROPS

The most disheartening trend change of all is the sudden drop. The GMMA is no more useful in the early detection of these sudden drops after unexpected bad news than any other indicator. However, the GMMA helps the traders understand what is happening in a fast-moving decline spread over several days. These declines are always led by traders and their activity has the effect of constantly probing the market for signs of weakness and strength. They react to bad news aggressively, sending prices downwards. The compression, crossover and reversal in this group is shown with ARB Corp (ARP) in Figure 18.3.

Observe how the short-term group behaves as it penetrates the long-term group. There is no sign of a rebound as everything just keeps on moving down. Additionally, the short-term group is widely separated, suggesting traders are desperate to get out. Instead of waiting for a price rise, shown by compression, they simply take whatever price is available. This pattern takes five days to

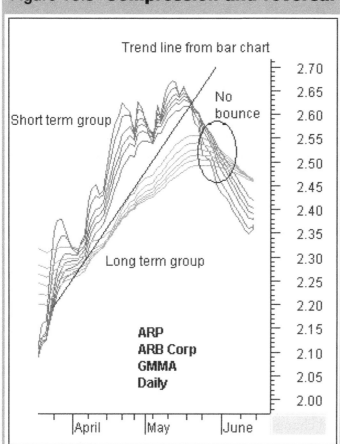

Figure 18.3 **Compression and reversal**

complete and gives the trader time to get out. It may not be at his preferred price but under these conditions an early exit in the face of a substantial trend change is an advantage. In the same five-day period the long-term group of averages quickly compresses and turns down, confirming a significant trend change is developing so the price dip is unlikely to be temporary.

The straight edge trend line plot gives early warning of a trend change when the short-term group of averages compressed and turned downwards, so why wait for this final GMMA confirmation signal? Experienced traders do not wait. The close below the trend line and the GMMA compression is enough to initiate the exit. Not all traders are experienced, or disciplined, so many wait for further evidence the trend has changed. They hope the price fall is temporary.

The GMMA evidence over the next five trading days should be enough to convince even the most hopeful investor this stock is heading for a significant change in trend. While we might dismiss the activity of traders, we cannot afford to ignore the activity of investors. As prices fall, the long-term group compresses and changes direction. This confirms the uptrend is seriously weakened.

The GMMA is not a predictive tool. It is used to understand the nature of the trend, and assists the trader in making a decision about the probability of trend continuation. When this balance of probabilities changes, the trader and investor may decide to modify their trade management tools, to take a protective exit, or to capture an unexpected profit.

The GMMA does not always protect the trader against a false exit, but it does clearly indicate when the trader needs to prepare for the worst. The prospect of a price collapse is a trader's constant nightmare, but another problem is the danger of being caught in a speculative bubble. These are clearly identified with a GMMA, and in the next chapter we look at the best bubble trading strategies. We may have entered a strong trend but when a bubble develops we have the opportunity to collect much better than expected profits.

CHAPTER 19

BUBBLE BATHS

A little bit of excitement in the market is good for the heart and the wallet. It sometimes appears after we have joined an established trend for all the best reasons. Instead of continuing steadily upwards, prices move rapidly upwards, creating a bubble. This is an opportunity and an invitation to disaster. Chinese traders see this situation and comment 'Zai nan cong tan yu fa shen' — disaster comes from greed. As trend traders we need to heed the warning. The Guppy Multiple Moving Average (GMMA) helps to identify the true bubble trading environment so we make better decisions about how to capture profits. Other traders look for these bubble situations, and trade them with specific momentum-driven strategies. The GMMA helps fine-tune both trading approaches.

In established uptrends, prices bubble above the trend and in overheated markets these bubbles extend well above the long-term trend line. Bubble tops are difficult to identify precisely. A conservative bubble trading strategy includes an entry made on the long-term trend line, and an exit made when predefined financial targets have been met. Traders who are late in seeing the opportunity wait until the bubble collapses back to the long-term trend line. Buy orders placed in advance on these trend line levels are filled on the pullbacks. This approach is appropriate where the underlying trend is stable.

Bubble trading is a speculative activity. It calls for good trading skills and excellent trading discipline. The objective is to ride the momentum-driven bubble for as long as possible. Exits are fine-tuned using a variety of volatility-based indicators and techniques. The end-of-day chart sets the general scene for the exit, but the actual exit is best managed using intra-day trading tools. Many traders avoid speculative bubble trading because it is so demanding. However, there are also times when we enter a trade which shows a steady trend, only to find a bubble develops. This poses several dangers and some temptations.

First the dangers. Bubbles inevitably burst and when they collapse prices often fall from a great height. In some cases this fall is fast and hard enough to seriously weaken the underlying trend. Bubble collapses wipe out not only bubble profits, but also profits accumulated over many weeks or months. Recognising these bubbles is a useful skill to develop because we limit the damage from a bubble collapse.

If we have not set out to trade a bubble we may be tempted to take profits from the temporary bubble as it develops. This is a sound strategy used to protect profits or take opportunity profits, while still intending to remain with the underlying trend. Many investors simply ignore the bubble, letting it collapse back to the trend. This may mean ignoring exit signals generated by other indicators. The bubble trade in this situation attacks our trading discipline because we are encouraged to ignore stop loss conditions. Traders need to be clear about when it is appropriate to ignore volatility-based stop loss indicators in this situation.

The GMMA is used to understand three types of bubbles:

- *The speculative bubble.* This is a distinct trading strategy. Trades are selected for this characteristic.

- *Bubbles in a strong trend.* Managing these bubbles means balancing temptation with danger, and understanding when it is appropriate to ignore other exit signals.

- *End-of-trend bubbles.* These are the most difficult to assess, because when they burst they take the trend with them.

Bubble identification

The Technology Investments (TIF) chart in Figure 19.1 shows the essential characteristic of a bubble. This is not a subtle chart development and most times it is very clear on the bar chart, as shown in the extract. What makes this a bubble is the change in the nature of the trend. This is not an accelerating or fast-moving trend. A bubble occurs in an established trend. It represents the final burst of speculative activity based on a developed trend. Just like a bubbling pot of soup, this price bubble lifts above the surface, bursts, and then collapses back to the surface.

The bubble should not be confused with the price action shown with Mincor Resources (MCR) in Figure 19.1. This is a dramatic and sudden change in price activity. This is a momentum-driven trade from beginning to end. This is not a bubble on an existing trend. The 'bubble' is the trend. When it collapses, or develops into a more stable trend, the starting point is well above the original trend or surface in area 1.

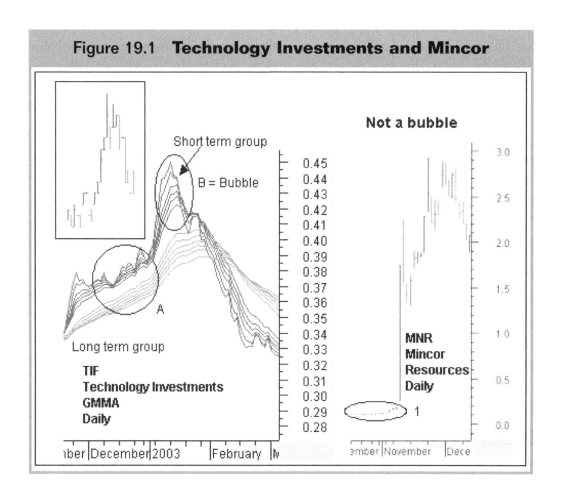

Figure 19.1 Technology Investments and Mincor

Price activity, and GMMA relationships, are different in the bubble. The trend in area A shows a steady and consistent degree of separation between the long-term and short-term groups of moving averages while area B shows a substantial widening of this gap. Prices shoot well above what investors are prepared to pay.

214

The trading activity of expansion and compression is not dramatic in area A. In area B, the expansion of the short-term group is significantly greater than in area A. The steepness of the slope increases, and the degree of separation within the short-term group also increases dramatically. The wider the spacing in this group the greater the level of over-excited competition amongst traders. They aggressively outbid each other to get stock. This simply cannot last for long because it calls for new money to buy at ever-increasing prices. When traders try to lock-in profits they do so aggressively. This means meeting the bid rather than waiting for prices to lift to their ask. The result is a sudden tumble in the short-term averages, which leads to a cascade of lower offers. Potential buyers no longer need to bid as high. Prices collapse as the bubble is pricked.

The final identification feature is the change in frequency of the traders' compression and expansion activity. Area A in Figure 19.1 covers four weeks and shows three peaks in the short-term group of averages. Area B covers a similar time period, but includes only a single peak. This is a change in the nature of the trading activity and signals a classic speculative bubble.

SPECULATIVE BUBBLES

The GMMA confirms the information on the bar chart for Essential Petroleum (EPR) in Figure 19.2. Trend line A defines the potential longer term uptrend with EPR. The momentum-driven bubble is defined by trend line B. This line hugs the fast and steep upwards move. The trader is attracted to this stock because the low price provides price leverage, and the breakout in December is fast. This price and volume change is detected with a basic database scan. The trader may have hoped to lock onto a speculative trade, and by the time the decision point arrives — shown by the vertical line — he clearly understands this is a speculative bubble trade.

The potential exit with EPR is based on the straight edge trend line. We might also choose to use a count back line, a 2×Average True Range calculation (2×ATR), an average dollar price volatility stop, a parabolic SAR, or some other volatility-based indicator.

In this type of trade we use the GMMA to confirm the existence of a bubble and to verify the exit signal. The GMMA is not used to initiate the exit. On the bar chart the exit signal is delivered by a close below the trend line. Although we have not shown the calculations, this close is still above the count back line, the 2×ATR calculation and a parabolic SAR indicator.

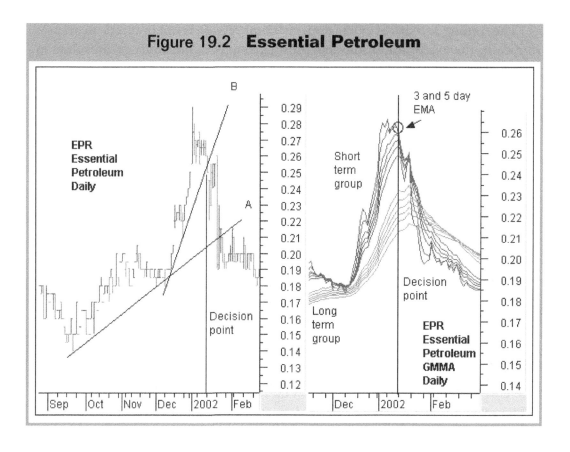

Figure 19.2 **Essential Petroleum**

Do we act on the next day to get the best possible exit? The decision is easier if one of the other volatility-based indicators is also flashing an exit signal, but in this case they are not. The GMMA acts as a confirmation. The 3- and 5-day moving averages have already turned down on the day of the decision point line. Wait another day and the compression of the 8-, 10- and 12-day averages is clear. The initial turndown of the 3- and 5-day moving averages at the top of this short-term group, in conjunction with the close below the trend line, confirms the exit decision.

Our trader gets out on the open at $0.245. If he delays for several days, prices lift back to $0.255. This is not the resumption of the uptrend, but it is an opportunity to get out at slightly better prices. When we apply the GMMA to assist in this type of exit it is within the context of an identified speculative bubble. With this knowledge we are prepared to apply the GMMA in the appropriate fashion.

BUBBLES IN A STRONG TREND

A bubble in a strong trend is an aberration. The trend is well-established and typically the trader or investor monitors this by observing the degree of parallel separation in the long-term group of averages. The GMMA display on the K&S Corp (KSC) chart in Figure 19.3 shows a sound, steady, well-developed trend.

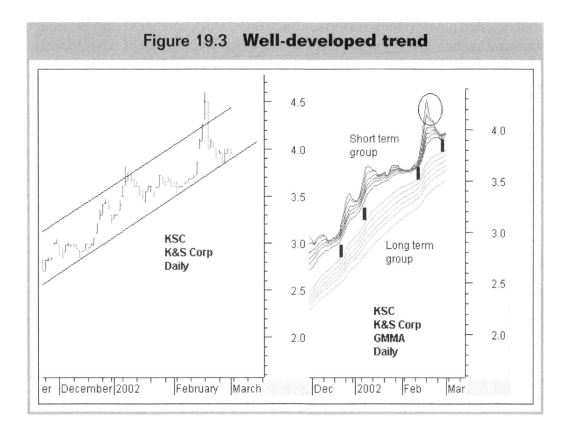

Figure 19.3 Well-developed trend

Our concern arises when the short-term group of averages moves rapidly upwards. This matches the three days on the bar chart which have a much greater price range than normal. These days also include gap openings where the open is higher than yesterday's high. Some temporary, exciting news is driving the price. This has the possibility of setting a new trend, or of being a short-lived rally. This is not the same as the speculative bubble because it is built on a well-established trend.

This bubble may attract some speculative activity. This is of no concern if we already hold the stock because any bubble collapse brings prices back to the underlying trend. Prospective buyers wait for the bubble to collapse.

The leading indication of the weak bubble is the sudden break downwards in the 3- and 5-day exponential moving averages, shown in the circle. The key confirmation comes when prices drop back to the trend line, and then bounce away. The short-term group of averages rapidly falls back, and then rebounds. The degree of separation between the two groups of averages at this compression and rebound point remains essentially unchanged when compared with previous rebound points, shown by the thick lines. When this consistent separation is also matched with a rebound from the trend line on the bar chart we are confident the underlying trend is intact. This combination of characteristics allows us to treat the sudden price rise as an unthreatening bubble. The development is very short-lived and it takes off from a very solid base. This is quite different from the bubble characteristic which threatens the end of the trend.

END-OF-TREND BUBBLES

Some bubbles smash down into the underlying trend and cause it to collapse. These are not benign bubbles, and they have several different characteristics from the weak bubble illustrated in KSC. The distinction starts with the nature of the underlying trend shown by the long-term group of averages in area A on the Newcrest Mining (NCM) display in Figure 19.4. The continued expansion in the long-term group confirms this trend is still developing. It is not stable as with KSC where the long-term group is broadly parallel.

The comparative lack of soundness is also evident on the bar chart. The NCM trend is easily defined with a straight edge trend line. The initial clue to the end of this fast-moving trend is proved by the close below the trend line. The final push in prices is consistent with this steep trend which means the final bubble is comparatively small when compared to the speculative bubble with TIF.

The GMMA relationship in area B signals the high potential for a bubble collapse leading to a trend change. In the days immediately prior to the decision point all the short-term averages turn down. By the time we get to point B there is a clear downtrend in this group and they crossover very quickly and clearly. The speed of this crossover tells us traders have dumped this stock in a major way.

If we wished to delay our exit decision, then the lack of any rebound activity confirms we should have made an exit a few days earlier when we had the opportunity. By then the long-term averages have all started to roll over, or move sideways. This provides additional confirmation of trend weakness.

The key confirmation is the close below the trend line. This is the leading indicator of trend change, and it is confirmed by the way the short-term group in the GMMA has already moved to a crossover point. Bubbles are managed using the GMMA as a confirming indicator. The nature of the bubble collapse and the nature of the underlying trend as revealed by the GMMA help the trader decide if the bubble is a temporary event or if it presages the collapse of the underlying trend.

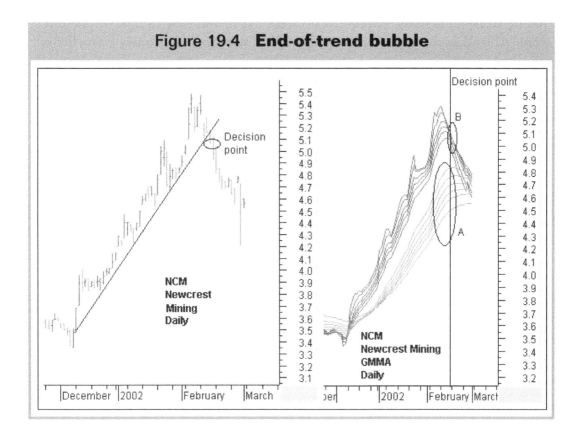

Figure 19.4 **End-of-trend bubble**

GMMA SUMMARY

The previous chapters have examined a variety of applications of the GMMA. This indicator tool is based on moving averages, but rarely does it apply the standard interpretation of moving averages, which tends to be fixated on the point of any crossover. Each group of averages in the GMMA is used to provide insights into the behaviour of the two dominant groups in the market — traders and investors. The indicator itself does not initiate an entry or an exit. It is used to confirm the signals delivered by other indicators. It allows the trader to understand the market relationships shown in the chart and so select the most appropriate trading methodology and the best tools.

The GMMA is applied as a broad tool for understanding trend behaviour, but there are also considerable benefits from applying more subtle interpretations. The GMMA is not a universal indicator. It is designed to help us understand the nature of trend activity. If there is no trend, then the tool cannot be usefully applied. Traders should not attempt to make it work in conditions to which it is unsuited.

When applied to breakout trading, to safe entries on temporary price weakness in an established trend, or to managing better bubble exits, the GMMA is a particularly useful tool. In trend trading we use it to filter out nasty trends with a bad nature and suspect character. The few stocks that pass this trend analysis test — step four in our series — are now subjected to an exacting price check to establish their suitability for effective trade management. We want trend winners, and we only have enough cash to back a single stock.

ANNEX TO CHAPTER 19

BUILDING A GMMA EXPERT IN METASTOCK

Indicator by Leon Wilson, author of The Business of Share Trading.
This article was originally published in Tutorials in Applied Technical Analysis.

The Guppy Multiple Moving Average is usually the common denominator in the tool box of nearly all successful traders. When we use our GMMA, most traders will either attach the indicator to a template or display as required, then delete. Because it can tend to be a little intrusive on our charts, we cannot leave it displayed permanently. To manually monitor the activity of the GMMA can become time-consuming if you visually assess many charts. What we can do is attach our GMMA as an expert and display in the form of a ribbon. By doing this we know which group of averages is dominant. We also become aware of crossovers without having to run an exploration or individually assessing our indicator on each chart, while leaving our chart clear for trend line placement and other analysis.

The GMMA expert does not provide trading advice or buy and sell signals. It is a convenient indicator display which visually highlights the points when a stock meets the set of conditions you have defined. It saves analysis time by highlighting the selected conditions. Traders use this as a starting point for further analysis.

For those of you who are not familiar with 'Experts', please do not skip this section prematurely. It is not as daunting as you may first think. With a little bit of practice, you will find that it is no harder than other MetaStock functions.

First click on the man with the hat — or as best described by Simon Sherwood in *MetaStock in a Nutshell*, the Charlie Chaplin icon — at the top of your screen. A screen will appear with default MetaStock experts. Now click on 'New'. We will do the easy bit first and name our new Expert as shown in Figure 19A.1.

Figure 19A.1 **New Expert**

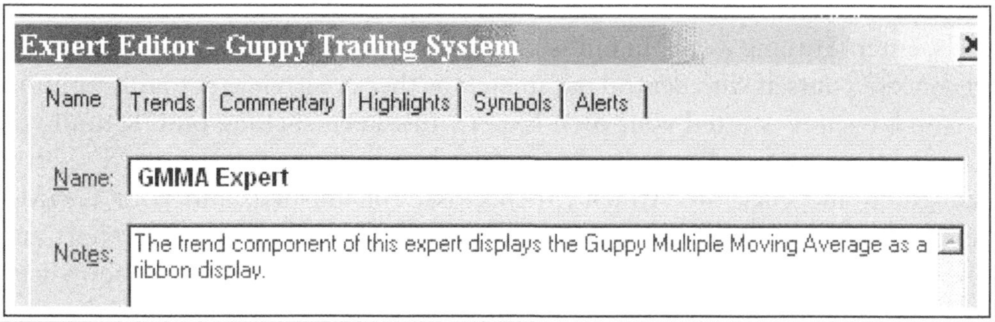

It is titled 'GMMA Expert' but feel free to give your expert a title to which you can relate. On the same screen you may wish to add a couple of lines in the 'Notes' section clarifying the objectives of your Expert. Remember, as your trading and your Expert grows, update your notes accordingly.

Now click on trends to bring the page to the front. You will notice the page is divided into bullish and bearish sections. Enter the following formulas into the appropriate sections. Note these are single lines of code. They are available from www.wilsontechstats.com and should be copied and pasted directly into MetaStock to avoid errors. Additional work with the GMMA for MetaStock is available from www.wilsontechstats.com.

Bullish

```
Value1:=(Mov(CLOSE,3,E)+Mov(CLOSE,5,E)+Mov(CLOSE,8,E)
+Mov(CLOSE,10,E)+Mov(CLOSE,12,E)+Mov(CLOSE,15,E));
Value2:=(Mov(CLOSE,30,E)+Mov(CLOSE,35,E)+Mov(CLOSE,40,E)+Mov
(CLOSE,45,E)+Mov(CLOSE,50,E)+Mov(CLOSE,60,E));Value1-Value2>=0
```

Bearish

```
Value1:=(Mov(CLOSE,3,E)+Mov(CLOSE,5,E)+Mov(CLOSE,8,E)
+Mov(CLOSE,10,E)+Mov(CLOSE,12,E)+Mov(CLOSE,15,E));Value2:=
(Mov(CLOSE,30,E)+Mov(CLOSE,35,E)+Mov(CLOSE,40,E)+Mov
(CLOSE,45,E)+Mov(CLOSE,50,E)+Mov(CLOSE,60,E));Value1-Value2<0
```

The Expert construction panel is shown in Figure 19A.2.

In the top right-hand corner of your trends page, shown in Figure 19A.3, click on ribbon. This brings up the ribbon page so you can set the ribbon parameters. On the top left-hand corner of your new page make sure 'Display ribbon on chart' is ticked. If you would prefer to have vertical lines displayed on your chart to clarify the precise points of change in the GMMA, then tick the 'Display vertical lines' command.

When it comes to the background, select green for bullish and red for bearish. For pattern, select 'None' for bullish and the sloping lines for bearish. For the labels, enter 'Trading Zone' in bullish and enter 'No Trade Zone' in bearish. Do not concern yourself with neutral parameters as they are irrelevant to this formula.

You have now started your own Expert. Just keep clicking on OK until you return to the very first Expert window. Check to make sure your new Expert is highlighted and click on 'Attach', then close. All finished, and your GMMA Expert should now be visible. If your ribbon has appeared on your chart and you would prefer to relocate it on your screen then left-click on the ribbon itself and, while holding the button down, move the ribbon to your preferred area.

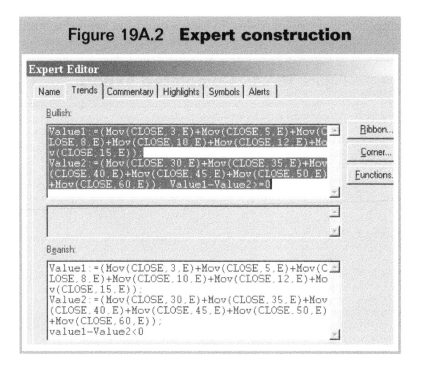

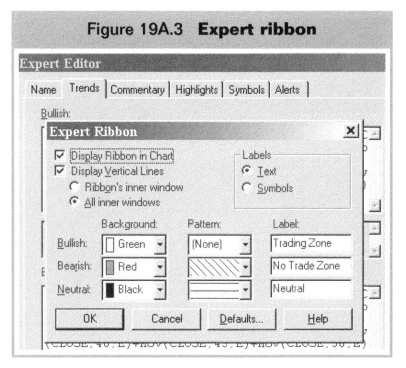

Your completed chart display should look something similar to Figure 19A.4.

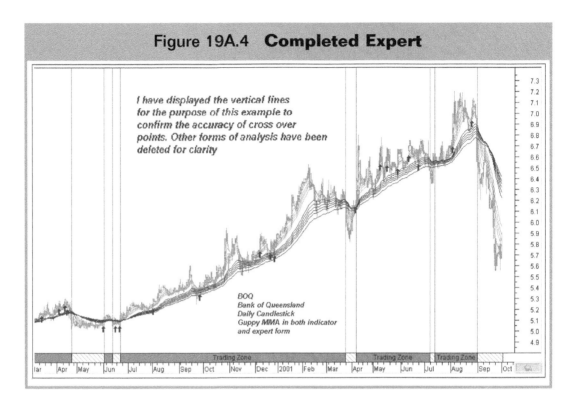

Figure 19A.4 **Completed Expert**

I have displayed the vertical lines for the purpose of this example to confirm the accuracy of cross over points. Other forms of analysis have been deleted for clarity

BOQ
Bank of Queensland
Daily Candlestick
Guppy MMA in both indicator and expert form

CHAPTER 20

NO SECRETS

Given the opportunity, only a few of our original test readers acted on the second set of potential exit conditions shown in the chart extracts at the end of the last 'No secrets' chapter. We give them a generous exit at $0.46 for a 43.75% return shown in Figure 20.1. This is not a nice thought for those who closed the trade earlier. Greed and fear have a significant impact on our trading results. The decision based on the information in the last chapter was a test of nerves as prices moved quickly upwards in a rally. Should we take the profit and run, or wait until we get more definite exit signals? We look at readers' answers below.

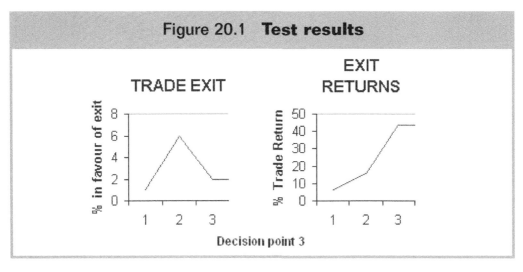

Figure 20.1 **Test results**

The traders who made an exit early in this trading series collected a 15.63% return. It looked good at the time, but the 43% return available from a rally exit makes the first trade profit look small.

OUR ANALYSIS

Based on the charts from the previous 'No secrets' chapter, reprinted as Figures 20.2 and 20.3, very few readers decided it was a good time to exit.

Most readers who exited cited the closes below the trend line as the main reason. They felt this trend line signal was supported by the MACD_Histogram but they seemed to ignore the consistent sell signals generated previously by the MACD_Histogram. A few traders applied a trend line to the Relative Strength Indicator (RSI) peaks and used this to confirm their exit decision. RSI trend lines are one of the least effective applications of RSI to stock trading, and the subsequent developments in this trade show why it is unwise to use this RSI technique.

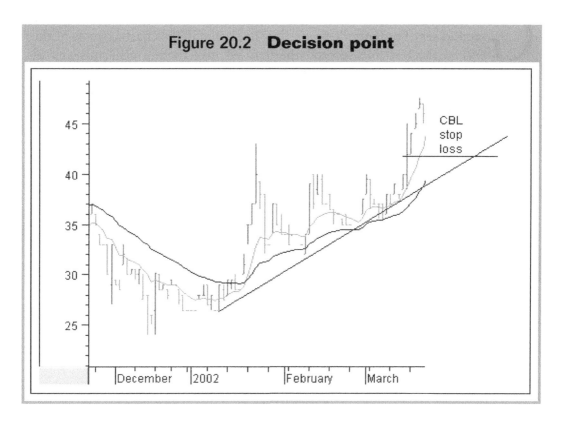

Figure 20.2 **Decision point**

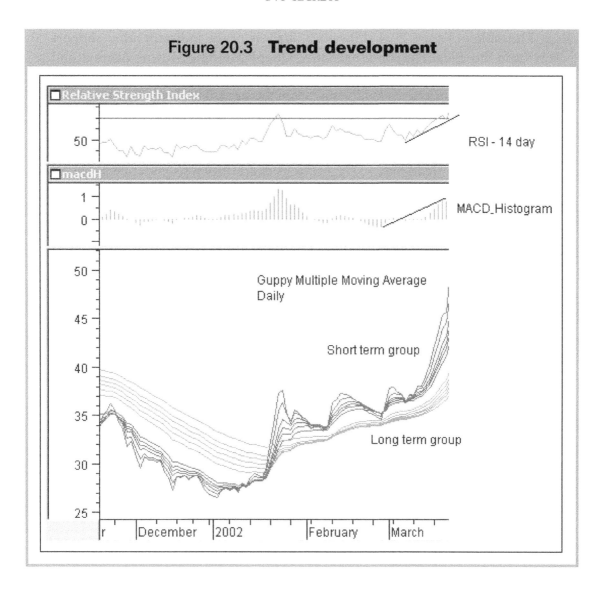

Figure 20.3 **Trend development**

This reaction reveals an interesting characteristic. Once we get one exit signal — the close below the trend line — we tend to look at other indicators with a bearish view. Instead of looking at them objectively, we go hunting for reasons to confirm the decision we have already made. Looking for confirmation is different from looking for verification. In assessing each indicator signal we must try to assess them on their merits, and not in a bullish or bearish light.

The table in Figure 20.4 shows our analysis of the indicators that support staying in the trade. The count back line, Guppy Multiple Moving Average and moving average signals do not flash any exit signals. Some traders use the MACD_Histogram as a reason for staying in the trade. This is a poor application of this indicator because it is unreliable. The MACD_Histogram flashed many exit signals when it remained below the zero reference line so it is only hopeful opportunism to use it now to support a stay-in-the-trade decision. The same applies to the RSI trend line. In the previous chart displays some traders placed a trend line on the peaks and suggested it confirmed a downtrend. They cannot have it both ways and still remain accurate. When multiple interpretations of an indicator are possible then we must either abandon the indicator or use it with extreme caution. An indicator should provide an objective analysis solution. If we can 'adjust' the indicator to suit our mood then it is not reliable.

Figure 20.4 **Analysis summary**

INDICATORS	STAY IN TRADE	EXIT TRADE
Count back line	No close below the CBL used as a trailing stop loss.	No signal.
Guppy Multiple Moving Average	Short-term group is well separated. It is also well above the long-term group. The long-term group is well separated and moving upwards. This is a strong trend.	Short-term group is moving to extremes. This is a fast trend that is likely to collapse quickly. Defensive exit.
Moving average crossover	No moving average crossover.	No signal.
RSI	No divergence signal but watch for new peak. RSI trend is up.	RSI has moved into overbought zone for the first time in this trade. This indicates the potential for a trend reversal and return to lower RSI levels.
MACD_H	MACD_H is strong and well above the zero reference line. MACD_H trend is up as shown by the trend line.	None applicable.
Trend line, support and resistance	Trend line still intact.	No signal.

TEST QUESTION

Do these new charts show a blow-off top or a rally spike or bubble? This is a difficult question. Price has continued to rally but are we seeing a bubble collapse strong enough to destroy the trend? The GMMA notes in the previous chapter may help you decide. We ask the same question again: 'Do you want to abandon the trade, or stay with it?' Do we act on gut instinct alone, or is it better to wait for our planned exit conditions? You do have a plan for this, don't you? Taking profits on spikes can be very profitable, but it can also be premature as prices move back to the trend line and continue powering upwards.

You must decide if the spike in Figure 20.5 is a sign of weakness, or a sign of strength. The indicator groups provide the opportunity to adjust the signals to reflect your mood. They also provide the means to make a major objective decision. How you apply them depends on the way you handle the impact of greed and fear found in every trading decision. Some traders aim for a defensive exit, trying to capture as much profit as possible. Other traders wait for the count back line exit signal.

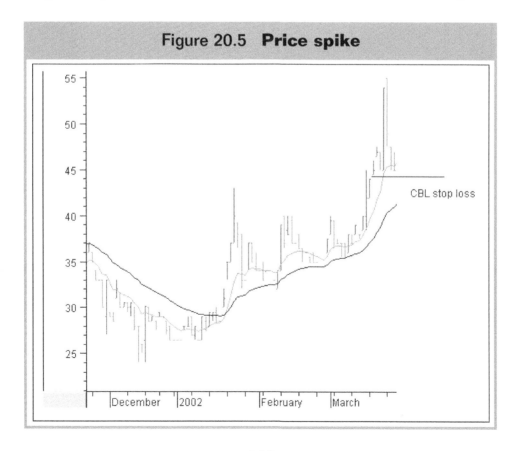

Figure 20.5   **Price spike**

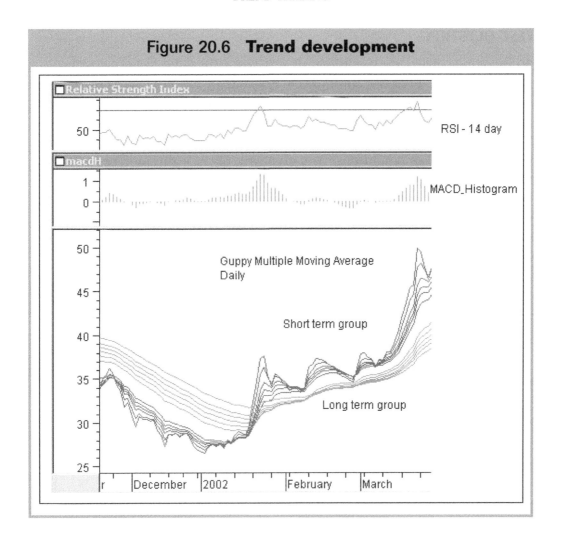

Figure 20.6 **Trend development**

If you believe there is a suitable time between the price action shown in the charts in Figures 20.5 and 20.6 and this latest chart to close the trade, then jot down your exit reasons on the opposite page. Alternatively, write down your trading plan and reasons for staying with the trade. At the end of the next section in the 'No secrets' chapter compare your notes with ours, and with the reasons given by other readers who took this test.

Notes:

_____

_____

_____

_____

_____

_____

_____

PART V

PRICE CHECK

CHAPTER 21

BREAKOUT CONFIRMATION

Seven tests are used to find and then reduce the list of potential trading candidates. They include an initial selection process to gather candidates followed by a visual test for trend direction. This is confirmed by applying a straight edge trend line, and those which pass are subjected to a trend character test using a Guppy Multiple Moving Average (GMMA).

We apply the count back line as test number five. The count back line has a long history and was introduced in my first book, *Share Trading*.[1] It is a versatile tool designed to confirm a trend breakout and to put precise numbers on entry, stop loss and protect profit conditions. Those stocks passing the count back line test get a tick and progress to test six. Stocks failing the count back line test are dropped. The stocks surviving all the way through from test one to test four are usually good trading opportunities. To pass tests five and six they must be excellent opportunities. It is easy to become confused at this stage of the testing process because we are surrounded by so many quality opportunities. We discard

---

1   The count back line is an extension of the 3-bar net line indicator developed by Joe Stowell, a US bond trader. The count back line includes some significant variations not found in Stowell's original 3-bar net line so we give it a different name to avoid confusion. Readers interested in the 3-bar net line will find more information in the July 1995 issue of *Technical Analysis of Stock and Commodities* magazine. It is included in *Tips for Traders and Investors*, by J. Stowell.

opportunities other traders might keep. We retain only those offering easy trade management because this reduces the chance of error as a result of our own trade mismanagement.

Although the count back line was originally applied to breakout trading, it also lays the foundation for trend confirmation and tracking. The calculation provides the most important figures we need to make a final selection between competing trading candidates. The count back line gives us the figures we use to calculate the risk in the trade, and the means to make this risk directly relevant to the logic of price activity. It is not enough to use just a financially based stop loss — such as the 2% rule discussed in Chapter 26.

We must not put at risk more than 2% of our total trading capital in any single trade, but unless this figure is directly related to the logical price activity on the chart, it remains a figment of our imagination and is easily overwhelmed by price action. When we select a stop loss point it must be at a level where the market is likely to pause and thus give us an opportunity to exit the trade with dignity at our preferred price level. The challenge, which we explore in the next section, is to match this logical stop loss with the final trade calculations to define risk.

This price check is vital in a breakout trade and it is just as important when we join a trend trade. In trend trading the count back line function of setting stop loss and protect profit conditions is most significant as our objective is to enter an established trend. However these functions are not easily separated from the initial use of the count back line as a breakout confirmation tool. Understanding how and why it is applied in this environment gives us the confidence to expand its application to the developing trend.

We complete a price check on every stock remaining on our short-list after the earlier tests. Our objective is again to reduce this list. Specifically we drop those stocks where the count back line has not been successful in identifying the breakout or defining the trend. We aim for simplicity of trade management and this is shown by the level of success in applying the indicator to the stock in the past. If it has worked in recent weeks and months, then it is likely to work in the coming weeks or months. The easier and more clearly the past trend is defined and managed, the better the chance of managing the future trend with confidence and discipline. The next two chapters may appear to detour from our focus on managing trend trades. Skip forward if you wish, but we believe an understanding of how the count back line is used to define the start of a trend develops the confidence to apply the count back line as a tool for managing an existing trend.

For traders who use the Guppy Traders Essentials charting pack, or the GTE tool pack reading MetaStock format data, or Ezy Charts, the construction details are unnecessary. These programs have a count back line tool which automatically calculates the placement of the count back lines when the cursor is placed over a price bar. MetaStock, OmniTrader, Supercharts and other charting program users have to complete these calculations by hand so it is helpful if traders know the correct starting point for the count back line calculation. These chapters are a detour designed to explain the construction process, and to show how the technique is integrated with other indicators. In Chapter 23 we use this knowledge to show how the count back line is applied as test five in the trade selection process.

BREAKOUT APPLICATIONS

The count back line is not designed as a stand-alone technique so it is used as step five in selecting a trade previously signalled by other indicators. Our preferred combination discussed in previous chapters includes the use of straight edge trend lines and the Guppy Multiple Moving Average. We use the count back line in a trend breakout situation to identify when a downtrend has turned into an uptrend, and the objective is to plan an entry as close as possible to the pivot point low. This low sets the ultimate low price bar of the downtrend. We cannot identify this price bar in real time as it happens. If we find this price bar as soon as possible after the downtrend low has been set then we have an advantage because we capture the early part of the trend change.

The count back line is a trend-following tool designed to confirm the reversal of a short-term trend. This is an important modifier. The count back line is not designed to identify and define a long-term trend. We use the Guppy Multiple Moving Average indicator for this. The count back line is used to select the better entry points once we have received trend change signals from other sources.

The count back line creates a short-term hurdle which must be overcome to develop confidence in a trend change. It consists of four applications:

1   The first is as a trend change verification tool.

2   The second is as an entry tool with a defined range of safe price levels.

3   The third is as a stop loss tool.

4   The fourth is related to the stop loss function when it is used as an exit tool.

Our objective is not to predict the future, but to put the balance of probability in our favour.

We start with the trend verification function. Assume for the moment the GMMA chart is already showing a strong potential for a trend reversal. We look for a trend change so we follow the downtrend until we get a definite signal the change is taking place. The count back line is used initially as a resistance line. It is calculated from the most recent low in the current trend. Any action between the count back line and the existing low point is ignored.

ENTRY APPLICATION

With each new low, we re-calculate the position of the count back line. We wait for a close above the count back line before acting. We take the count back line signal with confidence because we have already been alerted by the GMMA relationship, or a straight edge trend line break. The count back line confirms what we already know and as the trend continues down we re-calculate the count back line from every new low.

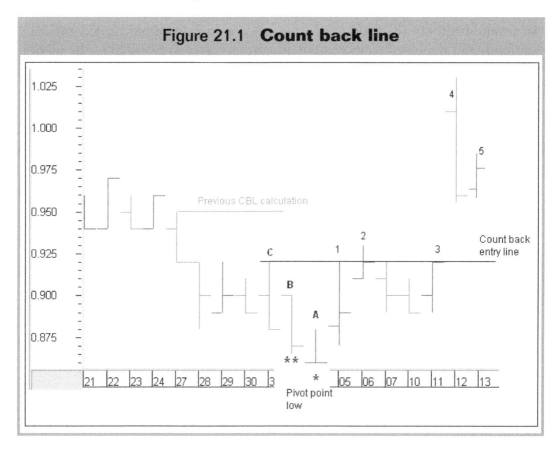

Figure 21.1 **Count back line**

A close above the short-term resistance level signals an entry. All of this is based on end-of-day downloads. We get the signal tonight and we get to take action tomorrow. The count back line defines the safe zone of entry. We need to know how far we can safely chase the price.

The chart extract in Figure 21.1 shows the simplest and easiest application of the count back line. Prices have been travelling in a downtrend, but there is some evidence from other indicators — such as the GMMA, a straight edge trend line, a stochastic or RSI — that a new uptrend is emerging. We have already made the decision about the potential for a trend trade. Now we apply the count back line to determine the exact entry conditions and prices.

We start with the most recent lowest low. This is marked with a * and shown as price bar A. This is the first *significant* price bar. We move to the top of the price bar and then move across to the left to locate the next highest price bar in the current downtrend. This is the next *significant* price bar. It is significant because it has a higher high than the first price bar. In this example this is shown as price bar B.

Then move to the top of price bar B, and across to the left to the next price bar with a higher high. This is the third *significant* price bar, shown as price bar C. Move to the top of this price bar and then plot a line extending to the right.

This is the count back line entry trigger line. No action is taken until there is a price close above this trigger line. We accept the price close is set by the smart money so we ignore temporary highs created by the bulls. In the chart the first higher price bar 1 sets a high equal to the count back line. No action is taken.

Price bar 2 pushes above the count back line for the high of the day, but the close is on the same level as the count back line. No action is taken. Price bar 3 also shows a close on the value of the count back line and this is ignored.

Price bar 4 delivers the signal for action with a close above the value of the count back line. Action is taken on the next day. This end-of-day indicator sets up an order for execution in the following day's market, shown as price bar 5.

We do not know at the time if price bar A will become the pivot point low of the downtrend. We only know this retrospectively. Every time a new low is made that is lower than the low used in the current count back line calculation, a new count back line calculation starts. The count back line calculation in Figure 21.1 is shown starting at the price bar marked as ** . As the downtrend develops, new count back line calculations are made with each new low, and the count back line entry line is lowered.

There are several variations on placing the count back line which confuses some users even though they may be using the automatic tools. Selecting the correct starting point for the calculation is vital. Select the incorrect point and the calculation does not confirm the entry signal at the correct time. In each of these chart illustrations we retain the A, B, C notation for each of the *significant* days used in the calculation. In the simplest application these three significant days equal three calendar days. This is not always the case as shown in Figure 21.2.

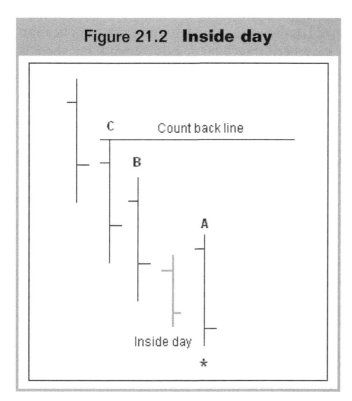

Figure 21.2 **Inside day**

The extract shows the first significant day, marked as bar A. The * marks the bar used as the start of the calculation point. It is preceded by an inside day shown as a thick line where the high of the day is lower than the high of the first significant day. When moving back from bar A we do not find the next highest bar until the third calendar day in this series. Bars B and C are the significant bars because each has a higher high. The inside day is ignored in making the count back line calculation so three significant bars occupy four calendar days.

There are no real limits on the number or combination of inside days which may be ignored in the search for three significant bars. In Figure 21.3 the three significant bars cover seven calendar days. The cluster of thick bars between bars B and C shows different types of price action. Some dip considerably lower than bar B, but not lower than bar A. None of the highs on this cluster of bars is higher than bar B. When bar C meets these conditions it becomes the final significant bar in this series.

Although the construction rules specify to use the lowest bar, some people are confused when there are several bars with equal lows. The extract in Figure 21.4 shows the most complex of these dilemmas. Bar A is preceded by a day with an equal low, shown as the thick bar on the left. Two days earlier another thick bar sets an equal low. Which one should be used as the calculation point for the count back line?

The construction rules specify we start with the lowest low in the current trend, and that is bar A. The start point of the calculation is shown by the * . This spreads the count back line calculation over seven calendar days.

A related area of confusion is created by equal highs appearing after one or more of the significant days, as shown in Figure 21.5. The same rules apply here as with inside days. A significant bar is always higher than the preceding significant bar. When we start with the top of bar A we move to the left, ignoring the first thick bar with an equal high. Likewise we ignore the two preceding days with lower highs and we also ignore the next thick bar which has an equal high. When

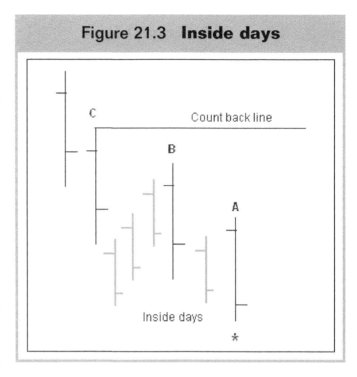

Figure 21.3 **Inside days**

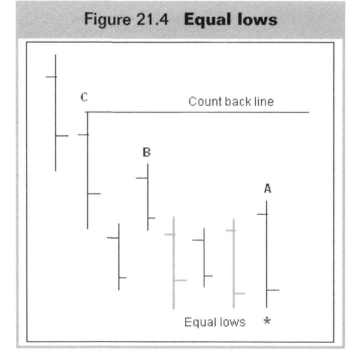

Figure 21.4 **Equal lows**

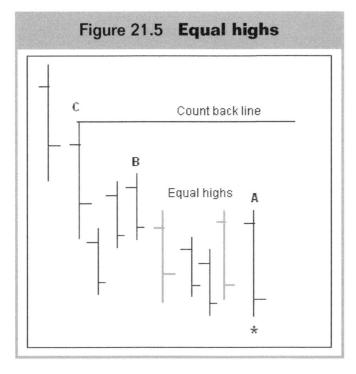

Figure 21.5 **Equal highs**

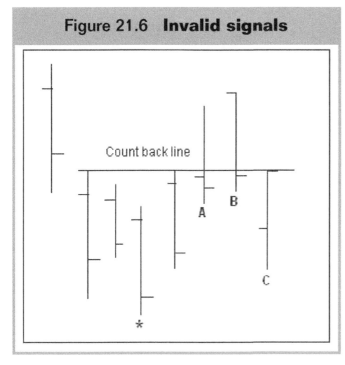

Figure 21.6 **Invalid signals**

we hit bar B with its higher high we set the next significant day. In this example the three significant days are found over nine calendar days.

A variety of invalid count back line signals are shown in Figure 21.6. Bar A shows a sharp intra-day rise which collapses, taking the close below the count back line so no entry is triggered. Bar B is similar, except the open is well above the count back line. This is unimportant. The trigger is activated by the position of the close and the close of bar B remains below the count back line. Although we might think it is time to act, no signal is created.

Bar C is the most tempting possible trigger signal. The close is at the same level as the count back line. We have shown it for clarity on the chart extract. This is not a count back line signal. The valid application of the entry technique depends upon a close above the count back line. We want a lead from the smart money in the market. If we include closes at the same value as the count back line, the reliability of the technique declines significantly.

WHEN TO USE THE COUNT BACK LINE

The count back line is a verification tool. We already know a downtrend is in place and it is often defined with a straight edge trend line as shown in Figure 21.7. We find this the most useful and reliable tool to apply before we reach for the count back line. The count back line is designed to answer one question: is the current close above the straight edge trend line a real breakout, or is it false?

The diagram in Figure 21.7 includes a price bar with a close above the trend line. If we act on this signal tomorrow, buying the stock in anticipation of a change in the direction of the trend, there is a low probability a new trend is developing. A close above the trend line is not a reliable signal. Markets are full of false breakouts where prices collapse very quickly and the downtrend resumes. The count back line is designed to protect us against these false breakouts by imposing another set of verification conditions.

The tool is used to verify a breakout from the *current* prevailing trend, and the verification process starts, not with the breakout bar, but with the previous lowest bar in the current downtrend being monitored, as shown in Figure 21.8. This lowest bar may be several days prior to the bar that breaks out above the trend line. In this diagram, the calculation bar is marked with a * . The movement in plotting the count back line is shown by the thick line. When these two relationships are met we have confidence the breakout above the trend line has a higher probability of being the start of a new uptrend.

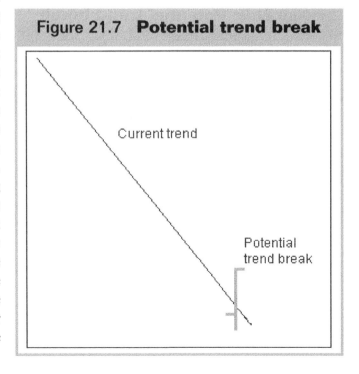

Figure 21.7   Potential trend break

Current trend

Potential
trend break

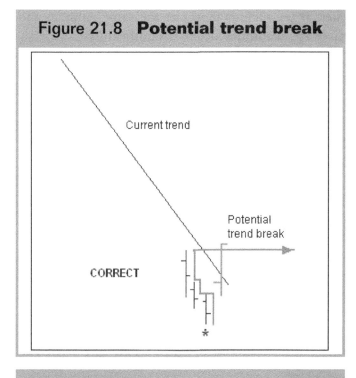

Figure 21.8 **Potential trend break**

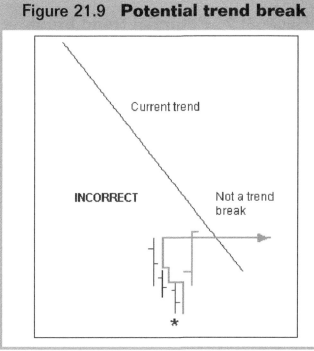

Figure 21.9 **Potential trend break**

Compare this to the situation where we see a count back line signal in Figure 21.9, but without a breakout above the straight edge trend line. The plot of the count back line is accurate, based on the lowest low of the period and with a close above the count back line calculation. However, the close is not also above the straight edge downtrend line. This count back line signal is false and unreliable. Used by itself, the count back line is not outstandingly reliable but the reliability of the signal is increased dramatically when combined with an initial breakout from a straight edge downtrend line.

The count back line is designed to trigger an entry as the trend changes from a downtrend to a new uptrend. A close above the count back line is the trigger. It is a clear-cut signal, and we look at this and at how the count back line is then used as a stop loss and protect profit tool in the next chapter.

CHAPTER 22

ENTRY MANAGEMENT

Traders use the count back line to follow a downtrend and alert them to a change in the trend signalled when prices close above the count back line. This close triggers an entry and sets two additional features in applying this technique. The first is a stop loss calculation. The second is a maximum chase level used to avoid the temporary rush of prices which then retrace and allow a cheaper entry point.

The focus is on breakout trading and the objective is to plan an entry as close as possible to the pivot point that sets the ultimate low point of the downtrend. This chapter is still part of the detour but it remains relevant to our trend trading objectives because there are times when price weakness in an established uptrend resembles the situation following the downtrend breakout discussed below. The Guppy Multiple Moving Average (GMMA) tells us the price dip is temporary, and the underlying trend is strong. This count back line technique confirms the rebound will hold, and provides us with figures for better risk management.

In this chapter we show how the count back line is used to confirm the reversal of a short-term trend and the continuation of an existing trend. The count back line consists of four applications:

1   The first is as a trend change verification tool — discussed in the previous chapter.

2   The second is as an entry tool with a defined range of safe price levels.

3   The third is as a stop loss tool.

4   The fourth is related to the stop loss function when it is used as an exit tool.

We start with the initial entry trigger and then consider the function used to define the maximum chase level. Trend breakouts rarely proceed upwards in a single movement. Often they make a short sharp run up and then collapse a few days later. This retracement is part of the test and re-test process common with new trends. Our objective is to avoid paying too much for the stock on the initial breakout. It is often better to resist the temptation to chase the price and wait for the temporary pullback before entering the trade.

The count back line provides two methods to deal with this behaviour. It stops us chasing price too far and it also provides a second point which prevents us from buying a breakout that later fails.

Our starting point is the classic count back line entry signal shown in Figure 22.1. The close is above the count back line, confirming the smart money is stronger than the most recent bearish strength. The smart money now agrees with the bulls and this is a necessary condition for any sustainable trend change. Trends feed on money flows and the larger the better. Smart money often means big money so when it is more enthusiastic than recent bullish sentiment, as shown by the three significant highs setting the position of the count back line, we have a higher level of confidence in the validity of the trend break.

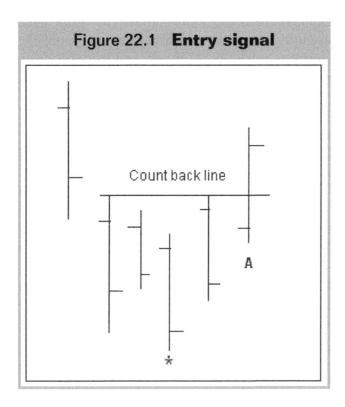

Figure 22.1 **Entry signal**

SEPARATING SIGNALS

At this count back line trigger point the nature of the trend, our analysis and the way we track subsequent developments all make a significant change. We have confirmed the downtrend has ended. The pivot point low of the downtrend, as shown by the * in Figure 22.1, is the starting point for the count back line entry calculation. Now it is time to switch our attention to verifying the continuation of the uptrend. We do this by reversing the initial count back line calculation.

The new current trend springs into existence the moment the break in the old downtrend is confirmed by a close above the count back line used as an entry tool. We start the new stop loss calculation with the first price bar with the highest high in this new uptrend, and we have marked this calculation point with a * in Figure 22.2. We show this as price bar 1 and it is the first *significant* price bar. We move down to the bottom of the price bar, and then move left until we encounter a price bar with a lower low than the first *significant* price bar.

This is shown as price bar 2. It is a *significant* price bar because its low is lower than price bar 1. Again, we move to the bottom of price bar 2 until we hit another price bar with a lower low. This is shown as price bar 3 and is the third *significant* price bar. From the bottom of this price bar we plot a line to the right and this becomes the count back stop loss line.

A close below this line confirms the current uptrend has failed. It is an exit signal.

CBL STOP LOSS

Once the new uptrend is established and we have taken a trade entry, we want to manage the trade carefully and within the

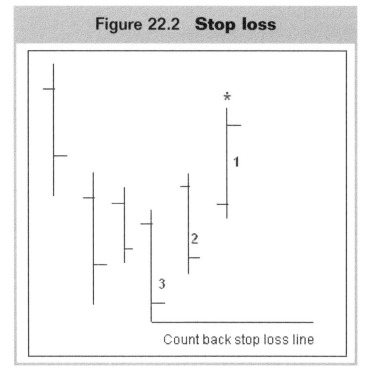

Figure 22.2 **Stop loss**

Count back stop loss line

ranges established by the most bearish recent activity. The three significant bars establish this maximum range. We are prepared to allow prices to range within this area, but if they close below the low point of this range, we get out. The count back line stop loss calculation defines the permissible range. In this example the stop loss line coincides with the pivot point low of the old downtrend. This is not always the case.

The diagram in Figure 22.3 shows the main complications which apply in calculating the placement of the stop loss line. The significant price bars used in the calculation are numbered while the unimportant price bars are shown with letters. We start with the relationship between price bar A and price bar 1. Price bar 1 is the significant bar because it is the most recent high in the series, coming after price bar A. When we have a choice between starting points set by two equal highs, we always start with the most recent high.

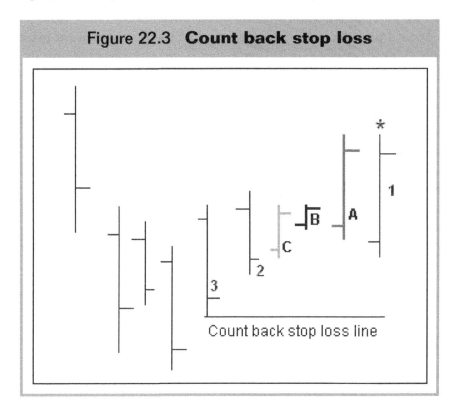

Figure 22.3 **Count back stop loss**

Count back stop loss line

Moving to the bottom of price bar 1, the objective is to locate the next significant price bar which is defined by a lower low, and this means both price bar A and B are ignored. Price bar C is also ignored as this has a low equal to the low of price bar 1. The next significant bar is shown as price bar 2. The third significant price bar is marked as price bar 3.

The stop loss calculation is simply a reversal of the way we apply the count back line calculations to follow a downtrend down. The breakout from the downtrend may be very rapid, creating one or more days of fast-moving gap activity, and Figure 22.4 shows an extreme example. The stop loss calculation starts with the most recent high, marked with a * . The breakout has defined a new trend, so we move to the next significant bar in the current trend. We drop down from bar 1 until we meet bar 2. We do not move across to a price bar in the old downtrend. The gap is ignored and we move directly to the next bar in the current trend. The same applies in the move from bar 2 to bar 3. Once the third significant bar is located, the stop loss line is plotted from the bottom of the bar, as shown.

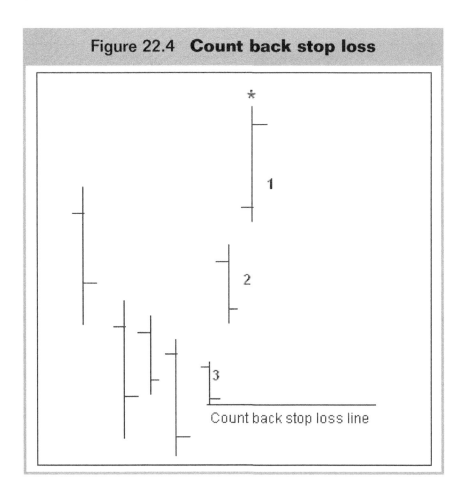

Figure 22.4 **Count back stop loss**

MAXIMUM CHASE LINE

The count back line used as an entry tool also protects us from embarrassment and greed. Once a breakout is confirmed it is tempting to chase the price rise to get on board before we miss the bus. The danger of this approach is shown in the diagram in Figure 22.5. Prices often rise very quickly in the initial stages of a breakout, only to be followed by a retreat. We want to avoid buying at the absolute high of the first temporary rally as there are often better opportunities to enter the new trend at cheaper prices once the initial enthusiasm dies down. This is the best buying zone. The bottom of this zone is defined by the count back line stop loss calculation. The top of the zone is defined by an additional count back line calculation we call the maximum chase line.

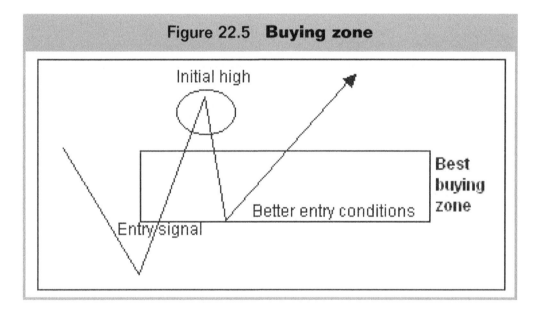

Figure 22.5 **Buying zone**

It is an arbitrary calculation, but we find it prevents traders from chasing prices too high. It provides a defined mechanism to encourage traders to wait until prices return to better levels. The calculation is automatic with the Guppy Traders Essentials package, but other charting program users have to complete the calculation by hand.

The maximum chase calculation uses the percentage difference between the count back entry point and the pivot point low, as shown in Figure 22.6. Perhaps the fall is 20%. This percentage value is then projected upwards from the count back line and sets the maximum chase line.

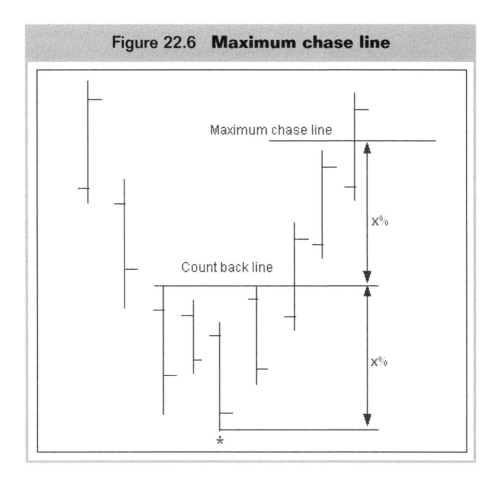

Figure 22.6 **Maximum chase line**

This maximum chase calculation is quickly completed on a spreadsheet. In the example in Figure 22.7 the pivot point low is at $0.10 and the count back line entry trigger is at $0.12. This is a 20% difference. Taking the value of the count back line at $0.12 we calculate the point 20% above this level. This sets the maximum chase level at $0.144. This does not mean you cannot chase prices higher than $0.144. There are many successful trades based on higher entries. However, once prices move above this point immediately after the initial breakout there is a high probability this rapid rise will be followed by a retreat into the buy zone. Paying too much doesn't kill the trade, but it does reduce profits, so waiting for a temporary retreat increases the profitability of the trade.

Initially we used a straight numerical count for the maximum chase line calculation. If the drop distance was $0.05 then we projected the maximum chase line upwards by $0.05 above the count back line entry trigger. However we found this lowered the maximum chase line and compressed the best buying zone too much. This meant some rebound trades were missed. Testing and experience have shown a percentage calculation is more effective.

Armed with this understanding we confidently apply the count back line as a stop loss and protect profit tool in an established trend. In the next chapter we examine how this is used in test five to weed out less-suitable trading opportunities.

Figure 22.7 Maximum chase line calculation

MANUAL CALCULATION OF THE MAXIMUM CHASE LINE

Pivot low	10
CBL level	12
Difference	2
Pivot Low to CBL % difference	20
Amount above CBL	2.4
Max entry price	**14.4**

Chapter 23

KEEPING THE MOST

A s soon as we buy a stock we face two critical issues. The first is to protect our trading capital. The second is to protect our profits. Both issues relate to our understanding of the trend and its ability to persist. The stop loss function of the count back line tool tells us when to act to protect our capital. Later in the trend, the count back line is used as a protect profit stop loss. The objective is to provide early warning of a trend break so we can exit and protect our accumulated profits.

We use the count back line in this way as our fifth selection test because we want to join an established trend and we favour those stocks where the count back line has proved an effective trade management tool in the past. Generally this means it has worked effectively as a trailing stop loss, and then later as a protect profit stop loss. These stocks pass test five because there is a higher probability they will continue to be managed successfully using count back line techniques.

However, when it comes to managing a trade in an established trend we do not always act on the count back line exit signal. Instead we must resolve the dilemma between a short-term exit signal and the strength of the underlying trend. This resolution comes from the Guppy Multiple Moving Average (GMMA). When the GMMA suggests the trend is strong we might choose to ignore the count back line exit signal. Later we might use the count back line as an entry tool to manage an additional entry into the strong trend as prices rebound. When the GMMA confirms the trend is weakening we act on the count back line protect profit signal. We look at these combinations below, although they are also relevant to the performance management section.

The count back line is used to verify the end of a downtrend and set the conditions for entry into a new uptrend. As part of this process the count back line is applied to the highest high in the new trend to calculate a stop loss line. This is an essential part of managing the entry process in a new trade.

The two figures — the entry price and the initial stop loss price — are combined with a position and risk sizing calculation to set the correct limits for the new trade. In this chapter we move beyond these applications and examine how the count back line is used, initially as a protect capital stop loss line and then later as a protect profit stop loss mechanism. Finally we show how it is used as an exit signal to end the trade as a trend reversal develops.

The count back line consists of four applications:

1 The first is as a trend change verification tool — Chapter 21.

2 The second is as an entry tool with a defined range of safe price levels — Chapter 22.

3 The third is as a stop loss tool to protect trading capital.

4 The fourth is related to the stop loss function when it is used as a protect profit exit tool.

CBL STOP LOSS

We start where we left off in the previous chapter with a classic stop loss calculation in Figure 23.1, but add two new days and a dot showing our original entry point. We add an additional line to show the final count back line placement for the entry trigger. The entry and the stop loss calculation occur simultaneously. Once the entry is made and prices move to a new high higher than bar 1 the count back line calculation starts again.

The stop loss line calculation is still based on bar 1 because neither of the two bars to the right are higher than bar 1. Some of these new bars are lower than bar 1 but this is unimportant. In tracking a new rising trend our interest is in the relationship between new highs as these define the limits of bullish strength.

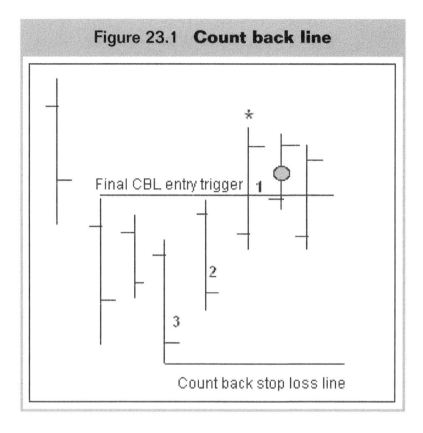

Figure 23.1 Count back line

Final CBL entry trigger

Count back stop loss line

The next diagram in Figure 23.2 shows several new features of the calculation. First is the shift in the significant bar to the right so the new high is a new price bar 1. We complete the stop loss calculation by moving down to the bottom of this price bar and then moving back to the left to the next lowest bar. This is shown as price bar 2. In the calculation in Figure 23.1 this price bar was irrelevant. Now it becomes part of the calculation because it is the first lowest bar after the new price bar 1.

We move down to the bottom of bar 2 and across to the left until we hit the next lowest bar, ignoring price bar A, because it has a higher low than bar 2. We also ignore bar B because the low is equal to the low of bar 2. It is not until we hit bar C that we find the next significant bar. We move to the bottom of this bar and draw a line to the right to define the new stop loss level.

The stop loss application is the exact reverse of the entry calculation. We use the highest high in the series as the starting point, and then calculate the cumulative three-day range using the next two significant bars. The calculation may extend over many more calendar days before we locate the significant bars.

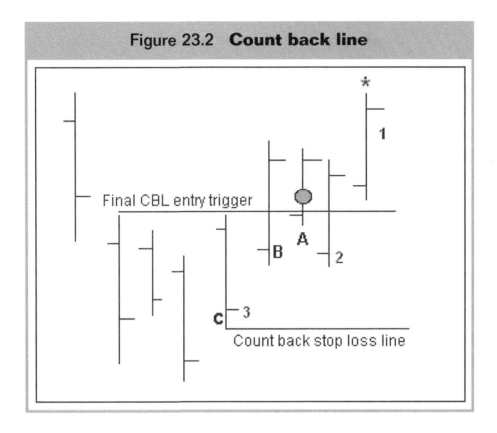

Figure 23.2 **Count back line**

The second point to note in Figure 23.2 is the calculation still acts as a protect capital stop loss. Should prices fall below this level we would exit the trade at a loss even though the current closing price suggests the trade is in profit when compared with the dot showing our entry point. The count back line stop loss calculation provides a signal telling us the new uptrend has ended. We get to act on this signal the next day in the market. While the stop loss line is below our original entry point the trade is still technically a loser because our trading capital is still at risk.

PROTECT PROFIT

As each new higher high is made, the count back line calculation is re-calculated. This example in Figure 23.3 illustrates two significant features. The first is the way the gap between bar 2 and bar 3 is ignored. When we encounter a gap we move to the next lowest bar in the current trend. The count back line is designed to give us information about the current trend so there is no value in extending the line all the way across to the left until we hit another trend.

The second feature is the way the nature of the count back line calculation has changed. It is no longer a protect capital stop loss. The count back line is now above the dot marking our entry point and this trade is now truly in profit. When we act on the exit signal generated by a close below the count back line the trade is closed with a small profit.

Until the new uptrend comes to an end, the count back line retains

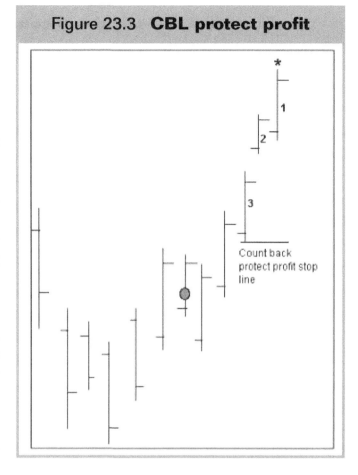

Figure 23.3 **CBL protect profit**

Count back protect profit stop line

this new character and acts as a protect profit trailing stop loss. With each new high, as shown in Figure 23.4, a new protect profit calculation is completed.

NASTY GAPS

Many traders are distracted by price gaps, believing they have some almost mystical significance, and must be 'filled'. Some price gaps are interesting and provide specific trading opportunities, as discussed in *Snapshot Trading*. Most gaps are unimportant. When we calculate the count back line as a breakout tool we ignore the gap. When we use it to set a trailing stop loss we also ignore gaps. Sometimes this is confused when traders fail to understand which trend they are tracking. It is useful to clarify two other aspects of the count back line calculation. The first is the idea of the current trend, and then how this impacts on the way we treat price gaps.

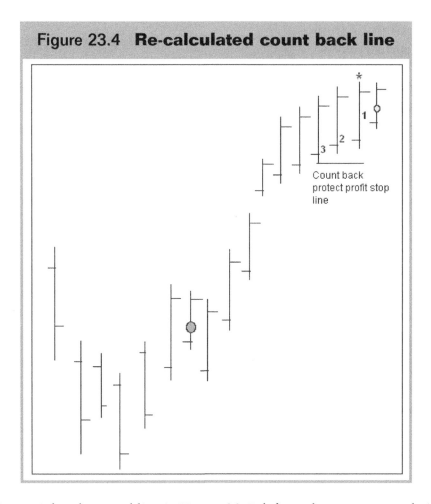

Figure 23.4 **Re-calculated count back line**

The straight edge trend line in Figure 23.5 defines the *current* trend. A close above the value of the trend line initiates the application of the count back line technique to verify that the apparent trend break has a high probability of success. In this series of prices we see a price gap.

The calculation of the count back line starts with the bar marked with a * — the lowest bar in the *current* trend in Figure 23.5 and shown by the thick line. Remember, we are trying to establish the conditions necessary for a breakout from the *current* trend. We are not interested in previous trends as these are not trends we are trading. The price activity and action in the current trend may be formed by a continuous series of overlapping bars, or it may include a number of price gaps. The gap is a reflection of volatility within the current trend. In deciding if a new trend is developing we must take into account the volatility and price behaviour of the current trend.

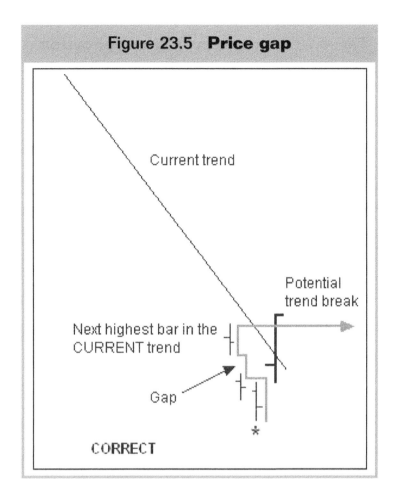

Figure 23.5 Price gap

Current trend

Potential
trend break

Next highest bar in the
CURRENT trend

Gap

CORRECT

By using the count back line in its correct sequence as a tool for verifying a breakout from an existing downtrend it is logical to apply it only to the price action in the trend we are tracking.

The final diagram in Figure 23.6 confirms the logic of the count back line application to the current trend. If the gap is ignored, then the calculation must travel all the way to the left until it intersects another price bar in an entirely *different* trend. As shown in the diagram, this price bar at the left of the diagram is in a trend that has clearly ended, and is clearly different in character from the *current* trend we are trying to monitor. The last bar in this series is part of an uptrend. The trend we are applying the count back line to is a downtrend. Proceeding with a count back line calculation in this way is incorrect because it is not applied solely to the current trend.

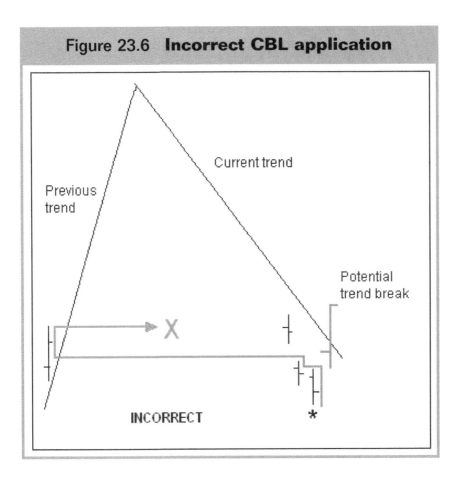

Figure 23.6 **Incorrect CBL application**

We have shown the count back line applied here to a trend breakout situation. The same conclusions apply when the count back line is used to manage an entry into an established uptrend, or to act as a stop loss point in a rising trend. Gaps are ignored and the calculation moves to the next bar in the *current* trend under consideration.

Gaps are also ignored when using the count back line as a trailing stop loss or protect profit calculation. When we look at Figure 23.7 we clearly see at least two trends. The first trend is the current trend. The second trend is the previous trend. In this example the previous trend is down, and the current trend is up. We confirm the previous trend has ended when prices close above the count back line used as an entry tool. When prices close above the bar marked X in Figure 23.7 we have confirmation of a trend change. A close below the count back line stop loss indicates the current uptrend has ended and a new downtrend has started.

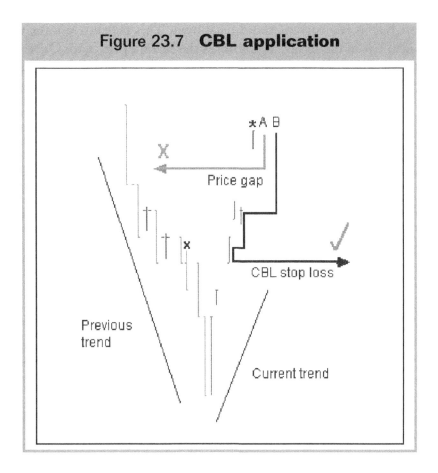

Figure 23.7 **CBL application**

When applying the count back line we always work with a current trend and the most recent previous trend. This is particularly important when we encounter price gaps. The calculation point for the count back line stop loss is shown by the * in Figure 23.7. The count back line calculation moves down to the bottom of the calculation bar, and then we move across to the left until we hit the next bar in the *current* trend. The process shown by thick line A is incorrect. We move to the bottom of this bar, but we do not move across to the left going through the price gap until we hit the next bar which is in the *previous* trend. Traders using Guppy Traders Essentials, the GTE toolbox or Ezy Charts do not have to worry about this problem as the calculations are done automatically.

The correct count back line calculation is shown by the thick line B. It moves down to the bottom of the first bar, then continues down in the current trend until we locate the next lower bar to the left in the *current* trend. Then we go to the bottom of this second significant bar, and continue down until we locate the next lowest bar in the current trend as shown. This process ignores the third chronological bar in the series, and ignores the second price gap. Once the third significant bar is located we move to the bottom of that bar, and project the line to the right to set the count back line stop loss value.

CLASSIC TREND EXITS

Traders should note that at the critical point where a downtrend changes to an uptrend, we do not verify any exit signal with a second indicator. While the count back line acts as a protect capital stop loss we act immediately on any exit. This is the weakest part of any new trend, and the most dangerous from a trading perspective. The risk of new trend failure is always high so we focus entirely on protecting capital. An exit to protect a profit is not always as straightforward so we consider the alternatives here. We start with the classic count back line exit designed to protect open profits.

The display in Figure 23.8 shows two trade entry points, marked by a large and small dot. The small dot shows an entry point in the developing uptrend. On the extract shown, the count back line protect profit stop loss is set at the bottom of bar 3. This bar is significant for both trades. A close below the line suggests the uptrend is weakening, and signals an exit. The first trader who entered as shown by the large dot gets out with a profit. The second trader who entered at the small dot exits with a small loss.

The new trader who entered on the small dot applies the same management techniques as the trader who entered with the large dot. His new trade does not become profitable until the value of the trailing stop loss line rises above the entry point.

A close below the count back line suggests the trend is changing direction. This is an early warning it is time to get out. The dip with price bar A is not an exit signal because the close is still above the value of the count back line. The close with bar B is below the count back line and signals an exit on the next day of trading. This is often difficult to act upon because greed gets in the way. This is particularly so if the next day opens higher. We look for excuses to hang on, and in certain circumstances, as shown below, this is acceptable. However, generally we should use this exit signal unless there are exceptional circumstances. Just as the count back line did not get us in at the very pivot point low of the downtrend, it will not get us out at the very pivot point high of the uptrend.

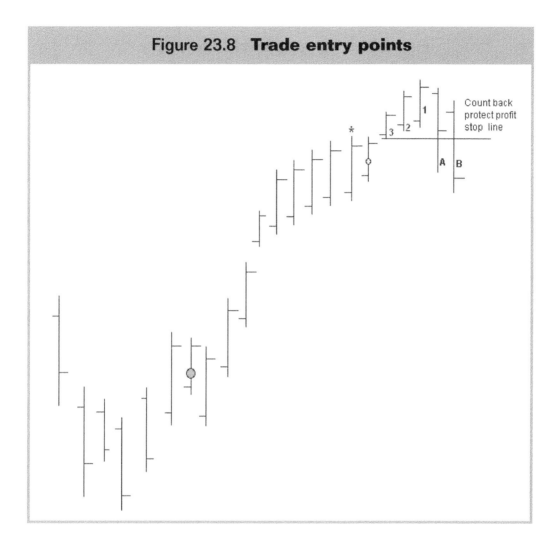

Figure 23.8 Trade entry points

As soon as the exit signal is generated by a close below the trailing stop loss count back line the trader immediately changes the application of the count back line entry technique. It reverts to its entry tool application and the significant bar is now the lowest bar in the new trend, shown by the * and marked as bar A in Figure 23.9. The next two significant bars are shown as bars B and C.

What new trend you may ask? The new trend starts as soon as the old trend is finished and this is signalled by the close below the count back line trailing stop loss. Using this trend definition, the new price action is a downtrend until prices close above the new count back line applied as an entry tool.

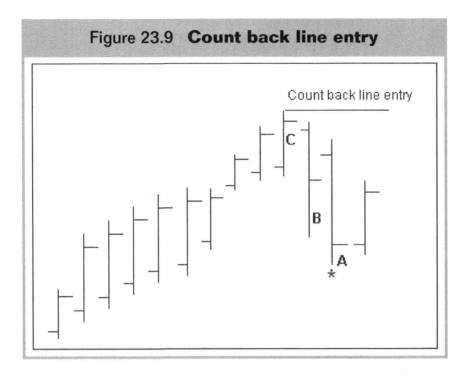

Figure 23.9 **Count back line entry**

This classic end-of-uptrend exit is confirmed by other indicator combinations. In this application we continue following the downtrend down, making a new count back line calculation with every new lower low and looking for a verified signal of a trend change as shown in Figure 23.10. This takes us back to the discussion in Chapter 21.

The count back line applies equally as effectively to trades from the short side as to trades from the long side. In the example shown in Figure 23.10 the count back line calculation remains the same, starting with the pivot point low in the new downtrend. For the trader going short with an entry at the dot, a close above the count back line signals an exit from short positions because it suggests there is an increased probability the downtrend has turned into an uptrend.

WHEN TO IGNORE EXIT SIGNALS

This discussion could be included in the trade management notes of the 'Performance plus' section. We include it here because it is a logical progression from the current discussion of when and how to use count back line exit techniques. Our objective is to understand when to ignore a count back line exit signal to avoid getting out on a false dip in the trend, as shown in Figure 23.11.

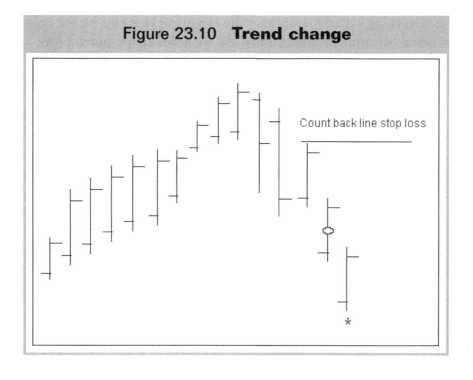

Figure 23.10 **Trend change**

Count back line stop loss

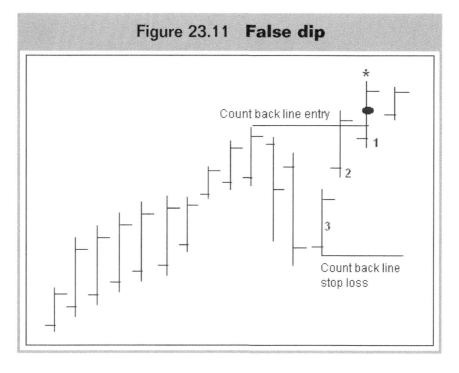

Figure 23.11 **False dip**

Count back line entry

Count back line
stop loss

Traders working with the temporary dip in a major trend ignore the count back line exit signal because other indicators like the GMMA do not confirm a trend change. This price dip signals the potential for a cheaper entry into an established trend, shown by the dot. The entry point is confirmed, along with trend strength, by a close above the new count back line. New traders interested in joining the trend use the same techniques to distinguish a temporary price dip from a trend collapse.

As soon as there is a close above the count back entry line the trader immediately applies the count back line as a stop loss tool. The significant bars are shown as 1, 2 and 3. A new trend has been established and will remain in place until there is a close below the new stop loss line.

In the period shown at the end of Figure 23.12, Lihir Gold (LHG) made a new high. When this was used as a calculation point for the next count back line protect profit exit point, traders found price had dropped below the line and an exit was signalled. Our trade objective is to benefit from a relatively short-term price move, so the trader acts immediately on the count back line stop loss signal.

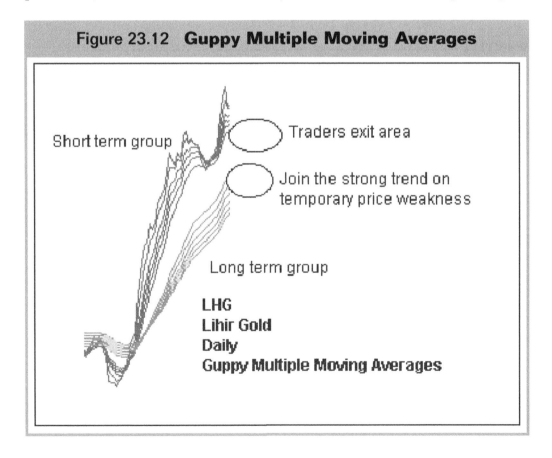

Figure 23.12 **Guppy Multiple Moving Averages**

The trend trader has a more difficult decision. The question he wants to answer about any price retreat triggering his stop loss is this: if I did not own this stock, would this price fall represent an opportunity to enter this strong trend at a point of temporary weakness? If the answer is 'Yes', then he may choose to ignore the immediate sell signal because the underlying trend is so strong. If the answer is 'No', then he acts immediately on the exit signal.

The trend trader's objective is to remain with the trend for as long as possible so he must understand the nature and character of the trend. The GMMA provides the solutions. The long-term group is well-separated showing a strong underlying trend. The distance between the long- and short-term groups suggests the current price pullback is not a threat to the underlying trend. His answer to the question above is 'Yes' so he ignores the count back line exit signal in this situation. The trend trader may buy more stock along with other investors who use this opportunity to join a strong trend on temporary price weakness.

Despite the extensive filtering process it is likely several trading candidates will have passed all the tests thrown at them so far. We give them one final hurdle to pass. The trade must meet financial conditions and offer the opportunity of a reasonable reward. This should be an objective process but it is marred by emotion and preconceptions that reflect the psychology of each trader. We examine some of these issues in the next section.

Before we move on, we finish this section with an example of how the count back line is used to effectively trade new floats, or initial public offers.

CHAPTER 24

IPO PROFITS

The count back line is used to define the stop loss limits on the initial entry into a trade. In the classic application this follows a breakout signal from a well-established existing downtrend. In this specialist application we apply it to trading new floats, or initial public offers (IPOs), which have just a few days of trading history.

The problem with IPOs from a trader's perspective is the lack of price history available to establish trend behaviour, support and resistance levels and rebound areas. Almost the entire arsenal of technical and chart trading tools are sidelined because we do not have enough price history available to apply them.

Trading IPOs can deliver some very good profits, but we need a method to distinguish between those which float and those which nosedive. Technical traders treat the fundamentals and hype associated with a new float with some skepticism. We want price action to tell us what the market really thinks. We cannot make an informed judgment about the future trend so we must focus purely on managing risk when we enter these types of trades.

The calculation starts with the bar created by the first day's trading. This is shown as a thick black bar in Figure 24.1. Either the high or the low will be used in the selection of the most appropriate count back line application. We do not know which one to apply until we get another two significant bars. Then we

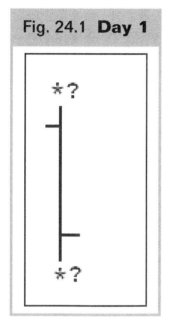

Fig. 24.1 **Day 1**

decide the probable direction of the trend, and develop a mechanism to enter the trade and protect profits.

Figure 24.2 shows the simplest way this trade may develop with the next two significant price bars appearing in quick succession. The starting thick bar is the first day of IPO trading and the next two days have higher highs. This combination provides the trader with three significant bars, labelled A, B and C. The count back line calculation starting point is shown by the * and applied as a standard trailing stop loss condition. This is similar to the way it is used to manage a mid-trend entry discussed in the previous chapter. Traders who act on the next day and take a position continue to apply the count back line as a standard trailing stop loss, and later as a protect profit stop loss until the new uptrend ends. In this example the trader is able to join the new IPO on the fourth day after listing.

The management of this trending trade does not require any moving averages, stochastics or RSI indicators. This trade relies entirely on bar chart relationships until there is sufficient price history available to apply other indicators.

Many IPOs sink quickly after listing. Some stocks stage a rebound and go on to develop a stable uptrend. We do not know if this will happen, so in this situation we apply the count back line in the standard entry application. The first day's trading for the IPO is shown as the thick black bar in Figure 24.3. Each of the following bars has a lower low. Bars are marked 1 through 3. As soon as the third significant bar is created we calculate the location of the count back line from the * . The line now acts in the same way as the classic count back line entry tool so we do not enter until there is a close above the count back line.

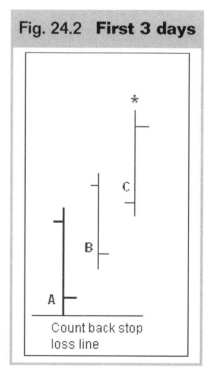

Fig. 24.2 **First 3 days**

Count back stop loss line

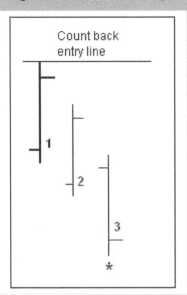

Fig. 24.3 First 3 days

Count back
entry line

1
2
3
*

We do not need weeks of previous price activity to establish a downtrend is in place. As soon as we have three significant downtrend bars the placement of the count back line confirms a downtrend is in place. We then treat the trade in the same way as we treat a potential trade in a well-established downtrend. We follow it down, looking for signs of a trend breakout.

Not all IPOs fly out of the starting gate. Many drift sideways for several days, or even weeks, before enough interest is generated to develop into an uptrend as shown in Figure 24.4. In this situation the position of the new highs is not always the same as the final position of the significant bars.

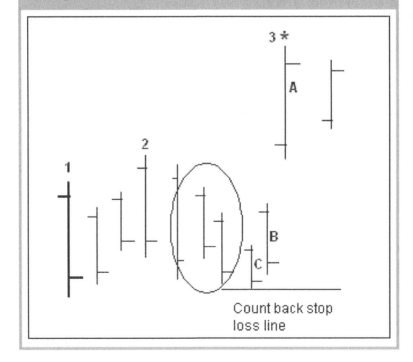

Figure 24.4 Price activity after listing

3 *
A
2
1
B
C
Count back stop
loss line

The initial bar setting the first high in the calculation is shown as bar 1. The next higher bar is bar 2. The two days of price activity in between do not set a new high and they do not set a lower low than bar 1. At this stage the price activity leans towards an uptrend.

It takes six days for the next highest high at price bar 3 to be established. The price action over this six days is erratic. No new highs are set, and although prices trend downwards in the area circled, there are still no lows lower than bar 1.

The trigger for the entry is the valid application of the count back line as used in the same way as the mid-trend entry approach discussed in previous chapters. We cannot complete the count back line calculation until the high at bar 3 is established, and this sets a paradox. Bar 3 is the trigger bar, but as soon as the calculation is made, bars 1 and 2 are no longer significant bars.

Instead we move to the bottom of bar A — a significant bar — to the next significant bar, which is bar B. The gap is ignored because we look for the closest low bar in the current trend. The third significant bar is bar C and the count back line stop loss is set from this point. It is higher than bar 1, set on the first day of IPO trading.

FUMBLE THE STOP

A good stop loss continues to rise behind the current price action and should not drop. In most cases the count back line moves consistently upwards, but there are situations in very volatile markets where the most recent count back line calculation might drop below the previous calculation, as shown in Figure 24.5.

In this example the valid count back line calculation starts with bar A, and uses bars B and C as the next significant days. The count back line protect profit is shown by the thin line.

The next day is a large price range day with extreme volatility. The low of this day, shown as bar 1, is lower than the low of bars A and B. Applying the count back line calculation from bar 1 we move down to the next significant bar which is shown as bar 2. The final significant bar has a low below the original count back line calculation. The new stop loss is shown as a thick line.

If we act on the new count back line calculation it overpowers our stop loss point. This is an incorrect application of the stop loss technique because it allows the risk to expand. The application of the calculation steps is correct — start at bar 1 and move to bar 3 — but the interpretation of the adjusted stop loss signal is not.

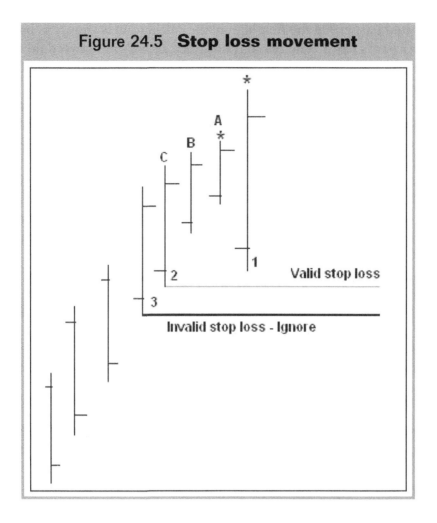

Figure 24.5 **Stop loss movement**

The stop loss should not be lowered. It is designed to protect capital and profits. Over-riding the level puts capital or profits at risk and this is unacceptable trading.

If the trend is strong, prices recover and set the new highs necessary for the count back line calculation, as shown by the thick bars B and A and the upper count back line stop loss in Figure 24.6.

If the trend weakens, then an exit is signalled by a close below the most recent valid stop loss line. A decline in the trend is shown by the thick bars 1, 2 and 3. The close below the most recent valid placement of the stop loss line, shown as the middle line, is a signal for the exit. We do not wait for a close below the low, invalid stop loss line. If we wait for a close below the invalidly placed stop loss line we put substantial profits and capital at risk.

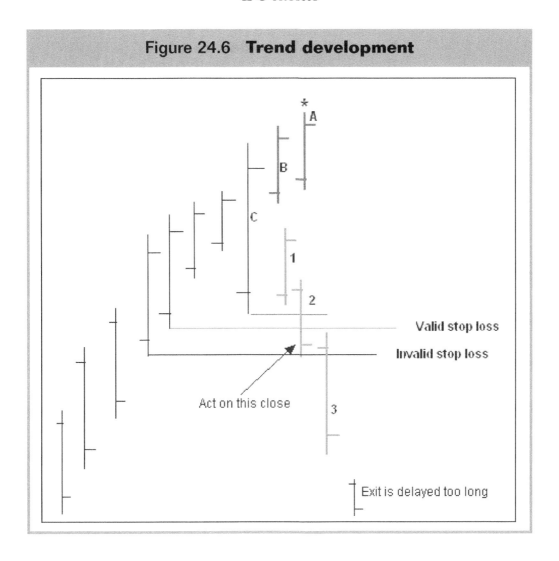

Figure 24.6 **Trend development**

INTRA-DAY APPLICATIONS

The count back line is generally applied to end-of-day charts. It is also applied to intra-day charts and used as a tool for managing open intra-day trades, as illustrated in Figure 24.7. A number of examples of this intra-day application are also discussed in *Snapshot Trading*. The same processes are used in this tighter timeframe. The only modification is to ensure the trade is managed consistently with bar intervals selected at the beginning of the trade. If the trade starts with five-minute bars then the trade should be managed using five-minute bars until it is closed. Do not shift to three-minute or to ten-minute bars part way through the trade.

273

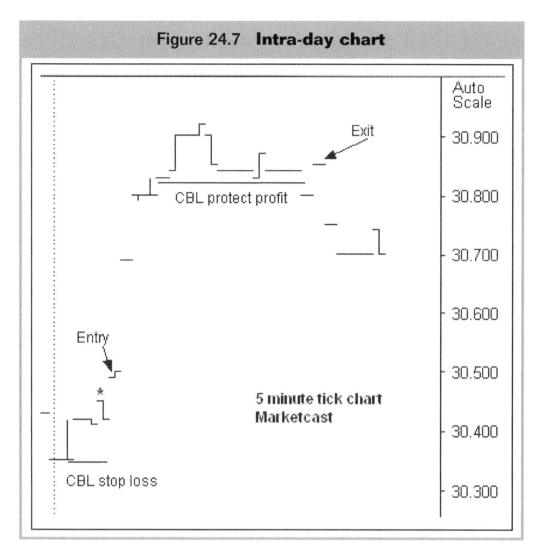

Figure 24.7 **Intra-day chart**

Such shifts in timeframe alter the ranging relationships between the bars and invalidate the count back line signals. The indicator relies on a constant time span for each of the bars used. In an end-of-day trade we use a bar representing a full day of price action. When the signal is generated, we take action on the next day. In an intra-day trade we may choose to work with five-minute bars. When a signal is generated we get to act in the next five minutes.

The count back line is designed to establish the cumulative range of price action to determine significant price action that triggers a trade entry or exit. It is a powerful technique but it should be applied in conjunction with other indicators to verify the nature of the trend.

CHAPTER 25

NO SECRETS

Are you still hanging onto this trade, or have you become a spectator by taking an exit based on the charts in the 'No secrets' chapter at the end of the last part?

In the original test series, some readers snatched quick profits while others grew nervous as profits exceeded 40%. The chart development shown at the end of the last part was the most challenging to date, with 68.75% return available. This is substantially better than the 43.75% return available to those who exited the trade in previous chapters.

Another 12% of readers in the original test decided it was time to take the money and run. The percentage of people in favour of an exit increased as shown in Figure 25.1, and this matches the increase in returns. The larger the return, the more people want to get out. In selecting a 68.75% return we generously allow traders to exit at a good price on the day of the price collapse. Is this the best exit decision?

Part of the answer lies in the way you approach the trade. Is this a short-term trade, a rally trade, a momentum trade, or a trend trade? They are all shown in Figure 25.2. The tools we select to manage the trade provide a clue to the nature of the opportunity. When the trade first starts we have an idea of how we want to trade it and this guides our choice of tools.

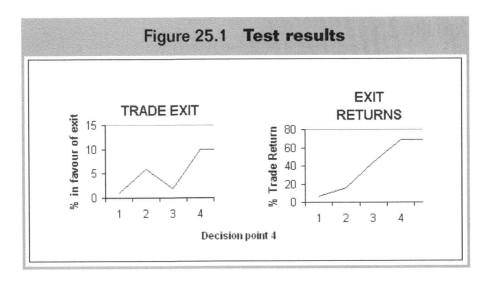

Figure 25.1 **Test results**

We took an entry consistent with the count back line technique, the Guppy Multiple Moving Average (GMMA), and a moving average crossover. We also included an RSI and MACD_Histogram display because we know many readers use these tools. The tools we choose are trend trading tools, and although there may be the opportunity to capture unexpectedly quick profits, in general we aim to ride the continuation of the trend.

When large profits beckon it is difficult to make good trading decisions. Greed gets in the way. It shows itself as fear of missing out on the profits already there. Traders who sent exit emails in the original test all mentioned the blow-off top shown by the large price range days and the subsequent price collapse. Many suggested they would get back into the trade as prices approached the value of the count back line. Climbing back into the trade is an honourable intention, but few traders have the discipline to do this. Instead they watch how price action develops, and if it rebounds they regret they did not follow their mental plan.

OUR ANALYSIS

The charts from Chapter 20 are reprinted here as Figures 25.2 and 25.3, along with our analysis notes and a summary of notes from other participating traders. The price spike is large, but it is also consistent with the character of this stock.

Two previous price spikes have collapsed and dropped price back to the value of the short-term moving average. The price fall does not trigger a stop loss exit condition. If we are managing the trade in a way consistent with our trading plan there is no exit signal generated.

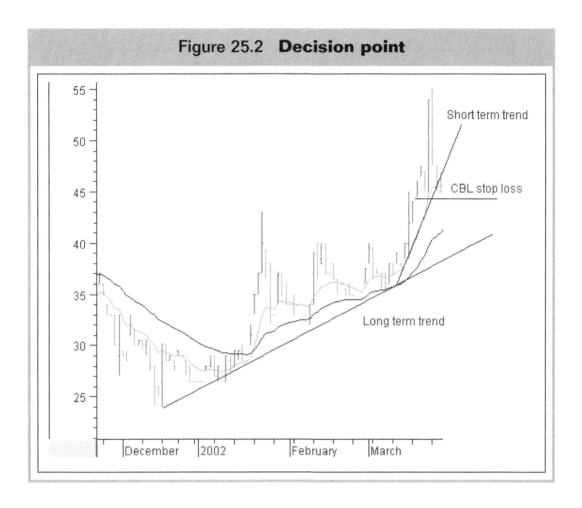

Figure 25.2 **Decision point**

Traders may use the same indicator combinations but interpret them in different ways. They may act in advance of the indicator signal, taking a defensive or fearful exit. Many readers in the original test series noted the short-term grouping of the GMMA had begun to turn down. This is a bubble, so an exit is called for, but they noted the potential to re-enter should there be a rebound.

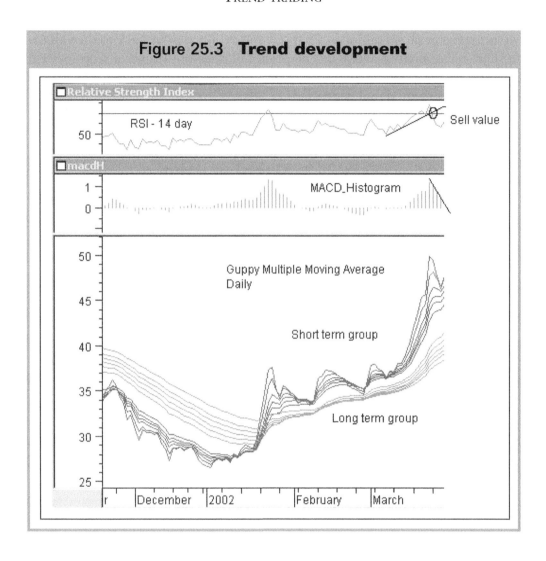

Figure 25.3 **Trend development**

It is interesting to observe the way readers selectively applied the RSI. This apparently objective indicator is open to many subjective interpretations. Different readers interpret the indicator in different ways, and this leaves open the possibility for any individual trader to interpret the indicator in a way that suits his emotional preconceptions about the trade. Want a reason to stay with a losing trade? Use an RSI. Want a reason to get out of the trade? Use the RSI.

Readers noted the RSI had dropped below the overbought zone and was sloping downwards in Figure 25.3. A move below the 70% line suggests this is a good time to sell and capture profits. The RSI value has also dropped below a straight edge trend line on the RSI.

The same type of subjective assessment applies to the MACD_H. Some readers noted the MACD_H was sloping down. A new down-sloping trend line is drawn as shown in Figure 25.3, and it reverses the previous uptrend line.

Once we decide it is time to exit we tend to look at other indicators with a bearish view. Some indicators lend themselves to this type of re-interpretation. Instead of looking at them objectively, we hunt for reasons to confirm the decision we have already made. Looking for confirmation is different from looking for verification. In assessing each indicator signal we must try to assess them on their merits, and not in a bullish or bearish light.

We treat this as a trend trade and it remains open. While it is tempting to take quick profits we need to exercise the discipline to stay with the conditions of the trade. Trend trading delivers substantial longer term profits but we need to give the trade time to continue to develop. Just staying with the trend is not a guarantee of better profits, but it provides a solid framework for decision-making. A summary of readers and our indicator analysis is shown in Figure 25.4. We also show the reasons for staying in the trade, and these include count back line, GMMA and moving average signals which do not flash an exit. As this trade develops over the next few chapters readers will get a better idea of how many traders make their exit decisions. Use this information to improve your own trading.

TEST QUESTION

The chart extracts in Figures 25.5 and 25.6 show how price action developed up until the next decision point. They suggest those who took the defensive exit made the right choice. However, we have one question for these traders: when are you going to re-enter the trade and under what conditions? They all claimed theirs was a defensive exit but it takes courage to get back into the trade.

Should we act on an exit signal on this chart, or should we treat this as a rebound opportunity? Use all the indicators available to decide where the balance lies for this decision. Which indicator takes the dominant place? Should you go with the majority of signals, or should you follow the lead indicator?

The indicator groups provide the opportunity to adjust the signals to reflect our mood. They also provide the means to make a major objective decision. How you apply them depends on the way you handle the impact of greed and fear present in every trading decision.

If you believe there is a suitable time between the price action shown in Figures 25.2 and 25.3 and these latest charts to close the trade, then write your decision in the space at the end of this chapter. At the end of the next part in the 'No secrets' chapter, compare your notes with ours, and with the reasons given by other readers who took this test.

Figure 25.4 Analysis summary

INDICATORS	STAY IN TRADE	EXIT TRADE
Count back line	No close below the CBL line used as a trailing stop loss.	No signal.
Guppy Multiple Moving Average	Short-term group is well-separated. It is also well above the long-term group. The long-term group is well-separated and moving upwards. This is a strong trend. Bubble collapse does not threaten the trend.	Short-term group has begun to turn down. This is a bubble, so an exit is called for. Potential to re-enter should there be a rebound.
Moving average crossover	No moving average crossover.	No signal.
RSI	No divergence signal. RSI peak is higher than previous peak.	RSI has dropped below the overbought zone and is sloping downwards. A move below the 70% line suggests this is a good time to sell and capture profits. The RSI value has also dropped below a straight edge trend line on the RSI.
MACD_H	MACD_H is weakening but still above the zero reference line. MACD_H trend is down, but this bearishness is outweighed by other indicators.	MACD_H is sloping down. A new down-sloping trend line can be drawn and it reverses the previous uptrend line.
Trend line, support and resistance	Longer trend line still intact.	The short-term trend line is broken, signalling an exit. (Note exit is well below the trade exit used here of $0.54.)

Figure 25.5 **Trend development**

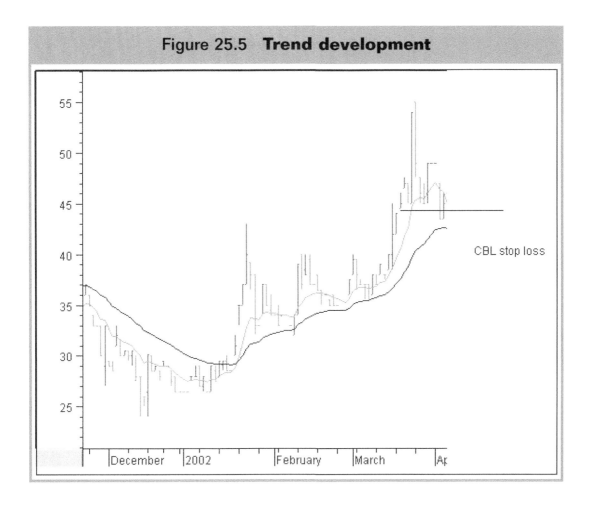

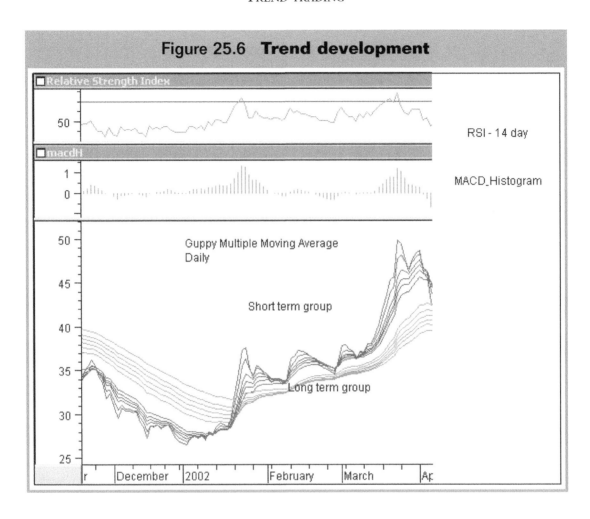

Figure 25.6 **Trend development**

Notes:

_____

_____

_____

_____

_____

_____

PART VI

CALCULATING SIZE

CHAPTER 26

THREE FIGURES

Three figures are used for trading success and they rest on a single rule or foundation. The first figure is the entry price. The second figure is the stop loss price. The third figure is the number of shares purchased. When combined, these form the sixth selection test. We started with a list of potential trading candidates and subjected them to a series of five tests — initial selection, visual, trend line management, trend character and a price check. Stocks failing any test were dropped. Occasionally no candidates make it through to this final test. When this test procedure reveals no trading candidate it is a good time to walk away from the market and go fishing, or hiking, or just relax. Opportunities appear every day so there is no rush.

Most times we face the opposite problem. We have several candidates and we must choose just one of them. We use the position sizing test calculations to make the final and best selection. These are elite candidates. It is difficult to knock any one of them out of the game at this stage. Ultimately we may be called upon to make an intuitive choice because this test may still leave two candidates standing and we have enough capital to trade just one of them. With time and experience traders learn to make the best selection from these excellent candidates.

FOUNDATION RULES

The challenge of position sizing — how many shares we buy — is to combine a financial and a chart-based calculation to arrive at a practical solution. The financial calculation is a money management tool. This foundation is the 2% rule, which tells the trader he can afford to risk no more than 2% of his total trading capital on any single trade. This formula uses the proposed entry price and sets a proposed stop loss exit price. This makes financial and mathematical sense but it is impractical. The price level reached via this calculation bears no relationship with market activity.

THE 2% RULE
Limit risk on any single trade to no more than 2% of total trading, or portfolio, capital

---

The chart-based calculation identifies a natural support level in the market. We prefer to base it on the value of a straight edge trend line, or the current value of a count back line. We anticipate price might fall to these levels, and then rebound as the uptrend continues. A close below these lines suggests the trend is weakening or has failed. It is an exit signal directly related to price activity.

The position sizing calculation matches our proposed entry price — our first figure — with the chart-based support level, which becomes our stop loss price — our second figure. These two figures are combined with the 2% rule in an equation used to calculate the number of shares we can afford to buy.

Our concern is how this rule is used as part of the selection process so we only summarise the application of the rule. Readers who are interested in a more detailed discussion of these money management solutions for controlling risk will find it in *Better Trading*.

If we have $100,000 in portfolio capital, this does not mean each trade is limited to a total of $2,000. It means the actual risk of the trade — the amount we are prepared to lose before we admit we are wrong — is not larger than 2% of our total trading capital. It means we get out of a trade if the current price shows we have lost more than $2,000.

If we buy a stock for $1.00 it does not mean we get out after a 2% loss when the stock trades at $0.98. Such action usually bears no relationship to chart-based support levels. The correct application of the 2% rule may mean the loss in a single individual trade grows to 10%, or 30%, or even larger. However, it will not exceed the dollar value of 2% of our total trading capital. In this example, it means not more than $2,000.

The diagram in Figure 26.1 shows how the percentage fall in an individual trade, shown on the left, is translated into a dollar figure and matched as a percentage of the total trading capital. When we talk of 2% it is calculated as a percentage of total trading capital. We use the 2% rule consistently in all our trading calculations and as a final selection filter. We use 2% because testing shows it is the optimum size for private traders with accounts under $1,000,000. New traders with less than $100,000 tread on dangerous ground and often have no choice but to let risk grow to 5% or more. This calls for extra caution in selecting only the very best trading candidates where there is an extremely high probability the uptrend will continue.

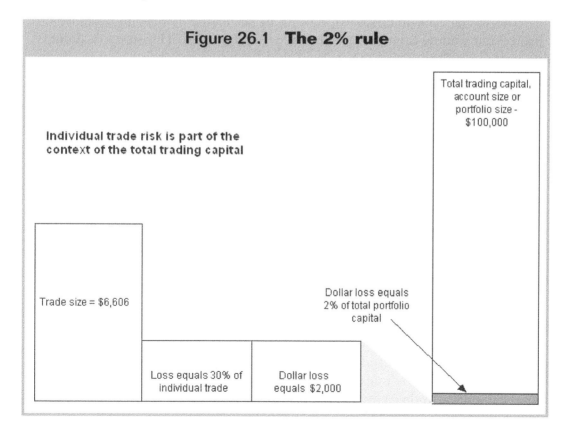

Figure 26.1 The 2% rule

Total trading capital, account size or portfolio size – $100,000

Individual trade risk is part of the context of the total trading capital

Trade size = $6,606

Dollar loss equals 2% of total portfolio capital

Loss equals 30% of individual trade

Dollar loss equals $2,000

The implications and operation of the 2% rule are vital, although many people who call themselves traders or investors do not understand. In the market it pays to commit this statement to memory: a 30% loss in a trade is acceptable if it is less than 2% of your total trading portfolio.

The percentage lost in an individual trade is unimportant. What really counts is how much the dollar loss represents as a percentage of your total trading portfolio capital.

APPLICATION

Matching the financial calculations of the 2% rule with an entry and exit price calls for a method to establish chart-based support levels. This is where we apply the count back line calculation. It is the final step in commitment to a trade and it fine-tunes the entry and exit conditions. Its primary purpose at this stage of trade selection is to generate the exact entry condition and the exact stop loss or protect profit exit conditions.

The count back line is used initially to set a stop loss point designed to protect our trading capital when the trade is first opened. This stop loss point is the price signalling an exit. Once the count back line stop loss level lifts above our original entry price, the count back line is used as a protect profit signal. An exit triggered by a close below the line now saves our open profits from being chewed up in a new trend collapse.

As discussed in Part V the count back line is applied to breakouts, mid-trend entries, and to points of temporary weakness in the trend. The mathematics of the position sizing calculation remains the same in each case.

In this penultimate test, the trader must decide between the advantages of liquidity with plenty of daily trading and the advantages of price leverage offered by lower priced stocks. Leverage means reward objectives may be reached more quickly, and there is a higher probability the reward target may be exceeded.

Leverage may come with lower liquidity which impacts on the size you can trade. It may be difficult to fill a $10,000 order and in this case a more liquid stock is a safer trading opportunity because it is easier to buy and sell the stock.

The position size test has a correct answer and it is 2%. The objective of these calculations is to ensure the potential dollar loss in the trade is no greater than 2% of our total trading capital. This simple financial calculation in Figure 26.2 is based on our entry price, our planned stop loss exit price and the total amount of trading capital — our portfolio size.

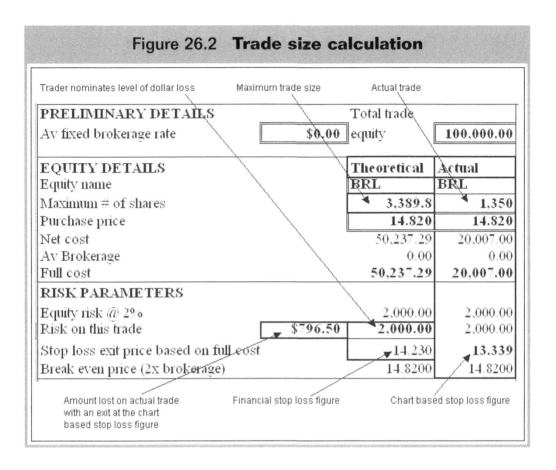

Figure 26.2 **Trade size calculation**

Trader nominates level of dollar loss   Maximum trade size   Actual trade

PRELIMINARY DETAILS		Total trade	
Av fixed brokerage rate	$0.00	equity	100,000.00

EQUITY DETAILS	Theoretical	Actual
Equity name	BRL	BRL
Maximum # of shares	3,389.8	1,350
Purchase price	14.820	14.820
Net cost	50,237.29	20,007.00
Av Brokerage	0.00	0.00
Full cost	50,237.29	20,007.00

RISK PARAMETERS		Theoretical	Actual
Equity risk @ 2%		2,000.00	2,000.00
Risk on this trade	$796.50	2,000.00	2,000.00
Stop loss exit price based on full cost		14.230	13.339
Break even price (2x brokerage)		14.8200	14.8200

Amount lost on actual trade with an exit at the chart based stop loss figure   Financial stop loss figure   Chart based stop loss figure

This means the percentage loss in the individual trade can be much greater than 2%. It may be as large as 30% to 60%. As long as the dollar loss in the individual trade remains less than or equal to 2% of our total trading capital the individual trade failure does not have the capacity to destroy our portfolio success.

A personal trade with Adelaide Brighton (ABC) in Figure 26.3 shows how these factors are combined.

Managing risk is at the heart of every trade so this is where we start our analysis. If we buy ABC at $1.04, how far is it likely to fall? To provide the answer we look at support levels, trend lines, support and count back line calculations. The support level is defined by the previous resistance level at $0.95 to $0.96. If prices fall, this is the level they are most likely to pause at, and this provides us with an opportunity to exit the trade.

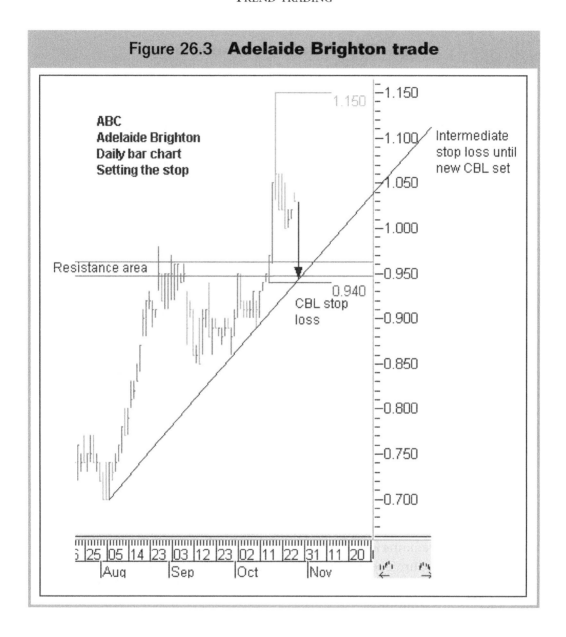

Figure 26.3 **Adelaide Brighton trade**

This support level is even more useful if it is related to other logical chart-based support features. This is a proposed trend trade and as the trade develops it is managed with a combination of count back line and trend line stop loss conditions. We start with the count back line. The current calculation based on the most recent high sets the count back line at $0.94. This is marginally below the support level and this is useful information. It suggests the count back line level is less likely to be triggered and this confirms the strength of the trend.

Based on the chart, a fall to the value of the straight edge trend line would call for an exit with a close below $0.95. As the trade continues we use the trend line as the primary exit trigger until such time as a new count back line stop loss point is calculated. Trade management relies on a combination of the straight edge trend line defining the trend and the count back line to capture the current volatility of price.

We have the first of our two required figures and it is an entry at $1.04. The second figure is the chart-based exit price at $0.95. Now we plug these figures into the spreadsheet in Figure 26.4 to get a maximum position size solution and then the optimal solution for our intended trading size.

Figure 26.4 Trade size calculation

EQUITY DETAILS	Theoretical
Equity name	ABC
Maximum # of shares	22,222.2
Purchase price	1.040
Net cost	23,111.11
Av Brokerage	0.00
Full cost	23,111.11
RISK PARAMETERS	
Equity risk @ 2%	2,000.00
Risk on this trade	$1,728.00 2,000.00
Stop loss exit price based on full cost	0.950
Break even price (2x brokerage)	1.0400

In this example we use a nominal portfolio capital of $100,000 and a planned position size of $20,000. Using the spreadsheet from the Trading Methods pak available from www.guppytraders.com, we enter figures into the black cells to establish the maximum permissible trade size. We plug in the total portfolio trading capital — $100,000 — the proposed purchase price, figure 1 — $1.04 — and the proposed exit price, figure 2 — $0.95. We also confirm the dollar amount we are prepared to risk on this trade. Traders may choose to reduce this amount, but it should never be increased beyond the 2% calculation shown in the cell immediately above the black cell. Brokerage rates vary so widely we do not include them in this example. Unfortunately, you must include this cost in your calculations.

The maximum permissible position size allows us to purchase 22,222.2 shares for a total cost of $23,111.11. If prices should fall to $0.95 then we lose $2,000, or 2% of our total trading capital. The problem is that we either do not have $22,111.11 to spend or we do not want to allocate this much capital to the trade. The optimal or preferred position size for our trading is $20,000.

We adjust the number of shares we purchase so we spend just under $20,000. Using our preferred position size of $19,968, this puts at risk $1,728 if price falls from $1.04 to the stop loss point of $0.95. The reduction in position size reduces the risk in the trade as shown in Figure 26.5.

The figure in the grey cell shows the difference between the theoretical and actual trade calculations, given an exit at the chart-based stop loss point. If prices fall to $0.95 and we get out we lose only $1,728, or 1.7% of our total trading capital. This is an important way of reducing risk in the trade, and in the next chapter we examine the way these calculations are used to select better trading candidates.

Figure 26.5 Reduced trade size

EQUITY DETAILS	Theoretical	Actual
Equity name	ABC	ABC
Maximum # of shares	22,222.2	19,200
Purchase price	1.040	1.040
Net cost	23,111.11	19,968.00
Av Brokerage	0.00	0.00
Full cost	23,111.11	19,968.00
RISK PARAMETERS		
Equity risk @ 2%	2,000.00	2,000.00
Risk on this trade ($1,728.00)	2,000.00	2,000.00
Stop loss exit price based on full cost	0.950	0.936
Break even price (2x brokerage)	1.0400	1.0400

CHAPTER 27

STOP

Stop loss is a deceptive concept. It sounds so simple, so logical, so sensible, and yet it is perhaps the single most difficult task the trader must face. Many who aspire to be traders never master stop loss successfully. In the previous chapter we looked at the theory of setting a stop loss point. Now we want to concentrate on ways to set the stop loss, and to increase our chances of acting on it.

Some traders believe setting a stop loss correctly is a matter of judgment but we believe it is a matter of skill. If the stop loss is set too tight — too close to the current price action — then it may be triggered unnecessarily. This means the trader exits the trade too early on a minor downtrend. He exercises stop loss discipline, gets out of the trade, and then watches in horror as the trend resumes strongly.

When this happens he believes his stop loss was set too tight, or too close, so in his next trade he shifts the stop loss a long way from the current price action. This gives the stock room to breathe and has an unintended consequence. Although the larger stop loss allows the trader to stay in the trade for longer, it also means he misses the vital price signal alert when the uptrend turns to a downtrend. The result is either a reduction in profits or a substantial loss of capital.

Eventually the trader decides stop losses are a waste of time and he stops using them. This also frees the trader from the need to exercise discipline and the result is usually a steady decline in trading performance and results.

These problems arise as a result of some very fuzzy thinking about the role of the stop loss and the relationship it has to price action. It is further confused by our emotional reactions to taking losses in the market. The better solution starts with the identification of a logical chart-based support level. Any effective stop must start with this analysis.

SETTING BETTER STOPS

The key question in setting a stop loss is to decide how far prices could fall. This is not an open-ended question and the traditional accepted answer is wrong. Risk does not equal reward. Trades with high rewards do not have to carry the same high levels of risk. The answer to how far prices might fall is supplied by the closest support level under the current price. The diagram in Figure 27.1 shows our proposed entry point into this trade, along with our proposed stop loss point and the nearest support level. All traders should be familiar with the concepts of support and resistance. These areas develop because price activity seems to pause at these levels. A price level signalling resistance in the past is most likely to act as a support level in the future when prices eventually break above the old resistance level.

When prices fall they are most likely to fall as far as the support level and then pause. The pause in price action provides the opportunity for traders to act. The support level acts as a rest area. Prices may rebound away from the support level, or they may slip slowly below it. How prices behave determines how the trader acts in relation to his stop loss. These levels act to dampen the velocity of price falls and the volatility of price action. The levels provide an opportunity for the trader to act and achieve an exit at the price he prefers.

Contrast this logical approach with an artificial, non–chart-based stop loss. This is a figure plucked out of the air. It may be based on a 5% retreat in prices, or a 10% fall. The percentage figure bears no relationship to price behaviour. It is simply a convenient figure selected by the trader, and it is often just as conveniently altered during the trade to avoid having to make an exit decision.

The stop loss figure might be related to a purely financial calculation. This is a misapplication of the position sizing formulas because the exit figure is related to the conclusion of the calculation and not to the market. In correct position sizing, the exit figure is part of the calculation prices and has an impact on deciding the position size.

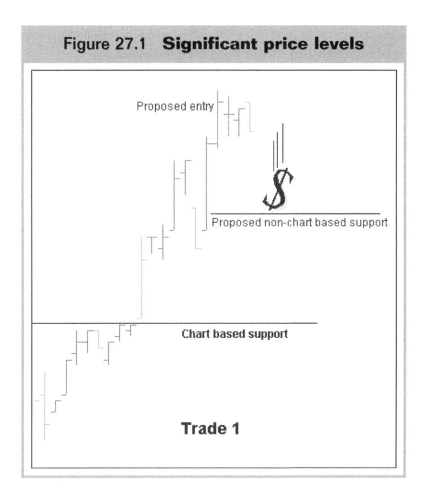

Figure 27.1 **Significant price levels**

No matter which way the non–chart-based stop loss figure is reached, it invariably sits in mid-air when plotted on a chart. The diagram shows the first important point when setting a stop loss. The most effective stop loss is based on a logical chart-based feature, such as an established support level. When prices fall they are most likely to fall quickly to the support level. The speed of this fall makes it very difficult for traders to execute an effective non–chart-based stop loss. It is difficult to capture price as it is falling. It is easier to capture price once it has paused.

This example uses a horizontal support level, but the level is also set using a variety of other methods. These include count back line and 2×Average True Range style calculations which are directly related to the volatility of price behaviour or the value of a moving average. The objective is to identify a price level where prices are most likely to pause, because when they pause we increase our chances of being able to exit at our preferred price.

The first part of the answer to the question of how to set stop losses is related to the way they are set. The second part of the question relates to the tightness of the stop. Many traders feel the stop should be well below their current entry price. They feel uncomfortable if they buy into the stock at $1.00 and have the stop loss set at $0.99. This is most often related to previous experiences where stops were incorrectly set, resulting in false exits from strong trends.

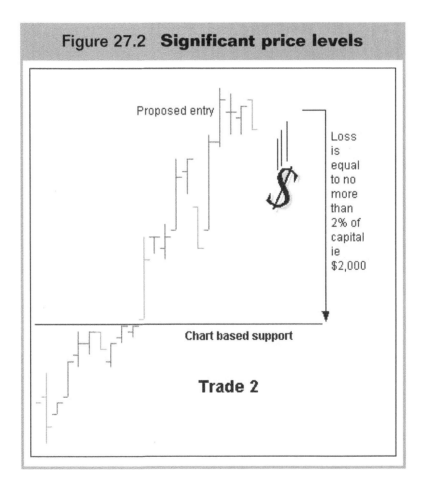

A more objective look at the process of setting accurate stop losses provides a different answer. In trade 2 shown in Figure 27.2 our proposed entry price is well above the support level. If we buy today and prices collapse tomorrow, how far could we expect them to fall? The answer is clear in trade 2. Price is likely to fall as far as the support level. A stop loss set at this level is effective because it is related to past price activity. In trade 2 the stop loss is set well below the proposed entry price.

The distance between the entry price and the logical stop loss price has a significant impact on the position size. It means we cannot buy a large position. The distance from our proposed entry point to the stop loss exit is calculated in dollars. How many dollars would we lose if prices fell to this level? The objective of position sizing is to keep the dollar value equal to or less than the maximum dollar value we can afford to put at risk in any one trade.

We use a standard portfolio capital size of $100,000 and the 2% risk rule. This means the trade puts at risk no more than $2,000. The only way we achieve this is by *reducing* our position size, or the number of shares we buy. If we do not do this, then the non–chart-based financial stop loss calculation may dictate an exit at a higher price with the same consequences as shown in trade 1. The result is our stop loss is too tight and we get out of the trade on a false signal because we cannot afford to lose any more cash. The financially calculated exit signal has no relationship to the character of price action. The further the chart-based stop is away from the proposed entry price, the smaller the permissible position size.

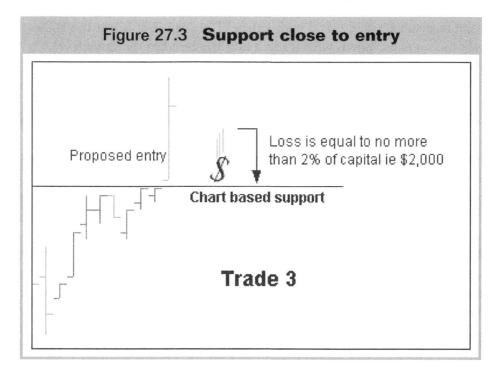

Figure 27.3 **Support close to entry**

Consider the proposed trade 3 in Figure 27.3. The entry price is very close to the stop loss level, perhaps as close as $0.01. Most traders think this stop is too tight because it takes just a very small move before the trader has to exit the trade. This reaction fails to understand the relationship between the stop loss and logical chart-based stop loss points.

The point of entry into the trade has no impact on the positioning of the support level. The support level is independent of our decision to enter the trade. In all these trade examples the support level remains at exactly the same point and we expect support to behave in exactly the same way. It does not matter if prices fall from a great height, as in trade 2, or just a few cents, as in trade 3. When price hits the chart-based support level we expect prices to pause around these levels and provide us with an opportunity to make an exit close to or at our preferred exit price.

In terms of the stop loss position and our reactions to it, there is no difference between trade 2 and trade 3. The only difference is the relationship between our position size and the amount we are prepared to put at risk. With a standard portfolio capital size of $100,000 and the 2% risk rule we put at risk no more than $2,000. We achieve this with a *larger* position size, or number of shares, in trade 3 when compared to the situation in trade 2. The fall from the proposed entry to the stop loss level is just a cent or two in trade 3 so we can increase our position size substantially, and with safety. The stop loss is not too tight. It is exactly the same as shown with trade 2 and triggered at the same level.

An effective chart-based stop loss point allows the trader to take a larger position size for the same level of risk as incurred with a smaller position size when the trade is entered at a higher price. This not only lowers risk but it increases the potential reward as the lower entry price leverages the impact of the developing uptrend.

Stops are set too tight when they do not relate to a logical chart-based support feature. Stops are set too loosely when they ignore chart-based support levels. Stops are set correctly when they accurately identify chart-based support levels where traders know prices have a higher probability of pausing after a price collapse or temporary trend break.

By understanding the nature of a price fall and the probability of support at selected levels we effectively enter a trade with a larger position size and still contain risk. The nature of the stop — too tight or too loose — does not depend on our entry point into the trade because the stop loss level is a function of price behaviour revealed on the chart.

KEEPING IT TIGHT

Despite this logic, some traders remain uncomfortable with entering a trade close to the stop loss level based on chart support. There is still a feeling the stop can be set too close, regardless of the means used to set it.

The key concern is the relationship between the stop loss point and the current volatility of the stock. These concerns go to the heart of the three main methods traders use to set a stop loss. The first method is logical and chart-based, and the second is volatility-based. The third method consists largely of pulling a stop loss point out of mid-air because we think 2% or 5% or 10% sounds like a good figure. Some traders warn against using round figures like $1.00 or $1.10 for setting stop loss points. These warnings fail to take into account how a stop loss is related to price action and not at all related to the wishes of the trader.

The first of the three methods mentioned above is based on an identified chart feature, usually a support level. It may have acted as a resistance level in the past, or it may be a newly developed support level. A breakout from an upward-sloping triangle with Hills Industries (HIL) in Figure 27.4 is a good example of this type of stop calculation. Support is now the old resistance level at $2.75. Any entry above this point uses the support level as a stop loss point. This is sometimes referred to as a natural stop loss point, although my preference is to refer to it as a logical chart-based stop loss point. This point does not shift. It remains in place and it

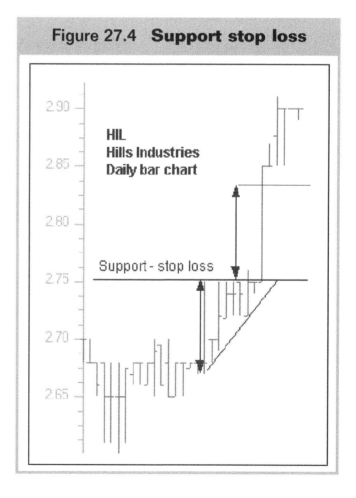

Figure 27.4 **Support stop loss**

HIL
Hills Industries
Daily bar chart

Support - stop loss

indicates an area where traders reasonably expect prices to pause before continuing a downtrend or resuming an uptrend. This pause makes it effective to use as a stop loss point.

REWARD DOES NOT EQUAL RISK

High rewards entail high risk, or so the common investment adage would have us believe. This suggests the upward volatility — the reward — is counterbalanced by an equal level of downward volatility — the risk. The idea suggests that risk and reward are equally balanced, but this is simply incorrect because a range of factors limit the potential downside risk in every trade. High rewards equal high risk only if we do nothing to manage risk. The stop loss solutions based on chart features limit risk and reduce the impact of downside volatility.

The second method of setting a stop loss point is based on volatility. This is more commonly used in short-term trading but it is also applied to longer term timeframes. The intention here is to work entirely with the volatility of the stock. It does not recognise support levels. Traders use an indicator to calculate the average volatility of the stock, and this figure, in cents, is used to set the potential range for prices on the next day.

The chart extract in Figure 27.5 shows a close, and the volatility calculation. The trader enters the trade as shown, and using a volatility-based stop, selects the lower value of the volatility reading as a stop loss

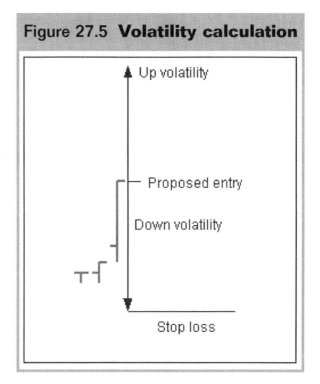

Figure 27.5 **Volatility calculation**

point. A close below this level is an exit signal. He does not expect to have an exit triggered as the volatility calculation defines the expected limits of volatility for the next day. At the end of the next day, the volatility-based stop loss is lifted as a new calculation is completed. The application of these volatility-based stop loss conditions is valid when the trader is chasing a momentum-driven trade because these indicators are consistent with the character of the trading opportunity. This is not always the case with many other types of trades. In these trades, volatility is a feature but its impact is contained by the presence of nearby support levels.

TAMING VOLATILITY RISK

The easiest way to explore the relationship is to look at the relationship in Figure 27.6. We have exaggerated the position of the volatility stop in this example to highlight the issues. The position of the volatility stop loss calculation is well below the chart-based support. The key question we want to answer is this: which is more powerful? The volatility calculation or the support calculation? The answer provides the key to setting tight stop losses in all conditions.

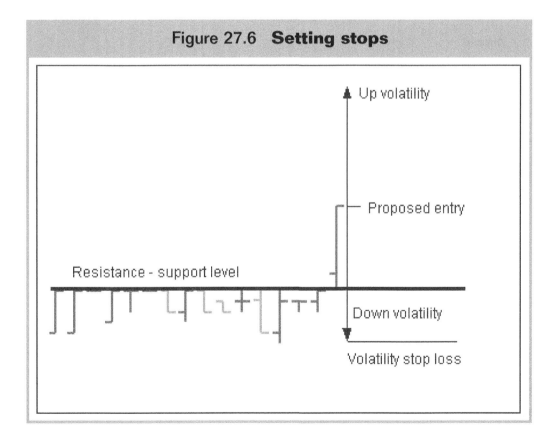

Figure 27.6 **Setting stops**

We start by examining the very strong chart-based support level. The old resistance level has been a dominant feature constraining price action for many days and once the breakout appears above this we reasonably expect the old resistance level to become a very strong support level. Compare this support level with the volatility-based calculation. By the very nature of the volatility calculation, this is a short-term support level. Most volatility calculations are based on 3-, 5-, 15- or perhaps 20-day volatility movements. These define the temporary and transient limits of support. They are important in a momentum-driven trade, but are less significant in a trade with a steady trend or trend continuation.

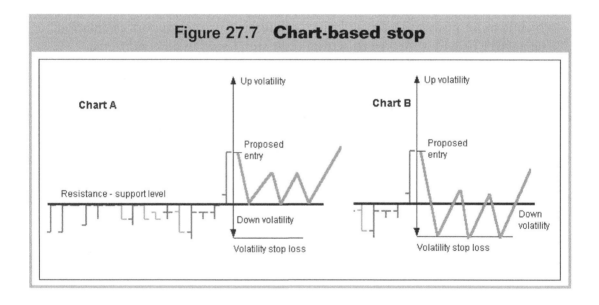

Figure 27.7 **Chart-based stop**

If we enter at the proposed entry point shown in Figure 27.7, what can we expect if prices take a tumble on the next day? The outcomes depend on the dominant feature of price. The risk does not equal the reward. This is where the value of the chart-based support level re-asserts itself. The support level is the dominant long-term feature on the chart extract and it has a dominant influence on price behaviour. It acts as a limit, or dampener, on price volatility calculations. Volatility is contained or limited by the position of the strong support level. The high reward outweighs the low risk.

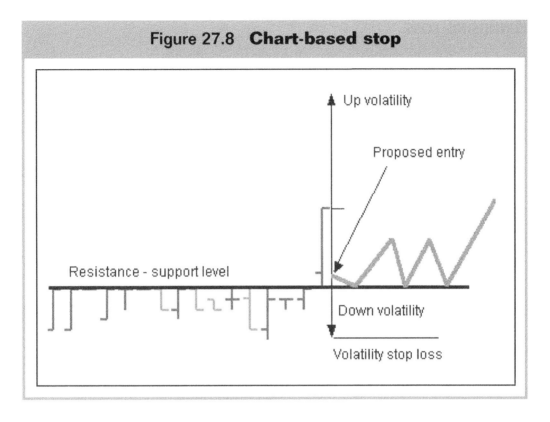

Figure 27.8 Chart-based stop

If prices fall we expect them to bounce off the support level. This price action is shown by the thick line in Figure 27.8. Support is less likely to fail so the volatility limit acts as a reserve support level. When a strong chart-based support level exists prices are unlikely to fall through support and use the volatility-based stop as a rebound point. The psychology of the support and resistance levels suggests these are points where many traders re-enter the market. This long-term behaviour is stronger than the short-term measure of volatility. The dominant feature is the support level, not the volatility limit. When prices fall, they pause at chart-based support and this allows the trader to pursue the same logic as discussed at the beginning of the chapter. In this example the high reward is pursued with a very small degree of risk.

Despite the wide volatility, we still enter at a point close to the support level. We expect any price fall to be arrested by the support level and not continue to the lower volatility extreme. In the battle between support and volatility, support is most often the winner and this knowledge allows us to place tighter and more effective stop loss points whenever we have identified a valid chart-based support level.

MINIMISING LOSS

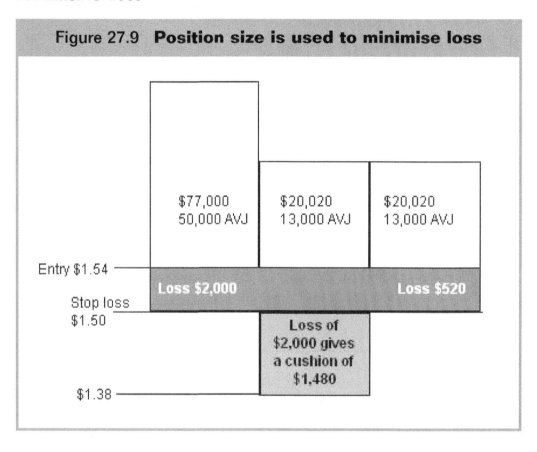

Figure 27.9 **Position size is used to minimise loss**

The advantage of taking an entry close to the stop loss level lies in the way this reduces the risk in the trade. An analysis of a proposed trade with AV Jennings (AVJ) in Figure 27.9 illustrates the impact. Portfolio size is $100,000 with a maximum risk of $2,000. The maximum size trade we could take buys 50,000 shares at a total cost of $77,000. With an entry at $1.54, any price fall to our stop loss at $1.50 triggers a $2,000 loss.

However, we want to limit trade size to $20,000. Spending $20,020 buys 13,000 shares at $1.54. Prices could drop to $1.38 before we incur a $2,000 loss. Our stop loss is set at $1.50. An exit at this level means we lose only $520. Instead of risking 2% of our total trading capital on this trade we risk just over 0.05%. The smaller trade, or position size, makes this a 'safe' trade because if it fails, there is a reduced impact on our trading capital. In the event of a larger than expected price fall that carries prices well below $1.50 there is still a very good chance we can exit with a loss smaller than 2% of our total trading capital. We have a safety cushion of $1,480.

There are many ways to set stop loss conditions and each trader applies his preferred method. Ultimately the success of a stop loss depends as much on the discipline of the trader as it does on setting the stop in the correct position. A correctly positioned stop is triggered less often. When it is triggered, it is a reliable indication the trend has ended and an exit is warranted. No matter how good the stop position is, the success of the stop loss techniques depends on the trader's ability to send a sell order to quickly cut the loss.

These are not the only methods of setting a stop loss but they are the methods we find successful and reliable. We use these as the final test to select the best candidate to trade. We look for a low-risk trade that allows us to trade at our preferred size and limits loss to less than 2% where possible. This is often achieved by entering the trade as close as possible to the stop loss level.

CHAPTER 28

A DANGER TO OURSELVES

When we start trading we tend to think there is a goal or objective to reach, and once reached, we like to believe nothing more is required as we are fully trained. This idea includes some very significant misunderstandings of the relationship between trading and the way our skills develop. More importantly, it ignores the way we develop as traders. An experienced trader is not just someone who knows more than the novice. The experienced trader is a different person from the person he was when he was a novice. As our skills change and our experience accumulates, we change and come to understand that trading is a process and not an objective.

This means solutions appropriate when we were novices are perhaps no longer appropriate as we become experienced traders. The personality changes develop in response to a range of factors. Among the most significant are:

☐ Our trading experience.

☐ We encounter a wider range of non–trading-related experiences which add to our maturity.

☐ Lifestyle changes not related to trading. This might include relationship breakups or experiencing a major trauma such as a car accident or a bushfire.

☐ Our age. Our approach to spending money is different when we are 30 to when we are 60.

When developing our trading strategies we must take into account the way we are changing, and the way the market is changing. It is dangerous to believe the myth that there is a single solution to trading. We readily accept no single 'black box' provides a solution, but we are less willing to accept that the trading solution we were comfortable with at age 40 is no longer appropriate at age 50. Our trading solutions are a combination of several shifting targets and by applying a closer analysis of our assumptions, we improve our trading responses.

The longer you trade the more you come to understand the vital part psychology has to play in your trading success. With our first trade we encounter unbridled fear, and we may also meet greed. Remember those nameless fears in childhood nightmares? When the market eats your hard-earned cash the feeling is the same, but now the fear has form and a partner we call greed. We react in unusual ways and some traders find these experiences so frightening that they leave the market in despair. When we move beyond the initial impact of these emotions we discover other factors which influence our decisions. Experienced traders know success comes from within themselves. Understanding their personal reactions and triggers for their behaviour is just as important as understanding the market. Some traders need to seriously address underlying psychological issues that stop them achieving trading success. These issues are also likely to play a role in their non-trading life. For most traders the issues are less crippling but still significant.

Assuming risk

Recognising repeated self-defeating behaviours, like failing to act on a stop loss, is the first step towards overcoming, changing or neutralising these responses. Ignoring them will not make them go away. Everybody has different psychological reactions in detail, but it is useful to examine some of the broad psychological factors inhibiting trading success.

One of the basic assumptions of trading success suggests that as our skill and experience grow it becomes easier to act with discipline when stop loss conditions are triggered. If we accept the need for a stop loss, then it is easier to move onto the next step, which allows risk to grow in dollar terms as long as it remains at or below 2% of total trading capital. This rule is a valid theoretical relationship, but it ignores the way the dollar value impacts on our ability to act. If the dollar size becomes too large it has a corrosive impact on our trading discipline. The result may mean we start to ignore stop loss points because we feel uncomfortable with the size of the dollar loss.

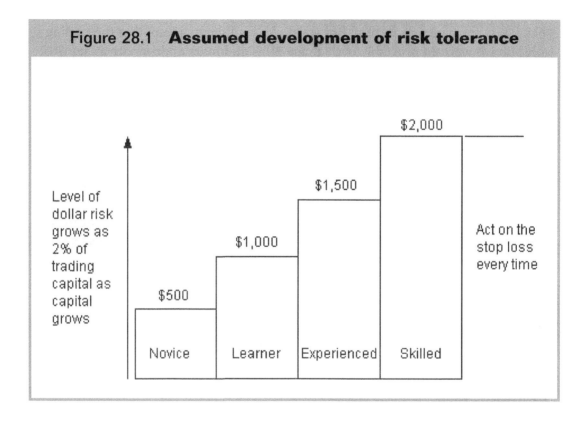

Figure 28.1 **Assumed development of risk tolerance**

The diagram in Figure 28.1 shows four traders. Each represents an individual stage of development we move through as traders. Risk is limited to 2% of total trading capital at each stage, but the dollar size grows. This is just $500 for trader Novice, and although $500 is nearly two-thirds of his weekly wage, he still feels relatively comfortable in crystallising a loss at this size if necessary. When the time comes to act he is not prevented by the size of the dollar loss. It hurts, but it is within acceptable limits.

The size of this loss horrifies those who are contemplating trading from the sidelines. It underlines the prevailing market myths about the danger of the market. Unfortunately those who are terrified by a loss of this size usually do one of three things. Many hand their money to professionals who often go on to lose a great deal more than just $500. This loss is hidden in fees and language describing negative returns. Somehow it does not seem to hurt as much.

Another group reaches for the illusion of expensive protection and purchases an $8,000 trading program. They seem to think that the higher the price, the more exclusive and effective the software. Too timid to face the loss of $500 they soon find their expensive program captures much larger losses as good risk control is often not a feature of these black box systems.

The final response is when a person decides he is an investor, in for the long term, so these painful fluctuations are minor on a 10-year time scale. This is true for investors who are asset income managers, but not true for those whose income depends on capital appreciation. Refusing to count up the losses does not make them disappear.

Trading and effective investment requires a commitment of time and money. There is no escape, but with good strategies you can reduce the cost of market tuition. A $500 loss hurts when you first start trading but it is an unavoidable learning experience.

Trader Learner has made a number of successful trades and grown his capital. He has much more confidence and is able to increase his loss per trade to $1,000. Just as he was when he was trading as a novice, he finds he can tolerate a loss of $1,000. Trader Experienced is also comfortable with a larger loss of $1,500 because he knows it is just 2% of his total trading capital. Trader Skilled has lifted his market performance to the level where $2,000 is an acceptable loss on any single trade.

We assume as our skill and patience grow there is no impediment to increasing the dollar size of the loss on any trade, as long as it remains no more than 2% of our total trading capital. This assumption is often wrong. Despite taking large profits and growing portfolio capital, the trader may not be comfortable taking a loss beyond a certain dollar limit. This reluctance may be due to a whole range of factors not directly related to trading, but this reluctance has a significant impact on his trading success.

A series of losses in the market may make the trader 'gun shy'. Markets change, and traders are not always quick to adapt. Systems that worked in the past may suddenly start to fail. The dollar loss acceptable in one or two losing trades scattered amongst a string of winners is no longer acceptable when losers start to outnumber winners. The usual suggested solution is to reduce position size, but this does not tackle the key psychological barrier preventing the trader from acting on his stop loss conditions.

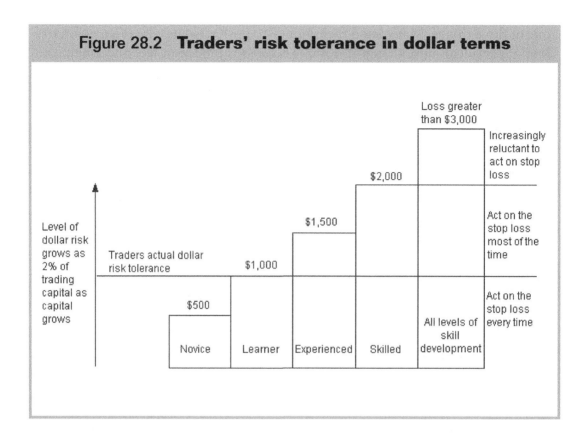

Figure 28.2 **Traders' risk tolerance in dollar terms**

The diagram in Figure 28.2 is a better representation of the relationship between risk, the dollar amount of loss, and the ability of the trader to take action. The acceptable dollar loss generated by the theoretical financial calculation based on portfolio size and the 2% rule is not necessarily the size of the dollar loss acceptable to the trader. In this diagram we show the acceptable dollar loss at $1,000.

What happens as we develop as traders? As a novice with limited capital, our dollar loss is under our $1,000 threshold. Developing discipline is easy. As we move to the Learner stage the acceptable dollar loss matches our tolerance level. This match means we might not even be aware of the role this plays in developing our trading discipline.

When we advance to the Experienced stage the mismatch between our preferred loss and the actual loss generated by our trading system becomes larger. Initially we are protected by our trading discipline developed when the dollar loss was kept at an acceptable level. It hurts much more than it should when we take the $1,500 loss. Our developing skill keeps the losing trades to an acceptable percentage of our performance and some losers are closed for less than a $1,500 loss.

Depending on market conditions, it may take some time before we realise there is a developing problem with our ability to act on stop loss points. One or two larger losses may creep in, even to the extent where the trade has bombed totally. Once the loss grows to $3,000 we freeze at the wheel, unable and unwilling to act. There is no way we take a loss of this magnitude because we simply do not feel comfortable with a loss at this dollar size.

Some of these big-time losing trades may come from stocks where prices gap dramatically below our stop loss point. There are early warning signs but they are too frequently ignored. Instead, when the stock price plummets many traders and investors go looking for excuses to stay with the trade because the size of the dollar loss was so large they found they could not act. We all have a dollar point beyond which we freeze. In the diagram this point is $1,000. In bullish market conditions we expect a fairly high success rate with trades. We may move from an experienced trader to a skilled trader without ever fully realising our growing inability to act once the dollar loss grows beyond $1,000. The clues are there, but we do not want to see them.

The clues include losing trades where the exit has been deferred. It includes one or two trading 'mistakes' where an exit was ignored because we felt we had placed our stops too tight. Inevitably there are times when we feel we are on top of the market so when the market does not behave as our trading plan has anticipated, we decide to hold onto the stock. One of the hidden reasons for this action may be because the dollar loss is greater than our tolerance level, even though it is within the 2% rule limits.

RECOGNISING CHANGE

These contradictions in our behaviour are revealed when circumstances change and it does not have to be a change in the market. Sometimes our tried-and-true trading approaches stop working in the current market. More often, it means we have changed as individuals, usually in response to external factors not related to the market. This affects our ability to act on stop loss points. The pattern of trading may include swift exit action where the stop loss point is less than $1,000 due to an accidental choice of position size or entry point. Combined with this pattern is a number of open, losing positions, where the loss is larger than $2,000 or 2% of total trading capital. Previous good exits made at less than a $1,000 loss obscure the growing problem with delayed exits where losses are greater than $2,000. Initially it is easy to hide the developing impact of these larger losses within the overall portfolio performance. Examine these trades and write down the list of excuses you use to avoid closing the trade. They can be quite interesting.

Unless you have excellent discipline, it is unlikely you will close these trades. However they are a particularly important signal warning of the need to change and re-assess your trading approach. A bullish market may obscure your true dollar tolerance level. A change in personal circumstance may change your dollar tolerance level and make it inappropriate to trade with stops set at these points.

The traditional advice when traders lose touch with the market is to reduce the position size. Instead of trading at $20,000 a trade, the trader trades at $10,000. By spending less in total on each trade, the trader gives himself time to develop and test new trading strategies at a lower cost. This solution is based on the assumption shown in the first diagram. It works if the trader still has the mental discipline and capacity to take a $2,000 loss. It does not work if the true dollar tolerance level is lower, at $1,000.

A better solution is to reduce the risk on each trade, not the size. We do this by scaling back the position size to the level where the dollar risk in each trade matches our dollar tolerance level; $1,000 in this example. This is achieved using the methods discussed in the previous chapter. Reducing position size is the standard solution for traders who find they have lost touch with the market. When combined with a reduction in the actual dollar loss, it is an effective solution. The second solution keeps the same position size, but the entry is closer to the logical chart-based stop loss point.

Reducing the dollar loss to under our tolerance level improves our ability to act on the exit signal. Markets change and we change as traders. We must recognise the psychological changes standing in the way of effective trading discipline. A string of losing trades is a warning sign. A growing portfolio of stocks where stops have been ignored is a clear signal you need to re-examine the level of dollar stop loss appropriate for you at this point in your trading development. The most effective solution is to reduce position size and to reduce the size of the dollar stop loss until you are able to act consistently and confidently when the stop is hit. It is better to start from the bottom, say $500, and work upwards until you hit your particular barrier level, say $1,000.

These psychological factors impact in different ways when we come to trade blue chip or speculative stocks. Handling losses is always difficult and there is some truth in the old market story about how to learn to trade. It suggests you start by dropping a $50 note over the balcony and onto a busy footpath. The objective is to develop the ability to calmly watch a complete stranger pick up this gift. This training continues until you are able to give away hundreds of dollars to complete strangers without getting too emotional. The objective is to develop a tolerance for small losses, so when it comes time to act to take a small loss on a stop loss, you will act.

As traders we change over time, so we are not quite the same person after five years of trading as we were when we first started. Our experiences in the market change the way we approach the market. Our experiences in life also affect the way we understand and participate in the market.

Our inconsistent approach to stop loss points is affected by these long-term changes, and also by immediate environmental events. Our stop loss discipline is always under attack from a multitude of sources. A string of successful profitable trades may encourage us to ignore a stop loss exit signal. We can afford to give some money back. Perversely, a string of trades where stops are hit may encourage us to ignore the next stop because we can no longer stand the pain of these small losses and the continued onslaught against our ability to successfully select a profitable trade.

When we experience profoundly emotional events, it impacts on our trading, even though we may not be consciously aware of it. In 1998, my office, books and research were washed away in the Katherine flood, along with hundreds of other homes. I believed I had coped well with this disaster, but my trading records over the next six months show otherwise. My capacity for risk had changed substantially. Trades I had been comfortable with were now uncomfortable and I found I cut profits short, and let losses run. There was always a different excuse for each disaster.

I keep records of all trades and examine them to establish patterns of destructive and positive behaviour. Within a few months the objective evidence was in my trade records. I could not return to my old levels of risk tolerance, so I had to adjust my trading strategies to take into account my new risk tolerance. Traders who lost friends on September 11, or who went through the Canberra bushfires, or have been involved in a car accident, experience a change in risk tolerance levels. We need to be alert for these changes.

STYLE AND RISK

The 2% rule sets the maximum we can afford to lose on a single trade and assumes the total trading capital is applied to the same type of trading opportunity.

This does not reflect reality because we usually hold a variety of stocks and we use the 'shoe box' approach to separate our holdings. Instead of treating our stocks as part of a single portfolio we split them. Speculative and trading stocks are held in a mental shoe box separate from our blue chip shares.

Let's assume we have $150,000 in total trading capital. The 2% rule says we can afford to lose a maximum of $3,000. This is not a problem if all our trades are simple trend trades which normally last from 4 to 12 weeks. These types of trades are easily identified and managed using just a simple combination of two moving averages. It is not brilliant trading, but it is steady, predictable, consistent trading. Setting a stop loss at $3,000 is a good solution.

Unfortunately very few traders, or investors, use just a single style. There are times when we want to chase a speculative stock, trade a fast-moving momentum trade, apply an overnight gap strategy, or chase a blue chip breakout from a downtrend. We all have several trading styles, and the $3,000 stop loss limit may not be appropriate for each of these styles.

The solutions usually include reducing our position size so the size of the loss is reduced by the time our stop loss is hit. We looked at these position size manipulation approaches in the previous chapter. We simply buy less stock, or we buy closer to the stop loss point, perhaps reducing the potential loss to $1,000. These are good solutions in theory, but they sometimes fall down in practice because at the back of our mind, we know we can 'afford' to lose $3,000. Remember, our tendency is to first deny, and then to lie to ourselves. In the market this means ignoring a stop loss point.

A better solution is found by recognising the sometimes radically different trading approaches we want to take. These fall into broad divisions between position trading and speculative trading. Readers who consider themselves as investors might divide their activity into investing and trading. The important feature is the two activities demand different levels of risk management. The 2% rule is still appropriate, but the dollar value used may not be appropriate to the trading style. A $3,000 loss on a speculative trade is not the equivalent to a $3,000 loss in a slow-moving blue chip stock because the probability of the loss is substantially different. One strategy carries a higher risk of failure than the other.

The diagram in Figure 28.3 shows a useful solution. By splitting the total trading capital into two segments we apply a more appropriate risk level to the different styles of trading. If we allocate $100,000 to position trading or investment the dollar loss is reduced to $2,000. If we allocate $50,000 to speculative trading the dollar risk is reduced to $1,000.

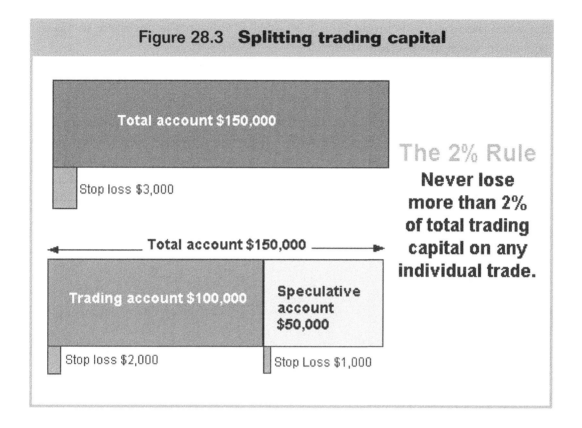

Figure 28.3 **Splitting trading capital**

There is a danger in this split. Some people who make this division consider the speculative account as money they can afford to lose. This is risk money. Instead of limiting risk to 2% of this value — $1,000 — they believe the entire $50,000 is risk money. This reflects the often quoted but dangerously misleading advice, to never use money in the market that you cannot afford to lose. Take this approach with you to the market and, beyond doubt, you will lose all your cash because you simply do not care about it. It is unwise to underestimate the psychological impact of believing you are playing with money you can afford to lose. The same impact occurs when we believe we are playing with the market's money generated by a series of winning trades.

Dividing trading capital into two separate accounts makes it easier to accept the risk on the trade is $2,000 or $1,000. This risk is reduced further by applying the position size and entry modifications. By treating each account as separate it is easier to consider the dollar risk appropriate to each style of trading. In an account where all trade calculations are based on $50,000 we have already mentally accepted $1,000 is the maximum allowable risk. It becomes easier to act when the stop loss is hit and this lower dollar value may contribute to more success in speculative-style trading.

Our psychological changes are often beyond our control. It takes a lifetime to develop behavioural habits, good and bad, and they are very difficult to modify. However, if we recognise our destructive behaviours we can take steps to minimise their impact on our trading. We do not stop the behaviour, we just make sure we limit the damage it causes. If we know we defer our stop loss decision until we reach our maximum dollar loss then there is no point in setting up a trade that asks us to act before this figure is reached because the odds are we will not act. By establishing a separate trading, or speculative, account and basing all stop loss calculations on the smaller account figure we are able to allow our behaviour — let stops run to the maximum dollar loss — to continue without inflicting damage on our total universe of market activity. It helps us get a better perspective on the trade.

CHAPTER 29

NO SECRETS

The nature of this trade example has changed in the time elapsed since the end of the last part. When you realised you had missed a good profit, how did you react? This is the second of three transformations in every trade. The first transformation is when the trade starts to make a profit and the temptation is to take profits quickly. This temptation fights against our more rational inclination to stay with the trade and let the trend develop fully before taking profits.

The second change comes when we miss the best profit available and we regret not acting sooner. At this stage traders construct a range of 'if only' scenarios to retrospectively prove a 2×ATR exit, a MACD indicator, a count back line signal, or just plain guesswork would have delivered a better result than the one they are currently contemplating.

The third transformation comes as prices continue to decline. Traders struggle with how to manage a potential loss to save a trade.

'If only' post-mortem analysis is important. Consistently delayed exits suggest the traders exit planning needs some attention. However we must expect to get out of some trades very close to the top, while others sacrifice a greater proportion of open profit. It is important to stand back from the individual trade result and assess the effectiveness of the exit strategies across a range of similar trades. If, on average, the exit is acceptable then we must expect some very good exits along with some other relatively poor exits.

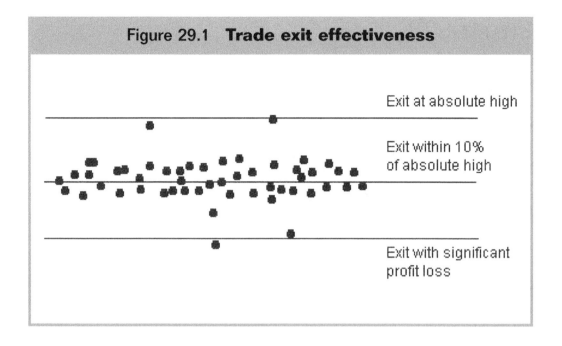

Figure 29.1 **Trade exit effectiveness**

Exit at absolute high

Exit within 10% of absolute high

Exit with significant profit loss

The schematic diagram in Figure 29.1 shows the preferred outcome. Only a few trades exit at the very high of the trend move. The majority of trades should cluster around 10% below the high in planned trend trades. A few of these trades suffer from a significant profit loss due to unexpected events, such as sudden profit downgrades. Note how these trades can fall below the lower line. While there is a cap on how good our exit can be compared with the absolute high, there is no cap on how bad our exit could be. We use a scatter diagram to decide if a poor exit is unusual and acceptable within the context of our normal exits, or if the poor exit is depressingly normal for our trading style.

Some traders use this type of diagram to lift their exit performance to an average of 5% of the absolute high. This type of measure is designed to assess the efficiency of the trading system and is more fully discussed by Le Beau and Lucas in *Computer Analysis of the Futures Market*.

TRADE MANAGEMENT

When the trade first starts we do not have the advantage of knowing how it is going to develop. We made an initial decision about the likely nature of the trade — breakout, rally or trend — and this decision impacts on the way we

318

apply, interpret and use a selected range of indicators. As the trade develops it may turn into something quite different from what we initially imagined. In these circumstances it may be appropriate to change the trading plan, but only in a way that increases our profit capture. The exit hurdle is lifted higher. It is not lowered to take into account falling prices. In this transformation we struggle with how to manage a profit.

In the coming 'No secrets' chart selections we examine the third transformation of the trade — how we manage a potential loss to save a trade.

The objective of the 'No secrets' exercise is to track how readers react in different ways to exactly the same information. The chart and indicator displays in the last 'No secrets' chapter were the most challenging to date, with a 68.75% return available. Those readers who did not snatch the profit showed trading discipline but they end up with a reduced return if they act on the close below the count back line. The results in Figure 29.2 show how readers in the original test behaved, with 32% taking an exit on the close below the count back line. We gave them a 40.63% return — and a free serving of regret.

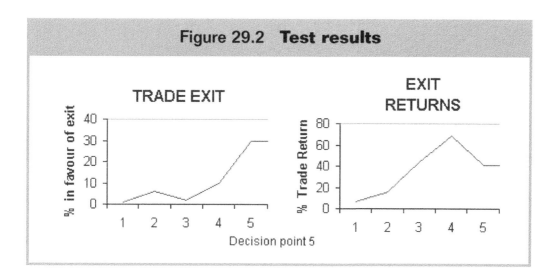

Figure 29.2 **Test results**

When the trade was opened we took an entry consistent with the count back line technique, the Guppy Multiple Moving Average (GMMA), and a moving average crossover. We also included a Relative Strength Indicator and MACD_Histogram display. These are trend trading tools, and although there may be the opportunity to capture unexpectedly quick profits, in general we aim to ride the continuation of the trend until the end of the trend is signalled by a close below the count back line and confirmed with a trend-following indicator. Our preference is to use the GMMA.

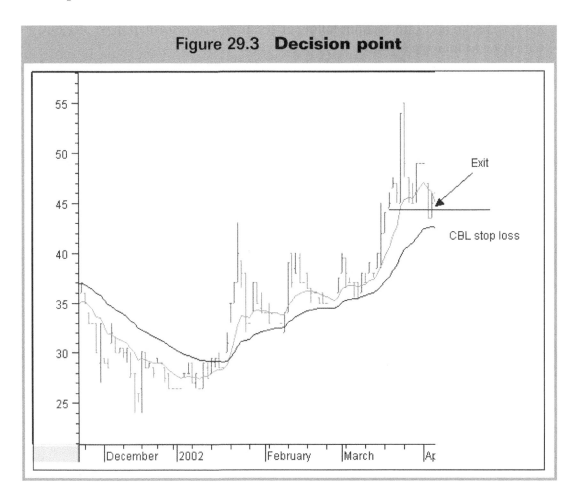

Figure 29.3 **Decision point**

The CBL exit at $0.45 delivers a 40.63% return and a landslide of exit emails from the participants in the original test. This exit is around 28% lower than the maximum return achieved by those who exited at the previous decision point. This decline in profits attacks our trading discipline. When large profits are surrendered it is difficult to make good trading decisions. Greed becomes a powerful force as we start counting the money we could have had if only we had plucked up the courage to exit at the previous decision point instead of waiting for the current exit signal.

OUR ANALYSIS

We know many readers held onto this trade despite the count back line exit signal. The notes below are culled from reader feedback in the original test and they may reflect your reasoning. The later close back above the count back exit line is the main feature keeping them in the trade. This is a legitimate response in some circumstances. When the exit signal with one indicator is counterbalanced by a potential entry signal with another indicator, we may be justified in treating this as a temporary pullback.

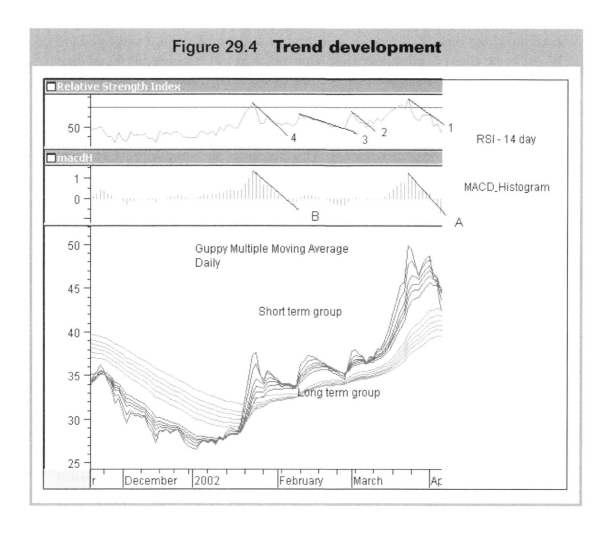

Figure 29.4 Trend development

The RSI in Figure 29.4, reprinted from the end of the previous 'No secrets' chapter, appears to confirm the exit decision. The trend line drawn along the current values shows a clear downward slope. The drop below the overbought zone, as with the previous charts, appears to confirm the general bearishness of the RSI values. Of course trend lines 2, 3 and 4 also show exactly the same relationships. Acting on any one of these took the trader out of the trade before the trend had time to develop.

We have suggested traders should use a combination of indicators to confirm any trading decision, so why not use the RSI for this decision? We believe its value as an indicator is severely diminished because of its level of reliability. Just as a broken watch is right twice a day, so too can a 'broken' indicator be right every now and then. Call bearish exits often enough and at some stage you are bound to be correct and this is what happened here. The successful signal does not indicate the RSI has suddenly become an accurate indicator. It simply tells us coincidences happen in the market, and this is one of them.

To a lesser extent the same applies to the MACD_H indicator. Some original test participants who sent emails noted the strong downtrend on the MACD_H and the move below the zero reference line. This is a classic and valid MACD_H signal and it appears in many textbook examples. Unfortunately the reliability of the signal is diminished when we compare it to exactly the same type of signal shown by trend line B. When trend line B appeared most traders chose to ignore its signal even though other indicators of trend strength — such as the RSI and the narrow band of long-term moving averages — suggested the trend might be in difficulty. We can pick and choose retrospectively, but it is more difficult in real time to decide which MACD_H signal should be acted upon and which should be ignored.

There are many stocks traded very effectively using nothing other than MACD_H or RSI. There are many more stocks where these indicators simply do not provide reliable signals. Careful observation of price history tells you if the indicator is reliable for any selected stock.

Most readers signalled an exit based on the close below the count back line and other features as shown in Figure 29.5. This poses a dilemma for those readers who have not yet made a decision. How long are they going to stay with this trade? The following charts show the next few days of price action, and the way indicators changed. For traders who took an early exit, this price dip provides an enticing entry point in anticipation of a rebound. If their analysis is correct then we should hold onto the trade and ride the rebound to do better than the 40.63% return collected by those who jumped ship based on the charts at the end of the last part.

Figure 29.5 Analysis summary

INDICATORS	STAY IN TRADE	EXIT TRADE
Count back line	Close above CBL on the day after the exit signal. Watch for rebound.	Close below the CBL used as a protect profit stop loss.
Guppy Multiple Moving Average	The long-term group is still well separated. Wait to see if short-term group rebounds from the long-term group.	The long-term group has turned over. The averages are moving downwards. There are early signs of compression.
Moving average crossover	No moving average crossover.	No signal.
RSI	No valid signal.	RSI values are showing a downtrend line and are below the overbought level and heading towards the oversold level.
MACD_H	None applicable.	MACD_H is sloping down. A new down-sloping trend line can be drawn and it reverses the previous uptrend line.
Trend line, support and resistance	Longer trend line still intact.	Long-term trend puts too much profit at risk, so other indicator signals should take precedence.

TEST QUESTION

The chart extracts in Figures 29.6 and 29.7 show the next decision point. Traders who took an exit in the previous week and suggested they would re-enter on a rebound provided some trading plans for this. Most said they would not re-enter the trade until it was able to take out the previous high at $0.55. Others were prepared to enter on evidence of a rebound from the current lows and the most recent chart poses a challenge for them. The RSI and MACD_H may support this decision.

Readers who believed they missed the boat have the opportunity to revisit their decision. They must decide if they will take the best exit possible in the next few days, or hold the trade open in anticipation of better profits.

Based on these charts, please note your reasons for staying with or leaving the trade at the bottom of the following page. In the next 'No secrets' chapter we show how the trade developed from this point.

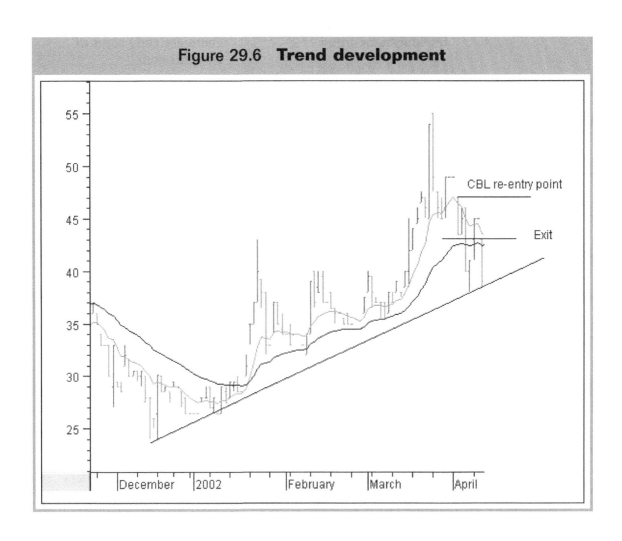

Figure 29.6 **Trend development**

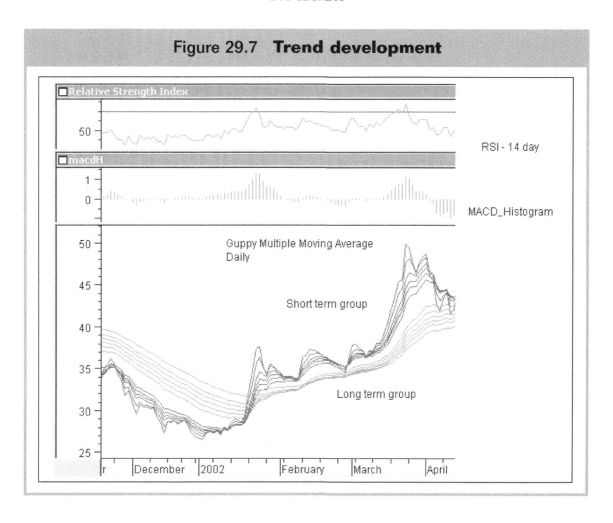

Figure 29.7 **Trend development**

Notes:

_____

_____

_____

_____

_____

_____

PART VII

MODERN DARVAS

CHAPTER 30

BOXING THE TREND

Trend traders are not interested in finding the beginning of a new trend so they leave this problem to breakout and rally traders. Trend traders essentially want to find a strong trend, jump on board, and then get off before the trend ends, or just after it turns into a downtrend. Trend traders make life unnecessarily difficult if they try to anticipate the end of an uptrend. Traders who take a bite out of the trend prefer these trades because they carry less risk. As soon as an uptrend comes to an end, it is difficult to decide when the new trend starts. At best this indecision means capital is trapped in a sideways price movement for an extended period so we stay with the trade. At worst, the uptrend ends quickly, exposing us to much more risk than anticipated.

How do you define a trend? The answer has been the focus many of the previous chapters. The classic answer is based on trend lines, moving averages and the ranging activity of price. A rising trend reflects changing perceptions of value over time and many indicators concentrate on tracking this behaviour in linear fashion. A moving average line may wriggle about but it is still a linear calculation based on the assumption of relatively smooth progress in a single direction. At their most basic, these indicators have a simple rule: if price stays above the indicator or line value, then the trend is upwards.

The Guppy Multiple Moving Average (GMMA) moves away from the classic linear understanding of the trend and it is used to understand the nature and character of the trend. We select stocks on the basis of direction — those moving up — but the GMMA is used to make an assessment about the probability of the trend continuing based on analysis of its strength. The GMMA is a behavioural tool for understanding the activity of traders and investors. Their competitive buying or selling establishes the nature of the trend and we use this information to select the most appropriate trading or investment strategies.

The count back line takes another step away from linear trend interpretations. Used purely by itself, the count back line defines a downtrend by the ability of price to close above a short-term resistance level. This is re-calculated every time there is a new significant bar. This is not a simple calendar-based or linear calculation. It relies on a measure of ranging activity in price and becomes a volatility-based indicator.

In an uptrend, the calculation is reversed. The uptrend is defined by the ability of the price to remain above a trailing stop loss calculation based on changes in the volatility of price. This measure self-adjusts to changes in trend behaviour. The end of the trend is signalled when price overcomes a defined resistance or support barrier. The count back line combines the idea of price change over time and the static concepts of support and resistance as an independent measure of trend activity. This indicator tool is best used in conjunction with other trend analysis tools, trend lines and the GMMA, because it is quite sensitive to trend changes. As shown with bubble trading, the trader and investor may not always wish to act on these subtle trend changes.

IGNORE THE CLASSICS

In this chapter, we discard completely the classic linear analysis of the trend and examine an approach based entirely on dynamic support and resistance concepts. This detour provides a completely different way of identifying, understanding and trading the trend. It is not one of the six tests discussed in previous parts. This is a complete and stand-alone trading approach of Darvas-style trading. It is not combined with straight edge trend lines, with moving averages, with the GMMA or count back line indicators.

Darvas defines an uptrend by constructing a series of imaginary boxes based on a price chart. Each box contains a set of price moves. Each new box sits on top of the previous box like a set of rising stairs. The continuation of a trend is confirmed when price moves above the upper edge of the box. The trend ends when prices close below the bottom of the current box. These upper and lower limits create a Darvas Box and define the acceptable bullish and bearish range of prices. Darvas Boxes provide an important alternative way to understand trend behaviour.

In this part we examine the complete Darvas strategy, and its modifications for modern markets. When we apply a Darvas strategy to a stock it must pass the specific selection tests covered in the following chapters, and they are different from the six selection processes detailed in previous parts. Our starting point, our fishing pool, is defined by stocks making new highs for the selected period. These are easily found in the Saturday edition of the *Australian Financial Review*. Look for the list of stocks that have made new highs for the rolling 12-month period. This is a public fishing spot, but not many traders make full use of this valuable information. You duplicate this information by conducting your own database search, looking for new highs for the selected period. Initial stock selection is based on price behaviour compatibility with the method. Look at the price history. If you had acted on the first Darvas Box plot, would you still be in the trend? If the answer is 'Yes' then this suggests the stock is effectively traded using a Darvas approach. If the answer is 'No' the stock is dropped in favour of those which are compatible with Darvas trading techniques.

Final selection depends on the position of price within the Darvas Box and price leverage. Performance management is built on strict stop loss management directly related to the Darvas Box calculation. This is the foundation of the strategy. The stop loss calculation is inviolable and directly related to the logic underpinning the construction of the box. There is no room to manoeuvre here. There is no arbitrary selection of a percentage-based retracement figure below the box because management is locked into the very structure of the Darvas Box construction.

WHY DARVAS?

Nicholas Darvas was a Hungarian-born dancer who successfully traded the market in the early 1960s. His book *How I made $2,000,000 in the Stock Market* is a classic. It describes a unique approach to understanding the nature of trend behaviour. His book was out of print for many years, although it was sometimes referred to in other market books. In a bull market, publishers search for out-of-print books, buy the rights, and issue them as reprints. This happened to Darvas's book and I read it on the way back from Los Angeles after completing a trading seminar presentation. What he wrote struck a chord in terms of trend trading and volatility.

There is some dispute about how ultimately successful Darvas was as a trader. This is quite irrelevant to the effectiveness of his trading method and I set out to understand his approach before testing it in modern markets. The first step was to clarify some confusing and contradictory sections in Darvas's original book and notes. Then we tested the approach in current markets and developed some modifications consistent with the logic of the Darvas method, but which took into account changes in volatility that characterise modern markets. These included applications to breakout trading using a different set of initiating triggers while applying the basic method. The results are discussed in the next few chapters where we examine our understanding and implementation of this technique in modern markets.

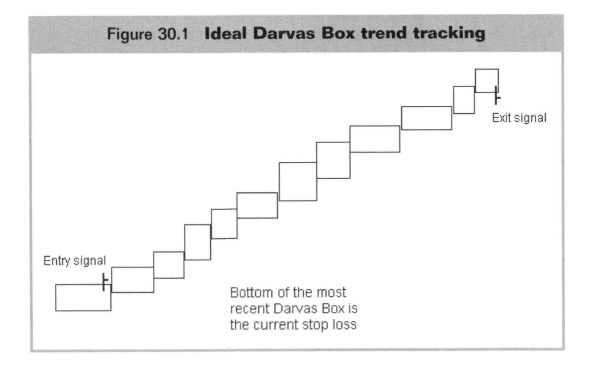

Figure 30.1 Ideal Darvas Box trend tracking

Exit signal

Entry signal

Bottom of the most recent Darvas Box is the current stop loss

The Darvas trading technique provides a useful way to manage longer term trending positions. It is designed as a method of capturing the strength of the trend. The buy signals are generated on new bullish strength and managed by using the six-day volatility range to set a stop loss. The limits of this strength and weakness set the perimeters of the Darvas Box. The bottom of the box is used as a stop loss point. Ideally, as shown in Figure 30.1, the box construction moves steadily upwards with the trend, with a trailing stop loss lagging just behind current price action. Nothing unusual here, but the Darvas approach uses a unique understanding of trend behaviour and is designed for long-term trend trading. It is a bullish approach most suited to trending stocks but it is also applied to breakout markets.

An additional important difference in the approach lies in the way Darvas was able to follow and trade stocks without the need for intra-day prices or even to have access to daily prices. This makes the approach particularly useful for readers who have full-time jobs, or who travel.

There are several charting methods — including Kagi, Renko, 3-line break, and to some extent, point and figure charting — that use various aspects of bullish and bearish behaviour to set breakout conditions and trigger signals for entry and exit. Some of these methods concentrate on tracking just one aspect of price behaviour and ignore other aspects of market sentiment. Others — including point and figure — rely on a somewhat arbitrary setting to define box size and reversal conditions.

The Darvas Box, or D_Box, uses a range-based measure of bullish and bearish sentiment to set the parameters of significant price action. The importance of a price breakout to a new high is confirmed when price overcomes a measure of immediate bullish strength. This combination provides greater certainty about the trend continuation, which is counterbalanced by an immediate measure of bearish strength. A close below this level set by the bottom of the Darvas Box suggests not just an exit from the trade, but a significant decline in trend strength and the potential for a trend collapse.

The unique feature of the Darvas approach is the way it uses a measure of both current bullish and bearish strength to define trend continuation. This means the method is used as a stand-alone approach to the market. Signals are not verified with a GMMA, a count back line or a straight edge trend line. The Darvas approach uses its own internal logic to understand trend behaviour and this leads to some counter-intuitive situations where classic indicators signal a trend exit but the D_Box remains intact. When applying this method traders ignore all other indicator-based signals.

BUY HIGH, SELL HIGHER

Many people believe the only way to make money in the market is to buy low and sell high. This will make money, but it is not the only strategy for success. The buy low and sell high strategy underpins breakout and rally trading strategies. Although it applies generally to a long-term trend trading strategy, it is not the most effective way to approach trend trades, so we prefer to 'buy high and sell higher'. This is the basis of Darvas trend trading objectives.

Buying breakouts to new highs for the year is not always an appealing strategy. We do not like the idea of paying more than necessary for an item — it goes against our instincts to search for a bargain. On a chart it is easy to compare what we have to pay today with what we could have paid a few days, weeks or months ago and we often decide a stock is too expensive.

This intuitive reaction keeps us out of very strong trend trades. Successful traders often find very good returns come from strategies which are counter-intuitive in the market. This does not mean buying a stock at $0.10 because it once traded at $10.00. Going against the crowd is not a very successful strategy when the trend is so strongly downwards.

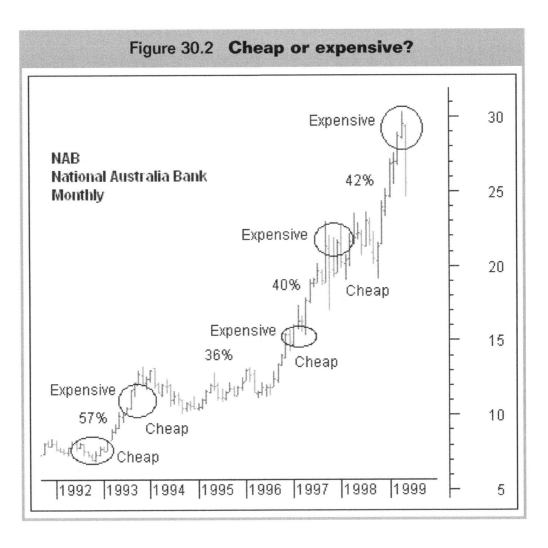

Figure 30.2   **Cheap or expensive?**

Counter-intuitive strategies work against our own intuitive reactions. We look at a stock trading at $11.00 on the chart of National Australia Bank (NAB) in Figure 30.2 and we think it is too expensive. We are right. It is expensive compared to its earlier trading price at $7.00. When NAB trades at $15.00 it is 36% higher than when it was 'expensive' at $11.00. The previous price high now looks cheap. When prices move 40% higher to $21.00 we regret we did not buy when it was trading more cheaply at $15.00. Our concepts of cheap and expensive change when price changes. These concepts of cheap and expensive do not serve us well in trend trading. If we step away from gut reactions and consider the situation more objectively we give ourselves a better chance to work with the market and enjoy the advantages of the trend.

Consider the logic of the rising trend. By definition it is an uptrend because it continues to make new highs. Each new low is higher than the previous low. It is like climbing a set of stairs. We want to take advantage of this continued bullish rise and we do this by applying a strategy based on buying new highs. This does not mean we actively look for the high of the day and try to buy at this price. It means we watch price performance, and when it makes a new high for the year we pay special attention.

A new high for the year means there are many people who believe this stock is good value. They buy at these new prices because they believe the stock is going to be worth a lot more in the future. When the new high for the year is also part of an established uptrend we get particularly interested. This is a very bullish or confident

Figure 30.3 **Price top**

We want to avoid buying here

situation. If we join in buying near the new highs for the year then we join part of an established trend. If we just want to take a bite out of the trend then this is a good strategy to identify strongly trending trades.

The danger in buying new highs is that it might be just a temporary event and this is a strategy for fools, highlighted in Figure 30.3. We buy at the top and it fills our worst nightmares. The price falls the next day, and keeps on falling. The approach developed by Darvas uses the new high as a starting point, and then waits for several confirming conditions to develop before acting on a buy trigger. These confirming conditions create the rules for constructing the Darvas Box. There are three variations to this strategy. We start with the classic Darvas approach, then we consider modern adaptations. Finally we look at Darvas trading applied to downtrend breakout opportunities. The differences, marked by squares, are summarised in Figure 30.4.

Figure 30.4 Darvas trading

CLASSIC

- Trade initiated by a new high for the rolling 12 month period.
- All decisions based on the high or low of the series.
- Action triggered by first trade at the trigger price.
- Method of stop loss calculation remains constant.
- Volume increase with breakout.

MODERN

- Trade initiated by a new high for the rolling 12 or 6 month period.
- All entry decisions based on the high of the series.
- All exit decisions based on the close of the series.
- Entry action triggered by first trade at the trigger price.
- Exit action managed on the day after the trigger close.
- Stop loss calculation uses 'ghost' boxes where necessary to handle modern volatility.

BREAKOUT

- Trade initiated by the second valid Darvas box after initial downtrend breakout.
- All entry decisions based on the high of the series.
- All exit decisions based on the close of the series.
- Entry action triggered by first trade at the trigger price.
- Exit action managed on the day after the trigger close.
- Stop loss calculation uses 'ghost' boxes where necessary to handle modern volatility.

There are five issues we want to consider with modern applications of this technique. They are:

1 The construction rules for the Darvas Box.

2 The classic implementation of a Darvas trading strategy.

3   Stop loss modifications for modern volatile markets.

4   Aggressive entry tactics for mid-trend entries.

5   Using the Darvas Box for trading downtrend breakout trades.

In Darvas-style trading a filter is applied to price movements to help determine which price moves are significant, and which are not. The objective is to determine what is a minor price move, and which is a significant price move. The significant price move is significant because it signals the end of a current trend, triggers a stop loss condition, or tips the balance of probability away from the current trend conditions continuing.

The market Darvas traded was different in another significant feature. Trading volumes were very low when compared with today's trading activity. The volume of weekly trading in the 1960s is now often exceeded by a single day of trading, and we know there are more participants with greater access to current information. The classic Darvas application looked for an increase in volume with a price breakout. Our research indicates this is no longer an important identification or verification feature.

Modern markets are deep and liquid enough for massive and sustainable volume to follow price movements for extended periods. Even in stocks with modest turnover, there is often enough trading activity to make good-sized trades achievable. Increasingly we observe that volume follows price, like a crowd gathering around a school-yard fight. As a result we only consider volume in terms of our ability to purchase the number of shares we require. We ignore volume in its original classic role as a breakout confirmation.

CONSTRUCTION RULES

This chapter ends with a summary of the construction rules and a perfect example of Darvas-style trading. In the next chapter we show in detail how they are applied. The rules are:

☐   The top of the Darvas Box is established when the price does not touch or penetrate a previously set new high for three consecutive days. This is essentially a four-day price pattern.

☐   The top of the Darvas Box always starts with a new high. This high must be followed by three days that have lower highs.

☐   The Darvas Box is based on a minimum of four days of price action.

The bottom of the Darvas Box is only calculated after the top of the Darvas Box has been confirmed. It is constructed in the opposite way to the top of the box:

□ The Darvas Box uses as its starting point the lowest low that occurs *after* the top of the Darvas Box is established.

□ The low is followed by three days of higher lows where the price does not touch or penetrate a previously set calculation low for three consecutive days. It is again a four-day pattern, but the calculation starts with the day the top of the box pattern is confirmed.

□ This means it takes a minimum of four days for a Darvas Box to be identified for both top and bottom.

□ The top of the Darvas Box is established in four days. The bottom of the box may take much longer to establish.

In addition to the filter idea, Darvas also uses stop loss orders and they fill two functions:

□ The first is to protect capital once the trade is opened. Darvas initially places the stop loss level at the exact bottom of the most recent box. This is essentially a volatility-based stop loss because the Darvas Box is built around the expected volatility of price and price ranges.

This sounds complicated, but in reality it is quite a simple concept. The Darvas Box captures the 'normal' range of price activity. A buy signal is generated when prices move outside this upper volatility box. A sell signal is generated when prices drop below the volatility band. When the trade is first entered, we do not know where the bottom of the new volatility band is going to be. As a result we use the bottom of the most recent box as the initial stop loss point.

Darvas does not move his stop loss point upwards until the bottom of the new box is established. This takes up to eight days. The upper level of the new box takes a minimum of four days to establish — a new high followed by three lower days. The bottom of the box may take another four days — a new low followed by three days with lows that are higher than the new low starting point.

□ The second function is to protect a profit once a trade starts to make money. As soon as the bottom of the new box is confirmed it becomes the calculation point for the next stop loss point. The stop loss is set one tick below the bottom of the new box. The exit is taken as soon as the price falls below the bottom of the box.

TRADING THE CLASSIC DARVAS BOX

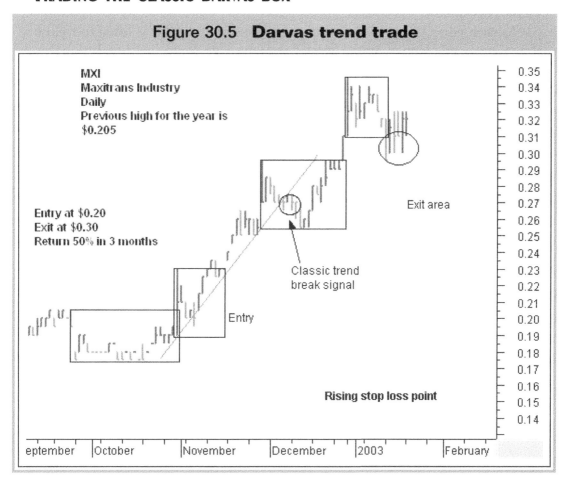

Figure 30.5 Darvas trend trade

MXI
Maxitrans Industry
Daily
Previous high for the year is
$0.205

Entry at $0.20
Exit at $0.30
Return 50% in 3 months

Classic trend
break signal

Exit area

Entry

Rising stop loss point

eptember October November December 2003 February

The chart of Maxitrans (MXI) in Figure 30.5 shows a summary of a classic Darvas trend trade. The buy signal is generated when prices move above the top of the first box on the left of the chart. This intra-day price move may be the high or the close for the day. The signal does not depend on the close being above the top of the box. Any breakout is sufficient, even if the close is at the low of the day. Darvas uses a contingent buy order to buy the stock as it moves above the top of the box and we get into this trade at $0.20.

In addition to the way the box defines bullish and bearish behaviour, Darvas uses stop loss orders. These are central to his approach. The stop loss orders allowed him to continue effective trade management while he was out of contact with the market. Since he was a night-club performer engaged in a global travelling schedule, his ability to manage his open trades by using stop loss orders was vital to his success.

As each new Darvas Box is confirmed, the stop loss level is lifted to follow the rising trend. Notice how a classic straight edge trend line break signal is generated around $0.27. If the trader had applied the usual trend trading strategies, this trade would have been closed when prices dipped below the trend line. The Darvas technique gives no exit signal because there is no price dip below the bottom of the Darvas Box. This highlights the independent, stand-alone characteristics of this trading approach. It is not applied in conjunction with other trend-following indicators.

The exit at $0.30 in this example is triggered by a price dip below the Darvas Box, and returns 50% over a three-month period from the strong uptrend.

The disciplined execution of stop loss orders is at the heart of success for this trading approach. In the next chapter we look in more detail at the construction rules and the application of the Darvas Box, and highlight the significance of the stop loss calculation and placement.

CHAPTER 31

BUILDING A BOX

Buying new highs is a foolish strategy unless we have confirmation the new high is part of a bullish continuation pattern. The Darvas approach creates the confirmation condition by plotting a Darvas Box (D_Box). The Guppy Traders Essentials charting package is one of the few charting programs to automatically plot the Darvas Box. This means most other charting software users must plot the boxes by hand. Fortunately it is not difficult or time-consuming. Even with an automatic tool, it is useful to understand the logic behind the box construction because it re-confirms the absolute necessity of applying the original Darvas stop loss rules.

The search for a valid Darvas Box starts with a new high for the selected period. We use either the results in the *Australian Financial Review* or the results of a database search. The MetaStock formula for this is detailed at the end of the chapter. The classic Darvas approach uses a new 12-month high. This is a good tactic for a strong and established bull market and has a good level of reliability of around 80%. In modern markets we found using a new high for the six-month period also returned good results with an acceptable level of reliability of around 70%, which puts this technique in the select group of very successful trend approaches.

Very aggressive applications of the Darvas technique use a new high for a three-month period. We find this a less-successful application, with reliability shrinking to between 50% and 60%. In strong bear markets the failure rate is much higher as there are generally many more false breakouts in bearish conditions. Our research suggests the early application of the Darvas technique to these bear-market breakouts has a reduced level of reliability. The technique can be used to capture early breakouts and developing trends, but there are many other more effective techniques for trading in these conditions.

SETTING THE TOP

When applying a Darvas approach, traders start with a new high for the selected period. This has the capacity to set the top of the D_Box if the correct conditions are established by subsequent price action.

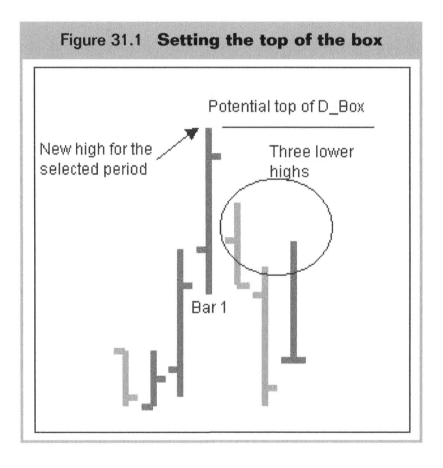

Figure 31.1 **Setting the top of the box**

Setting the top of the box takes exactly four days of price action. The high must be followed by three days of lower highs. This does not mean the highs are all descending highs where each one is lower than the previous high. The deciding factor is the three highs must all be lower than the initial high — bar 1 in Figure 31.1 — that triggered the start of the pattern. In the example shown the first two days show a pattern of descending bars, but the last day in the extract has a high that is higher than the previous day's bar. This is acceptable because the three most recent bars have highs that are all lower than bar 1.

The upper edge of the new box is always a four-day pattern. If one of the three days after bar 1 sets an equal high the calculation is abandoned and a new calculation commences. The new, most recent equal high is used as a new starting point. Alternatively, if one of the three days after bar 1 sets a high that is higher than bar 1, the current D_Box construction is abandoned and the new highest high for the period is used as a starting point for plotting a new D_Box.

The objective is to capture the high for the period and then plot the bullish strength over the next three days. No move is made to start calculating the bottom of the Darvas Box until the top of the box is confirmed. Once the top is verified our attention shifts to plotting the correct placement of the bottom of the box.

SETTING THE BOTTOM

The bottom of the D_Box defines the limits of bearish strength. When the box is completed it captures the bullish and bearish range of price, so breakouts above or below the box limits are particularly significant. This underpins the trend-following and stop loss strategies of the technique.

As soon as the top of the box is confirmed the trader looks for the most recent low occurring after and including bar 1 because this is the starting point for the calculation used to set the bottom of the D_Box. In most cases the lowest bar is below the low of bar 1 as shown in this example in Figure 31.2. The lowest bar is used as the start of the calculation point for setting the bottom of the Darvas Box and is set when the bar is followed by three days of higher lows. The starting point of the calculation captures the limits of bearish strength. After this low the bulls take charge and prices lift steadily.

We do not look for three consecutively higher lows where each low is higher than the low of the previous day. The defining feature is the way subsequent lows are higher than the low of the bar used for the starting point of the calculation of the D_Box bottom. In the example shown, the three bars have lows higher than bar A. The low of the last bar in the series is lower than the low of the previous day. This is acceptable because the lows of the days following bar A are all higher than the low of bar A.

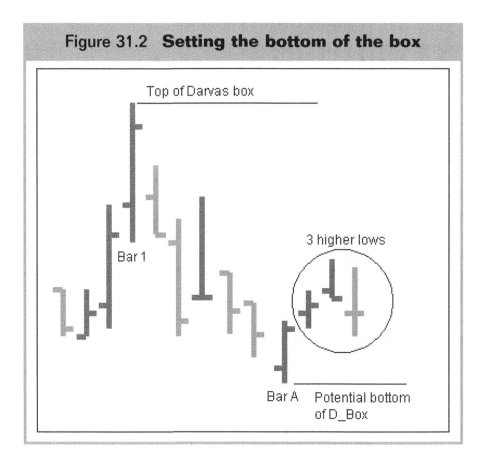

Figure 31.2 **Setting the bottom of the box**

We have used this example because it shows that once the top of the box is set it may take a few more days before we set the bottom of the box. Once the top of the box is set, the bottom of the box does not automatically start from the most recent low, ignoring any further lows. The bottom of the box is only set once the specified conditions have been met. If a new equal or lower low appears within three days of bar A, the current bottom-of-the-box calculation is abandoned and a new calculation starts from the most recent equal or lower low.

The final completed Darvas Box includes a high resistance level based on a single price point high. The low support level also swings off a single price point. These levels define the expected ranging activity of the stock over any given four-day period. This sounds restrictive, but the size of the box is determined by the low of the box. This low may take a week or more to establish. It may be significantly lower than the new high, and provides a considerable range for price activity before any stop loss exits are triggered.

TRICKY BITS AND WARNINGS

Although the D_Box is plotted with relative ease, there are three potential trip points. The first is a hangover from the way we treat equal highs in other indicator applications. The second relates to the application of the automatic Darvas tool. The third resolves a contradiction in some of the notes written by Darvas.

We start with equal highs. Cast your mind back to the discussion of count back lines and the way we treated equal highs. A new high equal to a previous high immediately cancels out any previous calculations. Like many indicators, the count back line uses the most recent new or equal high as the starting point. Not so the Darvas Box once it has been established.

The box starts with the placement of the upper line to define the top of the box and we use the most recent equal high, shown on the left of Figure 31.3, as the starting point. This is the same process used with many other indicator calculations but this changes once the top and the bottom of the Darvas Box have been confirmed. The Darvas Box consists of a resistance line and a support line, and once confirmed they remain in place until they are broken by a move above the resistance line — the top of the box — or a move below the support line — the bottom of the box. Once confirmed, the Darvas Box plot lines are not re-calculated until a break occurs beyond the perimeter of the box.

What happens after the top and the bottom of the box have been set is at the core of the application of the Darvas strategy. The box perimeter sets a trigger level for action. The placement or validity of the box is not affected by days with lows equal to the bottom of the box — as shown by bar X — or by days with highs equal to the top of the box — as shown by bar Y.

Once set, the perimeter of the box remains in place. New equal highs are only important if they appear *before* the top of the box is set and validated. Same with the bottom of the box, where new equal lows are only important if they appear *before* the bottom of the box is confirmed. The situation shown in the chart example does not call for the setting of a new D_Box. They are potential signals for a breakout as both the bulls and the bears test the limits of their previous range. Once the top and bottom of the Darvas Box are set, they remain unchanged until there is a price move beyond the confines of the box.

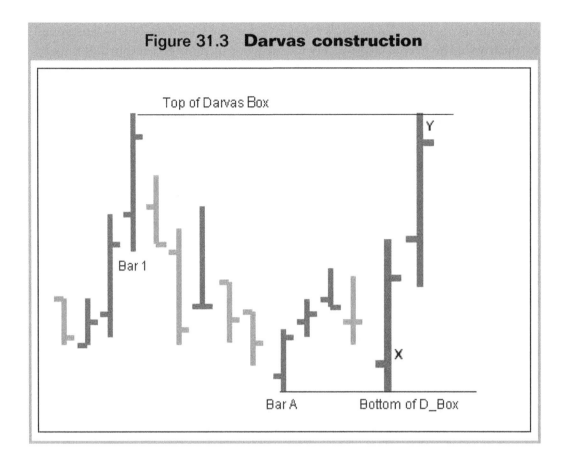

Figure 31.3 **Darvas construction**

Using the automatic Darvas plot calculation tool in the Guppy Traders Essentials charting package makes Darvas trade selection very easy. However, it carries an important warning. Once the tool is selected, it automatically places a box around any series of bars which meets the Darvas construction conditions — and this has one disadvantage.

The chart extract in Figure 31.4 shows two Darvas Boxes, one as a heavy black line, and the other as a thinner line. For clarity, both are shown just outside their calculation points. Both boxes meet the construction rules, but the light box is not a valid D_Box. The reason lies with the starting point for the construction calculation.

The D_Box starts with a new high for the selected period. In the classic application, this is a new high for the year. In some modified applications, this is a new high for a six- or three-month period. The choice is left to the user so the D_Box tool simply completes the calculations from any point selected by the user.

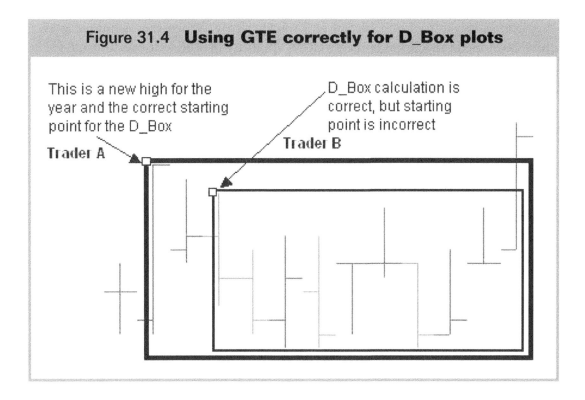

Figure 31.4 **Using GTE correctly for D_Box plots**

This is a new high for the year and the correct starting point for the D_Box

Trader A

D_Box calculation is correct, but starting point is incorrect

Trader B

Trader A has selected a new high for the year as the starting point for his D_Box, and the resulting calculation and plot is correct. Trader B has selected a starting point that is not a new high. His D_Box is structurally correct, but practically incorrect. When using an automatic Darvas tool it is important to select a starting point that is a new high for the chosen period.

SPECIAL CASE

Darvas is at times contradictory in the way he writes about the construction of the box. He appears to allow a special case when the day that sets the new high is followed by a string of inside days. In this special case he uses the initial bar to set both the top and the bottom of the box. Additionally, the pattern developing after a new high may include a range of other chart patterns, including bullish flags, up-sloping triangles, down-sloping triangles and pennants. The Darvas approach ignores these chart pattern developments and concentrates on the signals generated by price activity within, or outside, the box perimeters. The relationship between these boxes provides the basis of Darvas's trade management.

Darvas recognised one special and unusual case. When the technique was first developed the market had a different volatility profile so it was unusual for the starting bar of the calculation — bar 1 — to form both the high of the box and the low of the box. Darvas developed a special rule to deal with this exception. In modern markets we see more examples of this exception. The construction of the box proceeds in the normal fashion, but setting the bottom of the box is slightly different.

We start with a new high for the selected period — call it bar 1. We look for three days of lower highs as shown. The top of the box is plotted. As soon as the top of the box is in place we start looking for the lowest low of the period, starting with and *including* the low created by bar 1.

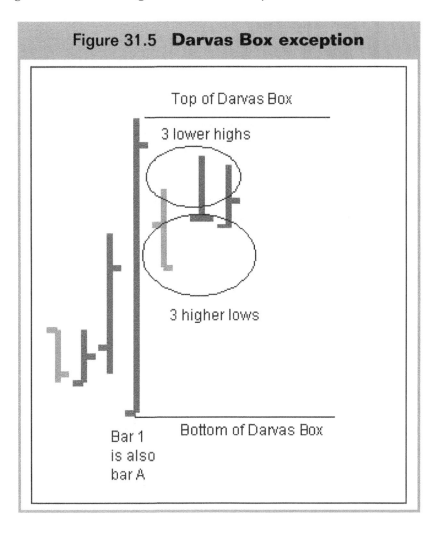

Figure 31.5 Darvas Box exception

In the example shown, bar 1 also has the capacity to become bar A used in the calculation for the bottom of the Darvas Box, where we look for three days of higher lows. We have used an extreme example in Figure 31.5. In this case the first three days of lower highs also show three days of higher lows. Once the top of the D_Box is set and the trader turns to the most recent low he finds bar 1 is also the lowest low for the period. In this case the following three days also show a pattern of lows that are higher than the low of bar 1. In this extreme example the top and the bottom of the box are set simultaneously.

It is not uncommon in today's volatile markets for the initiating bar — bar 1 — to also act as the confirming bar — bar A — for the bottom of the D_Box. What was an exceptional case at the time Darvas was trading is now much less unusual.

BOX LIMITS AND TRIGGERS

The triggers for action using the Darvas technique are set by price moves above the top of the box or below the bottom of the box. A price move above the top of the box is a signal for entry action using the classic Darvas approach. Again, because of modern volatility, we find the reliability of the method is improved if we wait for a close above the top of the D_Box. The default Darvas tool in the Guppy Traders Essentials charting package is programmed for the classic Darvas approach. Users can also select a modern Darvas application.

Two important things happen once we have a price move above the top of the box as shown in Figure 31.6. The first happens immediately and we use the bottom of the box as a stop loss level for the new trade. Aggressive traders act in anticipation of a D_Box breakout. They buy stock once the bottom of the box has been confirmed. They buy in anticipation of a breakout above the top of the D_Box and use the bottom of the D_Box as a stop loss point.

The second feature is a charting convenience. Once the breakout takes place, the Guppy Traders Essentials charting package plots a vertical line at the start and the end of the D_Box. This helps to visually confirm the concept of a 'box' and also reminds the trader this pattern has now been fully completed. Depending on the choice of line thickness, the D_Box vertical sides may obscure the underlying bars. In this extract we show the D_Box as thin lines.

The breakout above the top of the D_Box, by definition, sets a new high for the selected period. Traders immediately start to apply the conditions necessary to set a new D_Box. Once the new high is followed by three lower highs the top of a potential new D_Box is established. Once the bottom of the new D_Box is created the stop loss level is lifted to match the new D_Box. This is the essence of Darvas trade management.

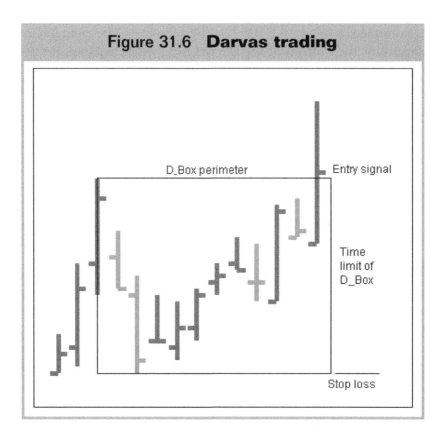

Figure 31.6 **Darvas trading**

The final D_Box configuration in Figure 31.7 is a D_Box failure. This happens when prices close below the bottom of the D_Box and signal an exit as it suggests the prevailing uptrend has come to an end. The classic application of the technique signals an exit as soon as there is a price move below the bottom of the D_Box. Our preference for Darvas in modern markets is to use a close below this level as a signal.

Once the D_Box is established there is no guarantee prices will provide an entry signal by closing above the top of the box. Some prices just continue to drift lower. Once they break below the bottom of the D_Box, the trade is closed or the potential trade is abandoned. No new action is taken until the stock is able to make a new high for the selected period. Once this occurs the trader applies D_Box construction techniques again.

The Darvas trading technique is easy to apply, either using an automated plotting tool or by hand. It provides a useful way to identify trends and to trade breakouts to new highs with a high level of confidence the high is not a blow-off top, but part of a strong bullish trend.

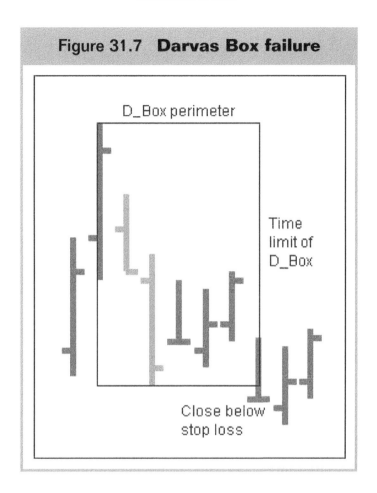

Figure 31.7 **Darvas Box failure**

DARVAS EXPLORATION FOR METASTOCK

This search finds stocks which have made a new 52-week high anytime over the last week. It is run once a week to find all stocks that have made a new 52-week high in the past five trading days.

Col A:	close	(CLOSE)
Col B:	prevH	{Previous 52-week High} Ref(HHV(H,52), -1)
Col C:	curntH	{Current 52-week High}
Col D:	vol	{Volume} V
Col E:	high	(HIGH)
Filter		colE>colB

CHAPTER 32

CLASSIC DARVAS

The classic Darvas trading approach remains a highly successful trend trading technique. We think it is even better after some adjustment to take into account modern volatile markets. In this chapter we examine the classic strategy, and consider some minor changes in the next chapter. We also look at the way aggressive and delayed entry techniques are applied after the initial trade opportunity has been identified.

The classic application of the Darvas technique has two steps. The first is the creation of a valid Darvas Box (D_Box) as soon as possible after a new high for the year is established. The second step is the confirmation signal when price moves above the value of the D_Box.

The classic rules are:

☐ Trade initiated by a new high for the rolling 12-month period.

☐ All decisions are based on the high or low of the price series.

☐ Action is triggered by the first trade above or below the trigger price set by the D_Box.

☐ Action is triggered by intra-day price moves.

☐ Volume increases as price breaks out above the D_Box.

☐ Method of stop loss calculation remains constant.

The chart in Figure 32.1 shows a classic implementation of the Darvas trading strategy to Singapore listed stock, Giant Wire. The stop loss points move smoothly upwards. The entry at $0.15 is an example of modern Darvas trading applied to a breakout situation, and this is discussed in Chapter 34.

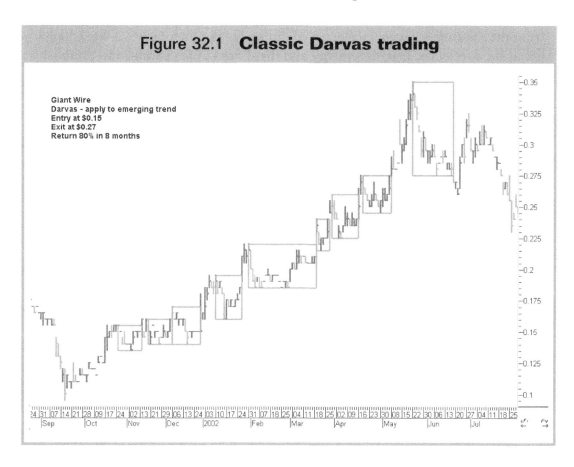

Figure 32.1 **Classic Darvas trading**

Despite the apparent simplicity of the approach, the practical application produces a number of selection and management problems. This is a working chapter so we show how the selection process is used to reduce the initial list of trading candidates to a manageable size. Traders always seem to be plagued by lack of money. We are surrounded by opportunities, but only have enough cash to explore one of them. In the previous test steps we used straight edge trend lines, Guppy Multiple Moving Average relationships and count back line points to weed out the less tradeable stocks. We apply a similar process with Darvas-based trading.

DARVAS TESTS

Our first objective is to find reasons for rejection. This process of elimination is designed to identify the best candidate at the end of the process. We start by scanning the database for stocks that have made a new high for the year some time in the last five days. Alternatively, we use the rolling year records page from the *Australian Financial Review*. Trading breakouts to new 52-week highs lies at the core of the Darvas strategy and these stocks are examined to establish if the new high is a breakout from a valid Darvas Box. The breakout from the D_Box confirms a higher probability of trend continuation.

Our first task is to eliminate those stocks that meet the mathematical conditions but do not meet trading conditions. The eight main reasons for rejections are:

1   Price activity is too erratic so the breakout is less likely to be significant.

2   The high is not really a new high for the year.

3   The high is part of a blow-off top or spike.

4   The high does not follow a valid D_Box.

5   It is prudent to wait for a new D_Box to be confirmed.

6   It is too late. Prices have moved on significantly and we do not want to chase prices further.

7   The stock is not appropriate for D_Box trading.

8   The stock is subject to takeover speculation. The takeover environment overrides pre-existing trend characteristics.

These eight conditions are used to weed out many of the stocks appearing on a database search. The final list might be honed down to perhaps two or three candidates. These are the stocks which require closer attention.

Selecting the best trading candidates is not just a matter of finding a stock that looks good. The selection process is improved if we know what types of stocks and chart conditions to avoid. All the stocks shown below appeared in a list of stocks making new highs for the year, and the notes show why we accept or reject them.

The Aliquot Asset chart in Figure 32.2 shows the classic price spike. This high is driven by a surge of volume in a sleepy stock. This is a rally or momentum-trading opportunity and not part of a genuine substantial long-term trend. The Darvas method is designed to capture the continuation of established trends.

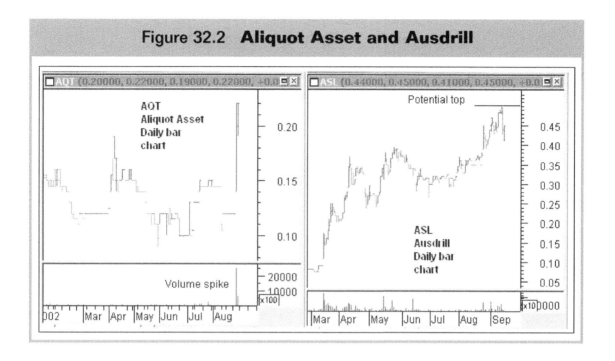

Figure 32.2 **Aliquot Asset and Ausdrill**

The Ausdrill chart in Figure 32.2 shows a new high and a price pullback. The top of a new D_Box could be established if the next day also has a lower high. Many traders prefer to wait for confirmation of this, and then adjust their trading strategy to take advantage of prices nearer the low of the new D_Box.

The Balmoral Group chart in Figure 32.3 highlights two issues with the Darvas scan. The first is related to the search. Not all the new highs for the 52-week period identified in this search are true new highs. The high in the area circled is an equal high for the year. Second, new highs on a chart which shows spotty price activity should be ignored. The volume of trading is very low. Price activity is a response to low liquidity, and not a response to a well-developed trend. Stocks with low trading activity are rejected as the Darvas trading technique does not apply in these situations.

The IWL chart in Figure 32.3 highlights the issue of strong resistance and an incorrect data scan identification. The very strong resistance level at $0.27 dominates this chart and makes it difficult to treat this as a good trend continuation opportunity because there is no pre-existing uptrend. Additionally, the most recent high at $0.27 is not a new high for the year. It is an equal high. A high at $0.28 would be a new high for the year.

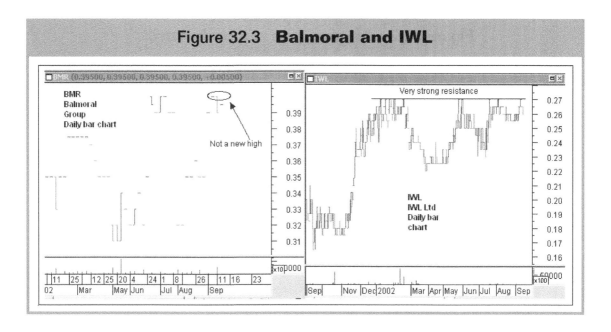

Figure 32.3 **Balmoral and IWL**

The Gunns chart in Figure 32.4 shows a false D_Box breakout. The high is a genuine new 52-week high, and already the top of the new D_Box has been confirmed. The problem is the new high is not a breakout from the most recent valid D_Box. This D_Box was broken on the downside in July. It is not valid to project the top of the D_Box forward into the future and then treat the new 52-week high as a breakout from the previous D_Box. The classic approach calls for the trader to wait until the new D_Box is confirmed and then to either enter in anticipation of a trend continuation or wait for a new D_Box breakout signal.

The Legal Co chart in Figure 32.4 shows a strong trend and a new 52-week high. This chart illustrates the final two reasons for rejecting charts with this type of price pattern. The first reason is the degree to which prices have moved above the most recent D_Box. This is an extreme example. This trend might be strong, but we do not want to chase it. The current price of $1.70 is simply too far above the top of the previous D_Box at $1.03. Equally important, the stop loss for this trade is still set at $0.90 if we use the bottom of the most recent valid D_Box. There are other ways of managing the stop loss in this situation, but the Legal Co chart highlights the problem of chasing runaway prices using classic Darvas methods.

Not all stocks are suitable for trading with Darvas methods. When the gaps between Darvas Boxes are very large or when it is difficult to plot previous

D_Boxes on the chart, it signals the Darvas technique may not be a suitable trading method. Ideally we look for stocks showing a steady uptrend which is compatible with Darvas-style management.

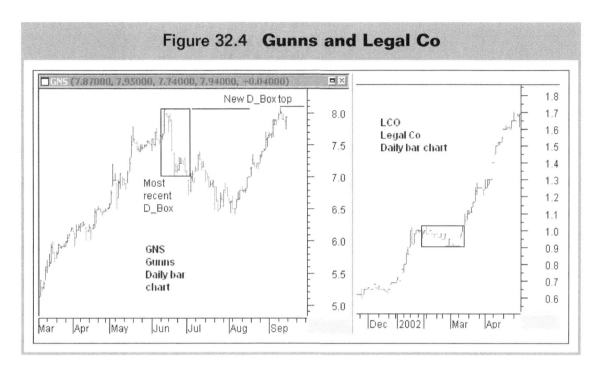

Figure 32.4 **Gunns and Legal Co**

RUNNING THE STOP

One of the appeals of the Darvas trading approach is the rigorous stop loss discipline. In the best of this style of trading, each new stop loss follows the rising trend fairly closely. Ideally each new stop loss point often overlaps the previous box, so the stop loss is ratcheted upwards steadily. This is obviously a very good protection device for open profits.

This rising stop loss relationship may well have been true in US markets in the 1960s and '70s when this method was used. In today's volatile markets this relationship is not as consistent, even in steadily trending stocks like Franked Income Fund (FIF) shown in Figure 32.5. This is both a good example of classic Darvas trading and an indication of the need to adjust the approach for modern markets. Unfortunately, there is no way to avoid the tedious detail when examining this example.

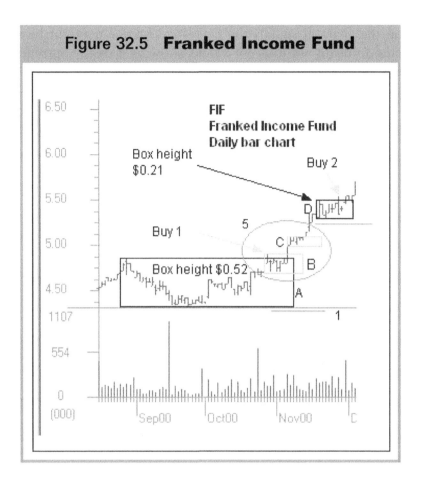

Figure 32.5 **Franked Income Fund**

Once the buy signal is delivered by a breakout above D_Box A, we start looking for the development of new Darvas Boxes. The light boxes at B and C are not genuine as explained in Figure 32.6. Box D is the first genuine new D_Box with the top at $5.51 and the bottom at $5.30. This gives a range of $0.21 with a stop loss exit at $5.29. After the trade entry around $4.85, as shown in Figure 32.5, this stop loss at $5.29 sounds attractive. This locks in a 9% profit in a developing trend.

This attractive result ignores the open nature of risk between the entry point and the next stop loss condition set around six weeks later. At any time in this period the trade is a loser because prices could tumble until they triggered the original Darvas Box stop loss at $4.32. This is a loss of 10.9%.

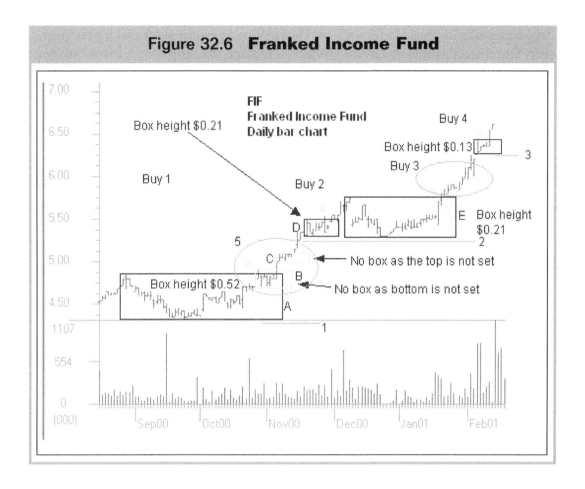

Figure 32.6 **Franked Income Fund**

Within seven days, a new breakout occurs above box D, as shown in Figure 32.6. Prices pull back, and the stop loss level lifts to $5.29, as shown by stop loss line 2. The top of the new Darvas Box, marked E, is established quickly at $5.75. The stop loss for new trades, and for established trades, remains at the bottom of box D. The new D_Box E creates a bullish range expansion where the upper limits are moved upwards, but the stop loss point remains the same. This allows for increased volatility without expanding the risk level significantly for existing trades taken at the first trade entry point. Traders who bought at the second buy point see no increase in downside risk.

This chart shows the way we expect the Darvas Box and stop loss system to work in steady trends. We expect overlapping so the stop loss is always close to current price action. When the third buy signal is generated, there is a considerable upward move in prices before a new Darvas Box is established and a new stop loss set, shown as line 3. Until D_Box F is created the stop loss remains at the level shown by line 2. This represents considerable risk for the first trades started at $4.85. It means trades started at the second and third buy points remain at risk of missing the potential profits because a stop loss would not be triggered until prices pulled back to the stop loss at line 2.

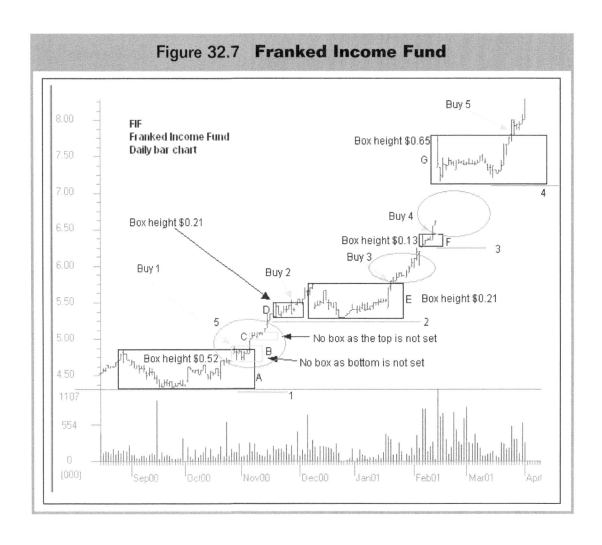

Figure 32.7 **Franked Income Fund**

The box shown as F is $0.13 high in Figure 32.7 and lasts for just the minimum number of days necessary to create the box. On the day the box is confirmed by the third higher low the price action breaks above the top of the box. Once the price moves above the top of the box, the trader places a buy order. This is a rare example where the box is both confirmed and broken on the same day.

The break above box F generates buy signal 4. Very rapidly, price gaps above this. With a few days of price action the new Darvas Box G is created. The advantage of this volatile action is the way a new stop loss point, shown as line 4, is quickly established. The height of the new box is $0.65. The value of the stop loss is $7.14. Prices spend six weeks in this box before breaking out and establishing buy signal 5.

The Darvas trading approach relies on setting buy signals based on new highs. It is well-suited to a bull market where the risk of trend collapse is slightly lower. The FIF action takes place in a bear market environment and the Darvas approach successfully captures these breakouts.

The real concern is the way this approach incorporates significant and unexpected risk factors. These are shown in the circled areas. The risk in these areas is of two types. The first is the increasing risk where price moves upwards but the stop loss point remains in place. This risk is compounded by the time it takes to establish a new Darvas Box, and adjust the stop loss conditions.

The second type of risk is the extended period in the market where the stop loss remains at the same level even though prices are moving to new highs. In nervous markets we may not be comfortable with waiting three to six weeks before adjusting our stop loss conditions. This puts a great deal of the open profit at unnecessary risk.

In the next chapter we look at alternative stop loss techniques using the Darvas methodology and logic to set new stop loss points in the gap period between boxes.

CHAPTER 33

MODERN DARVAS

The Darvas Box and trailing stop approach is designed to keep the trader in a long-term steady trend. In modern volatile markets, this sometimes exposes the trader to an unexpectedly high level of risk created by the way the stop loss level remains unaltered for extended periods in the face of some quite substantial price moves. The increased volatility of modern-day trading has reduced the risk control elements of the Darvas approach which was developed and applied to less volatile markets. We make five modifications to bring this classic approach into modern markets. Each modification is consistent with the underlying logic of the Darvas method. The new rules are shown in bold.

The modern rules are:

☐ **Trade initiated by a new high for the rolling 12- or 6-month period.**

☐ All entry decisions are based on the high of the price series.

☐ **All exit decisions are based on the close of the series.**

☐ Entry action is triggered by the first trade at the trigger price.

☐ **Exit action is managed on the day after the trigger close.**

☐ **Action is triggered by the close.**

☐ **Stop loss calculation uses 'ghost' boxes where necessary to handle modern volatility.**

The Darvas trading approach was developed in the late 1950s and worked in a market where high volatility was unusual. The original approach used the bottom of the most recent D_Box as a stop loss point. The stop loss point was only raised after a new D_Box had been formed. This was a fine strategy in a low-volatility market, so in many of the examples Darvas uses in his book *How I made $2,000,000 in the Stock Market* the D_Boxes overlap each other. The stop loss is lifted upwards on a regular basis and does not lag far behind the current price action.

GHOST BOXES

This is not the case today. Prices often move upwards very quickly in a typical momentum-driven sharp trend. There is no threat to the underlying trend in this action. But the speed of the move is not adequately managed using the Darvas stop loss approach. We use a 'ghost' D_Box to overcome the impact of volatility as illustrated in Figure 33.1.

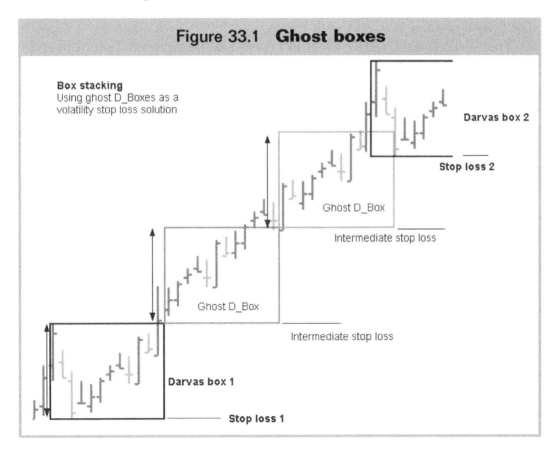

Figure 33.1 **Ghost boxes**

The ghost box uses the height of the last D_Box, measured in cents, to capture the current volatility of the stock. If a new D_Box does not develop quickly then we use a stepped trailing stop loss based on the height of the last box. To understand the reasoning behind using a ghost box we return to the original D_Box calculation, which essentially establishes the three-day bullish range — the top of the box — and the three-day bearish range — the bottom of the box.

Our solution uses the most recent calculation of these combined ranges. This calculation is easily identified by the most recent D_Box. The height of this D_Box is an important guide because it captures the bullish and bearish range. We project this range upwards above the existing D_Box as prices move. We do this by simply duplicating the box, and stacking it on top of the previous valid D_Box. This captures the permissible range of price activity.

The ghost D_Box is activated by a close above the value of the ghost box. The close tells us what the smart money is thinking. It is a useful calculation point that provides a margin of safety when changing the stop loss point. If we stay too close to bullish activity we may get shaken out of the trade too early. The Darvas strategy is to stay with trends.

The Adelaide Bank (ADB) chart in Figure 33.2 illustrates the problem and solution in a developing trade. The trader who purchased ADB at $5.93 based on the D_Box breakout watched price lift to $6.50 and higher without a new D_Box being created. This means the current ADB high of $6.62 still has a trailing stop loss based on the most recent D_Box at $5.87. This puts too much open profit at risk. This trade has clearly moved into a profit, and our stop loss should lift above our entry level so the profit is locked in.

On the chart extract the first ghost box swings into action as soon as the close occurs at point A1. The stop loss level is lifted to the bottom of ghost box A. This retains the same bullish and bearish volatility spread as the original D_Box. Prices still have plenty of room to manoeuvre in a way consistent with the developing trend.

This process is repeated whenever a new close takes prices above the current projected ghost box. On this chart display the most recent ghost box is box E. Ghost box F sets the upper reaches of the next price movement. A close above this level activates ghost box F and lifts the stop loss level again. This process continues until a new valid D_Box is created using the standard construction rules.

These fast-moving trends are characteristic of modern markets and Darvas does not provide a good way to manage the risk if the trend break develops in this way. However, once a new genuine D_Box is established the method provides a good way of monitoring trend activity as stability returns. When the initial

Darvas break signal is given we often cannot tell if the trend break will be slow or rapid. If the trend break does develop rapidly we apply ghost box methods until a new genuine D_Box is created.

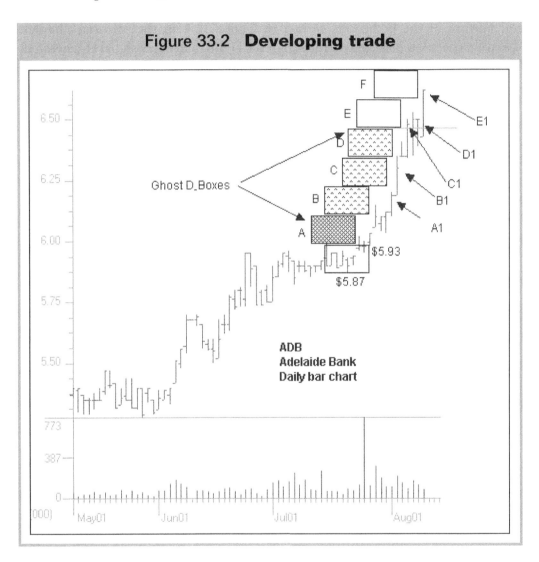

Figure 33.2 **Developing trade**

NERVOUS VOLATILITY

When the market is nervous we apply all trading techniques with caution. This is particularly true with techniques based on bullish breakouts and the continuation of trends. One method of risk reduction is to delay the entry until there is some proof the original signal is valid, or until there is an opportunity to enter the trade at a lower price and so reduce the risk. Entering a trade near the support level is one way to achieve this.

The classic Darvas trading approach rests upon the completion of the top and bottom of the D_Box as shown in Figure 32.1 in the previous chapter. When a trade takes place above the top of the D_Box, an entry signal is generated. In modern markets we use a close above the D_Box as a trigger signal.

The first modification to this classic approach in nervous markets works on anticipating the temporary collapse of the breakout rally. This is modified bargain hunting. It works in one of two ways, but both methods rest on the idea of getting an entry close to the bottom of the D_Box. The objective is, at the very least, to capture the range of bullish action as it develops in the box.

A box $0.02 high in a $0.10 stock offers a 20% return between the bottom and the top of the box, irrespective of any return available from the developing trend if prices break above the top of the box. This is an extension of aggressive techniques applied to D_Box trading in strong bull markets.

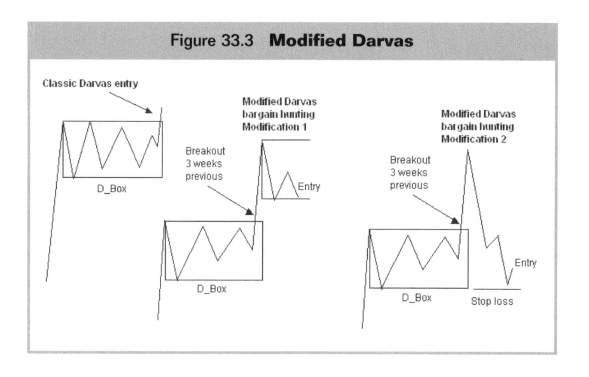

Figure 33.3 **Modified Darvas**

The trader looks for a confirmed breakout some weeks in the past and watches for the development of a new D_Box as shown in Figure 33.3. The objective is to enter as soon as the new D_Box has developed in anticipation that the trend, already verified by the first D_Box breakout, is likely to continue.

In applying classic Darvas trading we look back over the price history to see how applicable and successful the D_Box has been in capturing the trend. This modified entry technique deliberately searches for potential D_Box breakouts in previous weeks, with the objective of taking advantage of new D_Boxes as they form in confirmed trend strength.

The second modification is more appropriate for nervous markets where the D_Boxes are not as widely separated. This captures the gradual development of trends and, in some ways, is more consistent with the market behaviour when Darvas was trading. This creates the situation where there is a series of overlapping D_Boxes, so the stop loss is moved up in steady, small jumps. The objective is not to catch the D_Box breakout, but to wait for a price pullback towards the level of the previous D_Box stop loss. This allows the trader to take advantage of the potential price rebound from the bottom of the box to the top of the box and beyond. It also tightens the stop loss and lowers the risk in the trade.

Both of these modified approaches rely on identifying a pre-existing D_Box. Typically a D_Box takes between one and three weeks to develop, so we want to consider the market as it was three to four weeks before to today's date. We use MetaStock to complete a search on weekly data, looking for new highs for the year with a starting date, in this case, on August 26 as shown in Figure 33.4.

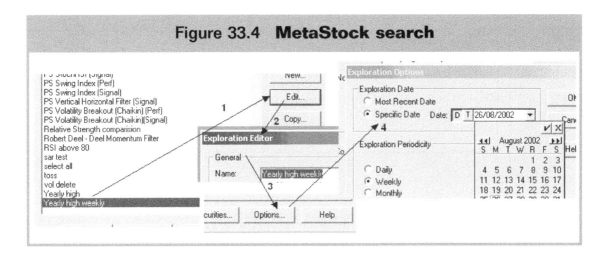

Figure 33.4 **MetaStock search**

Start by opening the EXPLORATION menu and select the search for YEARLY HIGH WEEKLY detailed at the end of the previous chapter. Highlight this and then select the EDIT button. This brings up the EXPLORATION EDITOR. From this sub-screen select the OPTIONS button. The default setting for exploration is the most recent date. We want to start the exploration from a specific date in the past so we select the SPECIFIC DATE option.

Either type the date in the box, or click to show the drop down menu. Select the starting date for the exploration, and make sure PERIODICITY is set to weekly. Click OK and return to the original exploration screen. Run the exploration, and use this as a starting point for further analysis.

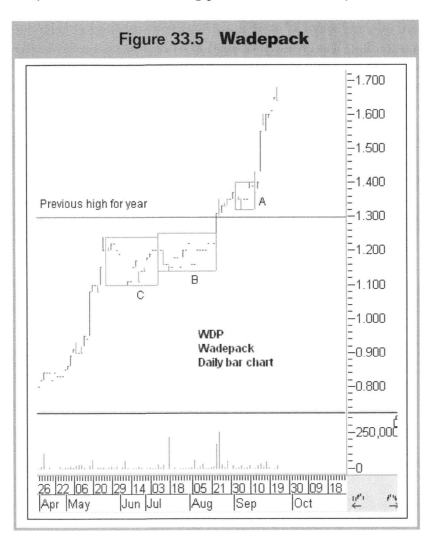

Figure 33.5 Wadepack

An exploration is adjusted to start from a date sometime in the past. This is a useful way of checking the validity of indicators because you see how they have developed after the exploration date. When the exploration is finished make sure to go back through the edit procedures and return the start date to the default setting of the most recent date.

The highs identified in this weekly scan may have been either a breakout from an existing D_Box or have the potential to set a new D_Box. Using the Darvas Box tool in Guppy Traders Essentials we locate the most recent valid D_Box from the high in the week ending August 26.

The Wadepack (WDP) chart in Figure 33.5 shows the disadvantages of this technique. The high for the year was not part of a D_Box development. A few days later a new higher high proved to be the start of a new valid D_Box, shown as box A. The box formed quickly, and the breakout from the box developed into a solid new uptrend. The two D_Boxes shown as box B and C are validly constructed, although they are invalid because they do not start with a new high for the year. However, their ability to effectively define the uptrend adds confidence to the applicability of this technique to this particular stock. Traders who identified the new high in mid-September used these previous D_Boxes as verification the breakout signal from box A was reliable.

HANDLING FAILURE

The Darvas trading technique, like all trading approaches, has its successes and failures. The successful application of the technique also rests upon the way traders are able to handle the times when the technique fails. One of the advantages of using this historical search modification is to establish how the breakouts from the D_Box have performed. In nervous markets we expect prices to pull back. The continuous breakout shown by WDP is unusual. In a bear market, we are often called upon to close trades as stop loss points are hit.

The exit on the Wattyl chart in Figure 33.6 shows our hoped-for orderly exit signal. Note the start of the D_Box covers the underlying bar. This is a classic D_Box, so it is closed when there is a price dip below the bottom of the D_Box. The trader has five days to act on this before prices start to fall more dramatically.

The exit with Schaffer Corp shows a more common exit signal in nervous markets, which tend to gap, and this wreaks havoc with stop loss signals. When the first exit signal is delivered here the trader has to act quickly to cut losses as the next day is likely to be worse. The Darvas technique by itself does not protect traders against trend failure and it does not limit losses. Nervous markets often drop more quickly than we expect.

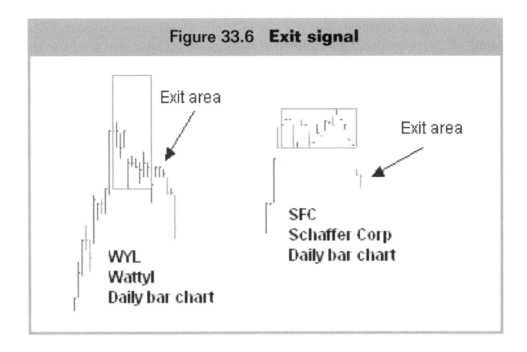

Figure 33.6 **Exit signal**

The solution to managing this volatility is to reduce the potential impact of any loss by shortening the distance between the entry point and the stop loss exit point as illustrated in Figure 33.7.

The analysis of Anvil Mining starts with D_Box B. This box developed after the high identified in the look-back scan starting on August 26. The first feature to note is that the box is based on a new high for the 12-month period. This makes it a valid D_Box and increases the reliability of the breakout signal.

The second feature is the validly constructed D_Box shown as box A. This box meets all the D_Box conditions except the high used as a starting point is not a new high for the year. Despite this, the box helps to verify that the Darvas technique has been successful in capturing the bearish and bullish range of prices and a continuation of the trend. In a bear market we do not expect to see a prolonged series of new highs for the year with a series of validly constructed and plotted D_Boxes. The breakout from each of these boxes is made on increased volume and this is an additional confirming feature traders might apply to any future breakout from the most recent D_Box.

The third feature is the validation of the new D_Box C in the weeks after the starting date for this scan. The top and the bottom of Box C have been confirmed but there is no indication of a break above this box.

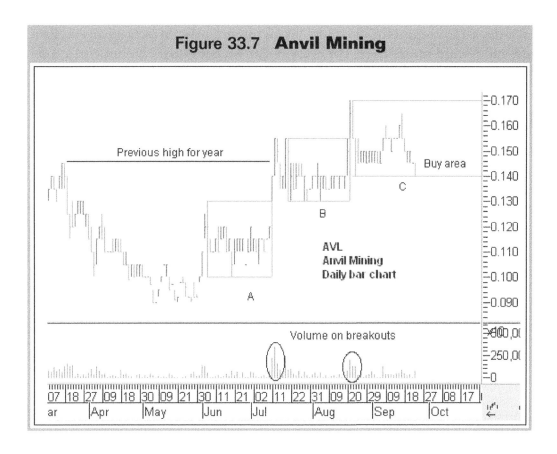

Figure 33.7 **Anvil Mining**

The fourth feature is the history of these D_Boxes. They include a small gap between each stop loss point. As each new D_Box is created it is close to, or overlaps, the previous D_Box so the new stop loss point is quickly lifted to nearer the most recent highs. Unlike the Wadepack example there is no large gap between successive boxes. This pattern of overlapping boxes makes it easier to control the risk in the trade.

Using this information we reduce the risk in the trade by taking an entry at $0.145. This buys 138,000 shares for a total cost of $20,010. Our stop loss is a close below $0.14. This is a tight stop loss based on the defined support level at $0.14. Prices could fall as low as $0.13 before we experience a $2,000 loss, which is 2% of our total trading capital and consistent with the 2% rule. A close below $0.14 may give us the opportunity on the next day to exit at $0.14.

There is an additional advantage in this approach. Our objective is to ride this trade to at least the top of the D_Box, and preferably beyond. We use the top of the D_Box as an initial profit calculation point where an exit at $0.17

provides a 17% return for the trade. Just as importantly, this sets up an excellent risk and reward ratio of 5:1. For every dollar we put at risk, we anticipate a $5 return.

Darvas dividends

Dividends provide four periods of interest to traders. The first is the announcement of the dividend amount. Prices often rise in expectation of the dividend announcement. If the dividend is below expectations then the price tends to fall very rapidly.

The second period is called the cum-dividend period. Although this really extends from the period starting as soon as the stock goes ex-dividend, other traders become aware of their entitlement to a dividend when the half-yearly results are released. This means everyone who holds the shares is entitled to receive the dividend. This tends to keep the price up, because a $10.00 share with a $1.00 dividend is really 'worth' at least $11.00 ($10.00 plus $1.00 dividend). Any shares sold in this cum-dividend period transfer the right to receive the dividend to the new shareholder. The old shareholder loses the right to collect the dividend.

The third period is when the shares go ex-dividend. From this time on, all shares sold do not carry an entitlement to receive the current dividend. The old shareholder retains the right to collect the dividend, even though he has sold the shares, while the new shareholder does not have a right to collect the dividend. Using the example above, we would expect the share price to decline by the value of the 'lost' dividend and fall from $11.00 to $10.00.

The fourth period is the book-closing date. This simply means this is the final date by which all share transaction during the cum-dividend period should be registered. The objective is to make sure everyone who is entitled to the dividend receives it. This book-closing date has no impact on the share price.

At the best of times, dividends cause a re-adjustment in price because the stock is suddenly worth less on the day it goes ex-dividend. Traders who purchase the stock on Monday pay $11.00 and this includes the value of a $1.00 dividend. On Tuesday, when the stock goes ex-dividend it means new buyers are no longer entitled to the $1.00 dividend. If all other factors remain unchanged, the stock is now worth $1.00 less than it was on Monday.

This rational decision is subject to a range of emotional factors. In a very strong bull market this stock might pull back by $0.50 on the day it trades ex-dividend. It does this because traders are more interested in the strong underlying trend. They believe the dividend value which has vanished will soon be replaced by continued price rises.

In a bearish market the value of the stock drops by at least the full value of the dividend, or perhaps even more because traders no longer have confidence the underlying trend is likely to continue. They want to collect profits as quickly as possible in case the trend collapses. This is a silly reaction, and some traders end up selling at a level much lower than the loss of the dividend would suggest. In a bear market many people get very emotional. The best trading strategy in this environment is to lock-in the value of the dividend by selling the stock before it goes ex-dividend.

In a nervous market after a long bear run we often see a much more dramatic result. As soon as the stock goes ex-dividend it is sold down by a much greater value than the dividend. The lost dividend is worth $1.00 but the stock falls by $1.50 and then keeps on falling. This happens because many people believe the company can no longer go on paying dividends at the same level. This fear causes substantial sell-downs, particularly in stocks already locked in long-term downtrends. We see this in poor dividend announcements, in failures to meet earnings forecasts and when stocks go ex-dividend.

These reactions create a dilemma for the Darvas trader. The traditional response when a stock goes ex-dividend is to temporarily move the value of the stop loss down by the value of the lost dividend. This approach is quite different from the way ex-dividend days are handled using Darvas trading techniques.

There is no adjustment to take into account the change in value due to ex-dividend trading. The United Energy (UEL) chart in Figure 33.8 shows an ex-dividend day based on a dividend payout of $0.10. The UEL stop loss set on the bottom of the most recent Darvas Box, at $2.86 as shown, remains unchanged.

The reason for this is consistent with the logic underpinning the construction of the Darvas Box. The D_Box perimeters are set to capture the proven bullish and bearish range of price behaviour. The upper level defines the bullish range of prices. If prices break above this level then it is a signal of bullish strength. The bottom of the current box defines the three-day bearish range of prices. This is as low as the bears have been able to push after the most recent new high was established. Essentially, this defines how far we are prepared to allow any bad news to push down prices. A close below this level tells us there is an increased probability the bears have taken over. It is our exit signal.

When a stock announces a dividend we see an increase in bullish activity. Although the dividend is payable at any time after the stock previously traded ex-dividend the value of the dividend is not confirmed until the next dividend announcement. In this sense, traders and investors become more aware of the additional value based on the current traded price. The result is usually a change in the perceived value, usually by around the value of the dividend. This is not a sudden jump, but rather a steady rise. Sometimes this rise is temporary, and prices slip back to the level of the previous trend. In either case, the dividend leads to an increase in bullish sentiment as investors become aware they are about to receive something extra.

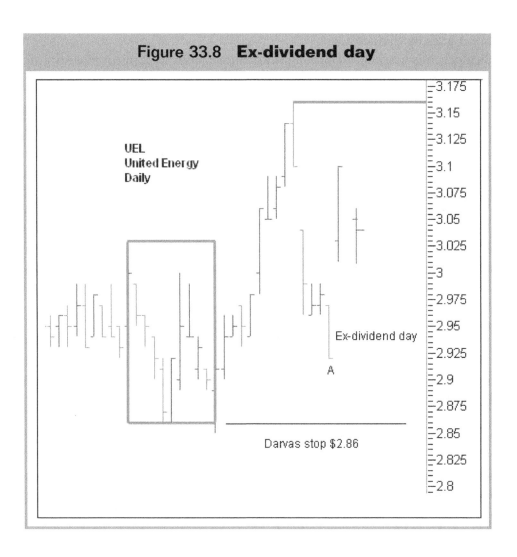

Figure 33.8 **Ex-dividend day**

There is no corresponding increase in bearish sentiment, and until the stock goes ex-dividend, the bulls have the upper hand. This may be strong enough to underpin a breakout to a new high, and sometimes leads to the development of an entirely new Darvas Box. With UEL, the lead up to the ex-dividend day resulted in a breakout to new highs and an increase in bullish sentiment.

When the stock goes ex-dividend we expect an increase in bearish sentiment — after all traders have just lost $0.10. However, this price retreat should be consistent with the previously defined limits of bearish behaviour so the decline should not be able to drop prices below the established D_Box level. Using the UEL example, this means prices do not close below $2.86. While prices remain above this level it confirms that the underlying trending activity remains well-supported. The decline establishes a new, adjusted, stop loss level based on three higher lows following the low shown by bar A on the chart.

With minor adjustments consistent with the logic underpinning the classic Darvas approach, this technique is fine-tuned to meet modern volatile market conditions. It does not get traders in at the very start of the trend nor does it get them out near the very top of the trend. It is designed to identify bullish strength, and then to exit when the bullish strength declines. Inevitably the trader is restricted to taking a bite, and sometimes a very good bite, out of a strong trend. Inevitably there are traders who wish to apply this approach to stocks beginning to trend upwards even though they have not made new highs for the year. These applications of Darvas techniques to breakout trends reduce the reliability of the approach, but they still provide a useful way of understanding trend behaviour. We show how they are applied in the next chapter.

CHAPTER 34

PLAYING WITH
THE EDGE

The classic Darvas trading technique is well-suited to bull markets. It is less suited to markets which have taken a temporary shock and which offer many downtrend reversal entry opportunities. The Darvas technique is modified to trade in these environments. With further modification, the approach is also applied to young bull markets. This is not true breakout trading, but it helps the trader to identify strong young trends. The base modern rules remain the same, but we add another, shown in bold. The breakout rules are:

☐ **Trade initiated by the second valid D_Box after the initial downtrend breakout.**

☐ All entry decisions are based on the high of the price series.

☐ All exit decisions are based on the close of the series.

☐ Entry action is triggered by the first trade at the trigger price.

☐ Exit action is managed on the day after the trigger close. Action is triggered by the close.

☐ Stop loss calculation uses 'ghost' boxes where necessary to handle modern volatility.

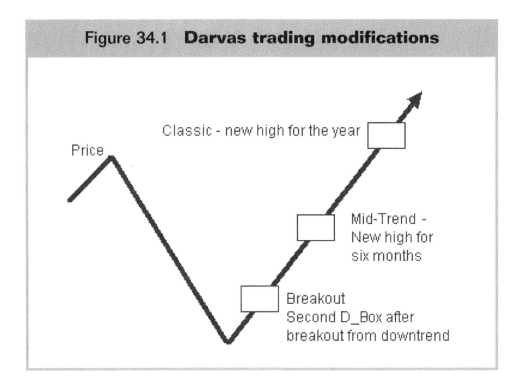

Figure 34.1 **Darvas trading modifications**

The techniques discussed in this chapter are an aggressive application of Darvas trading and they are illustrated in Figure 34.1. The Darvas technique is not designed to work with breakout trading. Darvas trading is based on new 12-month strength and bullish breakouts. As discussed below, we successfully modify this using six-month highs as a starting point. Once we move into smaller timeframes and apply the technique to breakouts, reliability is reduced.

If we apply Darvas to a breakout we are unlikely to get into the trade close to the point of the breakout. Instead we look for an entry point where there is greater confirmation the new breakout is likely to turn into a trend. The Darvas method is not applied until the breakout has been signalled, perhaps by a price and volume surge. We use the high of this initial rally to set the top of the first Darvas Box and then we set the bottom using the classic rules. The alert signal does not come until prices break above the initial high of the first box. The trade in Figure 34.2, with Singapore-listed Amtek, shows a successful application of this breakout trading.

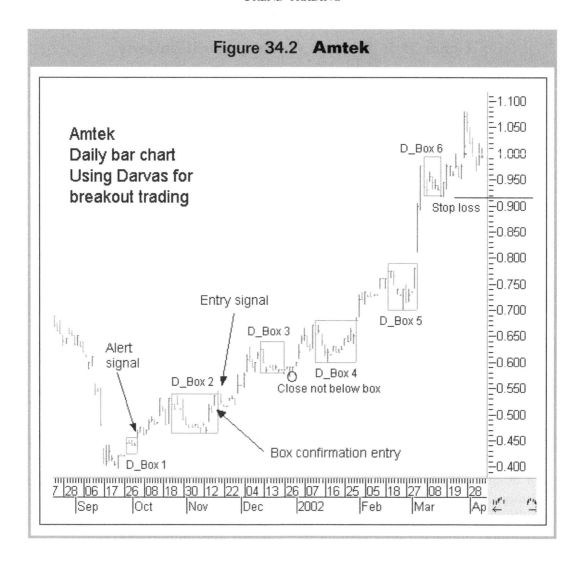

Figure 34.2 **Amtek**

Amtek
Daily bar chart
Using Darvas for
breakout trading

D_Box 6

Stop loss

Entry signal

Alert
signal

D_Box 3

D_Box 5

D_Box 2

D_Box 4

Close not below box

Box confirmation entry

D_Box 1

As soon as the top and bottom of the second Darvas box are confirmed, aggressive traders use this D_Box breakout signal as an early entry into new uptrends. Although the trader is conservative in waiting for the second D_Box, he is aggressive when it is confirmed, buying stock in anticipation of a trend continuation. Instead of waiting for price to close above D_Box 2, the trader buys stock as prices slip towards the confirmed bottom of D_Box 2. This allows greater participation in the developing trend.

Conservative traders prefer to wait for the breakout signal from the second D_Box as this increases their confidence in the stability of the new trend. The bottom of the second D_Box is now the stop loss point and there is a better probability of any price fall finding some nearby support. This makes it easier to implement the stop loss strategy.

The Darvas technique is not designed for trend break trading. It can be applied, but it is not successful in all cases. It works very well when uptrends do continue, and the technique provides a useful stop loss strategy. It does not provide a useful technique if the trend break slips into a prolonged sideways pattern. The Darvas approach is applied to trending stocks, but it does not in itself confirm the stock will trend after the trend break.

MID-TREND MODIFICATIONS

The classic Darvas trading technique is well-suited to bull markets. It is less suited to markets which have taken a temporary shock. The Darvas technique is modified to trade in these environments. The first of these modifications is the mid-trend entry point. This aggressive trading is often based on a six-month high. Although the classic Darvas trading technique does not swing into operation until a new high for the year is made, the logical basis of the technique also identifies other trading opportunities. In the classic application, Darvas is a bullish approach, buying new highs as stocks trend upwards. It identifies the opportunity and the strength of the developing trend by establishing the six-day bullish and bearish volatility.

If we think of the D_Box as a volatility box we can explore the opportunities. Once the D_Box is correctly plotted the aggressive trend trader has multiple entry opportunities available within the boundaries of the box. He enters this trade in anticipation of the breakout above the top of the D_Box.

On the chart extract in Figure 34.3 the D_Box width stretches from $0.70 to $0.85. Once the top and bottom of the box are confirmed and while prices remain above $0.70, the assumption is the trend is intact. For traders who wish to join the trend this confirmed volatility box is a potential entry point. By selecting an entry point close to the value of the bottom of the box, the trader has an advantage if the trend continues to develop.

For traders who entered after the breakout signal from the previous D_Box, the confirmation of the most recent D_Box is important. It allows them to set a stop loss condition designed to protect their profits. A tight stop loss based on an entry at $0.71 uses the bottom of the D_Box at $0.70. Conservative traders considering a mid-trend entry wait for prices to move above the top of the D_Box. They enter as close to this breakout level as possible, or they may also have the opportunity to enter at slightly better prices on any minor retreat. The breakout captures the growth in bullish sentiment so many times the entry is made at higher prices.

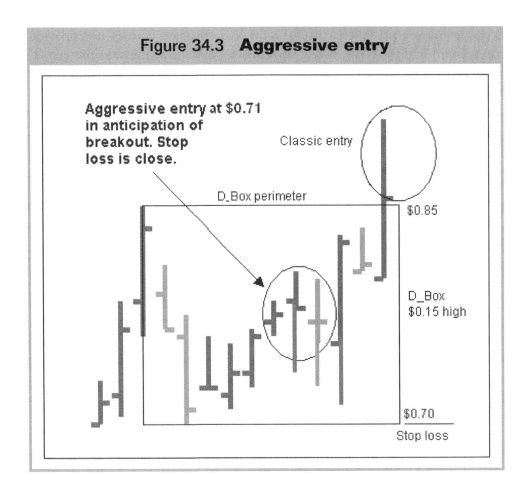

Figure 34.3 **Aggressive entry**

Once the break above the box occurs the stop loss remains set at the bottom of the D_Box at $0.70 until a new D_Box is confirmed. This is consistent with the classic Darvas application. Applying Darvas techniques to mid-trend situations carries a higher risk of failure than the classic application. The boxes still capture the range of bullish and bearish activity, but they do not have the added feature of capturing new bullish strength as shown by a breakout to new highs for the year. The probability of success is increased when the volatility box is associated with bullish confidence. Despite this lowering of probability, this technique is usefully applied in mid-trend situations where it is used only as a volatility measure.

The classic Darvas approach is a good example of the way trading techniques are applied and modified as markets change. As traders, we need to understand no single technique produces a perfect, or even a very good, solution to all trading situations. Success comes from the way we adapt and modify existing techniques to take into account new market behaviours. Markets do not stand still and we are constantly challenged to adapt, or get washed out of the market.

Darvas is not a detour. This approach represents an entirely different way of understanding trend behaviour and is consistent with our broad objective of entering a trend after it is established and leaving it as soon as there are signs of trend weakness. There is more than one way to take a healthy bite out of the trend.

CHAPTER 35

TECHNICAL DARVAS

Chapter contributed by Matthew Ford and originally published in Tutorials in Applied Technical Analysis.

The tool for plotting automatic Darvas Boxes is included in the Guppy Traders Essentials charting package. A classic Darvas expert can be created in MetaStock, and these detailed notes take readers through all the construction and application steps. MetaStock is very sensitive to spacing and layout errors. If you wish to apply these formulas we suggest you download them for free from www.guppytraders.com.

The first formula is 'Darvas High' which identifies new period highs followed by three lower highs.

Name of Indicator: **Darvas High**
Formula:
Periods:=100; {this is the only place the number of periods is set}
If((Ref(H,-3) ≻ Ref(HHV(H,Periods),-4))
    AND Ref(H,-3) >Ref(H,-2)
    AND Ref(H,-3) >Ref(H,-1)
    AND Ref(H,-3) >H,
  Ref(H,-3), PREVIOUS);

Notes: Negative references are used otherwise the indicator will not extend to the last day of the chart. Periods are a constant. We have not used an input statement because the formula is referenced by other formulas, and when that happens MetaStock only uses the default value of the input. Hence the user's input is ignored. Also, you do not usually plot this indicator.

Name of Indicator: **New Darvas High**
Formula:
dh:= Fml("Darvas High");
def:=IsDefined(dh) AND IsDefined(Ref(dh,-2));
(def AND Ref(def,-1)=0) + (dh AND Ref(dh,-1)<dh);

Notes: (dh AND Ref(dh,-1)<dh) gives a spike whenever a new Darvas High is found. The Ref(HHV(H,Periods),-4)) in the Darvas High formula cannot be calculated until (Periods + 4) data points from the beginning of the loaded data. The (def AND Ref(def,-1)=0) adds a spike one period after the Darvas High indicator can be calculated at the beginning of the plot. As illustrated later, the construction of the Darvas Box depends on these spikes.

Name of Indicator: **New Darvas Low**
Formula:
dh:= Fml("Darvas High");
ndl:=(Ref(L,-3) <Ref(L,-2) AND Ref(L,-3) <Ref(L,-1)
AND Ref(L,-3) <L AND Ref(H,-2) <dh
AND Ref(H,-1) <dh AND H <dh);
def:=IsDefined(dh) AND IsDefined(Ref(dh,-1));
(def AND Ref(def,-1)=0)+ (ndl AND (Ref(ndl,-1) <1))

Notes: This produces a spike each time a new Darvas low is found. In order to be a new Darvas Low, the low must be followed by three higher lows. The highs of these following three bars must be less than the current Darvas High. If there is a new high then the box is broken before it is completed. A spike is also added at the beginning of this plot.

Name of Indicator: **Darvas Low**
Formula:
If(Fml("New Darvas Low") , Ref(L,-3), PREVIOUS);

Notes: This indicator plots the latest Darvas Low. It moves up and down as new Darvas Lows are found.

Name of Indicator: **Darvas Box End**
Formula:
end:=BarsSince(Fml("New Darvas High")) <
    BarsSince(Ref(Fml("New Darvas Low"),-1));
def:=IsDefined(end) AND IsUndefined(Ref(end,-1));
(def AND Ref(def,-1)=0)+ (end AND Fml("New Darvas Low"))

Notes: This produces a spike for the first New Darvas Low that follows a New Darvas High. It also adds a spike at the beginning of the plot.
We are now in a position to plot the High and Low of the Darvas Box.

Name of Indicator: **Darvas Box High**
Formula:
dbe:=Fml("Darvas Box End");
dbhi:=If(dbe AND IsDefined(Ref(dbe,-1)), Fml("Darvas High"), PREVIOUS);
If(dbhi=0,H+0.0000001,dbhi)

Notes: Each time we find a Darvas Box End we update this plot to the current Darvas High. Before the first box is formed we just plot a line a little above the High of each bar. The IsDefined suppresses the effect of the initial Darvas Box End introduced above.

Name of Indicator: **Darvas Box Low**
Formula:
dbe:=Fml("Darvas Box End");
bl:=If(dbe AND IsDefined(Ref(dbe,-1)), Fml("Darvas Low"), PREVIOUS);
If(bl=0,L-0.0000001,bl)

Notes: Each time we find a Darvas Box End we update this plot to the current Darvas Low. Before the first box is formed we just run a line a little below the low of each bar.

Next we need to develop the Sell Indicator. First we look for possible sell signals.

Name of Indicator: **Darvas Poss Sell**
Formula:
dsl:=L <Fml("Darvas Box Low");
def:=IsDefined(dsl) AND IsDefined(Ref(dsl,-1));
(def AND Ref(def,-1)=0)+(dsl AND (Ref(dsl,-1)<dsl))

Notes: Since the classic Darvas Box is set by a price low, we use a price bar low below the Darvas Box Low as a possible sell. This formula produces a spike for each possible sell and a spike at the beginning of the indicator.

A Darvas Sell is the first Darvas Possible Sell after the formation of a valid Darvas Box. The next formula plots this.

Name of Indicator: **Darvas Sell**
Formula:
sell:=BarsSince(Fml("Darvas Box End")) <
BarsSince(Fml("Darvas Poss Sell"));
def:=IsDefined(sell) AND IsDefined(Ref(sell,-1));
((def AND Ref(def,-1)=0) + (sell = 0 AND Ref(sell,-1)=1))

Notes: Here we produce a spike when sell goes from 1 to 0. The spike in Darvas Possible Sell at the beginning of the plot is essential to the correct calculation of this formula. A beginning spike is also introduced here for Buy below.

Once we know the Sell points we can find the Buy points. In classic Darvas a buy is signalled by price high exceeding the Darvas Box High of the first valid Darvas Box formed after a Sell. In the modified modern version applied to more volatile markets we require a close above the Darvas Box High.

385

Name of Indicator: **Darvas Buy**
Formula:
dc:= Fml("darvas sell");
{ change the following line to H≥Fml("Darvas Box Hi") .. for Classic Darvas }
db:= C≥Fml("Darvas Box Hi") AND
**   (BarsSince(Fml("darvas box end")) <BarsSince(Fml("darvas sell")));**
dto:=If(db AND PREVIOUS=0,1,If(dc,0,PREVIOUS));
dto AND (Ref(dto,-1) =0)

Notes: dc is a Darvas Sell signal, db is a Darvas Possible Buy signal and dto is a Darvas Trade Open indicator. dto AND (Ref(dto,-1) =0) gives a Buy signal (spike) on start of trade open indicator. Subsequent possible buy signals are then ignored until the trade is closed by a sell signal.

Using these formulas it is simple to create a new MetaStock Expert Advisor for Darvas. Create a New advisor, call it Darvas and fill in the following tabs:

For the Trends tab I used the somewhat arbitrary:

Bullish   C ≥ Fml("Darvas Box Low");
Bearish   C <Fml("Darvas Box Low");

For Symbols tab use:

Buy: up arrow graphic, formula Fml("Darvas Buy")
Sell: down arrow graphic, formula Fml("Darvas Sell")

For Alerts tab use:

Buy: formula Fml("Darvas Buy") and some suitable text message such as
"buy on next open"
Sell: formula Fml("Darvas Sell") and some suitable text message such as
"sell on next open"

You can edit one of MetaStock's existing Expert Advisors to see what a completed advisor should look like.

Figure 35.1 shows the Darvas Expert Advisor using the modern modification of only buying on a close above the box. I have added the indicators Darvas Box High — upper thin line — and Darvas Box Low — lower thin line — to this chart. Remember these indicators only move up after a valid Darvas Box has been formed. The actual Darvas bBox is drawn to the left, by hand, as shown by the thick black box.

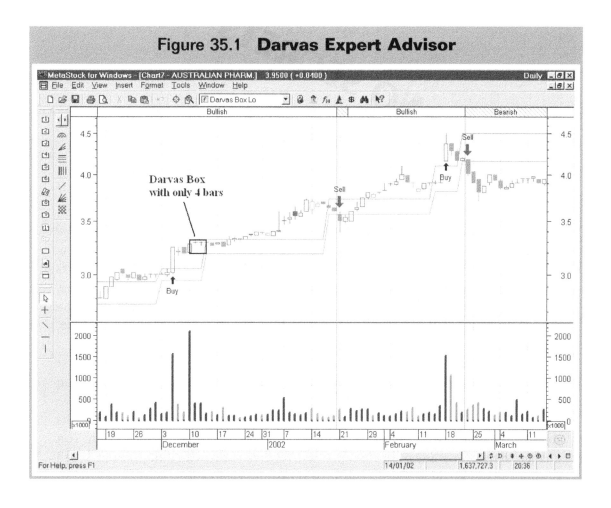

Figure 35.1 **Darvas Expert Advisor**

CHAPTER 36

NO SECRETS

Hope is a very strong driving force and perhaps this explains why so few readers in the original newsletter test took an exit based on the charts at the end of the last 'No secrets' chapter. Many people abandoned this trade, as shown by the chart, but there are many traders who held onto the trade. Are you one of them? A few jumped ship, but most stayed with the trade, apparently encouraged by the chart indicators.

Hope is the third transformation of our approach to a trade. The first transformation is when the trade starts to make a profit and brings the temptation to take quick profits. The second transformation is regret. It arrives when we realise we have missed the best profits available. The third transformation turns the losing trade into a potential winner based on hope. We believe there is a chance to recover some of the lost profits. We give readers an exit point at $0.43 during the week which gives a 34.38% return on the trade.

Only a handful of traders in the original test took this exit at this point, as shown in Figure 36.1. Why? The answer goes to the very heart of trading. A 34.38% return is very acceptable in any market conditions. Traders who have already taken an exit in this trade conclude the indicator combinations prove the trend has ended. They congratulate themselves on their exit decision.

Traders who still hold the trade look at the same charts and indicators and decide they show the beginnings of a new uptrend or rebound. They congratulate themselves on their decision to stay with the trade. They believe they can do at least as well as previous exits, and probably better.

Figure 36.1 **Actual test results**

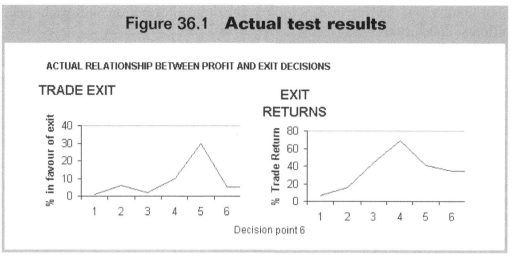

ACTUAL RELATIONSHIP BETWEEN PROFIT AND EXIT DECISIONS

TRADE EXIT

EXIT RETURNS

Decision point 6

It is an interesting rationalisation. They know how high prices managed to go in the past, in this case to $0.55. Armed with this knowledge, they believe they can manage a better exit near $0.54 and capture a very good return from the trade. They remain in the trade because they hope for recovery. They stay with the trade because they believe they can get an exit near the old highs because they feel they are now prepared to take the necessary action.

It is not our objective in these notes to provide traders with a definitive exit answer — at this stage.

Figure 36.2 **Expected test results**

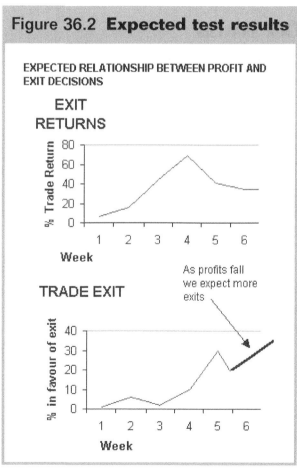

EXPECTED RELATIONSHIP BETWEEN PROFIT AND EXIT DECISIONS

EXIT RETURNS

TRADE EXIT

As profits fall we expect more exits

Our interest is in the way traders look at the same information and reach quite different conclusions.

The charts in Figure 36.1 track the returns from the trade, and the number of readers in the original test who indicated an exit. As returns peaked we see an increase in the number of traders who take an exit. As returns decline we see a decrease in exit decisions. This is counter-intuitive. We expect to see the number of exit decisions increase once the returns from the trade start to diminish. The results in Figure 36.1 should look like Figure 36.2, as more recent price action confirms the trend has ended. Rationality suggests people should abandon the sinking ship quickly. Instead the low number of exit emails from participants suggests many traders are clinging to the sides of this sinking ship hoping it will refloat, or rescue will arrive. The failure to exit as profit falls means traders are managing a losing trade rather than a winning trade.

OUR ANALYSIS

We have two groups of traders. Those who sold already want confirmation this was the correct decision. They want the indicators to prove they have made the right decision. The other group uses the same indicators to prove the trend is going to rebound — perhaps just enough to get out at a higher profit. In the notes and tables below we show how each group uses the indicator to reach quite different conclusions.

The count back line exit conditions are clear in Figure 36.3, reprinted from the previous 'No secrets' chapter. Prices are still well below the count back line which is now used as an entry calculation for the developing downtrend. Traders cannot use this count back line as a sign of trend recovery, but those holding onto the trade look for evidence prices can close above this level.

It takes just a little effort to adjust the straight edge trend line to confirm the long-term trend and treat the two price dips as a rebound from this line. The new line touches the major lows and is consistently applied. Traders who want an excuse to stay with the trade use this analysis to confirm the possibility of a rebound.

Rebounds require increased short-term activity and this means subsequent rebounds start from a higher point. Additionally, the height of the rebounds should be higher than the previous rebound. This is evidence the short-term traders are gaining momentum.

Figure 36.4 shows the relationships using a diagram of a Guppy Multiple Moving Average (GMMA) display. The important detail is the way the short-term averages behave when they rebound away from the long-term group of averages. The upper diagram shows a strong rebound, which suggests the uptrend is likely

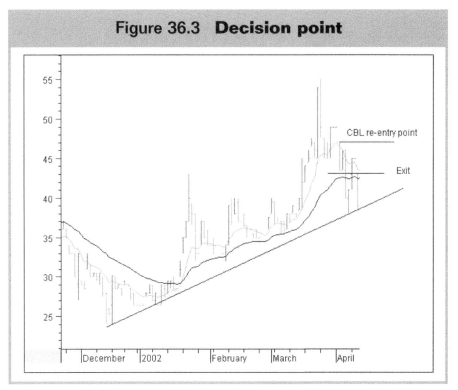

Figure 36.3 **Decision point**

to continue. The bottom of rebound point C is higher than rebound point A. Additionally, the peak of the second rebound, point D, is higher than the first rebound at point B. This is a bullish relationship showing short-term traders are regaining momentum.

The lower chart shows the bearish relationship. The rebound point C is lower than the initial rebound point A penetration into the long-term group of averages. Additionally, rebound D is not as high as rebound B. Short-term traders are unable to convince themselves of a rebound trend and selling intensifies, dragging the long-term group of averages with them.

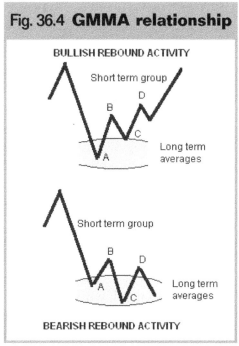

Fig. 36.4 **GMMA relationship**

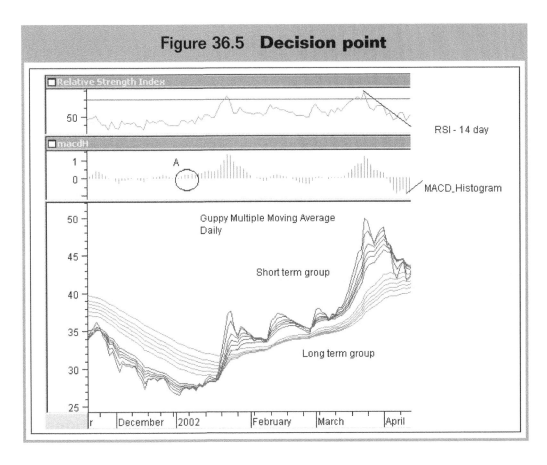

Figure 36.5 **Decision point**

The indicators are used to support each view. The GMMA is applied with subtlety as illustrated in Figure 36.5, reprinted from the end of the previous chapter. Traders who did not act on the count back line signal because the GMMA still signalled a strong trend carefully examined the relationships in the short-term group of averages. They wanted evidence the short-term traders were gaining momentum in any rebound. The relationships shown at this stage of the chart development do not confirm this momentum and so confirm the exit signal.

Traders hoping and holding onto stock focus on the separation in the long-term group in the GMMA display. This is still widely spread and the move towards compression has stopped. They use this as evidence the trend is still intact.

Drawing straight edge trend lines on the Relative Strength Indicator (RSI) is not a useful way to use this indicator. Despite this, the hopeful trader uses the breakout from a downtrend line on the RSI to boost his hope of trend recovery. Others note it is below the overbought area and so generates no buy signal. The most reliable use of the RSI is for its divergence signals.

The MACD_Histogram is open to manipulation by hopeful traders looking for an excuse to avoid action. They see a flattening of the MACD_Histogram and interpret this as a precursor to the development of a new uptrend. They project the line as shown on Figure 36.5. This is a valid projection as the line joins the slightly rising histogram bars. A third bar consistent with this trend is needed for confirmation. The trend line plot is correct, but this type of trend line analysis with the MACD_Histogram is less useful. Experienced traders note the start of this significant uptrend was not signalled by the MACD_Histogram in area A. If the MACD_Histogram fails to pick up this major trend change then it is unreasonable to expect it to pick up any new trend change.

Figure 36.6 Analysis summary

INDICATORS	STAY IN TRADE	EXIT TRADE
Count back line	New CBL entry line at $0.47. A close above this confirms a new uptrend.	Prices still below the CBL entry line.
Guppy Multiple Moving Average	The long-term group is still well-separated. Wait to see if short-term group rebounds from the long-term group.	The long-term group has stabilised, but the short-term group is dipping even lower into the long-term group. This suggests trend weakness. The rebound failures in the short-term group confirm trend weakness.
Moving average crossover	No moving average crossover.	No signal.
RSI	The RSI is above the downtrend defined by the straight edge trend line. Potential new RSI uptrend.	RSI value is below the overbought level.
MACD_H	MACD_H has stabilised. Watch for uptrend to develop.	MACD_H is below zero reference line.
Trend line, support and resistance	Replotting the trend line to take into account the new lows shows the long-term trend is intact.	Adjusted long-term trend puts too much profit at risk, so other indicator signals should take precedence.

TEST QUESTION

Readers who have not yet made an exit decision now face a dilemma. How long are you going to stay with this trade? The next few days of price action, and the way indicators changed, are shown in Figures 36.7 and 36.8.

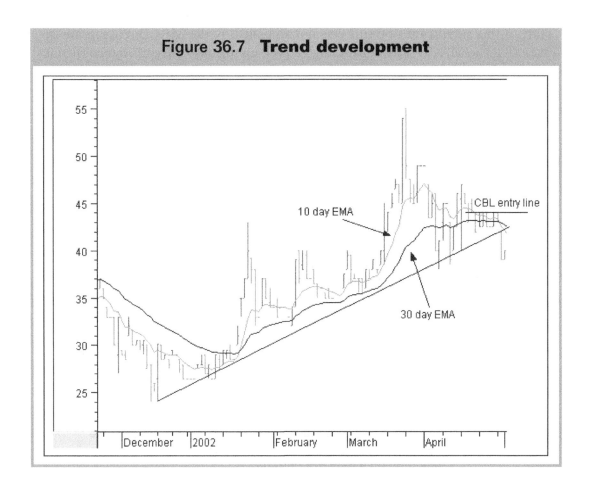

Figure 36.7 Trend development

Stay with the trade, or jump? This is the question for you to answer before turning to the concluding discussion in the next 'No secrets' chapter. Note the reasons for your decision at the bottom of the following page and compare them with our analysis at the end of the next part.

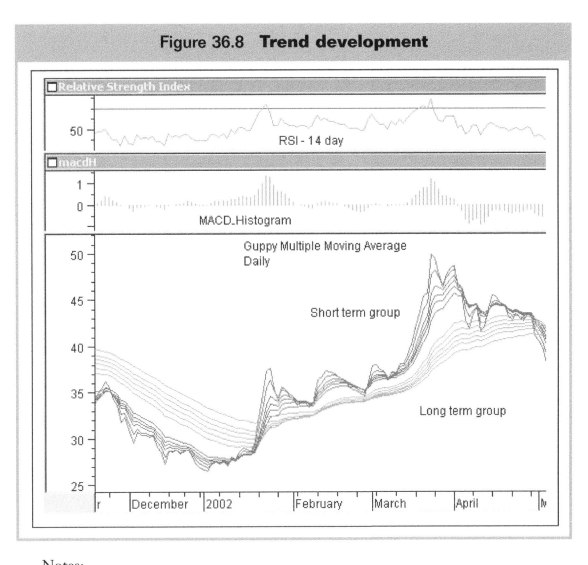

Figure 36.8 Trend development

Notes:

_____

_____

_____

_____

_____

PART VIII

PERFORMANCE PLUS

CHAPTER 37

PERSONALITY BLUES

*E*very trade provides an ultimate test of performance. This is where fantasy and planning are brought to an end with simple figures on your trading statement. Figures printed in black are good. Some figures printed in red are acceptable, while other, larger figures foretell financial ruin. Anyone can sit this test as long as they bring their own vehicle. You need a car for a driving test, and a stock for a financial market test. Many just walk in off the street, pay their entrance fee and fail. Others spend a lot of time reading, researching, developing and learning before taking the test. Many of them still fail.

You can take this final market performance test as many times as you wish. Passing the test calls for more than research and learning. It calls for skill, and this rests upon applied knowledge which is reflected in the choice of vehicle you select for the test. Making this choice is important, so we have subjected our stock to six previous selection tests, or filters. The tests are:

☐ An initial selection test to find a group of trading candidates.

☐ A visual test.

☐ A trend line test.

☐ A character test using a Guppy Multiple Moving Average.

☐ An entry test using a count back line.

☐ A position size or price test.

The closest we come to a performance test is the 'No secrets' chapter at the end of this part. Before we consider these results we explore some factors which cause failure despite extensive and accurate trade planning. Well-prepared students still flunk exams because they panic when the test is administered. In the financial market many people fail despite applying sound trend trading and selection approaches. It is not because they do not know enough, or have undertaken inadequate preparation. Failure often comes from more personal origins, so understanding some of the driving factors gives us the opportunity to take steps to change our behaviour, or minimise the damage the behaviour creates. Some must leave the market to others because the pressure of managing an open trade brings out the worst in them.

Running from mr hyde

Robert Louis Stevenson's story of the socially respectable Dr Jekyll and the socially irresponsible Mr Hyde holds a fascination for readers because it highlights the tendency we all have for a split personality. In ordinary life, we know people who are a small Jekyll and Hyde — nice and easy-going until they get behind the wheel of a car in city traffic, where Mr Hyde emerges. Perhaps Hyde is given the freedom to act because of the anonymity offered by driving just another car on the freeway?

In most circumstances our behaviour is modified by working with others around us. We might feel angry, frightened, fearful or greedy, but we are reluctant to show these emotions at full strength in a social situation. Trading is different. This is an emotional situation and we have the opportunity to give full and free reign to our emotions. Usually there is nobody to scold us if we surrender to greed and aim for an extra 10% on a trade that has already returned 100%. There is nobody to see our fear; even more so if we trade using an electronic order system. We do not even speak to a broker, so there is no chance he hears the catch of fear or the excitement of greed in our voice.

This loneliness and lack of normal social constraints makes trading an emotional experience for many, and this takes us back to Jekyll and Hyde. Giving the finger to another driver as he cuts in front of you is not the same as throwing another $10,000 into a losing position, but both actions stem from the same feeling of emotional freedom which often comes from the belief we will not be caught or held accountable for our actions. In the market our losses or profits are between ourselves and the market. The only public record is when we are forced to sell at a loss, or when we decide to sell at a profit. Once the hard figures are printed on the bank balance we must face up to the reality of our actions. We are caught. Until then we pretend we are rich. It is a very comforting delusion, and surrendering to this pretend world is one of the important, common reasons for trading failure.

It is almost as if we are two different people. We are Dr Jekyll when we open a trade, full of hope, confident we have made the right decision, and yes, a little greedy because we know this trade is going to make us money. We even have a plan to tell us when to get out to take a small protective loss, and when to get out to capture a good, but not too greedy, profit. On paper, we are the perfect Dr Jekyll. We are responsible, respectable, calm, rational and the model of a good trader. This is not accidental. All of us feel very much like this when we buy stock. We are backing our judgment and analysis, often with significant sums of money. We are intelligent people. We know and understand the consequences of surrendering to emotion, of ignoring losses and using the market as a tool to gamble on hope. We are not idiots, although later we might feel this way.

So what happens when we buy the stock? What does Dr Jekyll do? He turns into Mr Hyde. All our planning goes out the window as we surrender to our emotions, and this is made easier because we are not in a social situation. There is nobody to remind us we are doing anything wrong. Ignoring a stop loss is easy. Surrendering to irrational fear seems a natural response. We ignore losses by refusing to look at the trading screen. When the market report segment is due on the evening news, we go to the toilet. We find a delightful range of avoidance activities to prevent us from catching the important details about how our stock is performing. Yet, through this self-imposed fog of avoidance we still hear the commentator when he mentions that our share has gone up in price. We bring selective deafness to a new level not achieved since we were teenagers.

Hyde and seek

It does not get any better when the price goes up just as we expected, as illustrated in Figure 37.1. Now the price target that originally delivered a 15% return looks insignificant. This trade is going so well we shoot for 25%, or even more. The sky is the limit. It is just like being a teenager again. This trade is the elixir of youth, with the heady combination of the power to dream and the money to make it so.

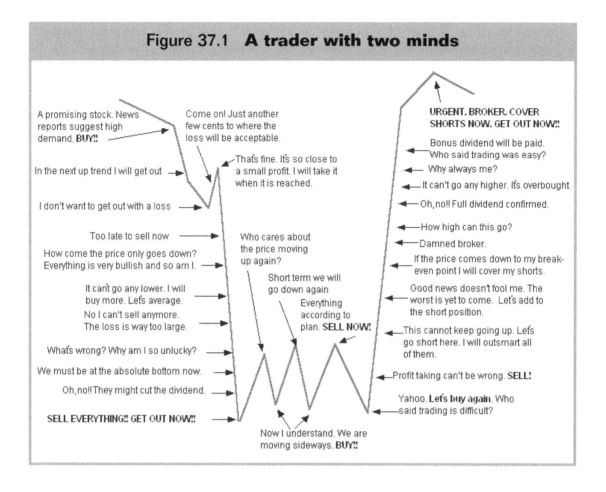

Figure 37.1 **A trader with two minds**

A promising stock. News reports suggest high demand. **BUY!!**

In the next up trend I will get out

I don't want to get out with a loss

Too late to sell now

How come the price only goes down? Everything is very bullish and so am I.

It can't go any lower. I will buy more. Let's average.

No I can't sell anymore. The loss is way too large.

What's wrong? Why am I so unlucky?

We must be at the absolute bottom now.

Oh, no!! They might cut the dividend.

SELL EVERYTHING!! GET OUT NOW!!

Come on! Just another few cents to where the loss will be acceptable.

That's fine. It's so close to a small profit. I will take it when it is reached.

Who cares about the price moving up again?

Short term we will go down again

Everything according to plan. **SELL NOW!**

Now I understand. We are moving sideways. **BUY!!**

URGENT. BROKER. COVER SHORTS NOW. GET OUT NOW!!

Bonus dividend will be paid. Who said trading was easy?

Why always me?

It can't go any higher. It's overbought.

Oh, no!! Full dividend confirmed.

How high can this go?

Damned broker.

If the price comes down to my break-even point I will cover my shorts.

Good news doesn't fool me. The worst is yet to come. Let's add to the short position.

This cannot keep going up. Let's go short here. I will outsmart all of them.

Profit taking can't be wrong. **SELL!**

Yahoo. **Let's buy again.** Who said trading is difficult?

Some traders find it relatively easy to cut big losing trades when they are winning on other trades. The real difficulty is when you've had a string of losses and yet another loss comes along. This makes it even more difficult to crystallise another loss, and the mess compounds. With multiple open trades it is easier for the Mr Hyde trading behaviour to dominate.

Win or lose in the trade, as soon as a trade is opened many people go from being rational traders to gibbering emotional wrecks when they are called to manage the trade. These reactions, just like Jekyll and Hyde, are directly opposed to each other. They concern the same trade, and just a single person. Why does an open trade bring out so many different behavioural characteristics? The behaviours might not be as severe or as prolonged as we have shown above, but for many traders this is just a matter of degree. Acknowledging these behavioural changes take place is an important first step in developing strategies that may help restore the emotional balance so we manage a trade with the same level of rationality we apply to planning the trade.

Why do we behave this way? What causes the Jekyll and Hyde effect? I believe it is a result of the way trading breaks the constraints of social behaviour, as discussed in the opening paragraphs in this chapter. However, I am more interested in solutions that do not require extensive psychoanalysis and therapy. Readers who want to explore the deeper psychological side to these questions will find a good starting point in: *The Psychology of Trading*, by A. Steenbareger; *Trading in the Zone*, by M. Douglas; *Trading to Win*, by A. Kiev; or *The Way of the Warrior Trader* by R. McCall.

Potential solutions fall into three categories. They are:

1 Internal solutions.

2 Social solutions.

3 External solutions.

There is no universal solution, and we offer a small selection of possibilities below. One might suit you, or the discussion may trigger some thoughts leading to a different personalised solution. These are not answers, but they are possibilities.

INTERNAL SOLUTIONS

The internal solutions are most difficult to implement. This means personally confronting the Mr Hyde aspects of our behaviour and turning them off. This calls for consistent trading discipline, and for most people who have a Jekyll and Hyde problem this is not an appropriate solution. Their failure to manage a trade once it is opened is the very behaviour that creates the problem. Our reactions are built on a lifetime of learning and experience. They are very difficult to change. It does not mean we should not try, but we should remember the one good thing about bashing your head against a brick wall is that it feels so good when you stop. In trading terms, this means it is easier to do nothing about a losing trade. Mr Hyde wins.

Some traders find it useful to deliberately set out to create a habit of checking the price of every one of their open trades every day, recording the amount of profit or loss. By creating a habit they reduce the tendency to avoid doing the task when it is unpleasant.

Handling greed is usually less of a problem unless your version of greed allows you to turn a wining trade into a losing trade. Handling a loss usually has the most corrosive impact when it comes to trading discipline. While the loss is on paper, it is easy to ignore.

If, at the end of each day, or each week, you transfer a sum equal to the amount of the loss from your trading account to your partner's account, or to charity, you may find it easier to treat the loss as a tangible event. The objective of this exercise is to transfer the loss from paper — which is easy to ignore — to reality — which is much more painful. This approach does not work for everyone. Those who have implemented this approach have found it both difficult and short-lived. They tend to find the transfer distasteful, so it is easier to observe the stop loss rather than continue to hand over money.

Our objective is to make it impossible to avoid the loss. A less painful method is to calculate the marked-to-market loss each day, print it out in 36-point type and stick it on the front of your computer monitor. During the day it is a constant reminder. You can test the psychological impact of this by calculating the loss of AMP shares purchased at $15.00 when they were trading at $10.00 and then later at $5.00. These are confronting figures, and may be enough to drive Mr Hyde away so that Dr Jekyll can take control of the trade.

SOCIAL SOLUTIONS

If Mr Hyde emerges because we are free from the normal social constraints, then he may disappear if we move trading into a more social environment. This was an interesting outcome of the growth of day trading services in the US in late 2000. Some traders moved from trading at homes, isolated from other traders, to the trading rooms where groups of traders used the same facilities. Now they were exposed to group pressure, so others knew if they failed, but if they won other traders congratulated them. Some found they became better traders because in the social situation of a trading room the group support mechanisms encouraged them to stick to their trading plans. Others found the environment less supportive, and in one American incident, a losing trader gunned down his colleagues before turning the weapon on himself.

Traders duplicate the positive aspects of group support by putting each active and open trade into a social situation. This may include the discussion of personal trades in an investment club situation. Although club decision-making is sometimes ponderous, it tends to be disciplined. Perhaps your investment club may also be happy to discuss the private trades of individual members.

Alternatively, you may find benefits in joining a traders' club. The objective is not to pick up investment advice, but to move into a social situation where there is group pressure on you to implement your trading plan. How you act in private is different from how you act in public. Use this difference to improve your management — not selection — of a trade. The Sunday Traders Club is found in most capitals, and details are available from Alan Hull: enquiries@alanhull.com. Closer to home it may be easier to discuss all open trades with your partner. Generally they are not particularly interested in the details you find so fascinating so they have just one concern: 'Show me the money.' It is quite demanding and it can be a very powerful force in encouraging you to stick with your trading plan. This does not mean you cannot make a loss. It simply means you must explain in advance to another person how much of a loss is acceptable, and when you intend to get out to protect capital or take a profit.

This does not have to be a confrontational affair. It is designed to create a social environment for your trading where Dr Jekyll's good trade planning gets to manage the trade when it is open. When my trading starts to slip due to a lapse in trading discipline I find it useful to discuss the progress of some trades with my office staff. Explaining why I am, or am not, taking a particular action helps crystallise my trade management. Additionally, the discipline of writing about trading solutions and management in weekly notional case study trades in the newsletter — a few of which are personal trades — also moves a private activity into a social situation.

An extreme implementation of this process is the Follow My Trade discussions on website forums like Reef Capital: www.reefcap.com. These solutions straddle the boundary between social and external solutions.

EXTERNAL SOLUTIONS

External solutions are the least used but, paradoxically, the most talked about solutions. When the trader blames his broker for bad advice, or for not telling him when to get out, the trader is desperately looking for an external solution.

On a personal level, the external solution means you make the trade selection and buy the stock. You then print out the full trading plan and hand it to your partner who becomes responsible for closing the trade according to the plan. This approach works where two people are fully in tune and accustomed to a joint relationship that magnifies their strengths and diminishes their weaknesses.

In the United States, the Robbins Trading Company service offers this type of facility where they automatically execute trades according to your plan.

In time, these third party execution services will be available in Australia. Already stop loss management services are offered by DataTech: www.datatech.com.au. Rather than automatic stop loss order execution, DataTech manages the stop loss exit to get the best possible price given the current market conditions.

Some foolish traders give their brokers discretionary control over their account. This is a carte blanche and means the broker opens and closes trades without reference to you, and without reference to your trading plan. This is a very unwise plan because our objective is not to surrender responsibility. If we want to surrender we simply select a fund manager and forget about performance while hoping it is good enough to fund our retirement.

Our objective as traders is to make better decisions and this may come from recognising the split-personality approach that separates good trade planning and identification from good trade management. The market gives us the opportunity to work in an environment free from the usual constraints of social behaviour, and where the financial rewards are often well beyond the pay packet we bring home each fortnight. Trading is an emotional minefield where greed and fear have the possibility of instant rewards. Be careful while you watch an open trade or you might find a change in personality creeping upon you. Mr Hyde has no place in the market, so it pays to recognise the situations in which he emerges and to put in place steps or processes to make it more difficult for him to take control of your trading.

Do this and it is possible to improve your performance results with skill — or is it just luck? We look at some ways to separate the two in the next chapter.

CHAPTER 38

LUCKY YOU

Tossed to the depths of despair, some trading victims start to believe odd market conspiracy theories or mutter darkly about the impact of inside trading. They make defamatory statements about leading business identities and become convinced the market is a cabal designed to keep ordinary people down. There is potential for this insanity in the market but it is not a path to success. Many trading victims come to believe market performance depends on luck and that success is as close as the next expensive lottery ticket. Distinguishing between bad luck and bad trading is an important way to survive in trading. There are times when our trade entry or exit benefits from good luck. We intend to get out at $0.12 and it looks as if prices will move to this level tomorrow. Overnight the DOW closes up dramatically, and the price for our stock gaps up. This is good luck, and we get out at $0.14. The trade plan does not change, but good luck helps us get a better-than-expected exit.

In some other trades the plan is excellent, but an unexpected event — bad luck — makes our exit much worse than we anticipated. We accept luck sometimes plays a role in our trading, but it is unwise to rely on luck to get us out of a hole. Good luck is a bonus but bad luck has the capacity to inflict serious financial damage to our account, so it is useful to distinguish between a run of bad luck and bad trading. Active traders find there are times when they lose touch with the market. Once successful trading techniques are no longer quite as successful. Good trades turn out badly and traders face a decision. Is it time to fine-tune their previously successful trading technique, or is this just a run of bad luck and not a reflection on the effectiveness of the trading plan?

The right answer sets us on the path to profitability while the wrong answer diverts us. By comparing selected periods of trading we develop a method of determining what results, or events, fall within a reasonable expectation of success, and which are random. No trading plan is perfect and we expect failures, but the rate and level of losses should be relatively small. They should also be consistent. A wide variation, or volatility, in losses suggests there are more random occurrences — more bad luck.

TRACKING LUCK

Although a random event is not the same as luck it is a useful way of understanding the role luck can play in trading. The diagrams illustrate the differences. To avoid clutter we show the outcome of 15 events, or trades, for three traders. This sample is too small to draw valid conclusions but when we turn the results into a percentage calculation we extrapolate the results with more validity. As traders we usually work with a small sample group because we cannot afford to gather a sample of 100 personal trades before undertaking analysis. The cost of a failing system is too great and our capital is likely to disappear before we are able to gather a sufficient sample size for valid statistical analysis. We have to make do with a smaller sample of trades and be hyper-alert for the leading indications of system failure.

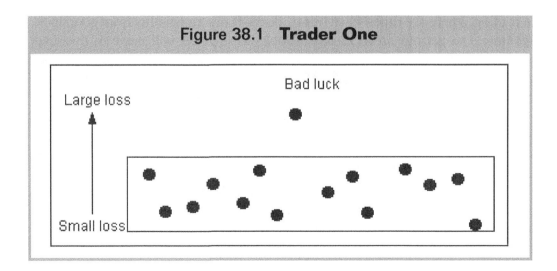

Figure 38.1 Trader One

The box in Figure 38.1 represents the value of 2% of total trading capital. The dots represent the losses incurred in 15 losing trades. Trader One enjoys steady trading success. He trades with discipline and skill so 14 of the trade losses fall within reasonable limits, as defined by the box. This is the expected range of losses for this trading system. We look at ways to determine these reasonable limits below. Only one trade has a loss much greater than the expected acceptable loss. This is a random event well outside the range of consistent results, so this trade is probably just bad luck. Trader One can afford to ignore this unusual event because it does not suggest something is wrong with his trading system.

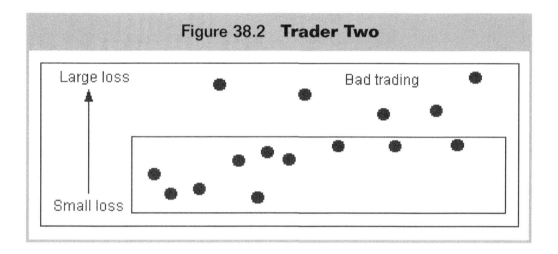

The character of losses for Trader Two — shown in Figure 38.2 — is quite different. This is a pattern of consistent failure. Ten of the losses still fall within the box area, which has the same value as the previous diagram and is set at 2% of total trading capital. This is not an ideal representation because 15 trades is too small a number to make an accurate assessment of a trading plan. We want to show the pattern of behaviour that separates bad luck from bad trading. The first feature is the way losses for Trader Two tend to cluster near the upper level of the box. This is not a definitive feature of a bad trading system, or a trading system in decline, but an increase in the number of losses near the maximum limit suggests this trading system may have a problem.

These losses are not the result of bad luck, as shown by the reduction in randomness of the number of very large losses that lie outside the box. Five large losses for Trader Two is not bad luck. Five large losses, or 33% of the sample, suggests this trading approach has problems. Trader Two is best advised to closely examine his trading system and trading discipline. The system might still be valid, but just inappropriate for the current market conditions. Dismissing this pattern of heavy losses as bad luck is inconsistent with the developing pattern of behaviour. The free spreadsheet discussed below provides a method of capturing this need for change.

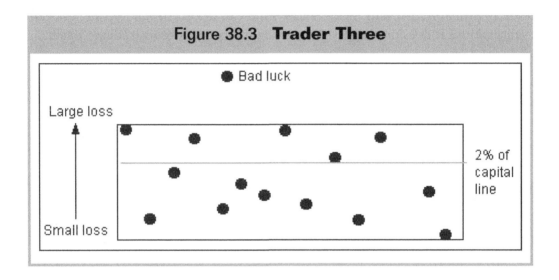

The difference between Trader Three and Trader One is the degree of spread in losses shown in Figure 38.3. There is still just one random loss — bad luck — and the remainder of the 14 trades are evenly spread within the box. The difference is the size of the box, which is much larger than 2% of trading capital. Trader Three is consistent, but the degree of loss is a problem. Trader Three's losses consistently exceed 2% of total trading capital, showing this trading system is marginal. Although the results are consistent, the level of loss makes it very difficult to get ahead. The single random, or bad luck, event is not enough to invalidate the system. However, the system needs adjustment to bring the consistent range of losses back below 2% of total trading capital.

DITCHING LUCK

To separate random or bad luck events from a true failure of the trading system we need a record of the *losses* for two separate periods of time. This allows us to compare changes in our trading behaviour. An active trader might compare this month with last month. A less active trader might compare this quarter's trades with the previous quarter. The time periods selected should be of the same length. It does not matter if the number of trades in each period is the same or different because we use the mean average for each period as a starting point for comparison. It is important that each period should contain at least five trades to ensure the comparison is valid. The more trades in each selected period, the more accurate the conclusions.

Our focus is on losses because they have the potential to damage our trading portfolio. The same analysis methods are applied to profits to help decide the extent luck plays in our trading success. This is a useful exercise and it can signal the need to fine-tune our profit-taking mechanism.

Once the two comparison sets of figures are collected the next step is to calculate one standard deviation from the mean. This tells us where two-thirds of all random occurrences — bad luck trades — are expected to fall. The objective is to separate consistent losses from random occurrences. The closer the results are together, the more consistent we are and the more control we have over our performance. This is a guide to the role luck plays in our trading. The key comparison result is the level of standard deviation from the mean. Low standard deviation shows consistent trading.

These spreadsheets are drawn from the excellent discussion of these issues and other aspects of disciplined trading in *The Market is Always Right* by Thomas McCafferty. We recommend this book to readers.

The spreadsheet extract in Figure 38.4 shows two comparison periods and the standard deviation for each period. The free spreadsheet

Figure 38.4 Period comparison

Period 1	Period 2
$ 370	$ 485
$ 250	$ 510
$ 12	$ 650
$ 900	$ 499
$ 85	$ 487
$ 1,635	$ 539
$ 78	$ 521
$ 23	$ 480
$ 600	$ 672
$ 140	$ 930
$ 80	
$ 55	
4.86	**1.41**
Inconsistent results	Trading system changed to achieve consistent results

available from www.guppytraders.com allows traders to enter up to six comparison periods. We have limited the number of trades for each period to 12, but this is changed simply by using the 'fill down' function after the protection feature on the spreadsheet has been unlocked. There is no password required for this.

The key result is the standard deviation result. The larger the figure, the larger the role 'bad luck' plays in our trading performance. In the first period the standard deviation was 4.86%. In the second period the standard deviation dropped to 1.41%. This trader is over three times more consistent in the second period in controlling losses. We equate the level of randomness, or lack of consistency in trading results, with luck. This is not, strictly speaking, correct, but it is a useful rule-of-thumb measure to use as a guide to the way our trading is developing.

Figure 38.5 **Period comparison**

Period 1	Period 2
$ 485	$ 370
$ 510	$ 310
$ 650	$ 18
$ 499	$ 500
$ 487	$ 90
$ 539	$ 1,900
$ 521	$ 72
$ 480	$ 34
$ 672	$ 589
$ 930	$ 154
$ 450	$ 70
$ 510	$ 155
1.34	5.22

Inconsistent results show the need for change

The second spreadsheet extract in Figure 38.5 shows a trading system that was in touch with market conditions but which has now slipped out of touch. Consistent losses within a narrow range have been replaced by a much higher level of volatility. There are more and larger losses and these cannot be put down to bad luck. The level of inconsistency has grown substantially. The trading system is now nearly four times as inconsistent as it was in the first period.

Changing our trading performance is not always a smooth task. There are times when a single bad luck trade distorts our true performance. This trader originally had a score of 1.34, but not satisfied, he tweaked his trading system to improve the results. Due to unfortunate circumstances — just pure bad luck — his new system incurred a massive losing trade of $1,500, as shown in Figure 38.6. This makes it difficult to decide if his new approach is really better than his original approach.

With a little manipulation we discount the impact of a bad luck trade by removing it from the calculation. The middle column on the spreadsheet shows a bad luck trade with a loss of $1,500. This is a single abnormal trade where the loss is substantially larger than the other losses. The trader is likely to remember the exact reasons for the failure of this trade. Include this large losing trade in the calculations and there appears to be little improvement in the trading system or approach over the two periods.

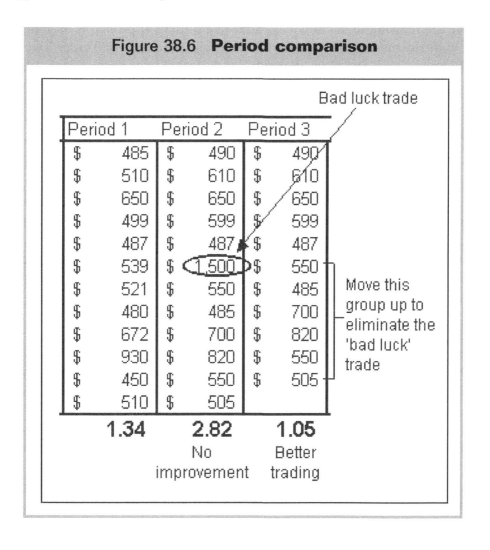

Figure 38.6 **Period comparison**

Bad luck trade

Period 1	Period 2	Period 3	
$ 485	$ 490	$ 490	
$ 510	$ 610	$ 610	
$ 650	$ 650	$ 650	
$ 499	$ 599	$ 599	
$ 487	$ 487	$ 487	
$ 539	$ 1,500	$ 550	
$ 521	$ 550	$ 485	Move this
$ 480	$ 485	$ 700	group up to
$ 672	$ 700	$ 820	eliminate the
$ 930	$ 820	$ 550	'bad luck'
$ 450	$ 550	$ 505	trade
$ 510	$ 505		
1.34	**2.82**	**1.05**	
	No improvement	Better trading	

To obtain a valid comparison we must remove the abnormal trade, but if we remove this single 'bad luck' trade by replacing the loss with a zero it increases the range of results achieved and expands the standard deviation result. The trade must be removed completely from the spreadsheet by moving the later results upwards, as shown in the third column of Figure 38.6. The calculation is now a more accurate reflection of the improvement of the trading system. Consistency, excluding the bad luck trade, has been reduced, or improved, to 1.05%. By discounting a bad luck trade the trader knows his new system is better than the original.

Removing a single bad luck trade is one way of verifying if a trading system is effective. If we find ourselves removing two, or three, or four 'bad luck' trades then we are refusing to acknowledge that our trading approach is no longer in touch with the market. This performance is closer to that of Trader Two. We must be honest with ourselves about the level of trading consistency we achieve. This spreadsheet provides a tool to help us with this calculation and assessment.

COMPARING SYSTEMS

The volatility of returns — the consistency of our trading — is an important foundation of long-term trading success. The rate of return from trading must be related to a low volatility. It is no good making an 80% annual return on capital if there is a good chance next year we might make an 80% loss. If you have a good rate of return, but your volatility is very large, then you should be nervous about your trading future. The risk of high volatility is that you could make a large fortune, or lose one. When high volatility in returns are matched with a low standard deviation in losing trades it suggests you have good control of your trading. You can breathe easier. To rest comfortably the next step is to measure your maximum draw-down, or largest loss. If this, in total, is less than 5% then you can invest in your trading approach with confidence.

The winning trading approach has a combination of generating profits while controlling risk. This is the profile we want to develop, and the second part of the spreadsheet gives us some tools to monitor and assess this.

This is based on the Sterling ratio developed by Deanne Sterling Jones and discussed in *The Market is Always Right* by Thomas McCafferty. It is one solution to resolving the risk/reward equation. Ideally you need three years of trading performance to get accurate figures. However, with caution, the same principles are applied over a shorter period. Use the results as a guide to assessing how effectively your rewards offset the risks of your trading approach.

The Sterling ratio compares your average percentage return over three consecutive years (or periods) with your largest realised percentage loss in equity in the same period. The formula then adds 10% to this loss. This adjustment is used to compensate for differences in the short-term draw-down which are usually understated when compared with the annual draw-down figure.

The result is also used to compare the relative performance of two trading systems, or two traders, or investment managers. The spreadsheet in Figure 38.7 applies the analysis to three trading systems. Trading system A has an average return of 40% over the past three years with the average draw-down at 15%. Trading system B has a lower return of 35%, but also a lower draw-down. Trading system B lost an average of only 10%. Trading system C delivers wild swings with high returns and big draw-downs, or losses. Which of these systems has the best risk/reward relationship?

Figure 38.7 The Sterling ratio

	System A	System B	System C
3 period average % return	40	35	45
Largest average % loss for 3 period	15	10	40
Sterling ratio (*Highest is best*)	1.600	1.750	0.900

It is easy to eliminate system C as an answer, but more difficult to decide between systems A and B. The Sterling ratio provides a quick answer. The higher the Sterling ratio the better the relationship between risk and reward.

Although trading system A has an annual return on capital track record 5% higher than trading system B, the second system is better adjusted for risk. The excellent annual returns for system C are destroyed by the very large draw-down. System C is not much better than gambling when all your trading capital can be won or lost with almost equal ease.

The Sterling ratio is also used to assess improvement in your trading performance. Instead of system A, B and C, this may become period A, period B and period C. This allows you to compare how you were trading in 1999 and 2002 with how you are trading in 2004.

As a private trader it is important to become consistent because it is easier on your nerves. Wild swings in returns are exhilarating when there are profits, but terribly depressing when there are losses. This does not mean losses should be about as large as profits. It means losses should be very small in relation to the return. By using stop loss methods discussed earlier we have the ability to limit our losses and let our profits run. Consistency, as measured in the standard deviation section of the spreadsheet, and a high Sterling ratio are a good guide to how consistently you are performing as a trader. Luck is a fortune but good traders do not mistake it for skill.

CHAPTER 39

NO SECRETS

There are no secrets, and with eight parts in the book it is no secret this is the conclusion of the trading exercise. If you are reading these conclusions immediately after completing Chapter 4 we encourage you to stop now and work through each of the developing examples at the end of each part. It is not just a matter of measuring your judgment against the decisions made by all the readers who took this original test in our weekly trading newsletter in real time. More importantly, this series of notes illustrates how we skew objective analysis according to the dictates of our fear, greed or other emotions. Despite all the tools of trend trading success covered in this book you still have the capacity for self-destruction in the marketplace. Acknowledging this capacity is perhaps the most important step in becoming a successful trader or investor because these are problems we can resolve.

We applied six tests in identifying and selecting the final trading candidate. The seventh and final test is applied by the market and the mark you achieve appears in your bank statement. The final mark depends on your ability to manage the trade and, as discussed in previous chapters, there is an unusual and unexpected range of emotional and psychological factors which influence and divert our best intentions. We cannot apply this test in this book, but as a substitute we use the 'No secrets' trade example to illustrate the way these external factors interfere with trading management and our interpretation and application of technical indicators. Our objective is to help you to learn from the experiences of others so their mistakes do not become yours.

The charts at the end of the last 'No secrets' chapter gave a clear, unequivocal exit signal. The close below the up-sloping trend line and the moving average crossover left no doubt it was time to abandon the trade. Those readers who held the stock hoping the trade would rebound were disappointed. Not surprisingly we saw an increase in exit emails from readers who took the original test and this is summarised in Figure 39.1. Unlike readers of this book, they did not know when the test was going to end with the last set of charts.

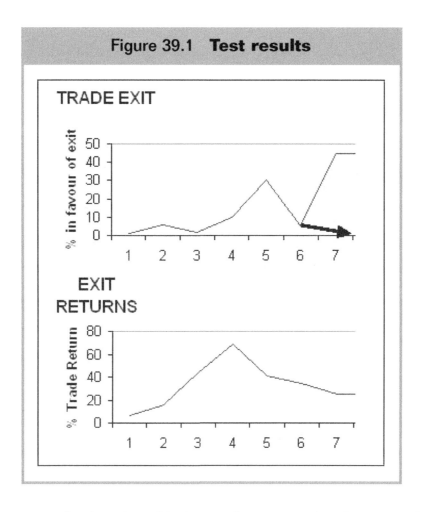

Figure 39.1 **Test results**

The reasons for the exit at this time are best summed up by one reader who wrote: 'Too late! It's starting to look a bit like crap around now.' We are generous with this exit so we set the exit at the high of the day following the moving average crossover. This gets traders out at $0.40 and locks-in a 25% return. This looks poor when compared to the best return of 68.75% taken by those who jumped ship at the top of the bubble. It is slightly worse than the exit based on the close below the count back line, which delivered a 40% return. It is, however, better than those traders who jumped the gun with an exit near the top of the first rally. They collected 15.53% from the trade before the trend had time to develop.

Readers of our newsletter are more informed than the general public. They have, or are developing, better trading skills. We suspect if the general public had been following a trade like this the number of exit emails would have declined, following the path shown by the thick line on the chart. The reason is simple. Most people do not have the discipline to exit a trade once the exit signal is given; even more so if the trade has once delivered a good profit — 68% in this case — and the exit signal delivered a substantially lower profit — 25% in this example.

KEEP GREED AT BAY

We must be careful to keep greed at bay and in perspective in this discussion. None of the exits show a loss. A 25% return over 14 weeks is not as good as a 68% return over 12 weeks but it is still not bad. There are many traders who would be more than satisfied with these returns.

When the first exit signal comes people tend to hold on, hoping even more fervently for a price rise. In time, if prices continue to fall, they slip the trade into the bottom drawer and forget it. Our objective is to understand our reactions and to trade better than the general public.

The relationships between the percentage return from the trade and the exit emails are interesting.

The thin line in Figure 39.2 tracks closing prices at each decision point. The thick line shows the percentage of readers in the original test who sent exit emails. The bubble peak attracted a few sellers. Their reasons for exiting the trade were sound, but they were generally not consistent with the trading plan or the indicators used for analysis. This was a judgment call which allowed them to lock-in profits, but in some cases it is difficult to distinguish the reasons for this later exit from the reasons used by traders who jumped ship near the top of the first rally in week two. Experience and the Guppy Multiple Moving Average (GMMA) play a role in recognising a rally peak and a bubble peak.

419

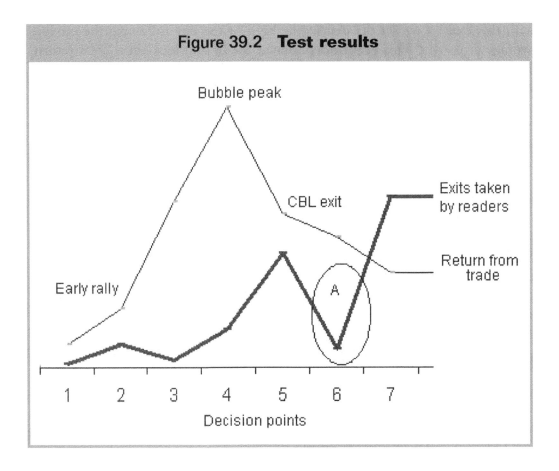

Figure 39.2 **Test results**

However, this discussion misses an important point. We must make a choice between intuitive trading decisions and those based on the application of a consistent trading plan. Intuitive decision-making slips dangerously close to guesswork and gambling. The intuitive exit taken near the bubble top is difficult to duplicate in the next trade, or consistently apply over a series of trades. Experienced traders apply their judgment skills to trading decisions, but this is not a good option for new traders to pursue.

The sample trade showed no evidence of behaviour contrary to the original plan to trade the developing trend until an exit signal was delivered. Our preferred application uses the count back line, and the exit signal saw a surge in email exits in the original test. Although the exit did not lock-in the best profits available, the discipline of the exit serves the trader well. In the next trade the same discipline may get him out very close to the top. When a trade starts we cannot determine in advance the exact nature of the trade. We may lock onto a trade perfectly suited to the count back line approach and capture an excellent trade. In others the result may be closer to that shown in the example.

The particularly interesting relationship is the behaviour after the count back line exit signal in area A. It took a lot of twisting to make the indicators suggest there was the possibility of a trend rebound. This is the area of greatest hope for traders. It soon became clear there was little hope of a rebound and the sensible strategy was to act on the count back line signal. Instead most traders held on, waiting for confirmation the worst scenario was true. If this did not come they believed the situation must improve, so they held off selling. Despite the decline in price and the clear exit signals, readers held on in hope.

The rational decision was to join the selling after the count back line close. The emotional decision was to hold on and hope. This is what many traders did, as shown by the very low number of exit emails. Finally when the death knell had been delivered, the body placed in the coffin and the grave filled in, many more traders decided it was time to exit. The relationship is not quite inverse. The time of maximum profits sees an increase in sell orders. The time of maximum or confirmed loss also sees an increase in sell orders. The real concern is area A where many traders seem paralysed by the need to make a decision. This has the capacity to turn a reasonable trade into a poor trade.

No secrets — really

This series of trading decision points was designed to provide an answer to the perennial question: are there trading secrets? The question is also a variation on: if everybody follows technical analysis won't it destroy any technical advantage? Our trading edge comes from what we do with information, and it is not related to when we get it or if others have access to the same information. The most exciting conclusion in the financial market is that we can all use the same information and we can all make money. This trading example shows that differences in returns come directly from our ability to analyse the information objectively and act with trading discipline to follow our trading plan.

The answer is confirmed by the behaviour of our readers in the original real-time test. They all had exactly the same information, used the same indicators, were shown the same trading plan in advance and had the same time available to make a decision. Despite the clear trade plan exit when prices closed below the count back line, many readers did not close the trade. They hung in, hoping for a price rise. It is not until the very end of the trade, when they were overwhelmed by exit signals with closes below the trend line and moving average crossovers, that they accepted the trade was dead.

Despite the clear trading plan some traders made a judgment choice and exited the trade near the top of the first rally, or at the top of the bubble. The underlying conclusion is the same. We all used exactly the same data and exactly the same indicators. We all got the information at exactly the same time. There has been no inside trading as the chart was deliberately anonymous. In an ideal world — a world where the effectiveness of the trading methods we teach is diminished as more people use them — we would expect to see the vast majority of exit emails coming in when the count back line exit is triggered.

Even if this had happened, the price action shows traders would still be able to exit with profits around 40%. Everybody who selected this exit condition would have made money. The exit decision has a great deal more to do with trader psychology — with greed, fear and the level of our trading skill and discipline — than it does with the indicators we use. A group of people can start from exactly the same point, follow exactly the same data, use exactly the same group of indicators and end up with very different profits from the trade.

Trading success depends upon the way tools are applied and not on the tools used. Our trading edge comes from what we do with what we have. Our edge is not created by having information others do not have, be it data, news or secret indicators. It comes from making better use of the information we all have.

OUR ANALYSIS

The chart in Figure 39.3 shows the final exit signals. At the very least, prices need to close above the count back line before we accept the possibility of a new uptrend. The movement of the short-term GMMA below the long-term group confirms the downtrend is dominant. Unless we want to stretch the plot of a straight edge trend line beyond all reasonable limits, there is no doubt the current trend defined by a straight edge trend has ended.

The more complex indicators, MACD_H and RSI shown in Figure 39.4, have already shown they are unreliable when applied to this stock. There is no reason to treat their signals with any level of confidence or importance in the current chart. They are simply irrelevant to the management of this trade. In some stocks these indicators do provide reliable and consistent signals. It is important to decide prior to trade entry just how reliable these indicators are with the stock you are trading. If they pass the reliability test on recent data they can be applied to the new trend. If they do not pass the reliability test, the indicators should not be used to manage the current trade.

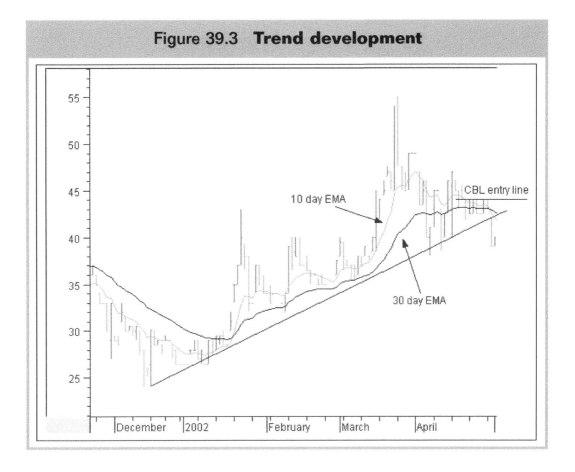

Figure 39.3 Trend development

As expected the summary notes in Figure 39.5 show no reason for staying with this trade.

The readers who participated in the original exercise helped develop a quantitative analysis of how traders use the same information to reach quite different decisions. This gives all traders an opportunity to closely examine the relationship between the indicators they use, their trading skill and the results they achieve. Trading success rests heavily on disciplined stop loss and disciplined application of trading plans developed before the trade is ever taken.

The conclusion is clear. There are no trading secrets. It seems a pity to have read so much to reach this conclusion, but it is a conclusion that very few people accept until it is examined in detail. Success is available to all but achieving it calls for skill and discipline.

Figure 39.4 **Trend development**

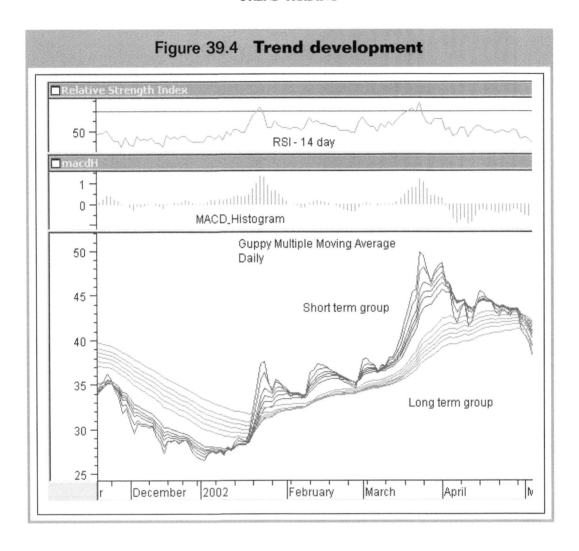

Figure 39.5 **Analysis summary**

INDICATORS	EXIT TRADE
Count back line	Prices below the CBL entry line.
Guppy Multiple Moving Average	Long-term group is compressing, turning down, and short-term group is compressed and moving below the long-term group.
Moving average crossover	Moving averages have crossed over.
RSI	Indicator is not useful except for divergence signals.
MACD_H	MACD_H is too unreliable to apply to this stock.
Trend line, support and resistance	All straight edge trend line plots are broken.

Chapter 40

FOUND IN TRANSLATION

I have found one of the most deceptive book titles I have encountered is *Chinese Language Made Easy*. This is closely followed by *Financial Markets Made Easy*. For some time I have been learning to speak, write and read basic Mandarin Chinese. An increasing level of work in Asia and China has made this a useful skill to develop. At first the spoken and written language was completely baffling and confusing, but as time passes it becomes less so.

Many people find their experience of the financial market is similar to my experience in learning Chinese. It is difficult to make sense of the language, the terms and the charts. They are compelled to make an attempt because they are embroiled in an escalation of expectations by government and others that they will be responsible for their financial future in retirement. When they first start to explore this area through choice or necessity, they find the language confusing. For many people the first steps into the market are as far as they go because the language of the market is so intimidating — particularly when spoken by some brokers and advisers who are empowered to act as a translator between the common man and the market.

Those who venture further and explore other aspects of market behaviour and analysis are asked to grapple with an entire range of new specialist terms. This applies to charting and technical analysis approaches I have discussed in this and other books. Understanding the market from a technical perspective appears at first incomprehensible because of the specialist chart displays used to describe the price action. At first glance a bar chart or a candlestick chart looks as foreign as a written Chinese character. By the time the display includes several indicators, the newcomer to the market is completely bewildered.

Just like the Mandarin language of China, the market has a logic and structure of its own. Learning the language inevitably means we learn about the ways of thinking captured by the structure of the language. If we can crack the code then understanding becomes easier. Profits accumulate and mistakes become less harmful. The development of skill is slow. Charts that once looked incomprehensible do not suddenly make sense. There is no epiphany, so do not expect a sudden leap of understanding. Instead there is a slow growth of comprehension. Gradually the charts and indicators do make sense. We learn to apply effective analysis almost by stealth because at each stage we continue to grapple with the new material and challenges thrown up by the market. Distracted by new problems we easily forget just how much we have learned.

Trapped in taxis and traffic jams in Singapore or Hong Kong I used to while away the minutes picking out the few Chinese characters in shop signs that I could read. It was an excruciatingly slow process. Now I am able to spend traffic jam time reading the headlines in the local Chinese language newspaper. It is only when we pause and look back that we understand how far we have come. It is only then that we realise how worthwhile the journey has been.

Just as with life, the market is a journey not a destination. The more we learn the more we know we need to learn. Not everyone feels comfortable with this awareness but it is an important requirement for survival and success in the market. Once I was satisfied with being able to return a Chinese politeness with Xie Xie — thank you. Now I want to say more, read more and write more. Market newcomers who were once satisfied with making an occasional profit based on simple chart analysis recognise this was the result of guesswork. Now they find they want to push their boundaries further. Some move on to use quite complex indicator combinations and develop sophisticated trading systems. Others explore the same territory and then return to a carefully selected combination of relatively basic analysis techniques. They acquire knowledge through learning.

A complex Chinese society is built upon apparently simple concepts of benevolence and morality largely recorded by Confucius in *The Analects* in 497 BC. An apparently complex profitable trading result can be built on the classic foundation concepts of trends and trend analysis. The purpose of this book has been to illustrate how the foundations of trend analysis are used to build consistently successful trades. We use straight edge trend lines, the Guppy Multiple Moving Average and count back line techniques.

We all have a choice of going forward and taking control, or being taken for a ride as a passenger. Some baulk at the first language bar created by the financial market. They completely surrender their financial future to a small army of commission-based advisers. Others take the plunge and make an effort to master the language, the written graphics of market charts, and they learn to read the market. Some go it alone, while others use this knowledge to ensure their chosen translator is making an accurate translation.

'Have I passed onto others anything that I have not tried out myself?' Tseng Tzu asks in *The Analects*. This responsible approach to knowledge is the mark of a good teacher. I write only about the techniques I have used in my own trading. In my books I have tried to unravel the language and show how charts and technical indicators are used to understand market behaviour. My objective is to speed up the democratisation of market activity and break down the barriers erected by those who claim the area is so specialist that you have no choice but to go to them for advice. I have tried to make the language and concepts of the financial market accessible.

This book is designed to help you understand the written character of the chart so you can learn to read price and trend behaviour. Beneath the broad concepts are levels of subtlety. Every written Chinese character encapsulates centuries of inferred meaning which gives an unexpected depth and richness to even simple statements. Every chart, or indicator, captures an inference about market behaviour. Use this knowledge to more fully understand the nature and the character of the trend in the market or stock that you have chosen to trade or invest in.

Gathering knowledge every day will make the financial market less 'foreign'. Learn the language to ensure that your financial objectives are not lost in translation. Listen carefully and trade well.

INDEX

DISCOUNT COUPON – TRADING WORKSHOPS

10% off the regular seminar fee – single and group rates. (These workshops are held in Australia, Asia, China, the USA, the UK and Europe.)

Trading looks easy, but it takes skill. How best to approach your market and survive is a skill that can be learned, and improved. Trading success means knowing how to GET IN by identifying a trade. It means knowing how to manage the trade so you GET OUT with an overall profit.

You can become a better trader by attending a half-day or full-day workshop because Daryl Guppy will teach you how to understand the market from a private trader's perspective, how to use your advantages, and how to manage a trade to lock in capital profits.

All traders – those considering entering the market and those who want to improve their trading – benefit from these workshops.

Nobody can give you the ultimate trading secret, but Daryl Guppy will show you, using local examples selected by the audience on the day, how a private trader identifies and manages a trade. You will enter the market better informed than your competitors.

Daryl Guppy holds regular trading workshops. Dates and details are posted on www.guppytraders.com eight weeks before each workshop.

How to claim your workshop discount

When you book your seminar mention that you own *Trend Trading* and get 10% off the advertised fee. Bring this book with you to confirm your discount. It can be autographed for you if you wish.

Some comments from workshop participants

"The workshop, like your book, was practical and informative. I enjoyed it, and more importantly, I learned from it. For me it brought a lot of the theory into perspective." – Private equity trader

"The workshop covered all the essential building blocks of the trade better and more effectively than any book that I have come across." – Hong Kong equity analyst

"In my seven years attending continuing education programs I have never found a session as useful and interesting as the one which you have conducted." – Remisier, Singapore

"On the subject of the seminar, I must say that it was an inspiring night. Daryl was energetic, spontaneous and his comments were thought provoking. Additionally, he was very generous with his time, staying back after the official closing time to discuss specific issues with us. I've not been to a trading seminar before where the examples used during the evening were drawn from the audience (not pre-planned)." – Private equity and derivatives trader

Printed and bound by CPI Group (UK) Ltd, Croydon, CR0 4YY

15/05/2024

14502436-0001